HISTORY

OF THE

UNITED STATES,

FROM THE

DISCOVERY OF THE AMERICAN CONTINENT.

BY

GEORGE BANCROFT.

VOL. VI.

SEVENTH EDITION.

BOSTON:
LITTLE, BROWN AND COMPANY.
1857.

Stereotyped by John F. Trow,
49 Ann Street, New-York.

PREFACE.

The present Volume completes the History of the American Revolution, considered in its causes. The three last explain the rise of the union of the United States from the body of the people, the change in the colonial policy of France, and the consequences of the persevering ambition of Great Britain to consolidate its power over America. The penal Acts of 1774 dissolved the moral connection between the two countries, and began the civil war.

The importance of the subject justified comprehensive research. Of printed works my own collection is not inconsiderable; and whatever else is to be found in the largest public, or private libraries, particularly in those of Harvard College, the Boston Athenæum, which is very rich in pamphlets, and the British Museum, have been within my reach.

Still greater instruction was derived from manuscripts. The records of the State Paper Office of Great Britain best illustrate the colonial system of that country. The opportunity of consulting them was granted me by the Earl of Aberdeen, when Secretary of State, and continued by Viscount Palmerston, by Earl Grey, and by the Duke of Newcastle. They include the voluminous correspondence of all military and civil officers, and Indian Agents, employed in America; memorials of the American Commissioners of Customs; narratives, affidavits, informations, and answers of witnesses, illustrating the most important occurrences; the journals of the Board of Trade; its Representations to the King; its intercourse with the Secretary of State; the instructions and letters, sent to America, whether from the King, the Secretary of State, or the Board of Trade; the elaborate abstracts of documents prepared for the Council; opinions of the Attorney and Solicitor General; and occasionally private letters. I examined these masses of documents slowly and carefully; I had access to every thing that is preserved; and of no paper however secret it may have been in its day, or whatever its complexion, was a copy refused me.

I owe to Lord John Russell permission to extend my inquiries to the records of the Treasury, of which he at the time was the head; so that all the volumes of its Minutes and its Letter-books, which could throw light on the subject of my inquiries, came under my inspection.

The proceedings in Parliament till 1774 had something of a confidential character; from sources the most various, private letters, journals, and reports, preserved in France, or England, or in America, I have obtained full and trustworthy accounts of the debates on the days most nearly affecting America.

Many papers, interesting to Americans, are preserved in the British Museum, where I have great reason to remember the considerate attention of Sir Henry Ellis. At the London Institution, in Albemarle Street, also, the Secretary, Mr. Barlow, obtained for me leave to make use of its great collection of American military correspondence.

It was necessary to study the character and conduct

of the English Ministers themselves. Of Chatham's private letters perhaps few remain unpublished; Mr. Disney imparted to me at the Hyde, two volumes of familiar notes, that passed between Chatham and Hollis, full of allusions to America. The Marquis of Lansdowne consented to my request for permission to go through the papers of his father, the Earl of Shelburne, during the three periods of his connection with American affairs; and allowed me to keep them, till by a continued examination and comparison they could be understood in all their aspects. Combined with manuscripts which I obtained in France, they give all the information that can be desired for illustrating Lord Shelburne's relations with America. My thanks are also due to the Duke of Grafton, for having communicated to me unreservedly the autobiography of the third Duke of that name, who besides having himself been a Prime Minister, held office with Rockingham, Chatham, Lord North, and Shelburne. The late Earl of Dartmouth showed me parts of the journal of his grandfather, written while he occupied the highest place at the Board of Trade.

Of all persons in England, it was most desirable to have a just conception of the character of the King. Mr. Everett, when Minister at the Court of St. James, keeping up in his busiest hours the habit of doing kind offices, obtained for me from Lady Charlotte Lindsay, copies of several hundred notes, or abstracts of notes from George the Third to her father Lord North. Afterwards I received from Lady Charlotte herself communications of great interest, and her sanction to make such use of the letters, as I might desire, even to the printing of them all. Others written by the King in his boyhood to his governor Lord Harcourt, Mr. Harcourt was so obliging as to allow me to peruse at Nuneham.

The controversy between Great Britain and her Colonies attracted the attention of all Europe, till at length it became universally the subject of leading interest. To give completeness to this branch of my inquiries, in so far as Great Britain was concerned either as a party or an observer, the necessary documents, after the most thorough and extensive search, were selected from the Correspondence with Ministers, Agents, and others in France, Spain, Holland, Russia, Austria, Prussia, and several of the smaller German Courts, especially Hesse Cassel and Brunswick. The volumes examined for this purpose were very numerous, and the copies for my use reach to all questions directly or indirectly affecting America; to alliances, treaties of subsidy, mediations, and war and peace.

The relations of France to America were of paramount importance. I requested of Mr. Guizot, then the Minister, authority to study them in the French Archives. "You shall see every thing that we have," was his instant answer, enhancing his consent by the manner in which it was given. The promise was most liberally interpreted and most fully redeemed by Mr. Mignet, whose good advice and friendly regard lightened my toils, and left me nothing to desire. Mr. Dumont, the Assistant Keeper of the Archives, under whose immediate superintendence my investigations were conducted, aided them by his constant good will. The confidence reposed in me by Mr. Guizot was continued by Mr. Lamartine, Mr. Drouin de Lhuys, and by Mr. de Tocqueville.

As the Court of France was the centre of European diplomacy, the harvest from its Archives was exceedingly great. There were found the reports of the several French Agents sent secretly to the American colonies; there were the papers tracing the origin and progress of the French Alliance, including opinions of the Ministers, read in the Cabinet Council to the King. Many volumes illustrate the direct intercourse between France and the United States. But besides these, I had full opportunity to examine the subject in its complication with the relations of France to England, Spain, Holland, Prussia, Russia, and other Powers; and this I did so thoroughly, that when I took my leave, Mr. Dumont assured me, that I had seen every thing, that nothing, not the smallest memorandum, had been withheld from me.

Besides this, I acquired papers from the Ministry of the Marine, and from that of War. The Duke de Broglie gave me a most pleasing journal of his father when in America; Mr. Augustin Thierry favored me with exact and interesting anecdotes, derived from Lafayette; and my friend Count Circourt was never weary of furthering my inquiries.

My friend Mr. J. Romeyn Brodhead, was so kind as to make for me selections of papers in Holland, and I take leave to acknowledge, that Mr. J. A. de Zwaan of the Royal Archives at the Hague, was most zealous and unremitting in his efforts to render the researches undertaken for me, effective and complete.

I have obtained so much of Spanish Correspondence, as to have become accurately acquainted with the maxims by which the Court of Spain governed its conduct towards our part of America.

Accounts of the differences between America and England are to be sought not only in the sources already referred to, but specially in the correspondence of the Colony Agents resident in London, with their respective Constituents. I pursued the search for papers of this class, till I succeeded in securing letters official or private from Bollan; Jasper Mauduit; Richard Jackson,—the same who was Grenville's Secretary at the Exchequer, a distinguished Member of Parliament, and at one time Agent for three Colonies;—Arthur Lee; several unpublished ones of Franklin; the copious and most interesting, official and private Correspondence of William Samuel Johnson, Agent for Connecticut; one letter and fragments of letters of Edmund Burke, Agent for New-York; many and exceedingly valuable ones, of Garth a Member of Parliament and Agent for South Carolina; and specimens of the Correspondence of Knox and Franklin, as Agents of Georgia.

Analogous to these are the confidential communications which passed between Hutchinson and Israel Mauduit and Thomas Whately; between one of the Proprietaries of Pennsylvania and Deputy Governor Hamilton; between Cecil Calvert and Hugh Hammersley, successive Secretaries of Maryland, and Lieutenant Governor Sharpe; between Ex-Governor Pownall and Dr. Cooper of Boston; between Hollis and Mayhew and Andrew Eliot of Boston. Of all these I have copies.

Of the letter-books and drafts of letters of men in office, I had access to those of Bernard for a single year; to those of Hutchinson for many years; to that of Dr. Johnson, the patriarch of the American Episcopal Church, with Archbishop Secker; to those of Colden; to those of Lieutenant Governor Sharpe. Many letters of their correspondents also fell within my reach.

For the affairs of the Colonies I have consulted their own Archives, and to that end have visited in person more than half the old thirteen colonies.

Long continued pursuit, favored by a general good will, has brought into my possession papers, or copies of papers, from very many of the distinguished men of the country in every colony. Among those who have rendered me most valuable aid in this respect, I must name in an especial manner the late Mr. Colden of New-York, who intrusted to me all the manuscripts of Lieutenant Governor Colden, covering a period in New-York history of nearly a quarter of a century; the late Mr. Johnson of Stratford, Connecticut, who put into my hands those of hi father, containing excellent contributions alike to English and American history; my friend Dr. Potter, the present Bishop of Pennsylvania, who furnished me numerous papers of equal interest and novelty, illustrating the history of New-York and of the Union; Mr. Force of Washington City, whose success in collecting materials for American History is exceeded only by his honest love of historic truth; Mr. J. F. Eliot of Boston; Mr. William B. Reed, Mr. Langdon Elwyn, and Mr. Edward D. Ingraham of Philadelphia; Mr. Tefft of Georgia, and Mr. Swaine of North Carolina, who show constant readiness to further my inquiries; the Connecticut Historical Society; the President and Officers of Yale College, who sent me unique documents from the Library of that Institution; Mr. William C. Preston of South Carolina, to whom I owe precious memorials of the spirit and deeds of the South.

The most valuable acquisition of all was the collection of the papers of Samuel Adams, which came to me through the late Samuel Adams Welles. They contain the manuscripts of Samuel Adams, especially drafts of his letters to his many correspondents, and drafts of public documents. They contain also the complete journals of the Boston Committee of Correspondence, drafts of the letters it sent out, and the letters it received, s far as they have been preserved. The papers are very numerous; taken together they unfold the manner in which resistance to Great Britain grew into a system, and they perfectly represent the sentiments and the reasonings of the time. They are the more to be prized, as much of the correspondence was secret, and has remained so to this day.

If I have failed in giving a lucid narrative of the events which led to the necessity of Independence, it is not for want of diligence in studying the materials, which I have brought together, or of laborious care in arranging them. The strictest attention has been paid to chronological sequence, which can best exhibit the simultaneous action of general causes. The abundance of my collections has enabled me, in some measure, to reproduce the very language of every one of the principal actors in the scenes which I describe, and to represent their conduct from their own point of view. I hope at least it will appear, that I have written with candor, neither exaggerating vices of character, nor reviving national animosities, but rendering a just tribute to virtue wherever found.

New-York, 13th May, 1854.

CONTENTS.

CHAPTER XXV.

THE CHARTER OF MASSACHUSETTS BAY IN PERIL.—THE FALL OF THE ROCKINGHAM ADMINISTRATION. May—July, 1766.

CHAPTER XXVI.

COALITION OF THE KING AND THE GREAT COMMONER AGAINST THE ARISTOCRACY. —THE ADMINISTRATION OF CHATHAM. July—October, 1766.

CHAPTER XXVII.

CHARLES TOWNSHEND USURPS THE LEAD IN GOVERNMENT.—CHATHAM'S ADMINISTRATION CONTINUED. October, 1766—January, 1767.

CHAPTER XXVIII.

THE BRITISH ARISTOCRACY REDUCE THEIR OWN TAXES.—DEFEAT OF CHATHAM'S ADMINISTRATION BY THE MOSAIC OPPOSITION. January—March, 1767.

CHAPTER XXIX.

PARLIAMENT WILL HAVE AN AMERICAN ARMY AND AN AMERICAN REVENUE.—CHARLES TOWNSHEND'S SUPREMACY IN THE ADMINISTRATION. March—July, 1767.

CHAPTER XXX.

HOW TOWNSHEND'S AMERICAN TAXES WERE RECEIVED BY FRANCE AND AMERICA.—COALITION OF THE KING AND THE ARISTOCRACY. July—November, 1767.

CHAPTER XXXI.

MASSACHUSETTS CONSULTS HER SISTER COLONIES.—HILLSBOROUGH'S ADMINISTRATION OF THE COLONIES. November, 1767—February, 1768.

CHAPTER XXXII.

AN AMERICAN EMPIRE IS IN THE DIVINE DECREES.—HILLSBOROUGH'S ADMINISTRATION OF THE COLONIES CONTINUED. February—March, 1768.

CHAPTER XXXIII.

AN ARMY AND A FLEET FOR BOSTON.—HILLSBOROUGH'S ADMINISTRATION OF THE COLONIES CONTINUED. April—June, 1768.

CHAPTER XXXIV.

DOES MASSACHUSETTS RESCIND?—HILLSBOROUGH'S ADMINISTRATION CONTINUED. June—July, 1768.

CHAPTER XXXV.

THE REGULATORS OF NORTH CAROLINA.—HILLSBOROUGH S ADMINISTRATION OF THE COLONIES CONTINUED. July—September, 1768.

CHAPTER XXXVI.

THE TOWNS OF MASSACHUSETTS MEET IN CONVENTION.—HILLSBOROUGH'S ADMINISTRATION OF THE COLONIES CONTINUED. September, 1768.

CHAPTER XXXVII.

THE CELTIC-AMERICAN REPUBLIC ON THE BANKS OF THE MISSISSIPPI. September—October, 1768.

CHAPTER XXXVIII.

THE KING AND THE BRITISH PARLIAMENT AGAINST THE TOWN OF BOSTON.—HILLSBOROUGH'S ADMINISTRATION OF THE COLONIES CONTINUED. October—December, 1768.

CHAPTER XXXIX.

A WAY TO TAKE OFF THE INCENDIARIES.—HILLSBOROUGH'S ADMINISTRATION OF THE COLONIES CONTINUED. December, 1768—February, 1769.

CHAPTER XLVI.

THE ORIGIN OF TENNESSEE.—HILLSBOROUGH'S ADMINISTRATION OF THE COLONIES CONTINUED. October, 1770—June, 1771.

CHAPTER XLVII.

GREAT BRITAIN CENTRES IN ITSELF POWER OVER ITS COLONIES.—HILLSBOROUGH'S ADMINISTRATION OF THE COLONIES CONTINUED. June, 1771—August, 1772.

CHAPTER XLVIII.

THE TOWNS OF MASSACHUSETTS HOLD CORRESPONDENCE. August, 1772—January, 1773.

CHAPTER XLIX.

VIRGINIA CONSOLIDATES UNION. January—July, 1773.

CHAPTER L.

THE BOSTON TEA PARTY. August—December, 1773.

CHAPTER LI.

THE KING IN COUNCIL INSULTS THE GREAT AMERICAN PLEBEIAN.
December, 1773—February, 1774.

CHAPTER LII.

THE CRISIS. February—May, 1774.

THE CRISIS.

HOW GREAT BRITAIN ESTRANGED AMERICA.

CHAPTER XXV.

THE CHARTER OF MASSACHUSETTS IN PERIL.—THE FALL OF THE ROCKINGHAM ADMINISTRATION.

MAY—JULY, 1766.

CHAP. XXV. 1766. May.

THE satisfaction of America was not suffered to continue long. The King, regarding the repeal of the Stamp Act as "a fatal compliance,"[1] which had for ever "wounded the majesty" of England, and "planted thorns" under his own pillow,[2] preferred the hazard of losing the colonies[3] to tempering the British claim of absolute authority. Their denial of that claim and their union were ascribed by his friends to the hesitation of his Ministers, whose measures, they insisted, had prevailed by "artifices" against the real opinion of Parliament; and "the coming hour" was foretold, "when the British Augustus would grieve for the obscuring of the glories of his reign by the loss, not of a province,

[1] George the Third to Lord North, 4 February, 1776.

[2] A short history, &c., &c., &c., 18, 19.

[3] Considerations on the Present State of the Nation, &c., &c., by a late Under-Secretary of State, 50.

CHAP. XXV. 1766. May.

but of an empire more extensive than that of Rome; not of three legions, but of whole nations."[1]

No party in England could prevent an instantaneous reaction. Pitt had erected no stronger bulwark for America than the shadowy partition which divides internal taxation from imposts regulating commerce; and Rockingham had leapt over this slight defence with scorn, declaring the power of Parliament to extend of right to all cases whatsoever. But they who give absolute power, give the abuse of absolute power; —they who draw the bolts from the doors and windows, let in the robber. When the opinions of Bedford and Grenville became sanctioned as just principles of constitutional law, no question respecting their policy remained open but that of its expediency; and country gentlemen, if they had a right to raise a revenue from America, were sure that it was expedient to ease themselves of one fourth of their land-tax by exercising the right. The Administration were evidently without vitality; "they are dead and only lying in state," was the common remark. Conway avowed himself eager to resign;[2] and Grafton not only threw up his office, but, before the House of Lords, addressing the Prime Minister, who regarded the ascendency of the old whig aristocracy as almost a part of the British constitution, called on him to join in a willingness to be content with an inferior station, for the sake of accomplishing a junction of the ablest and most experienced statesmen of the country.[3]

On the resignation of Grafton, Conway, with his accustomed indecision, remained in office, but seized

[1] Lloyd's Conduct of the Late Administration, &c., &c.

[2] Conway to Grafton, 23 April, 1766, in Grafton's Autobiography.

[3] See Grafton's own account of the incident in his Autobiography.

CHAP. XXV. 1766. May.

the occasion to escape from the care of America[1] to the Northern Department. There appeared a great and general backwardness[2] to embark with Rockingham. Lord North[3] had hardly accepted a lucrative post, before he changed his mind and excused himself. Lord Howe would not serve unless under Pitt.[4] Lord Hardwicke also refused the place left vacant by Grafton; so did his brother, Charles Yorke; and so did Egmont; till at last it fell to the husband of Conway's step-daughter, the liberal, self-confident Duke of Richmond; who added grace and courtesy of manners to firm affections, but was swayed by a violent and undiscerning ambition, that far outran his ability.[5] He, too, shunned[6] the conduct of American affairs, and they were made over to a new Department of State, which Dartmouth was to accept,[7] and which Charles Townshend avowed his hope of obtaining from a future Administration. Once, to delay his fall, Rockingham suggested a coalition[8] with the Duke of Bedford. In saloons, female politicians, at their game of loo, divined the ruin of the Ministry, and were zealots for governing the colonies by the hand of power.[9]

In America half suppressed murmurs mingled with the general transport. Arbitrary taxation by Parliament[10] began to be compared with restrictions on in-

[1] De Guerchy, the French Ambassador at London, to Choiseul, 22 May, 1766.
[2] Grafton's Autobiography.
[3] Lord North to Rockingham, 24 May, 1766.
[4] Lord Hardwicke's Memorial. Albemarle's Memoirs of Rockingham and his Contemporaries, i. 335.
[5] Albemarle, i. 340.
[6] Garth, member of the House of Commons, and Agent for South Carolina, to the Committee of South Carolina, 6 June, 1766.
[7] De Guerchy to Choiseul, 22 May, 1766.
[8] Duke of Richmond's Journal in Albemarle, i. 349.
[9] Rigby to Bedford, in Bedford Cor., 4 June, 1766.
[10] Philalethes in Holt's Gazette, No. 1218, 8 May, 1766.

CHAP. XXV. 1766. May.

dustry and trade, and the latter were found to be "the more slavish thing of the two," and "the more inconsistent with civil liberty." The protesting Lords had affirmed, that if the provinces might refuse obedience to one statute, they might to all,—that there was no abiding place between unconditional universal submission and independence. Alarmed that such an alternative should be forced upon them, the colonists, still professing loyalty to a common sovereign, drew nearer and nearer to a total denial of the power of the British Legislature. "I will freely spend nineteen shillings in the pound," said Franklin, "to defend my right of giving or refusing the other shilling; and, after all, if I cannot defend that right, I can retire cheerfully with my little family into the boundless woods of America, which are sure to afford freedom and subsistence to any man who can bait a hook or pull a trigger."[1] "The Americans," said the press of Virginia,[2] "are hasty in expressing their gratitude, if the repeal of the Stamp Act is not at least a tacit compact that Great Britain will never again tax us;" and it advised "the different Assemblies, without mentioning the proceedings of Parliament, to enter upon their journals as strong declarations of their own rights as words could express."[3]

To the anxious colonies, Boston proposed union as the means of security. While within its own borders it sought "the total abolishing of slavery," and encouraged learning, as the support of the constitution

[1] Franklin's Hints for a Reply to the Protests of Certain Members of the House of Lords against the Repeal of the Stamp Act.

[2] Gage to Conway, 1766.

[3] A British American, Virginia, 20 May, 1766, reprinted in Holt's Gazette, 1226; 3 July, 1766. Compare Moore to the Secretary of State, 11 July, 1766.

CHAP. XXV. 1766. May.

and the handmaid of liberty, its representatives[1] were charged to keep up a constant intercourse with the other English governments on the continent, to conciliate any difference that should arise; ever preferring their friendship and confidence to the demands of rigorous justice. Henceforth its watchword was union, which the rash conduct of the dismayed[2] officers of the crown contributed to establish. Bernard was elated at having been praised in the House of Lords by Camden for one set of his opinions, and quoted in the Bedford Protest as an oracle for the other. There was even a rumor that he was to be made a baronet. His superciliousness[3] rose with his sense of personal safety; and he gave out, that on the meeting of the legislature, he should play out his part as Governor.

In choosing the new House in Massachusetts, many towns, stimulated by the "rhapsodies" of Otis,[4] put firm patriots in the places of the doubtful and the timid. Plymouth sent James Warren, the brother-in-law of Otis; and Boston, at the suggestion of Samuel Adams, gave one of its seats to John Hancock, a young merchant of large fortune and a generous nature. At their organization, on the last Wednesday in May, the Representatives elected James Otis their Speaker, and Samuel Adams their Clerk. Otis was still the most influential Member of the House; had long been held in great esteem throughout the province; had been its Delegate to the New-York Congress; and had executed that trust to universal acceptance.[5] Though irritable, he was also placable,

[1] Records of the Town of Boston for 26 May, 1766. Boston Gazette, 2 June, 1766; 583, 2, 1.

[2] Hutchinson to Richard Jackson, 11 June, 1766.

[3] Diary of Oakes Angier.

[4] Advertisement by Otis, 14 April, 1766.

[5] John Adams: Diary, 203.

CHAP. XXV. 1766. May. and at heart was truly loyal. Bernard ostentatiously negatived the choice. The negative, as unwise as it was unusual, excited in the whole colony[1] undefined apprehensions of danger; but the House, deferring to legal right, acquiesced without complaint, and substituted as its Speaker the respectable but irresolute Thomas Cushing.

In the afternoon of the same day, at the choice of the Council, the four Judges of the Supreme Court, of whom Hutchinson was the Chief, the King's Attorney, and Oliver, the Secretary and late Stamp-master, all Members of the last year's Board, were not re-elected; for, said Samuel Adams, "upon the principle of the best writers, a union of the several powers of government in one person is dangerous to liberty."[2] The ballot had conformed strictly to the charter[3] and to usage, and the successful candidates were men of prudence, uprightness, and loyalty. But Bernard "resented"[4] the exclusion of the crown officers, and from the whole number of twenty-eight he rejected six[5] of the ablest "friends of the people in the board."[6] He had the legal right to do so; and the Legislature submitted without a murmur.[7]

Here the altercation should have terminated. But on the following day, Bernard—an "abject" coward,[8] where courage was needed, and now insolent when

[1] Compare Boston Gazette, 17 November, 1766; 607, 1, 1.

[2] Samuel Adams to Dennys De Berdt, 1766.

[3] Compare the Answer of the House to Governor Bernard, 2 June, 1766.

[4] Compare Bernard to Hillsborough, 30 May, 1768.

[5] Thomas Hutchinson to his son, then in England, 29 May, 1766.

[6] John Adams: Diary in Works, ii. 204.

[7] Samuel Adams to Arthur Lee, 19 April, 1771.

[8] See the Journal of Captain Conner of the Romney, and the letters of Lieutenant-Colonel Dalrymple, Commodore Hood, &c., &c., as well as the Boston Gazette.—Grenville Papers, iv. 375.

he should have been conciliatory—sought to constrain the election of Hutchinson, Oliver, and two others,[1] and accused the House of having determined its votes from "private interests and resentment and popular discontent," disguised "under the borrowed garb of patriotism." "It were to be wished," he continued, "that a veil could be drawn over the late disgraceful scenes. But that cannot be done till a better temper and understanding shall prevail. The recent election of Councillors is an attack on government in form, and an ill-judged and ill-timed oppugnation of the King's authority."[2]

CHAP XXV. 1766. May.

June.

Concurrently, Rigby, as the leader of the Bedford party,[3] on the third day of June, proposed in the British House of Commons an Address to the King, censuring America for its "rebellious disposition," as well as the Ministry for its dilatoriness; pledging Parliament to the coercion of the colonies; and praying that there might be no prorogation till positive assurances should be received from the provincial Governors of the return of the people to obedience.[4]

From the ministerial benches Charles Townshend, professing to oppose the motion, spoke substantially in its favor. "It has long been my opinion," said he, in conclusion, "that America should be regulated and deprived of its militating and contradictory charters, and its royal Governors, Judges, and Attorneys be rendered independent of the people. I therefore expect that the present Administration will, in

[1] Bernard to the Lords of Trade, 7 July, 1766.

[2] Speech of Governor Bernard to the Council and House of Representatives, 29 May, 1766, in Bradford's Massachusetts State Papers, 74.

[3] Rigby to the Duke of Bedford, 4 June, 1766, in Bedford Correspondence, iii. 336.

[4] Journal of the House of Commons, xxx. 841.

CHAP. XXV. 1766. June. the recess of Parliament, take all the necessary previous steps for compassing so desirable an event. The madness and distractions of America have demanded the attention of the Supreme Legislature, and the colony Charters have been considered and declared by judges[1] of the realm, inconsistent, and actually forfeited by the audacious and unpardonable Resolves of subordinate Assemblies. This regulation must no longer be trusted to accidental obedience. If I should differ in judgment from the present Administration on this point, I now declare, that I must withdraw, and not longer co-operate with persons of such narrow views in government. But I hope and expect otherwise, trusting that I shall be an instrument among them of preparing a new system."[2]

Rigby was ably supported by Lord North and Thurlow; and especially by Wedderburn, who railed mercilessly at the Ministers, in a mixed strain of wit, oratory, and abuse;[3] so that, notwithstanding a spirited speech from Conway, and a negative to the motion without a division, their helplessness stood exposed. America was taken out of their control and made the sport of faction.

The very same day on which Townshend proclaimed a war of extermination against American Charters, similar threats were uttered at Boston. In communicating the circular letter from Conway, proposing "to forgive and forget" the incidents of the

[1] The allusion is probably to the Speech of the Lord Chancellor, Northington, in the House of Lords, February 3, 1766.

[2] Manuscript Report of the Conclusion of Townshend's Speech, in my possession. The manuscript appears to me to be in the handwriting of Moffat of Rhode Island, and was obtained from among the papers of the late George Chalmers, after their sale.

[3] Rigby to Bedford, 4 June, 1766.

Stamp Act, and directing the several Governors to "recommend" to the Colonial Legislatures an indemnification of all sufferers by the riots which it occasioned,[1] Bernard renewed his complaints that the principal crown officers had been dropped from the Council. "If," said he, "this proceeding should be justified by asserting a right, the justification itself would serve to impeach the right."[2] And inviting them again[3] to choose among others Hutchinson, whom, after thirty years' uninterrupted concern in public affairs, the thought of a retreat, though with the occupation of Chief Justice and Judge of Probate, had plunged into melancholy,[4] he added, "The fate of the Province is put in a scale, which is to rise or fall according to your present conduct."

CHAP. XXV. 1766. June.

"The Requisition[5] is founded upon a Resolution of the House of Commons," he continued, employing the word which that body, after debate, as well as Conway, had purposely avoided. "The authority with which it is introduced should preclude all disputation about complying with it."

The patriots of Massachusetts could hardly find words[6] fit to express their indignation. Bernard's speeches fell on the ear of Samuel Adams, as not less "infamous and irritating" than the worst "that ever came from a Stuart to the English Parliament;"[7] and with sombre joy he called the Province happy in having for its Governor, one who left to the people no

[1] Prior Documents, 89.

[2] Speech of Governor Bernard to the Legislature, 3 June, 1766, in Bradford's Massachusetts State Papers, 81.

[3] Bernard to Lords of Trade, 7 July, 1766.

[4] Hutchinson to Bollan, 2 June, 1766.

[5] Bernard in Bradford, 82.

[6] John Adams's Private Diary. Works, ii. 204.

[7] Samuel Adams to Arthur Lee, 19 April, 1771.

CHAP. XXV. option, but between perpetual watchfulness and total ruin.

1766. June. "The free exercise of our undoubted privileges," replied the House,[1] "can never, with any color of reason, be adjudged an abuse of our liberty. We have strictly adhered to the directions of our Charter and the laws of the land. We made our election with special regard to the qualifications of the candidates. We cannot conceive how the assertion of our clear Charter right of free election can tend to impeach that right or Charter. We hope your Excellency does not mean openly and publicly to threaten us with a deprivation of our Charter privileges, merely for exercising them according to our best judgment."

"No branch of the Legislature," insisted the Council,[2] "has usurped or interfered with the right of another. Nothing has taken place but what has been constitutional and according to the Charter. An election duly made, though disagreeable to the Chair, does not deserve to be called a formal attack upon Government, or an oppugnation of the King's authority."

Mayhew, of Boston, mused anxiously over the danger, which was now clearly revealed, till, in the morning watches of the next Lord's Day, light dawned upon his excited mind, and the voice of wisdom spoke from his warm heart, which was so soon to cease to beat. "You have heard of the communion of churches," he wrote to Otis; "while I was thinking of this in my bed, the great use and importance

[1] Answer of the House, in Bradford, 88.

[2] Answer of the Council, in Bradford, 86.

of a communion of colonies appeared to me in a strong light. Would it not be decorous for our Assembly to send circulars to all the rest, expressing a desire to cement union among ourselves? A good foundation for this has been laid by the Congress at New-York; never losing sight of it may be the only means of perpetuating our liberties."[1] The patriot uttered this great word of counsel on the morning of his last day of health in Boston. From his youth he had consecrated himself to the service of colonial freedom in the State and Church; he died, overtasked, in the unblemished beauty of manhood, consumed by his fiery zeal, foreseeing independence.[2] His character was so deeply impressed on the place of his activity, that it is not yet grown over. Whoever repeats the story of American liberty renews his fame.

CHAP. XXV. 1766. June.

The time for intercolonial correspondence was not come; but to keep up a fellow-feeling with its own constituents, the House, setting an example to be followed by all representative bodies, opened[3] a gallery for the public to attend its debates. It also sent a grateful Address to the King,[4] and voted thanks[5] to Pitt and to Grafton; and, among many others, to Conway and Barré, to Camden and Shelburne; to Howard, who had refused to draw his sword against the colonies; to Chesterfield, who left retirement for their relief. But as to compensating the sufferers by the late disturbances, it upheld its

[1] Jonathan Mayhew to James Otis, Lord's Day Morning, 8 June, 1766. See Bradford's Life of Mayhew, 428, 429.

[2] Compare Thomas Hollis to Andrew Eliot, 1 July, 1768.

[3] Vote of the House of 12 June, 1766.

[4] Address to the King, in Bradford, 91.

[5] Vote of Thanks, &c., &c., 20 June.

CHAP. XXV. 1766. June. right of deliberating freely, and would only promise at its next session to act as should then appear just and reasonable.[1]

Connecticut,[2] overjoyed at the repeal of the Stamp Act and applauding its connection with Great Britain, elected as its Governor the discreet and patriotic William Pitkin, in place of the loyalist Fitch.

The Legislature of South Carolina, retaining, like Georgia,[3] its avowed sentiments on internal taxation, marked its loyalty by granting every requisition, even for doubtful purposes; at the same time, it asked for the pictures of Lynch, Gadsden, and Rutledge; and on the motion of Rawlins Lowndes, remitted a thousand pounds towards a statue of Pitt. Still they felt keenly that they were undeservedly distinguished from their happier fellow-subjects in England by the unconstitutional tenure of their judges during the King's pleasure. They complained, too, that ships, laden with their rice for ports north of Cape Finisterre, were compelled, on their outward and return voyage, to touch at some port in England; and they prayed for modifications of the Navigation Act, which would equally benefit Great Britain and themselves.[4]

At New-York, on the King's birthday, the bells rang merry peals to the strains of martial music and

[1] House to the Governor, 25 June—Governor to House, 27 June—House to Governor, 28 June,—all in Bradford. Also, Bernard's Observations, in Prior Documents, 107. Further: Letters from Bernard of 29 June, and 19 July, 1766.

[2] Gov. Pitkin to Secretary Conway, 4 Aug., 1766.

[3] Sir James Wright (nephew to the Lord Chancellor, Northington) to the Secretary, 23 July, 1766.

[4] South Carolina Committee of Correspondence to Garth, a Member of Parliament, their Agent, 2 July, 1766. Compare his answer of 26 September, 1766.

CHAP. XXV. 1766. June.

the booming of artillery; the Fields near the Park were spread for feasting; and a tall mast was raised to George the Third, William Pitt, and Liberty. At night enormous bonfires blazed; and all was as loyal and happy, as though freedom had been brought back with ample pledges for her stay.

The Assembly came together in the best spirit. They passed over the claims of Colden,[1] who was held to have been the cause of his own griefs; but resolved by a majority of one to indemnify James.[2] They also voted to raise on the Bowling Green an equestrian statue of George the Third, and a statue of William Pitt, twice the Preserver of his Country. But the clause of the Mutiny or Billeting Act, directing colonial legislatures to make specific contributions towards the support of the army, placed New-York, where the head-quarters were established, in the dilemma of submitting immediately and unconditionally to the authority of Parliament, or taking the lead in a new career of resistance.[3] The rescript was, in theory, worse than the Stamp Act. For how could one legislative body command what another legislative body should enact? And, viewed as a tax, it was unjust, for it threw all the burden on the colony where the troops chanced to be collected. The Requisition of the General, made through the Governor, "agreeably to the Act of Parliament," was therefore declared to be unprecedented in its character and unreasonable in its amount; yet in the exercise of the right of free

[1] Lieut. Gov. Colden to General Amherst, 24 June, 1766.

[2] Colden to Conway, June, 1766.

[3] Moore to Conway, and Gage to Moore, in Prior Documents, 94, &c.

CHAP. XXV. 1766. June.

deliberation, every thing asked for was voted, except such articles as were not provided in Europe for British troops which were in barracks.

The General and the Governor united in accepting the grant; but in reporting the affair, the well-meaning, indolent Moore reflected the opinions of the army, whose officers still compared the Americans to the rebels of Scotland, and wished them a defeat like that of Culloden.[1] "My message," said he at the end of his narrative, "is treated merely as a Requisition made here; and they have carefully avoided the least mention of the Act on which it is founded. It is my opinion, that every Act of Parliament, when not backed by a sufficient power to enforce it, will meet with the same fate."[2]

From Boston, Bernard, without any good reason, chimed in with the complainers. "This Government," said he, "quickened and encouraged by the occurrences at New-York, cannot recover itself by its own internal powers." "The making the King's Council annually elective, is the fatal ingredient in the constitution. The only anchor of hope is the sovereign power, which would secure obedience to its decrees, if they were properly introduced and effectually supported."[3] And he gave himself no rest in soliciting the interposition of Parliament, and the change of the Charter of Massachusetts.[4]

[1] Leake's Life of John Lamb.

[2] Gov. Moore to Conway, 20 June, 1766.

[3] Bernard to Lords of Trade, 7 July, 1766.

[4] Bernard to Conway, 19 July, 1766.

CHAPTER XXVI.

COALITION OF THE KING AND THE GREAT COMMONER AGAINST THE ARISTOCRACY—THE ADMINISTRATION OF CHATHAM.

JULY—OCTOBER, 1766.

CHAP. XXVI. 1766. July.

THE obnoxious clauses of the Billeting Act had been renewed inadvertently by Ministers, who had designed to adopt a system of lenity. They proposed to remove Bernard from Massachusetts, in favor of Hutchinson,[1] whom Conway had been duped into believing a friend to colonial liberty. Reviving against Spain the claim for the ransom of the Manillas, they suggested in lieu of it a cession of the island of New Orleans; though the Spanish ambassador took fire at the thought, saying, "New Orleans is the key to Mexico."[2] With equally vain endeavors, they were forming new and milder instructions for the government of Canada,[3] in the hope to combine respect for the municipal customs and religion of its old inhabitants, with the safeguards of the English criminal law.[4] The conquest of New France

[1] Thos. Hutchinson, jr., to Thos. Hutchinson, July, 1766.

[2] Durand to Choiseul, 27 June, 1766.

[3] Hardwicke's Memorial.

[4] Paper in the Lansdowne House Manuscripts endorsed, "Relative to the present State of Quebec, 17 May, 1767."

CHAP. XXVI. 1766. July. subjected to England one more country, whose people had not separated from the Church of Rome. At first, the English penal laws were extended to the banks of the St. Lawrence; but the British Government was soon compelled to take initiatory steps towards Catholic emancipation. Canadians, without altering their faith, were permitted to serve as jurors,[1] and it was proposed to make them eligible as Justices of the Peace and as Judges.[2] But Northington, in very ill humor, thrust forward vague objections;[3] and as his colleagues persevered, he repaired to the King to advise their change.[4]

The time was now come for the eclipse of the genius and of the glory of William Pitt. Unrelenting disease and the labors of the winter session had exhausted his little strength, and irreparably wrecked his constitution. Had he remained out of place, and appeared at intervals in the House of Commons, he would have left a name needing no careful and impartial analysis of facts for his apology. As it is, I have to record, how unsuccessfully he labored to diminish the aristocratic ascendency in England; to perpetuate colonial liberty; to rescue India from the misrule of commercial cupidity; how, as he rose to guide the destinies of a great people in the career of freedom, along the unknown future, he appeared

Like one who had been led astray
Through the Heaven's high pathless way.

Farming, grazing, haymaking, and all the charms of rural life in Somersetshire could not obliterate

[1] Additional Instructions to the Governor of Quebec, of 24 Feb. 1766. Dr. Adam Mabane to General Murray, 26 August, 1766.

[2] Duke of Richmond's Journal, in Albemarle, i. 353.

[3] Duke of Richmond's Journal, in Albemarle, i. 351.

[4] Rockingham to C. Yorke, 4 July, 1766, in Albemarle, i. 357.

from his mind the memory of days of activity, when, as he directed against the Bourbons the treasure and the hearts of the united empire, his life was the life of the British people, his will was their will, his uncompromising haughtiness was but the image of their pride, and his presumptuous daring the only adequate expression of their self-reliance. His eager imagination bore him back to the public world, though to him it was become a riddle, which not even the wisest interpreter could solve.[1]

While he was in this tumult of emotions, a letter was brought from the King's own hand, reminding him that his last words in the House of Commons had been a declaration of freedom from party ties,[2] and inviting him to form an independent Ministry.[3] The feeble invalid, whose infirmities inflamed his constitutional hopefulness, bounded at the summons of his sovereign, and flew, as he expressed it, "on wings of expedition, to lay at the King's feet the poor but sincere offering of the remnant of his life, body, heart and mind."[4]

He arrived in London on Friday, the eleventh of July, by no means well;[5] but his feverishness only bewildered his judgment and increased his self-confidence. On Saturday he was barely able to have a short interview with the King, and obtain consent to take the actual Administration as the groundwork of his own;[6] even though Newcastle and Rockingham

[1] Pitt to Countess Stanhope, 20 June, 1766. In Mahon's History of England, v. Appendix, vii.

[2] Rigby to Bedford, 24 April, 1766. Bedford Correspondence, iii. 333.

[3] The King to Pitt, 7 July, 1766. Chatham Correspondence, ii. 436. Northington to Pitt, 7 July, 1766. Chat. Cor. ii. 435.

[4] Pitt, in Chat. Corr. ii. 435.

[5] Pitt to Lady Chatham, 12 July, 1766. Chat. Corr. ii. 439.

[6] That Pitt stated this on Saturday the 12th appears from the King's secret note of the 15th July.

CHAP. XXVI. 1766. July.

should retire.[1] True to his affections, he next invited Temple, the beloved brother of his wife, the head of her family, and their common benefactor, to become the First Lord of the Treasury. But Temple, who had connected himself with Grenville[2] and the party of Bedford, refused to unite with the friends of Rockingham; and, having told the King, "he would not go into the Ministry like a child, to come out like a fool,"[3] he returned to Stowe, repeating this speech to the world, dictating a scurrilous pamphlet against his brother-in-law, and enjoying the notoriety of having been solicited to take office and been found impracticable.

The discussion with Temple and its issue, still further aggravated the malady of Pitt. He was too ill, on the eighteenth, to see the King, or even the Duke of Grafton, and yet, passing between all the factions of the aristocracy, he proceeded to form a Ministry. Grafton, to whom, on Saturday, he offered the Treasury, was one who did not see far before him, and was always making mistakes. His judgment was often in error; though his candor remained unimpaired. Without consultation, he went directly to Charles Townshend, by whose assiduous court and rare abilities he had been "captivated;" and found him "eager to give up the Paymaster's place for the office of Chancellor of the Exchequer;" which must have seemed to him "the readiest road to the upper seat." When informed of this proposal, Pitt, who

[1] Camden to Thomas Walpole, 13 July, and 19 July, 1766. In Campbell's Chancellors, v. 257, 258.

[2] Geo. Grenville to Bedford, 15 July, 1766, in Bedford Corr. iii. 340.

[3] Inquiry into the Conduct of a late Right Honorable Commoner, Durand, to Duc de Choiseul, 3 Juillet, 1766. Temple to Lady Chatham, Chat. Corr. ii. 469.

better understood Townshend's character, said every thing to dissuade Grafton from taking such a man as his second; warning him of the many unexpected disappointments which he was preparing. But "I was weak enough, very unwisely, to persist in my desire," Grafton afterwards wrote, more anxious to manifest the integrity of his intentions, than to conceal the consequences of his advice. Pitt loved to oblige those in whom he confided, and at last gave way, though much against his inclination, as well as his opinion; insisting, however, that Townshend was not to be called to the Cabinet.[1] On learning this exclusion, Townshend hesitated; but, finally, on the twenty-sixth, pleading "the express commands" of the King, he acquiesced. "I sacrifice," said he, "with cheerfulness and from principle, all that men usually pursue." Affecting to trust that this merit would be acknowledged by posterity, he pledged himself, in every measure of business and every act of life, to cultivate Pitt's confidence and esteem; and, to Grafton he said, "My plan is a plan of union with your Grace; words are useless; God prosper our joint labors, and may our mutual trust, affection, and friendship grow from every act of our lives."[2] Thus he professed himself a devotee to Pitt and Grafton, being sure to do his utmost to thwart the one, and to supersede the other.

CHAP. XXVI. 1766. July.

The lead in the House of Commons was assigned to Conway, as one of the Secretaries of State; the care of America to the Earl of Shelburne, notwithstanding he suffered under the King's extreme dis-

[1] Grafton's Autobiography.

[2] C. Townshend to Grafton, 25 July, 1766, in Grafton's Autobiography; and C. Townshend to Pitt, 26 July, 1766. Chatham Corr. ii. 464, 465.

CHAP. XXVI. 1766. July.

like.[1] The seals of the highest judicial office were confided to Camden, who had called taxing America, by Act of Parliament, a robbery. The former Chancellor became President of the Council; while the Prime Minister's own infirmities, which should have forbidden him to take office at all, made him reserve for himself the quiet custody of the Privy Seal. Taken as a whole, the Cabinet—of which the Members were Pitt, Camden, Grafton, Conway, Shelburne, and the now inactive Northington—was the most liberal that had been composed in England. "If ever a Cabinet," wrote a sagacious observer,[2] "can hope for the rare privilege of unanimity, it is this, in which Pitt will see none but persons whose imagination he has subjugated, whose premature advancement is due to his choice, whose expectations of permanent fortune rest on him alone."

Of the friends of Rockingham, Lord John Cavendish set the example of refusing to serve under Grafton; but he insisted to Conway that acts of civility would satisfy the heads of his party. At this suggestion, Pitt, on the twenty-seventh of July, went to pay Rockingham a visit of respect; and had passed the threshold,[3] when the young chief of the great whig families, refusing to receive him, turned the venerable

[1] Walpole's George the Third, ii. 349.

[2] Durand to Choiseul, 30 July, 1766. Referring not to Chatham's Ministry, but to the modifications which Grafton afterwards made in it by a junction with the Bedfords, Chesterfield called the Cabinet a piece of "Mosaic." Burke appropriated the metaphor, and applied it wrongfully; yet in rhetoric so splendid, that every one is inclined to forget historic exactness, and quote his brilliant epigrams. Chatham's Ministry was at first less of a Mosaic than Rockingham's, and very much less of a Mosaic than the Opposition, of which Burke was now to form a part.

[3] Pitt to the Duke of Grafton, Sunday, 27 July, 1766, in Grafton, 135. Walpole, ii. 356. Albemarle's Rockingham, ii. 4. Rockingham to Pitt, and Rockingham to Conway.

man of the people from his door. But he was never afterwards able to resume office, except with the friends of the Minister he now insulted; and his followers never gained continuing power, till, after many vacillations and many coalitions with other branches of the aristocracy, they gave up something of their exclusiveness, and, in an alliance with the people, renounced their worn out policy, to advocate reform.

The Old Whig party which, in 1746, deserted the public service only to force their restoration on their own terms, which eleven years later kept England, in time of war, in a state of anarchy for ten weeks till their demands could be satisfactorily compromised, had, in 1765, owed office to the King's favor, and now fell powerless, when left to themselves. The Administration of Rockingham brought Cumberland into the Cabinet; took their law from Mansfield; restored Lord George Germain to public life; and would willingly have coalesced with Bedford. Yet a spirit of humanity ruled their intentions and pervaded their measures; while their most pernicious errors sprung from their attempt at a compromise with the principles of their predecessors. They confirmed the rights of persons by condemning general warrants, and adhered to those friends of liberty who had run hazards in its cause. They abstained from some of the worst methods of corruption usual to their party in its earlier days; they sold no employments, and obtained no reversions. Opposed by placemen and pensioners, they had support in the increasing confidence and good will of the nation. Still they had entered the Cabinet in violation of their essential doctrine, at the wish of the King, superseding

CHAP. XXVI. 1766. July.

men who were dismissed only for maintaining Privilege against Prerogative; and if they mitigated taxation in America by repealing the Stamp Act, they boasted of having improved the revenue raised there from trade,[1] renewed the unconstitutional method of making parliamentary Requisitions on colonial Assemblies, and in the Declaratory Act introduced into the statute book the worst law that ever found a place there, tyrannical in principle, false in fact, and impossible in practice.

The incapacity of Pitt's new Administration was apparent from its first day, when he announced to his astonished and disheartened colleagues his purpose of placing himself as the Earl of Chatham in the House of Lords. During the past year such an elevation in rank had often been suggested as his due, and would have been no more than a moderate distinction for merit far inferior to his own. Besides, he was too much "shattered" to lead the Commons; and if the King should grow weary of his counsels, he might wish secure dignity for his age.[2] But in ceasing to be the Great Commoner, he veiled his superiority; and made a confession of the utter ruin of his health. "My friend," said Frederic of Prussia on hearing of it, "has harmed himself by accepting a Peerage."[3] "It argues," said the King of Poland, "a senselessness to glory to forfeit the name of Pitt for any title."[4] "The strength of the Administration," thought all his colleagues, "lay in his remaining with the Commons." "There was but one voice among us," said Grafton,

[1] Edmund Burke's Short Account of a late Short Administration.

[2] De Guerchy to Choiseul, 19 Dec. 1766.

[3] Andrew Mitchell to Chatham, 17 Sept. 1766; Chat. Corr. iii. 70.

[4] Charles Lee to King of Poland, 1 Dec. 1766; Lee's Life, 187.

"nor indeed throughout the Kingdom."[1] The lion had left the forest, where he roamed as the undisputed monarch, and of himself had walked into a cage. His popularity vanished, and with it the terror of his name. He was but an English Earl and the shadow of a Prime Minister; he no longer represented the enthusiastic nationality of the British people. He had, moreover, offended the head of every faction, whose assistance he yet required; Camden, his Chancellor, had not the qualities of a great statesman, and wanted fidelity; Grafton, on whom he leaned, was indolent and easily misled; Conway, one of his Secretaries of State, always vacillated; Shelburne, his firm, able, and sincere friend, was, from the first, regarded at court with dislike; and the King himself agreed with him in nothing but the wish to humble the aristocracy.

Aug. At the time of Chatham's taking office, Choiseul, the greatest minister of France since Richelieu,[2] having assigned the care of the navy to his brother, had resumed that of Foreign Affairs. He knew the gigantic schemes of colonial conquests which Pitt had formerly harbored; and weighed the probabilities[3] of an attempt to realize them by a new war against France and Spain. The agent whom he had sent in 1764 on a tour of observation through the British colonies, was just returned, and reported[4] how they abounded in corn, cattle, flax, and iron; in trees fit for masts; in pine timber, lighter than oak, easily wrought, not liable to split, and incorruptible; how

[1] Grafton's Autobiography.

[2] Chatham in Walpole, iv. 279.

[3] Choiseul to Durand, 24 August, 1766.

[4] Durand to Choiseul, 3, 7, and 24 Aug. 1766; Choiseul to Durand, 15 Sept. 1766.

CHAP. XXVI. 1766. Aug.

the inhabitants, already numerous, and doubling their numbers every twenty years, were opulent, warlike, and conscious of their strength; how they followed the sea, especially at the north, and engaged in great fisheries; how they built annually one hundred and fifty vessels to sell in Europe and the West Indies, at the rate of seven pounds sterling the ton; and how they longed to throw off the restraints imposed on their navigation. New-York stood at the confluence of two rivers, of which the East was the shelter to merchant vessels; but its roadstead was also a vast harbor where a navy could ride at anchor. The large town of Philadelphia had rope-walks and busy ship-yards; manufactures of all sorts, especially of leather and of iron. In the province to which it belonged, the Presbyterians outnumbered the peaceful Quakers; and Germans, weary of subordination to England and unwilling to serve under English officers against France, openly declared that Pennsylvania would one day be called Little Germany. In all New England there were no citadels, from the people's fear of their being used to compel submission to Acts of Parliament infringing colonial privileges. The garrison at Boston was in the service of the Colony. The British troops were so widely scattered in little detachments, as to be of no account. "England," reasoned the observer, "must foresee a Revolution, and has hastened its epoch by emancipating the Colonies from the fear of France in Canada."[1]

Simultaneously with the reception of these accounts, Choiseul was reading in the Gazette of Leyden the Answer lately made by the Assembly of Massa-

[1] Report of Pontleroy, the French Emissary, made through Durand to Choiseul, Aug. 1766.

chusetts to its Governor, and learned with astonishment that colonies which were supposed to have no liberties but by inference, spoke boldly and firmly of rights and a Constitution.[1] In this manner, time was bringing him some assuagement of his former deep humiliation.

CHAP. XXVI. 1766. Aug.

Could Chatham have regained his health, he would have mastered all difficulties, or fallen with dignity. Jealous of the Bourbon courts, he, too, thought of the possibility of war, and urged the improvement of the harbor of Pensacola, which, it was said, could be made to admit vessels of the heaviest burden, shelter at least forty ships of the line, and hold in check all the commerce of Vera Cruz.[2]

Sept.

The rival statesmen, with eyes fixed on America, were, all the while, competing for European alliances. No sooner had Chatham entered on the ministry, than he rushed with headlong confidence into the plan of a great Northern League to balance the power of the Bourbons; and hastily invited Frederic of Prussia and Catherine of Russia to connect themselves intimately with England. But, at all courts, his accepting a Peerage robbed him of his lustre; and Frederic, disliking George the Third, retaining the rankling memory of having been deserted in 1763, doubting the fixedness of any Ministry in England, put the invitation aside. Choiseul was as superior in diplomacy, as his opponent had been in war; and with steady purpose and consummate skill, was establishing such relations with every power of Europe, that, in the event of new hostilities respecting America, France would have Spain for its partner, and no enemy but England.

[1] Durand to Choiseul, 27 Aug. 1766.

[2] Durand to Choiseul, 23 Aug. 1766.

CHAP. XXVI. 1766. Sept.

Chatham grew sick at heart, as well as decrepit. To be happy he needed the consciousness of standing well with his fellow-men. But he whose voice had been a clarion to the Protestant world no longer enjoyed popularity at home, or influence abroad, or the trusting affection of the Colonies. Cheering sympathy could scarcely have wrought the miracle of his restoration; but now the sense of his loneliness on his return to power, crushed his vigor of will. He who had been most imperative in command knew not how to resolve. Once, at Grafton's earnest solicitation, Charles Townshend was permitted to attend a consultation on European alliances.[1] The next day Chatham, with the cheerful consent of the King,[2] retreated to Bath; but its springs had no healing for him. He desired to control France by a northern union; and stood before Europe without one power as an ally. He loved to give the law to the Cabinet; and was just admitting into it a restless intriguer, who would not fear to traverse his policy. He gloried in the unbounded confidence of his sovereign; and the King wanted nothing of him but "his name."[3] He longed for the love of the people of England; and he had left their body for an Earldom. He would have humbled the aristocracy; and "the nobility" not only "hated him"[4] with vindictive arrogance, but retained strength to overwhelm him, whenever he should lose the favor of the Court.

Oct. Yet the cause of liberty was advancing, though Chatham had gone astray. Philosophy spread the knowledge of the laws of nature. The Empress of

[1] Grafton's Autobiography.

[2] King to Chatham, 25 Sept. 1766; Chat. Corr. iii. 75.

[3] Letter of the King to Lord North.

[4] Bollan to Hutchinson, 25 Sept. 1766.

CHAP. XXVI. 1766. Oct.

Russia with her own hand minuted an edict for universal tolerance. "Can you tell me," writes Voltaire[1] exultingly to D'Alembert, "what will come within thirty years of the revolution which is taking effect in the minds of men from Naples to Moscow? I, who am too old to hope to see any thing, commend to you the age which is forming." But though so far stricken in years, Voltaire shall himself witness and applaud the greatest step in this progress; shall see insurgent colonies become a Republic, and welcome before Paris and the Academy of France a runaway apprentice as its envoy to the most polished Court of Europe.

Meantime Choiseul dismissed from the Council of his King all former theories about America, alike in policy and war;[2] and looked more nearly into the condition of the British colonies, that his new system might rest on the surest ground.

[1] Voltaire to D'Alembert, 15 Oct. 1766.

[2] Choiseul to Durand, 15 Sept. 1766.

CHAPTER XXVII.

CHARLES TOWNSHEND USURPS THE LEAD IN GOVERNMENT—
CHATHAM'S ADMINISTRATION CONTINUED.

OCTOBER, 1766—JANUARY, 1767.

CHAP. XXVII. 1766. Oct.

THE people of Massachusetts lulled themselves into the belief that they were "restored once more" to the secure enjoyment "of their rights and liberties." But their secret enemies, some from a lust of power, and others from an inordinate love of money,[1] still restlessly combined to obtain an American army and an American tribute, representing them in numerous letters as necessary for the enforcement of the Navigation Acts, and even for the existence of Government. When the soldiers stationed in New-York had, in the night[2] of the tenth of August, cut down the flagstaff of the citizens, the General reported the ensuing quarrel as a proof of "anarchy and confusion," and the requisiteness of troops for the support of "the laws."[3] Yet the New-York Association of the Sons of Liberty had been dissolved; and all efforts to keep up "its glorious spirit," were subor

[1] Candidus [Samuel Adams], in Boston Gazette, 9 Sept. 1771.

[2] Holt's Gazette, 1232; 14 Aug. 1766, and 1233, 21 Aug. 1766. Dunlap's History of New-York, i. 433; Isaac Q. Leake's Life of John Lamb, 36.

[3] General Gage to Secretary Richmond, 26 Aug. 1766.

CHAP. XXVII. 1766. Oct.

dinated to loyalty.[1] "A few individuals"[2] at Boston, having celebrated the anniversary of the outbreak against the Stamp Act, care was taken to report, how healths had been drunk to Otis, "the American Hampden, who first proposed the Congress;"[3] "to the Virginians," who sounded the alarm to the country; to Paoli and the struggling Corsicans; to the spark of Liberty that was thought to have been kindled in Spain. From Bernard, who made the restraints on commerce intolerable by claiming the legal penalty of treble forfeits from merchants whom his own long collusion had tempted to the infraction of a revenue law, came unintermitted complaints of illicit trade. At Falmouth, now Portland, an attempt to seize goods under the disputed authority of Writs of Assistance, had been defeated by a mob;[4] and the disturbance was made to support a general accusation against the Province. At Boston, Charles Paxton, the Marshal of the Court of Admiralty, came with the Sheriff and a similar warrant, to search the house of Daniel Malcom[5] for a second time; but the stubborn patriot refused to open his doors, which they dared not break down, so doubtful were they of their right; and when the altercation attracted a crowd, they withdrew, pretending to have been obstructed by a riotous and tumultuous assemblage. These incidents, by themselves of little moment, were secretly

[1] Isaac Sears, John Lamb, and others to Nicholas Ray, New-York, 10 Oct. 1766.

[2] Andrew Oliver to Thomas Whately, 7 May, 1767, in Letters, &c., 19.

[3] Tenth Toast at Liberty Tree, 14 Aug. 1766.

[4] Bernard to the Board of Trade, 18 Aug. 1766, and Inclosures; Same to Shelburne, 3 Sept. 1766; Shelburne to Bernard, 11 Dec. 1766.

[5] Bernard to Shelburne, 10 Oct. 1766, with inclosures of Depositions, taken ex Parte; Letter from the Town of Boston to Dennys De Berdt, 22 Oct. 1766, with other Depositions. Boston Gazette, 13 Oct. 1766; 602, 1, 1 and 2.

CHAP. XXVII. 1766. Oct.

reported as a general rising against the execution of the Laws of Trade. But the chief reliance of the cabal rested on personal importunity; and the untiring Paxton, who had often visited England, and was known to possess as much of the friendship of Charles Townshend as a selfish client may obtain from an intriguing patron, was sent over as the representative of the colonial Crown Officers,[1] with special authority to appear as the friend of Oliver[2] and of Hutchinson.[3]

We are drawing near the measures which compelled the insurrection of the colonies; but all the stars in their courses were harbingers of American Independence. No sooner were the prairies of Illinois in the possession of England than Croghan, a deputy Indian Agent, who from personal observation knew their value, urged their immediate colonization. Sir William Johnson; William Franklin, the royalist Governor of New Jersey; several fur-traders of Philadelphia; even Gage[4] himself eagerly took part in a project by which they were to acquire vast estates in the most fertile valley of the world.[5] Their proposal embraced the whole Western territory bounded by the Mississippi, the Ohio, a line along the Wabash and Maumee to Lake Erie, and thence across Michi-

[1] Candidus, in Boston Gazette, 9 Sept. 1771.

[2] Compare Oliver to Whately, 7 May, 1767.

[3] Hutchinson to R. Jackson, introducing Paxton; date not given, but evidently of Oct. 1766.

[4] Gage to Secretary of State, 28 March, 1766, referred to the Lords of Trade in May.

[5] Reasons for establishing a British Colony at the Illinois, 1766; Sir William Johnson to Secretary Conway, 10 July, 1766; Lords of Trade to the King, 3 Sept. 1766, before the above named papers were received; Letters of William Franklin and Benjamin Franklin, 1766; Franklin's Writings, iv. 233, &c. This plan for a colony in Illinois should not be confounded with the transactions respecting Vandalia, or as it has been called, Walpole's Grant, which was a tract south of the Ohio.

CHAP. XXVII. 1766. Oct.

gan, Green Bay, and the Fox River, to the mouth of the Wisconsin.[1] The tract was thought to contain sixty-three millions of acres, the like of which could nowhere be found. Benjamin Franklin favored the enterprise which promised fortune to its undertakers, and to America some new security for a mild colonial Administration. It was the wish of Shelburne,[2] who loved to take counsel with the great philosopher on the interests of humanity, that the Valley of the Mississippi might be occupied by colonies enjoying English liberty. But the Board of Trade, to which Hillsborough had returned,[3] insisted that emigrants to so remote regions would establish manufactures for themselves; and in the very heart of America, found a power, which distance must emancipate. They adhered, therefore, to the Proclamation of 1763, and to the range of the Alleghanies as the frontier of British settlements.

But the prohibition only set apart the Great Valley as the sanctuary of the unhappy, the adventurous, and the free; of those whom enterprise, or curiosity, or disgust at the forms of life in the old plantations, raised above royal edicts;[4] of those who had nowhere else a home; or who would run all risks to take possession of the fine soil between the Alleghanies and the Ohio.[5] The boundless West became the poor

[1] From the Reasons, &c., section

[2] B. Franklin to his son, 11 Oct. 1766.

[3] Franklin, iv. 235.

[4] Lieutenant Governor Fauquier to the Lords of Trade, 22 May, 1766: "In disobedience to all proclamations, in defiance of law, and without the least shadow of right to claim or defend their property, people are daily going out to settle beyond the Alleghany Mountains. They flock there just now more than usual," &c., &c. Same to same, 4 Sept. 1766; Proclamation by Fauquier [in the summer of 1766] against making Settlements westward of the Alleghany Mountains.

[5] Lieut. Gov. Fauquier to Shelburne, 18 Dec. 1766.

CHAP. XXVII. 1766. Oct.

man's City of Refuge,[1] where the wilderness guarded his cabin as inviolably as the cliff or the cedar-top holds the eagle's eyrie. The few who occupied lands under grants from the Crown, could rely only on themselves for the protection of their property, and refused to pay quit-rents till their legal right should be acknowledged. The line of "straggling settlements" beyond the mountains, extended from Pittsburg up the Monongahela[2] and its tributaries to the banks of the Greenbriar and the New River,[3] and to the well-known upper valley of the Holston,[4] where the military path from Virginia led to the country of the Cherokees. But as yet there was no settlement in Kentucky, and James Smith, who, with three others from Pennsylvania, went this year from the Holston, by way of Cumberland River, to the Ohio, and so to the mouth of the Tennessee, left no memorial of his passing by but the name of Stone, one of his companions, which he gave to a branch above Nashville.[5] Most of the party proceeded to the country of the Illinois.

In North Carolina, the people along the upland frontier, many of whom had sprung from Scotch-Irish

[1] Fauquier to Earl of Shelburne, 15 Nov. 1766.

[2] For the Official Papers of 1766, respecting the settlements on the Monongahela, especially at Redstone, see the Minutes of the Provincial Council of Pennsylvania, vol. ix. Compare also, J. L. Bowman in the American Pioneer, for February, 1843; Craig's History of Pittsburg, 98, 99; Day's Historical Collections of Pennsylvania, 336.

[3] Compare Monette's History of the Discovery and Settlement of the Valley of the Mississippi, i. 345.

[4] That lands in the Holston Valley were sought for as early as 1756, see the proof in Ramsay's Annals of Tennessee, 66.

[5] Remarkable Occurrences in the Life and Travels of Colonel James Smith, by himself. Reprinted in 1849, at Abingdon, Va., in Mirror of Olden Time Border Life. This narrative is adopted by John Haywood in his Civil and Political History of the State of Tennessee, from its earliest Settlement up to the year 1796, 35, 36. Ramsay in his Annals of Tennessee, 69, adopts Smith's narrative from Haywood. Collins in the chronological table to his Historical Sketches of Kentucky, accepts it also.

CHAP. XXVII. 1766. Oct.

Presbyterians,[1] suffered from the illegal exactions of Sheriffs and officials, whose pillaging was supported by the whole force of Government. "The Sons of Liberty," said they to one another, "withstood the Lords of Parliament in behalf of true Liberty; let not officers under them carry on unjust oppression in our province."[2] Some of those who were wronged hardly gained by their utmost efforts a scanty subsistence for their families.[3] All were loyal; regarding the British form of government as "the wholesomest Constitution in being." But they were goaded "by the corrupt and arbitrary practices of nefarious and designing men, who, being put into posts of profit and credit among them, and not being satisfied with the legal benefits which arose from the execution of their offices, had been using every artifice, practising every fraud, and where these failed, not sparing threats and menaces whereby to squeeze and extort from the wretched poor."[4]

To meet this flood of iniquity, the most approved advice came from Herman Husbands,[5] an independent farmer, who dwelt on Sandy Creek, then in Orange, now Randolph County, where he possessed an ample freehold of most fertile land, and cultivated it so well, that his fields of wheat and his "clover meadow"[6] were the admiration of all observers. Each neighborhood throughout Orange County came together

[1] Compare Foote's Sketches of North Carolina, chap. xi.

[2] No. 1, Advertisement C. Aug. 1766. In Tryon to Secretary of State, 24 Dec. 1768; Martin's North Carolina, ii. 217; Jones's Defence of N. C.

[3] Compare Petition prepared by Fanning, and sent the Regulators by Fanning's friend, Ralph McNair.

[4] Plain and Simple Narrative of Facts.

[5] Compare A Plain and Simple Narrative of Facts.

[6] Compare North Carolina Gazette of 15 July, 1771, copied into Boston Gazette of 15 July, 1771; 348, 2, 1 and 2.

CHAP. XXVII. 1766. Oct.

and elected Delegates to a General Meeting. "They are judiciously to examine," such were the instructions given them by their simple-hearted constituents, "whether the freemen of this County labor under abuses of power, and in particular to examine into the public taxes, and inform themselves by what laws, and for what uses they are laid, in order to remove some jealousies out of our minds; and the Representatives, Vestrymen, and other officers are requested to give the Members of said Meeting what information and satisfaction they can; so far as they value the good will of every honest freeholder and rendering the execution of the public offices pleasant and delightsome."[1]

In October, chosen men, about twelve in number, assembled at Maddock's Mill, on Enoe River, just outside of Hillsborough. Some of the officers had expressed their willingness to meet the people; but none appeared. A second invitation was sent to them; but no answer came, except from Edmund Fanning.[2] A favorite and at a later day the son-in-law of Governor Tryon, he was at that time the Representative of the County, one of its magistrates, the highest officer under the Crown in its militia; and was amassing a fortune by oppression as an attorney, and by extortion as Registrar, loading titles to estates with doubts,[3] and charging illegal prices for recording Deeds.[4] He was, above all others, justly obnoxious to the people; and his message to them

[1] Meeting of the Neighborhood of Deep River, the 20th Aug. 1768.

[2] Plain, Simple Narrative of Facts.

[3] Compare Sabine's American Loyalists, at the word Edmund Fanning.

[4] For Proofs of Extortion, see Records of the Court held at Hillsborough, September, 1768, printed by Husbands, and reprinted in Wheeler's North Carolina, ii. 322. Tryon admits the Fact.

CHAP XXVII. 1766. Oct.

ran, that their proposition to inquire "judiciously" implied an intention of setting up a jurisdiction, and looked more like an insurrection than a settlement. "We are no critics in words," replied the Meeting;[1] "we know not how many different constructions the term 'judiciously' may bear; as to ourselves, we meant no more by it, than wisefully, carefully, and soberly to examine the matter in hand." Their wrongs were flagrant and undeniable. "Grievous now it is to us," they said, "to have our substance torn from us by those monsters in iniquity, whose study it is to plunder us." And since their "reasonable request" for explanations was unheeded, they resolved on "a meeting for a public and free conference yearly, and as often as the case might require," that so they might reap the profit of their right under "the Constitution of choosing representatives and of learning what uses their money was called for."[2] Yet their hope of redress was very distant. How could unlettered farmers succeed against the undivided administrative power of the Province? And how long would it be before some indiscretion would place them at the mercy of their oppressors? The apportionment of Members of the colonial Legislature was grossly unequal; the Governor could create Boroughs; the actual Legislature, whose members were in part unwisely selected, in part unduly returned, rarely called together, and liable to be continued or dissolved at the pleasure of the Governor, increased the poor man's burdens by voting an annual poll-tax

[1] Plain, Simple Narrative of Facts.

[2] Paper No. 3. Proposal at a Meeting of the Inhabitants of Orange County, at Maddock's Mill, on Enoe, Monday, 10 Oct. 1766; Martin's North Carolina, ii. 218; Jones's Defence of North Carolina, 41.

CHAP. XXVII. 1766. Oct. to raise five thousand pounds, and the next year ten thousand more, to build a House for the Governor at Newbern.[1]

In Boston, the General Court resumed its session near the end of October; and received petitions from Nov. the sufferers by the Stamp Act. The form of its answer was suggested by Joseph Hawley, the Member for Northampton. He was the only son of a schoolmaster, himself married, but childless; a very able lawyer, of whose singular disinterestedness his native town still preserves the tradition. Content with a small patrimony, he lived securely in frugal simplicity,[2] closing his house door by a latch, without either bar or bolt. Inclined by temperament to moods of melancholy,[3] his mind would again kindle with a brighter lustre, and be borne onwards by its resistless impulses. All parties revered his purity of life and ardent piety; and no man in his neighborhood equalled him in the public esteem. He opposed[4] relief, except on condition of a general amnesty. "Of those seeking compensation," said he, "the chief is a person of unconstitutional principles, as one day or other he will make appear."[5] The Resolves of Parliament were cited in reply. "The Parliament of Great Britain," retorted Hawley, "has no right to legislate for us." At these words Otis, rising in his place, bowed and thanked him, saying, "He has gone further than I myself have as yet done in this House."[6] It was the first time that the

[1] Martin's North Carolina, ii. 227, 228, 229, 230; Wheeler, i. 55.

[2] From a Paper by Sylvester Judd, from the Reminiscences of Benjamin Tappan of Northampton.

[3] Compare his own MSS.

[4] Bernard to Shelburne, 14 Nov. 1766.

[5] Hutchinson to J. Williams, of Hatfield, 7 Dec. 1766; and J. Williams in reply, 5 Jan. 1767. Hutchinson to Charles Paxton, then in London, Dec. 1766.

[6] Bernard's very long letter to Shelburne, of 24 Dec. 1766.

power of Parliament had been totally denied in a colonial Legislature. "No Representation, no Taxation," had become a very common expression; the Colonies were beginning to cry, "No Representation, no Legislation."[1] Having never shown bitterness of party spirit, Hawley readily carried the Assembly with him, from their great opinion of his understanding and integrity; and a Bill was framed, "granting compensation to the sufferers and pardon to the offenders," even to the returning of the fines which had been paid. A recess was taken that members might consult their constituents, whose instructions were strictly regarded.[2] Yet before the adjournment complaint was made of the new zeal of Bernard in enforcing the Navigation Acts and sending to England injurious affidavits secretly taken. "I knew the time," interposed a member, "when the House would have readily assisted the Governor in executing the Laws of Trade." "The times," replied Otis, "are altered; we now know our rights."[3]

While the mercenary motives which prompted the Governor's sudden eagerness to suppress illicit trade, incensed the people still more at the captious restraints on navigation, Shelburne sought to recover the affections of the Colonies by acquiring and deserving their confidence.[4] "Assure the Assembly of Massachusetts," he said with "frankness"[5] to their

[1] Hutchinson's History of Massachusetts, iii. 164.

[2] Speaker of Massachusetts House to its Agent, 11 Nov. 1766; Samuel Adams to Dennys De Berdt, 12 Nov. 1766.

[3] Bernard to Shelburne, 24 Dec. 1766.

[4] Durand to Choiseul, 14 Aug. 1766.

[5] This description of Shelburne is by the Agent of the Massachusetts Assembly in London. See his Letter to the Speaker, 19 Sept. 1766. American Newspapers of 1766, Boston, 10 Nov.; New Hampshire, Gazette, 14 Nov. 1766. Bradford omits the sentence; Bradford Papers, 102.

CHAP. XXVII. 1766. Nov. correspondent, "they may be perfectly easy about the enjoyment of their rights and privileges under the present Administration." He enjoined moderation on every Governor, and was resolved to make no appointments but of men of "the most generous principles." To Bernard, whom he directed to pursue conciliatory measures,[1] he wrote no general approval of his conduct, no censure of the Assembly, no unqualified assertion of the legislative power of Parliament; but invited the colonial Legislature of itself to fall upon measures for terminating all local difficulties. The country people, as they read the letter, which was printed at the request of the Council, agreed with one another that the compensation it recommended, should be made. "The King," said they, "has asked this of us as a favor; it would be ungenerous to refuse."[2]

Dec. On the re-assembling of the Legislature, Hawley's Bill prevailed by large majorities; yet it was also voted that the sufferers had no just claim on the Province,[3] that the grant was of their own "free and good will,"[4] and not from deference to "a Requisition." The Governor assented to an Act in which a colonial Legislature exercised the prerogative of clemency; and Hutchinson, saying "beggars must not be choosers," gave thanks, at the bar of the House, to his benefactors. But he treasured up the feeling of revenge, and the next year taking offence at some ex-

[1] Shelburne to Bernard, 13 Sept. 1766.

[2] John Adams's Diary.

[3] Resolves of the House of Representatives on Compensation to the Sufferers, by the Riots of 1765, [adopted in December, not in October]. Bradford Papers, 100, 101.

[4] Preamble to "An Act for granting Compensation to the Sufferers, and General Pardon, indemnity and oblivion to the offenders, in the late times." Bradford Papers, 98 Note.

planatory publication by Hawley,[1] dismissed him arbitrarily from practising in the Superior Court. CHAP XXVII. 1766. Dec.

The patriots of New England did not doubt Shelburne's attention to its real interests and respect for its liberties; but they were exquisitely sensitive to every thing like an admission that the power of taxing them resided in Parliament. Bernard was rebuked, because, with consent of Council, he had caused the Billeting Act to be printed by the printer of the Colony laws; and had made that Act his warrant for furnishing supplies at the Colony's expense to two companies of artillery,[2] who, in stress of weather, had put into Boston. Otis attributed the taxing of America by Parliament to Bernard's advice. "I know," said he, "the room, the time, and the company, where the plan was settled." And he added publicly, "Those who are appointed to the American Governments are such as are obliged by their crimes or their debts to fly their country."[3] The debates unmasked the hypocrisy of Hutchinson; and roused the public to a sense of danger from Paxton's[4] voyage to England. The jealous Legislature dismissed Richard Jackson from the service of the Province; and the House elected the honest, but aged Dennys De Berdt as its own particular Agent.

This is the time from which Hutchinson dated the revolt of the Colonies; and his correspondence and advice conformed to the opinion.[5] But Samuel

[1] Hutchinson to Bollan, 31 Oct. 1767; same to another, 10 Nov. 1767.

[2] Bernard to J. Pownall, 16 Dec. 1766; same to Shelburne 6 and 24 Dec. 1766.

[3] Bernard to Shelburne, 22 Dec. 1766.

[4] Hutchinson to Paxton, Dec. 1766.

[5] Hutchinson's History, iii. 173. "The revolt of the Colonies ought to be dated from this time, rather than from the Declaration of Independence."

CHAP. XXVII. 1766. Dec.

Adams was gifted with a sagacity which divined the evil designs, now so near their execution. He instructed De Berdt to oppose the apprehended establishment of a military force in America, as needless for protection and dangerous to liberty. "Certainly," said he, "the best way for Great Britain to make her Colonies a real and lasting benefit, is, to give them all consistent indulgence in trade, and to remove any occasion of their suspecting that their liberties are in danger. While any Act of Parliament is in force, which has the least appearance of a design to raise a revenue out of them, their jealousy will be awake."[1]

At the same time he called across the continent to the patriot most like himself, Christopher Gadsden of South Carolina. "Tell me, sir," said he[2] of the Billeting Act, "whether this is not taxing the Colonies as effectually as the Stamp Act? And if so, either we have complained without reason, or we have still reason to complain. Grenville was told, that he should have stationed a sufficient number of troops in America before he sent over the Stamp Act. Had that been the case, your Congress might have been turned out of doors. New-York has had regular troops among them for some months. I never could hear a reason given to my satisfaction why they were ordered to remain there so long. A standing army, especially in a time of peace, is not only a disturbance, but is in every respect dangerous to the civil community. Surely, then, we cannot consent to their quartering among us; and how hard is it for us to be obliged to pay our money to subsist them!"

[1] Samuel Adams to D. De Berdt, 16 Dec. 1766; and 18 Dec. 1766.

[2] Samuel Adams to Christopher Gadsden, 11 Dec. 1766.

CHAP. XXVII. 1766. Dec.

But Gadsden had already met patriots of South Carolina under the Live Oak, which was named their Tree of Liberty,[1] had set before them the Declaratory Act, explained to them their rights, and leagued with them to oppose all foreign taxation.

Every Colony denied the right of Parliament to control its Legislature. Moffat, of Rhode Island, asked relief for his losses; founding his claim on the resolves of the British House of Commons, and the King's recommendation.[2] "Neither of them," said the Speaker of the Assembly, "can ever operate with me; nor ought they to influence the free and independent Representatives of Rhode Island Colony." Moffat had leave to withdraw his first petition and substitute an inoffensive one, which was received, but referred to a future session.

At New-York the soldiery continued to irritate the people by insolent language, and by once more cutting down their flagstaff;[3] so that the Billeting Act could find no favor. Shelburne[4] sought to persuade their Assembly to obedience, holding forth hope of a change of the law on a well-grounded representation of its hardship; and a prudent Governor could have avoided a collision. But Moore was chiefly bent on establishing a Play-house[5] against the wishes of the Presbyterians, and his thoughtless frivolity drove the House to a categorical conflict with

[1] Drayton's Memoirs of the American Revolution, ii. 315; Johnson's Traditions and Reminiscences of the American Revolution, 27, 28, 29, 35; Wm. Johnson's Life of Greene, ii. 266.

[2] Thomas Moffat to a Member of Parliament, "Mr. Burke's cousin." 12 Dec. 1766; Moffat's Account sent to the same M. P., and to Sir George Saville and others.

[3] Dunlap's New-York, i. 433; Leake's Lamb, 32, 33; Holt's Gazette, 14 Aug. and 21 Aug. 1766, and 25 Sept. 1766.

[4] Shelburne to Sir Henry Moore, 9 Aug. 1766.

[5] MSS. of Judge Livingston, 1766.

CHAP. XXVII. 1766. Dec.

the Act of Parliament, when they had really made "provision for quartering two battalions and one company of artillery." They did but exercise a discretion of their own, and refused to be "guilty of a breach of trust," by imposing heavier burdens than the people could support.[1] This prudent reserve secured unanimity in the Assembly and among their constituents.[2] In New-York as well as over all North America, the Act declaratory of the absolute power of Parliament was met by "the principle of the supreme power of the people in all cases whatsoever."[3]

Before American affairs engaged the attention of Parliament, the power of Chatham's Ministry was shaken by Camden's indiscretion. On occasion of a scarcity, the Ministry had prohibited the export of corn. Camden defended the measure as "not only excusable but legal;" and to the complaints of its arbitrariness, rashly answered: "The Crown may do whatever the safety of the State may require, during the recess of Parliament, which is at most but a forty days' tyranny." This dangerous opinion Chatham rejected, and Mansfield triumphantly overturned.

The waves thus raised had not subsided, when traces began to appear of the influence of Paxton, who had arrived from Boston, to tell his stories of rebellion against the Navigation Act, and to be congratulated on the accession to power of his patron, Charles Townshend. In Parliament a spirit was rising very different from that which had prevailed in the previous winter. "So long as I am in office," said

[1] Address of the Assembly of New-York to the Governor, delivered 18 Dec. 1766, in Prior Documents, 120; Holt's N. Y. Gazette, 1251, 24 Dec. 1766.

[2] Gov. Moore to Board of Trade, 19 Dec. 1766, and to Shelburne, 19 Dec. 1766.

[3] Colden to Shelburne, Dec. 1766.

Townshend on the floor of the House, "the authority of the laws shall not be trampled upon. I think it the highest injury to the nation to suffer Acts of the British Parliament to be broken with impunity."[1] He did not fear to flatter the prejudices of the King, and court the favor of Grenville and Bedford; for he saw that Chatham, who had "declared to all the world, that his great point was to destroy faction," was incurring the hatred of every branch of the aristocracy.[2] Eight or nine[3] Whigs resigned their employments, on account of his headstrong removal of Lord Edgecombe from an unimportant post.[4] Saunders and Keppel left the Admiralty, and Keppel's place fell to Jenkinson. The Bedford party knew the weakness of the English Ximenes, and scorned to accept his moderate bid for recruits. But the King continually cheered him on "to rout out" the Grandees of England, now "banded together."[5] "Their unions," said Chatham in return, "give me no terrors." "I know my ground," he wrote to Grafton;[6] "and I leave them to indulge their dreams. Faction will not shake the King nor gain the public. Indeed, the King is firm, and there is nothing to fear;" and he risked an encounter with all his adversaries.

To Shelburne, who was charged with the care of the Colonies, he gave his confidence and his support. He claimed for the Supreme Government, the right of dominion over the conquests in India, and the

[1] R. Nugent, 13 Dec. 1766, to a Gentleman in Boston, printed in Boston Gazette, 2 March, 1767; Diary of Oakes Angier.

[2] Lord Barrington to Sir Andrew Mitchell, 14 Dec. 1766.

[3] Chesterfield to Stanhope, 9 Dec. 1766.

[4] Charles Townshend to Grafton, 2 Nov. 1766, in Grafton's Autobiography; Conway to Chatham, 22 Nov. 1766, Chat. Corr. iii. 126.

[5] King to Chatham, 2 Dec. 1766.

[6] Chatham to Grafton, 3 Dec. 1766, in Grafton's Autobiography.

CHAP. XXVII. 1766. Dec.

disposition of its territorial revenue; and as Townshend crossed his plans and leaned to the East India Company, he proposed to Grafton the dismissal of Townshend as "incurable."[1] Burke indulged in sarcasm at "the great person, so immeasurably high" as not to be reached by argument, and travestied the litany in a solemn invocation to "the Minister above." "Have mercy upon us," he cried, while the Opposition applauded the parody; "doom not to perdition the vast public debt, seventy millions of which thou hast employed in rearing a pedestal for thy own statue."[2] And the very next day, in the House of Lords, Chatham marked his contempt of the bitter mockery of Rockingham's partisans by saying to the Duke of Richmond, "When the people shall condemn me, I shall tremble; but I will set my face against the proudest Connection of this country." "I hope," cried Richmond, "the Nobility will not be browbeaten by an insolent Minister," and Chatham retorted the charge of insolence.[3]

But it was the last time during his Ministry that he appeared in the House of Lords. His broken health was unequal to the conflict which he had invited. On the eighteenth of December,[4] he repaired to Bath with a nervous system so weak that he was easily fluttered, and moved to tears; yet still in his infirmities he sent to the Representatives of Massachusetts his friendly acknowledgment of their vote of gratitude.

Jan. Townshend saw his opportunity, and no longer

[1] Chatham to Grafton, 7 Dec. 1766, in Grafton's Autobiography.

[2] Sir Matthew Fetherstonehaugh to Lord Clive, 30 Dec. 1766, in Chat. Corr. iii. 145, 146, Note.

[3] Walpole, ii. 411, Chat. Correspondence, iii. 138; Duke of Bedford's Journal, for 10 Dec. 1766.

[4] De Guerchy to Choiseul, 19 Dec. 1766.

concealed his intention. Knowing the King's dislike of Shelburne, he took advantage of his own greater age, his authority as the ablest orator in the House of Commons, his long acquaintance with American affairs, and the fact that they turned chiefly on questions of finance, to assume their direction. His ambition deceived him into the hope of succeeding where Grenville had failed; and in concert with Paxton, from Boston, he was devising a scheme for a Board of Customs in America, and duties to be collected in its ports. He would thus obtain an American fund for a civil list, and concentre the power of government, where Grenville looked only for revenue. He expected his dismissal if Chatham regained health; and he also saw the clearest prospect of advancement by setting his colleagues at defiance. He therefore prepared to solve the questions of Asia and America in his own way; and trod the ground which he had chosen with fearless audacity. On the twenty-sixth day of January, the House of Commons, in Committee of Supply, considered the estimates for the land forces and garrisons in the Plantations. Grenville seized the opportunity to declaim on the repeal[1] of the Stamp Act. He enforced the necessity of relieving Great Britain from a burden which the Colonies ought to bear, and which with contingencies exceeded £400,000; reminding the country gentlemen that this sum was nearly equal to one shilling in the pound of the land tax. He spoke elaborately; and against Chatham was even more rancorous than usual.[2]

"Administration," replied Townshend, "has applied

[1] De Guerchy to the Duke of Choiseul, 27 Jan. 1767.

[2] Beckford to Chatham, 27 Jan. 1767.

CHAP. XXVII. 1767. Jan.

its attention to give relief to great Britain from bearing the whole expense of securing, defending, and protecting America and the West India Islands; I shall bring into the House some propositions that I hope may tend, in time, to ease the people of England upon this head, and yet not be heavy in any manner upon the people in the Colonies. I know the mode by which a revenue may be drawn from America without offence."[1] As he spoke the House shook with applause; "hear him," "hear him," now swelling loudest from his own side, now from the benches of the Opposition. "I am still," he continued, "a firm advocate for the Stamp Act,[2] for its principle and for the duty itself,[3] only the heats which prevailed made it an improper time to press it. I laugh at the absurd distinction between internal and external taxes. I know no such distinction. It is a distinction without a difference; it is perfect nonsense; if we have a right to impose the one, we have a right to impose the other; the distinction is ridiculous in the opinion of every body, except the Americans." Looking up where the Colony Agents usually sat, he added with emotion, "I speak this aloud, that all you who are in the galleries may hear me;[4] and, after this, I do not expect to have my statue erected

[1] Garth to Committee of South Carolina, 31 Jan. 1767; Grafton's Autobiography.

[2] Charlemont to Flood, 29 Jan. 1767.

[3] Shelburne to Chatham, 1 Feb. 1767; Chat. Corr. iii. 184, 185.

[4] W. S. Johnson to Gov. Pitkin, 12 Feb. 1767. I follow the Account of Johnson from his MSS., of which I took and preserve copies. The story in Pitkin's Political and Civil History of the United States, i. 217, seems to me to have been fashioned by verbal tradition. I was told the same story, but not as to be found in the MSS. One English historian has quoted from Pitkin the passage, which might seem to prove that Townshend acted on a sudden impulse. The supposition would be erroneous. Townshend's policy was adopted deliberately.

CHAP. XXVII. 1767. Jan.

in America."[1] Then laying his hand on the table in front of him, he declared to the House, "England is undone, if this taxation of America is given up."[2]

Grenville at once demanded of him to pledge himself to his declaration; he did so most willingly; and his promise received a tumultuous welcome.[3]

Lord George Sackville pressed for a revenue that should be adequate; and Townshend engaged himself to the House to find a revenue, if not adequate, yet nearly sufficient to meet the military expenses when properly reduced.[4] The loud burst of rapture dismayed Conway, who sat in silent astonishment at the unauthorized but premeditated rashness of his presumptuous colleague.[5]

The next night, the Cabinet questioned the insubordinate Minister, "how he had ventured to depart, on so essential a point, from the profession of the whole Ministry;" and he browbeat them all. "I appeal to you," said he, turning to Conway, "whether the House is not bent on obtaining a revenue of some sort from the Colonies." Not one of the Ministry then in London, had sufficient authority to advise his dismission; and nothing less could have stopped his measures.[6]

[1] Letter cited in Wirt's Patrick Henry, 96. This last clause is not in W. S. Johnson's report.

[2] George Grenville, in Cavendish Debates, ii. 35.

[3] Grafton's Autobiography.

[4] Shelburne to Chatham, 1 Feb. 1767; Chat. Corr., iii. 184, 185.

[5] Grafton's Autobiography; Walpole, ii. 413, 414, tells nothing of this debate, but what his hatred of Grenville prompted. Grenville was in a minority on his motion, but triumphed in his policy.

[6] Grafton's Autobiography.

CHAPTER XXVIII.

THE BRITISH ARISTOCRACY REDUCE THEIR OWN TAXES—DEFEAT OF CHATHAM'S ADMINISTRATION BY THE MOSAIC OPPOSITION.

JANUARY—MARCH, 1767.

CHAP. XXVIII 1767. Jan. THE day after Townshend braved his colleagues the Legislature of Massachusetts convened. Hutchinson, having received his compensation as a sufferer by the riots, restrained his ambition no longer, and took a seat in the Council as though it of right belonged to the Lieutenant Governor.[1] The House resented "the lust of power," manifested by his intrusion into an elective body of which he had not been chosen a member.[2] The Council, by a unanimous vote, denied his pretensions. The language of the Charter was too explicit to admit of a doubt;[3] yet Bernard, as the accomplice of Hutchinson, urged the interposition of the central Government.

Feb. Men feared more and more the system which Paxton had gone to mature. With unshaken confidence in Hawley, Otis, and Samuel Adams,[4] they

[1] Bernard to Secretary of State, 7 Feb. 1767, and 21 Feb. 1767.

[2] Answer of the House, 31 Jan. 1767, in Bradford, 104; and Letter from the House to Dennys De Berdt, 16 March, 1767

[3] Opinion of the Attorney General in England, cited in "a Minute relative to Massachusetts Bay," 1767.

[4] Freeborn American, in Boston Gazette, 9 March, 1767.

scanned with increasing jealousy every measure that could imply their consent to British taxation. They inquired if more troops were expected; and when the Governor professed, "in pursuance of the late Act of Parliament," to have made provision at the Colony's expense for those which had recently touched at Boston Harbor, they did not cease their complaints, till they wrung from him the declaration that his supply "did not include articles prescribed by that Act," but was "wholly conformable to the usage of the Province."[1] Upon this concession, the House acquiesced in an expenditure which no longer compromised their rights; and they also declared their readiness to grant of their own free accord such aids as the King's service from time to time should require.[2]

By the authority of the same Act of Parliament, Gage demanded quarters for one hundred and fifty-eight recruits, of the Governor of Connecticut; but that Magistrate refused compliance with the Requisition, and did nothing, till he was duly authorized by an Act of the Colonial Assembly.[3]

The Crown Officers in the Colonies busied themselves with schemes to check every aspiration after Independence. Carlton, the able Governor of Canada, advised against granting legislative immunities to its people.[4] The more he considered the state of affairs, the more he was convinced, that it was indispensably necessary to keep Crown Point and Ticon-

[1] Bernard to Shelburne, 14 Feb. 1767, 18 Feb. 1767; House to Bernard, and Bernard to the House, Feb. 1767; See Bradford's State Papers, 105, 106, 107; Prior Documents, 133.

[2] Message from the House to the Governor, 4 Feb. 1767.

[3] Gage to Shelburne, 20 Feb. 1767, and accompanying papers; Prior Documents, 130, &c.

[4] Compare Carlton to Shelburne, 20 Jan. 1768.

CHAP. XXVIII. 1767. Feb.

deroga in good repair; to have a citadel and place of arms in New-York, as well as a citadel in Quebec; and to link the two provinces so strongly together, that on the commencement of an outbreak, ten or fifteen thousand men could be moved without delay from the one to the other, or to any part of the continent. No pains, no address, no expense, he insisted,[1] would be too great for the object, which would divide the Northern and Southern Colonies, as well as secure the public magazines.

For Chatham, who wished to keep the affections of the colonists, the future was shrouded in gloom. He could not suspend the Act of Parliament; but through Shelburne, he enjoined the American Commander-in-Chief to make its burden as light, both in appearance and in reality, as was consistent with the public service. He saw that the imperfect compliance of New-York would open a fair field to the arraigners of America,[2] and between his opinions as a statesman and his obligations as Minister, he knew not what to propose.[3] The Declaratory Act was the law of the land, and yet was as a barren fruit-tree, which, though fair to the eye, only cumbers the earth, and spreads a noxious shade.[4]

Shelburne was aware also, that if the Americans "should be tempted to resist in the last instance," France and Spain[5] would no longer defer breaking the peace of which they began to number the days. Spain was resolved not to pay the Manilla ransom,

[1] Carlton to Gage, Quebec, 15 Feb. 1766; compare Shelburne to the Board of Trade, 5 Oct. 1767.

[2] Chatham to Shelburne, Bath, Feb. 3, 1767; Chat. Corr. iii. 188; Chatham to Shelburne, Bath, Feb. 7, 1767; Chat. Corr. iii. 193; Shelburne to Chatham, Feb. in Chat. Corr. iii. 186.

[3] H. Hammersley to Lieut. Gov. Sharpe, 20 Feb. 1767.

[4] Farmer's Letters.

[5] Shelburne to Chatham, 16 Feb. 1767; in Chat. Corr. iii. 209.

was planning how to drive the English from the Falkland Islands, and called on France to prepare to go to war in two years; "for Spain" said Grimaldi, "cannot longer postpone inflicting chastisement on English insolence."[1] "This is the rhodomontade of a Don Quixote," said the French Minister, and Choiseul kept the guidance of affairs in his own hand, and for the time was resolved not to disturb the peace.

Executive moderation might still have saved England from a conflict. Undismayed by the disorder in the cabinet, the ill health of Chatham, the factions in a corrupt Parliament, or the unpromising aspect of foreign relations, and impressed with the necessity of giving up trifles that created uneasiness,[2] Shelburne proceeded diligently to make himself master of each American[3] question, and to prepare its solution.

The subject of the greatest consequence was the forming an American fund. To this end, without exercising rigor in respect to quit-rents long due, he proposed to break up the system of forestalling lands by speculators, to require that the engrossing proprietors should fulfil the conditions of their grants, and to make all future grants on a system of quit-rents, which should be applied to defray the American expenses then borne by the Exchequer of Great Britain.[4]

[1] The Marquis de Grimaldi to Prince Masserano, 20 Jan. 1767; De Guerchy at London to Choiseul, 12 Feb. 1767; D'Ossun at Madrid to Choiseul, 24 Jan. 1767. Compare Choiseul to De Guerchy of 2 Jan., and Choiseul to D'Ossun, 27 Jan. 1767.

[2] Richard Jackson to Hutchinson, Jan. 1767.

[3] Paper indorsed, "Things to be considered of in North America," in Lansdowne House MSS. Compare the Justice and Policy of the late Act of Parliament for Quebec, 1774, 17.

[4] Circular of Shelburne to all the Governors in America, 11 Dec. 1766; Shelburne to General Gage, 11 Dec. 1766; Shelburne to Chatham, 1 Feb. 1767.

CHAP. XXVIII 1767. Feb.

Relief to the mother country being thus derived from an income which had chiefly been squandered among favorites, he proposed to leave the Indian trade to be regulated under general rules by the respective Provinces at their own cost.[1]

Resisting those who advised to concentrate the American army in the principal towns, he wished rather that the military should be disposed on the frontiers among the younger Colonies, where their presence might be desired.[2]

The people of America, even a majority of those who adhered to the Church of England, feared as yet to see an American Episcopate, lest ecclesiastical courts should follow; Shelburne expressed his opinion openly, that there was no manner of occasion for American Bishops.[3]

He reprobated the political dependence of the judges in the Colonies; and advised that their commissions should conform to the precedent in England.[4]

The grants of lands in Vermont under the seal of New Hampshire, he ordered to be confirmed, and this decision was not less wise than just.[5]

Massachusetts and New-York had a controversy about limits, which had led to disputed land-titles and bloodshed on the border; instead of keeping the question open as a means of setting one Colony against another, he directed that it should be definitively settled; and Massachusetts did not scruple to

[1] Compare Shelburne to Gage, 11 Dec. 1766.

[2] Shelburne to Gage, 11 Dec. 1766.

[3] Rev. Dr. Johnson to Sir William Johnson, 6 July, 1767.

[4] Garth to South Carolina, 12 March, 1767. Compare Sir Henry Moore to Shelburne, 1 Feb. 1767.

[5] Shelburne to Moore, 11 April, 1767.

place Hutchinson at the head of its boundary Commission.[1]

CHAP. XXVIII

1767. Feb.

The Billeting Act for America, which the Rockingham Ministry had continued for two years, so that it would not of itself expire till the twenty-fourth of March, 1768, constituted the immediate difficulty. It was contrary to the whole tenor of British legislation for Ireland, and to all former legislation for America. Shelburne disapproved its principle, and, corresponding with the Secretary at War, sought to reconcile the wants of the army with the rights of America; being resolved "not to establish a precedent, which might hereafter be turned to purposes of oppression."[2]

The American Continent was interested in the settlement of Canadian affairs; Shelburne listened to the hope of establishing perfect tranquillity, by calling an Assembly that should assimilate to the English laws such of the French laws as it was necessary to retain, and by rendering the Canadian Catholics eligible to the Assembly[3] and Council.

But the more Shelburne showed his good disposition towards America, the more the Court spoke of him as "an enemy."[4] The King had long been per-

[1] Shelburne to Bernard, 11 Dec. 1766; Bernard to Shelburne, 28 Feb. 1767; Same to Same, 23 March, 1767, and very many letters.

[2] Shelburne to Chatham, 6 Feb. 1767, and 16 Feb. 1767; Chat. Corr. iii. 193, 208, 209. Compare the paper indorsed, "Remarks on the Present State of America, April, 1767, from Mr. Morgan." Lansdowne House MSS. "There are strong reasons against the principles of this Act," &c. Morgan condemns the Act utterly. "There is no bottom to the impropriety of *enacting* that those Assemblies should *enact*."

[3] Paper in Lansdowne House marked, Lord Shelburne to the Board of Trade on the Appointment of an Assembly, and other things necessary to the Settlement of Canada: indorsed, Relative to the Present State of Quebec, 17 May, 1767. The paper seems to have been drafted by an Under Secretary for Lord Shelburne's consideration; perhaps by L. Macleane.

[4] Grafton's Autobiography.

CHAP. XXVIII 1767. Feb.

suaded[1] that the Colonies shared in the licentiousness of opinion, which he thought was infusing itself into all orders of men; and that a due obedience and submission to law must in all cases go before the removal of grievances. "Otherwise," said he, "we shall soon be no better than the savages."[2] He was now accustomed "to talk a great deal about America;"[3] and he told Shelburne plainly that the Billeting Act "should be enforced;" though he declined "to suggest the mode." Besides; the dependence of the Colonies was believed by the public to be at stake;[4] and New-York "underwent the imputation of rebellion."[5]

The difficulties that beset Shelburne were infinitely increased by the condition of parties in Great Britain. The old Whig aristocracy was passing out of power with so ill a grace, that they preferred the immediate gratification of their passions to every consideration of wisdom and expediency. America was the theme in all companies, yet was discussed according to its bearings on personal ambition; justice and prudence were lost sight of in unreflecting zeal for a momentary victory. Men struggled for a present advantage more than for any system of government; and the liberties of two millions of their countrymen, the interests of a continent, the unity of the British empire, were left to be swayed by the accidents of a Parliamentary skirmish.[6]

[1] Compare Secretary Calvert to Lieut. Gov. Sharpe, June, 1763.

[2] King to Conway, 20 Sept. 1766, 8 minutes past 9 P. M.

[3] Bristol to Chatham, 9 Feb. 1767; Chat. Corr. iii. 199.

[4] Shelburne to Chatham, 16 Feb. 1767; Chat. Corr. iii. 207, 209.

[5] Shelburne to Chatham, Feb. 1767; Chat. Corr. iii. 187.

[6] W. S. Johnson to Pitkin, 12 Feb. 1767.

Merchants of New-York, at the instigation of a person much connected [1] with Charles Townshend, had sent a very temperate Petition,[2] setting forth some of the useless grievances of the Acts of Trade, and praying for the free exportation of their lumber and an easier exchange of products with the West Indies.[3] The reasonable request provoked universal dislike; Grenville and his friends appealed to it as fresh evidence, that nothing would give satisfaction to the Colonists, but a repeal of all restrictions on trade, and freedom from all subordination and dependence. Besides; Townshend, whom Chatham had thrice [4] denounced to Grafton as "incurable," was more and more inclining to the same views, and in giving them effect, exercised over Grafton the superiority, which intellectual vigor and indefatigable activity are sure to win over self-indulgent indolence and sluggish, well-intentioned dulness. CHAP. XXVIII 1767. Feb.

At this critical conjuncture, when nothing but Chatham's presence could restore activity to the Administration, and draw Parliament from its lethargy,[5] the gout had returned upon him at Marlborough on his way to London.[6] But business would not wait. On the eighteenth of February, there appeared in the account of the Extraordinaries, a large and unusual expenditure on the continent of America.

[1] Shelburne to Chatham, 6 Feb. 1767; Chat. Corr. iii. 191; S. Sayre to J. Reed, 3 Sept. 1766.

[2] Prior Documents, 165.

[3] W. S. Johnson's Journal, Monday, 16 Feb. 1767; Garth to Committee of S. C., 12 March, 1767.

[4] Chatham to Grafton, 7 Dec. 1766, MS.; Chatham to Grafton, 23 Jan. 1767. This letter is printed in the Chat. Corr. iii. 200, with the erroneous date of Feb. 9. The third letter of Chatham to Grafton, in which he calls C. Townshend incurable, is a letter really dated 9 Feb. 1767. See Grafton's Autobiography for all three.

[5] De Guerchy to Choiseul, 3 Feb. 1767.

[6] Chatham to Shelburne, 16 Feb. 1767, Marlborough.

CHAP. XXVIII 1767. Feb. Grenville advised to lessen the expense, and charge upon the Colonies the whole of what should remain. There was a general agreement, that America ought to alleviate the burdens of England. Every speaker of the Opposition directly inveighed against Chatham, whom no one rose to defend. Rigby, stinging the self-love of the Ministers, reproached them with being but the servile instruments of their absent chief; incapable of acting but on orders from his lips. To prove his independence, Townshend explained his own system for America, and openly combated Chatham's of the year before.[1] "I would govern the Americans," said he, "as subjects of Great Britain. I would restrain their trade and their manufactures as subordinate to the mother country. These, our children, must not make themselves our allies in time of war, and our rivals in peace." And he concluded by adopting substantially the suggestions of Grenville in favor of retrenchment and an American duty.[2] None heeded the milder counsels of Conway. The mosaic Opposition watched every opportunity to push the Ministry upon extreme measures.[3] A week later, Camden, who had pledged himself "to maintain to his last hour, that Taxation and Representation are inseparable," that Taxation without Representation is a "robbery," seized the occasion to proclaim as loudly, "that his doubt respecting the right of Parliament to tax America, was removed by the declaration

[1] Compare Guerchy to Choiseul, 20 Feb. 1767.

[2] W. S. Johnson to Jared Ingersoll, 18 Feb. 1767; Charlemont to Flood, 19 Feb. 1767; Garth to Committee of South Carolina, 12 March, 1767; Walpole's Memoirs, ii. 417; Compare Grafton to Chatham, 13 March 1767; Chat. Corr. iii. 233.

[3] H. Hammersley to Lieut. Gov. Sharpe, 20 Feb. 1767.

of Parliament itself; and that its authority must be maintained."[1]

By this time the friends of Grenville, of Bedford and of Rockingham, men the most imbittered against each other by former contests, and the most opposite in character and tendencies, were ready to combine to aim a deadly blow at the existing Ministry, whatever might be the consequence of its destruction.[2] During the war, and ever since, the land-tax had been at the nominal rate of four shillings in the pound, in reality at but about nine pence in the pound. On Friday, the twenty-seventh of February,[3] Dowdeswell, the leader of the Rockingham party, regardless of his own policy when in the treasury and his knowledge of the public wants, proposed a reduction in the land tax, nominally of a shilling, but really of only about nine farthings in the pound. Grenville, with more consistency, supported[4] the proposal, which, it was generally thought, must bring in its train a tax on the Colonies.[5] The question was treated in the debate, as one between the Americans and the landed interest of England; and the Chancellor of the Exchequer was reminded of his pledge to derive this very year some revenue from America. On the division Edmund Burke, "too fond of the right" to vote against his conscience, and not enough fond of it to vote against his party, staid away; the united factions of the aristocracy mustered two hun-

[1] Garth to the Committee of South Carolina, 12 March 1767; Walpole, ii. 418.

[2] Compare Grenville in his Diary, Papers, iv. 214.

[3] Even in Grenville's Diary dates can be wrong. Grenville Papers, iv. 211; King to Conway, 27 Feb. 1767, in Albemarle, ii. 430; Grafton to Chatham, 28 Feb.; King to Chatham, 3 March.

[4] Guerchy to Choiseul, 3 March, 1767.

[5] Letter from London, of 4 April 1767, in Boston Gazette, 637, 2, 1, 15 June 1767.

CHAP. XXVIII 1767. Feb. dred and six against one hundred and eighty-eight for the Ministry. But not one of those who planned this impolitic act, derived from it any advantage. The good sense of the country condemned it; the city dreaded the wound given to public credit; Grenville, who joyfully accepted the congratulations of the country gentlemen, deceived himself in expecting a junction with Rockingham, and had in the King an inflexible enemy.[1] The ancient whig Connection, which had ruled England so long and still claimed to represent the party of Liberty, by creating an apparent excuse for Townshend's system of American taxes, only doomed itself more surely to a fruitless opposition. For so small a benefit, as a reduction on but one year's rental of nine farthings in the pound, and for a barren parliamentary triumph, it compromised its principles, and risked a continent.

March This was the first overthrow on an important question, which the Government had sustained for a quarter of a century. On hearing the news, Chatham rose from his bed, and ill as he was, hastened to London. Charles Townshend "was warm in the sunshine of majesty;"[2] but as Chatham attributed the disaster to his lukewarmness and wished to dismiss him, the King readily assented; and Lord North was invited to become Chancellor of the Exchequer. Townshend knew well what was passing;[3] and in the debates on the East India question, with easy confidence gave a defiance,[4] by asserting his own opinions. "I expect to be dismissed for it," said he openly; but Lord North

[1] Compare Grenville's Diary in the Grenville Papers, iv. 212, with Sir Geo. Saville to Rockingham in Albemarle's Rockingham, ii. 41.

[2] Trecothick in Cavendish, i. 212.

[3] Shelburne to Chatham, 13 March 1767.

[4] De Guerchy to Choiseul, 8 March, 1767.

would not venture to supersede him. Whom will Chatham next recommend? asked the King, through Grafton; and no other could be named. This was a new humiliation. Chatham saw his adversary exposed defenceless to his will; and the shaft which his aged and enfeebled hand tremulously hurled at him, fell harmless at his own feet. He could endure no more. "We cannot remain in office together;" said he of Townshend, and he asked the Duke of Grafton himself to call the next Council at his own house.[1] The accumulation of grief destroyed what little of health remained to him; he withdrew from business and became invisible even to Camden and to Grafton.

Here, in fact, Chatham's Administration was at an end.[2] Transmitting to his substitute every question of domestic, foreign and colonial policy unsettled, the British Agamemnon retired to his tent, leaving the subordinate chiefs to quarrel for the direction.

[1] Chatham to Grafton, Wednesday, 11 March 1767, in Grafton's Autobiography.

[2] Grafton's own statement in his Autobiography.

CHAP. XXIX.
1766. Dec.

CHAPTER XXIX.

PARLIAMENT WILL HAVE AN AMERICAN ARMY AND AN AMERICAN REVENUE.—CHARLES TOWNSHEND'S SUPREMACY IN THE ADMINISTRATION.

MARCH—JULY, 1767.

THE eclipse of Chatham left Charles Townshend the lord of the ascendant. He was a man of wonderful endowments, dashed with follies and indiscretion. Impatient of waiting, his ruling passion was present success. He was for ever carried away by the immediate object of his desires; now hurried into expenses beyond his means, now clutching at the phantoms of the stock market or speculations in America. In social circles he was so fond of taking the lead, that to make sport for his companions, he had no friendship which he would not wound, no love which he would not caricature. In the House of Commons his brilliant oratory took its inspiration from the prevailing excitement; and careless of consistency, heedless whom he deserted or whom he joined, he followed the floating indications of the loudest cheers. Applause was the temptation which he had no power to resist. Gay, volatile and fickle, he lived for the hour and shone for the hour, without the thought of founding an enduring name. Finding Chatham not likely to reappear, his lively imagination was for ever on

CHAP. XXIX. 1767. March

the stretch, devising schemes to realize his ambitious views; and he turned to pay the greatest court wherever political appearances were most inviting.[1]

In the Cabinet meeting held on the twelfth of March at the house of Grafton, Townshend assumed to dictate to the Ministry its colonial policy. Till that should be settled, he neither could nor would move the particular sum necessary for the Extraordinaries in America. "If," said he, "I cannot fulfil my promise to the House, I shall be obliged to make it appear that it is not my fault, and is against my opinion."[2]

A letter from Shelburne explained to Chatham the necessity that Townshend should no longer remain in the Cabinet. But Chatham was too ill to thrust his adversary out, or give advice to his colleague. Nor could Shelburne by himself alone abandon the ministry; for such a resignation would have seemed to his superior a desertion or a reproach. He continued, therefore, to protect American liberty as well as he could, but had no support, and was powerless to control events; for Grafton and even Camden yielded to Townshend's impetuosity, and were very ready to sacrifice Shelburne to the royal resentment.

The disappearance of Chatham reanimated the dissatisfied factions of the aristocracy; yet, in case of success, they had no agreement respecting ulterior measures or the distribution of influence. They had only a common desire according to the traditions of the old Whig party, to make the King so far subordinate to his ministers, that it should be "impossible

[1] Grafton's Autobiography.

[2] Shelburne to Chatham, 13 March, 1767; Chat. Corr. iii. 233.

CHAP. XXIX. 1767. March

for him not to give them his support." Respecting measures, Rockingham gave assurances that his friends, without whom, he persuaded himself, nothing could be carried by the Bedfords, would not join in any thing severe against America.[1] But he was all the while contributing to the success of the policy which he most abhorred.

The King would not recede from the largest claim to authority on behalf of the imperial Legislature. Great pains had been successfully taken to irritate the people of England, especially the freeholders, against the Americans. "Our interests," it was said, "are sacrificed to their interests; we are to pay infinite taxes and they none; we are to be burdened that they may be eased;"[2] and they would brook no longer heavy impositions on themselves, which were not to be shared by the Colonies.[3] The merchants complained of a want of gratitude, and of the failure to make remittances; many were incensed at the Petition from New-York for a relaxation of the Navigation Acts; still more at the partial refusal of that Province to billet the troops; and the angry feeling was exasperated by the report from its Governor, that it would never again pay obedience to British statutes, which there was not an army to enforce. Since the last winter, America had lost friends both in and out of Parliament. Conway, who kept his old ground, was only laughed at. "He is below low-water mark," said Townshend to Grenville.

[1] W. S. Johnson's Diary, 30 March, 1767.

[2] W. S. Johnson to Lieut. Gov. Trumbull, 14 March, 1767.

[3] W. S. Johnson to Gov. Pitkin, 19 March, 1767.

On the thirtieth of March,—two days after news had arrived, that in one of their messages the Representatives of Massachusetts had given a formal defiance to Parliament, as well as encouraged the resistance of their sister Colony, New-York, to the Billeting Act,—the American papers which Bedford had demanded were taken into consideration by the House of Lords. Camden opened the discussion by declaring New-York to be in a state of delinquency;[1] and receding from his old opinions, he justified his change.[2] Grafton said well, that "the present question was too serious for faction," and promised that the Ministers would themselves bring forward a suitable measure. But the Lords wearied themselves all that day and all the next, in scolding at the Colonies with indiscriminate bitterness. They were called, "undutiful, ungracious and unthankful;" and "rebels," "traitors," were epithets liberally bestowed. Some wished to make of New-York an example that might terrify all the others; it was more generally proposed by Act of Parliament to remodel the government of them all.[3] America had not yet finished the statues which it was raising to Chatham; and Mauduit artfully sent over word, that the plan for reducing America would be sanctioned by his name.[4]

CHAP. XXIX. 1767. March

April

On the tenth of April, Massachusetts was selected for censure; and Bedford,[5]—notwithstanding the sud-

[1] Israel Mauduit to Hutchinson, 11 April, 1767.

[2] Walpole's Memoirs, ii. 448.

[3] W. S. Johnson's Journal for 30 and 31 March; W. S. Johnson to Col. Walker, 31 March, 1767; W. S. Johnson to A. Tomlinson, 31 March, 1767; W. S. Johnson to E. Dyer, 10 April, 1767.

[4] De Guerchy to Choiseul, 17 March, 1767; Bristol to Chatham, 23 March, 1767, to be taken in connection with Israel Mauduit's Letter to Hutchinson of 11 April, 1767.

[5] Bedford's Journal for 10 April, 1767.

CHAP. XXIX. 1767. April. den death of a son, who left infant children, and one of the loveliest women in England a heart-broken widow to weep herself to death for sorrow,—came to the House of Lords to move an Address, that the King in Council would declare the Massachusetts Act of Amnesty null and void.[1] The Ministry contended truly, that the motion was needless, as the Act would certainly be rejected in the usual course of business. "Perhaps we had best look into the Massachusetts Charter before we come to a decision," said one of the Administration. "No!" cried Lord Townshend. "Let us deliberate no longer; let us act with vigor, now, while we can call the Colonies ours. If you do not, they will very soon be lost for ever."

Lord Mansfield[2] spoke in the same strain, descanting "upon the folly and wickedness of the American incendiaries," and drawing an animated picture of the fatal effects to England and to the Colonies, which the "deplorable event of their disjunction must produce."[3]

All that he said carried conviction to the House of Lords,[4] and hastened the very event which he deplored. In the six hours' debate, the resistance of New-York and Massachusetts[5] had been so highly colored, that Choiseul began to think the time for the great American insurrection was come. He resolved, therefore, to send an emissary across the Atlantic, and selected for that purpose the brave and upright De

[1] Journals of the Lords, xxxi. 566.

[2] W. S. Johnson to Pitkin, 11 April, 1767; W. S. Johnson's Journal, 10 April, 1767; De Guerchy to Choiseul, 11 and 13 April, 1767; Horace Walpole to Mann, 17 April, 1767; Walpole's Memoirs, ii. 454.

[3] Mauduit to Hutchinson, 11 April, 1767; Note to Hutchinson's Hist. iii. 171.

[4] Extract of a letter from London.

[5] Benj. Franklin to Ross, London, 11 April, 1767; W. S. Johnson to Dyer, 10 April, 1767.

Kalb, a Colonel of Infantry, from Alsace, able to converse with Americans of German parentage in their own tongue. His written instructions, dated on the twenty-second day of April, enjoined him to repair to Amsterdam, the free city which was the great centre of commercial intelligence, and to examine the prevailing report respecting the English Colonies. If it should seem well founded, he was ordered to go to them; to ascertain their wants, in respect of engineers and artillery officers, or munitions of war, or provisions; the strength of their purpose to withdraw from the English government; their resources in troops, citadels and intrenched posts; the plan on which they projected their revolt, and the chiefs who were to assume its direction.

"The commission which I give you," said Choiseul, "is difficult, and demands intelligence. Ask of me the means which you think necessary for its execution; I will furnish you with them all."[1]

The eagerness of the Minister suffered his hopes to run ahead of realities; for a Frenchman could not compute the power of Anglo-American forbearance; nor had the brave officer whom he employed, sagacity enough to measure the movement of a revolution; but from this time Choiseul sought in every quarter accurate accounts of the progress of opinion in America, alike in the writings of Franklin, the reports current among the best informed merchants, and even in New England sermons, from which curious extracts are tc this day preserved among the State Papers of

[1] Choiseul to De Kalb, 20 April, 1767; Special and Secret Instruction to Lieut. Col. de Kalb, put into his hands, 22 April, 1767; De Kalb to Choiseul, 24 April, 1767; Choiseul to De Kalb, 2 May, 1767.

CHAP. XXIX. 1767. April. France. His judgment on events, though biassed by national hatred, was more impartial and clear than that of any British Minister who succeeded Shelburnes; and his conclusions were essentially just.

The English Ministry were misled by those in whom they trusted. The civil and military officers of the crown in America were nearly all men of British birth, who had obtained their places for the sake of profit; and had no higher object than to augment and assure their gains. For this reason they wished to become independent of colonial Legislatures for their support, and to strengthen the delegated executive power. The Commander-in-Chief was of a kindly nature, but without sagacity, or any one element of a statesman; reasoning about the debates of free legislative Assemblies as he would about the questioning of military orders; entering complaints against Georgia,[1] South Carolina, and other Colonies, and holding up New-York as preeminent in opposition. The letters of Moore, who had been appointed Governor of New-York by the Rockingham Ministry, advocated an independent civil list and more troops. The same views were maintained by William Franklin of New Jersey, and by the able, but selfish Tryon, who, under a smooth exterior, concealed the heart of a savage. The Lieutenant Governor of South Carolina was a man of sense; but his moderation was soon to draw upon him a rebuke. Sir James Wright, in Georgia, and Carlton, in Quebec, were strenuous supporters of power. The attention of the British Government and of Parliament was drawn chiefly

[1] Gage to Shelburne, 7 April, 1767.

CHAP XXIX. 1767. April.

towards Massachusetts, where Bernard,[1] Hutchinson, and Oliver,[2] with perseverance equalled only by their duplicity, sought to increase their emoluments, to free themselves from "their dependence on the people for a necessary support," and to consolidate their authority by the presence of a small standing army. The opinions of Hutchinson were of peculiar importance, for while he assented to Bernard's views, and was forming relations with Israel Mauduit and Whately, and through them with Jenkinson, Grenville and Wedderburn, his plausible letters to Richard Jackson had so imposed upon the more liberal statesmen of England, that they looked forward with hope to his appointment as Bernard's successor.

We are arrived at the last moment in American affairs, when revolution might still have been easily postponed; and must pause to ask after the points in issue. As yet they were trifling. The late solemn deliberation of the Peers was but a frivolous caviling on the form of a royal veto.[3]

The People of Massachusetts, seeing a disposition to mar its Charter, and use military power in its government, needed more than ever an Agent in England.[4] Bernard insisted that no one should receive that appointment without his approval; and repeatedly negatived the dismissal of the last incumbent. But

[1] Bernard to Shelburne, 6 May, 1767.

[2] Oliver to T. Whately, 7 May, 1767.

[3] The papers are many on a very trifling matter. Board of Trade to the King, 6 Dec. 1766; Reference in Council, 13 April, 1767; Subject considered in Council, 1 May, 1767; Opinion of Attorney and Sol. General, ordered 4 May; Phil. Sharpe to Att. and Sol. Gen. 4 May; Decision of the Council, 9 May; Final Order in Council, 13 May, 1767; Address of Commons for Papers, 14 May, 1767; Papers laid before Parliament, 18 May, 1767. The subject need have had no notice at all but in the ordinary course of business.

[4] Bernard to Shelburne, 28 March, 1767.

CHAP. XXIX. 1767. April.

Shelburne held that the right of nomination should rest essentially with the Representatives, so that this dispute could not become serious while he remained in the Ministry.

The Lieutenant Governor, in spite of his want of an election, had taken a seat in the Council, pleading the Charter as his warrant for doing so; but the Attorney General in England, to whom the case was referred, gave his opinion that "the right could not be claimed by virtue of any thing contained in the Charter or the Constitution of the Province."[1]

Bernard wished to control the election of Councillors; and gave out that by the use of his veto, he would always keep places open for Hutchinson and Oliver.[2] The menace was a violation of the spirit of the Constitution; its only effect was to preserve two perpetual vacancies in the Council.

The Council itself Bernard advised to alter from an elective body to one of royal nomination. The change would have been an act of aggression, and an unwarranted breach of faith, for no Council in any one Colony had more uniformly shown loyalty than that of Massachusetts. Hutchinson perceived this so clearly, that he at heart disapproved of the measure which from personal motives he advocated. The perfidious advice would be harmless, if England would only respect the Charter it had granted, and which nearly a century's possession had confirmed.

There remained no grounds of imminent variance except the Navigation Acts, the Billeting Act, the Acts restraining industry, and the Slave Trade.

[1] Opinion of the Attorney General, quoted in the "Minute relative to Massachusetts Bay," 1767.

[2] Bernard's Letters on the Rejection of Hutchinson and Oliver; but particularly, Bernard to Shelburne, 6 June, 1767.

CHAP. XXIX. 1767. April.

To the latter Virginia led the opposition. Towns at the North, especially Worcester, in Massachusetts, protested against the system; but opinion through the country was divided; and complaints of the grievance had not been made in concert.

The restraints on some manufactures, especially of wool and iron, were flagrant violations of natural rights; but the laws, so tyrannical in their character, were not of recent date, and as they related to products of industry which it was still the interest of the people to import, were in a great degree inoperative and unobserved.[1]

By the Billeting Act, Great Britain exposed its dignity to the discretion or the petulance of provincial Assemblies. There was no bound to the impropriety of Parliament's enacting what those Legislatures should enact, and accompanying the statute by a Requisition from the throne. Is the measure compulsory and final? Then why address it to Assemblies which are not executive officers? Does it not compel obedience? Then the Assemblies have a right to deliberate, to accept in whole or in part, or to reject. And indeed the demand of quarters and provisions without limitation of time or of the number of troops, was a reasonable subject for deliberation. Such was the opinion of the very few in England who considered the question on its own merits, and not merely as a test of authority.[2] Besides: no Province had absolutely refused to comply with the spirit of the

[1] Moore to Lords of Trade, 12 Jan. 1767; Gov. Penn of Pa. to Same, 21 Jan. 1767; and many other letters.

[2] See the Paper on the Subject by Morgan, in Lansdowne House MSS.; Compare Shelburne to Chatham, Chat. Corr. iii. 192, and for the opinion of Grenville, Chat. Corr. iii. 208.

CHAP. XXIX. Act. A slight modification, leaving some option to the Colonies, would have remedied this disagreement.

1767. April. The Navigation Acts were a perpetual source of just and ever increasing discontent. But no public body in America had denied their validity; nor was there any reluctance to subordinate American commerce to the general interests of the empire; the relaxations which America most desired were very moderate, relating chiefly to intercourse with the West Indies, and the free export of such of its products as Great Britain would not receive. The illicit trade was partly owing to useless laws, but more to the prevailing corruption among the servants of the crown. No practical question existed, except that which Otis had raised, on the legality of the Writs of Assistance first issued by Hutchinson; and while it was even suggested by one person at least to construe some reported declarations of Otis[1] as proofs of treason, and to bring him to trial in England on an impeachment by the House of Commons, the Attorney and Solicitor General of England, established his opinion that the Writs themselves, which had begun the controversy, were not warranted by law.[2]

[1] Lansdowne House MS., indorsed, "Remarks on the Present State of America," April, 1767, from Mr. Morgan; Compare Bedford's Opinion, in Lyttelton to Temple, 25 Nov. 1767, in Phillimore's Life and Correspondence of Lyttelton, 743.

[2] The opinion of the Attorney and Solicitor General, I could not find in the State Paper office, nor at the Treasury; but that it was adverse to the views of Charles Townshend appears from a letter of Mr. Grey Cooper to Mr. Nuthall, 14 Feb. 1767, in Treasury Letter Book, xxiii. 416, directing him "forthwith to lay this matter before Mr. Attorney and Mr. Solicitor General, together with the case and their opinion, for their reconsideration." That there was in "the reconsideration" no change of the adverse opinion, may be inferred from the fact, that the Treasury gave up the question, took no step against Malcom, and introduced into the American Revenue Biil just the clause which, from Towns-

CHAP. XXIX. 1767. May.

"In America," said the calm Andrew Eliot, of Boston, "the people glory in the name, and only desire to enjoy the liberties of Englishmen."[1] "There is not the least foundation for the suspicion, that they aim at independence. If we have no forces, or new Stamp Act, I would almost answer for them. Our warmest patriots speak of our connection with Great Britain as our felicity; and to have it broken, as one of the greatest misfortunes that could befall us. We are not so vain as to think we could be able to effect it; and nothing could influence us to desire it, but such attempts on our liberties as I hope Great Britain will be just enough never to make. Oppression makes wise men mad."[2]

To tranquillize America nothing more was wanting than a respect for its rights, and some accommodation to its confirmed habits and opinions. The Colonies had, each of them, a direction of its own and a character of its own, which required to be harmoniously reconciled with the motion impressed upon it by the imperial Legislature. But this demanded study, self-possession and candor. The Parliament of that day esteemed itself the absolute master of America; and recognising no reciprocity of obligations, it thought nothing so wrong as thwarting the execution of its will. It did not doubt its own superiority of intelligence, and to maintain its authority and reduce every refractory body to obedience, appeared to it the perfection of statesmanship, and the true method

hend's point of view, an adverse opinion would have rendered necessary. Besides, had the opinion been favorable to the Crown Officers, it would have been made use of in America.

[1] Andrew Eliot to T. Hollis, 13 May, 1767.

[2] Andrew Eliot to Archdeacon Blackburne, 3 May, 1767.

CHAP XXIX 1767. May. of colonial reform. A good system would have been a consummate work of deliberative wisdom; the principle of despotic government acted with more speed and uniformity, having passion for its interpreter, and a statesman like Townshend, to execute its impulses.

That statesman had no ear except for complaints against the Colonies, and for men like Paxton, who blinded him to every thing but what suited their cupidity. It was his purpose[1] to effect a thorough revolution in colonial government, and to lay the foundation of a vast American revenue.

The American merchants and friends to the Colonies took the utmost pains to moderate resentments and to extinguish jealousies. Their committee, with Trecothick at its head, interposed with Townshend; but he answered: "I do not in the least doubt the right of Parliament to tax the Colonies internally; I know no difference between internal or external taxes; yet, since the Americans are pleased to make that distinction, I am willing to indulge them, and for that reason choose to confine myself to regulations of trade, by which a sufficient revenue may be raised." "Perhaps the army," rejoined Trecothick, "may with safety be withdrawn from America, in which case the expense will cease, and then there will be no further occasion for a revenue." "I will hear nothing on that subject," such was Townshend's peremptory declaration; "the moment a resolution shall be taken to withdraw the army, I will resign my office and have no more to do in public affairs. I insist, it is absolutely necessary to keep up a large

[1] Compare Trecothick in Cavendish, i. 212.

CHAP. XXIX. 1767. May.

army there and here. An American army and consequently an American revenue, are essential; but I am willing to have both in the manner most easy to the people."[1]

On the thirteenth day of May, Townshend came to the House of Commons, in the flush of his reputation and the consciousness of his supremacy. A more eventful day for England had not dawned in that century. When the resolutions for the Stamp Act were voted, Parliament was unenlightened. Now it had had the experience of taxing America, and of repealing the tax through fear of civil war. What is done now cannot easily be revoked. A secret consciousness prevailed that a great wrong was about to be done. The liberty and interests of America were at issue, and yet the doors of the House of Commons were, by special order, shut against every Agent of the Colonies, and even against every American merchant.

Townshend opened the debate[2] with professions of candor and the air of a man of business. Exculpating alike Pennsylvania and Connecticut, he named as the delinquent Colonies, Massachusetts, which had invaded the King's prerogative by a general amnesty, and, in a message to its Governor, had used expressions in derogation of the authority of Parliament; Rhode Island, which had postponed, but not refused an indemnity to the sufferers by the Stamp Act; and

W. S. Johnson to the Governor of Connecticut, 16 May, 1767.

[2] De Guerchy to Choiseul, 14 May, 1767. I have very full reports from Garth, Agent for South Carolina, and member of the House of Commons, who was present, and from W. S. Johnson, who got reports from Whately and from Richard Jackson, and from Trecothick. Compare Walpole's Memoirs, iii. 28; Cavendish Debates, i. 38, 39, 213; Franklin's Writings, vii. 333.

CHAP. XXIX. 1767. May. New Jersey, which had evaded the Billeting Act, but had yet furnished the King's troops with every essential thing to their perfect satisfaction. Against these Colonies it was not necessary to institute severe proceedings. But New-York, in the month of June last, beside appointing its own commissary, had limited its supplies to two regiments, and to those articles only which were provided in the rest of the King's dominions; and in December had refused to do more. Here was such clear evidence of a direct denial of the authority of Parliament, and such overt acts of disobedience to one of its laws, that an immediate interposition was most strongly called for, as well to secure the just dependence of the Province, as to maintain the majesty and authority of Government.

It became Parliament, not to engage in controversy with its Colonies, but to assert its sovereignty, without uniting them in a common cause. For this end he proposed to proceed against New-York, and against New-York alone. To levy a local tax would be to accept a penalty in lieu of obedience. He should, therefore, move that New-York, having disobeyed Parliament, should be restrained from any legislative act of its own, till it should comply.

He then proceeded to advocate the establishment of a Board of Commissioners of the Customs, to be stationed in America.

"Our right of taxation," he continued, "is indubitable; yet to prevent mischief, I was myself in favor of repealing the Stamp Act. But there can be no objections to Port Duties on wine, oil and fruits, if allowed to be carried to America directly from Spain and Portugal; on glass, paper, lead, and colors; and especially on tea. Owing to the high charges in England,

America has supplied itself with tea by smuggling it from the Dutch possessions; to remedy this, duties hitherto levied upon it in England are to be given up and a specific duty collected in America itself. A duty on china can be obtained by repealing the drawback. On salt it was at first intended to lay an impost; but this is abandoned [1] from the difficulty of adjusting the drawback to be allowed on exports of cured fish and provisions, and on salt for the fisheries." CHAP. XXIX. 1767. May.

The American revenue, it was further explained, was to be placed at the disposal of the King for the payment of his civil officers. To each of the Governors, an annual salary was to be assigned of two thousand pounds sterling; to each of the Chief Justices, of five hundred pounds.

This speech, pronounced with gravity and an air of moderation by an orator who was the delight of the House, implied a revolution in favor of authority. The Minister was to have the irresponsible power of establishing by sign manual a general civil list in every American province, and at his pleasure to grant salaries and pensions, limited only by the amount of the American revenue; the national exchequer was to receive no more than the crumbs that fell from his table.[2] The proposition bore on its face the mark of owing its parentage to the holders and patrons of American offices;[3] and yet it was received in the House with general favor. Richard Jackson was not regarded, when he spoke[4] against the duties themselves, and foretold the mischiefs that would ensue.

[1] Franklin's Writings, x. 371.

[2] Hartley's Letters on the American War, 59.

[3] Compare De Kalb to Choiseul, 16 Oct. 1768; and Franklin, iv. 388.

[4] Richard Jackson to W. S. Johnson, 5 April, 1774; and Same to Same, 30 Nov. 1784.

CHAP. XXIX. 1767. May. Grenville who must have shed tears of spite, if he could not have "croaked out" a presage of evil,[1] heard with malignant joy one of the repealers of his Stamp Act propose a revenue from Port Duties. "You are deceived," said he; "I tell you, you are deceived. The Americans will laugh at you for your distinctions." He spoke against legalizing a direct trade between Portugal and America. As to taxes, he demanded more; all that were promised were trifles. "I," said he,[2] "will tell the Honorable gentleman of a revenue that will produce something valuable in America; issue paper bearing interest upon loan there, and apply the interest as you think proper."

Townshend, perceiving that the House seemed to like the suggestion, stood up again, and said that that was a proposition of his own, which he had intended to have made with the rest, but it had slipped his memory; the Bill for it was already prepared.

The debate would not have continued long, if there had not been a division of opinion as to the mode of coercing New-York. Edmund Burke, approving a local tax on importations into that province, opposed the general system. "You will never see a single shilling from America," said he prophetically;[3] "it is not by votes and angry resolutions of this House, but by a slow and steady conduct, that the Americans are to be reconciled to us." Dowdeswell described the new plan as worse than to have softened and enforced the Stamp Tax. "Do like the best of physicians," said Beckford, who alone seemed to understand the subject of American discontents,

[1] Burke's Works, i. 255. Am. ed.

[2] Franklin, vii. 339.

[3] Edmund Burke's Account of what he said, in Cavendish, i. 39.

and whom nobody minded; "heal the disease by doing nothing."[1] CHAP. XXIX. 1767. May.

Others thought there should be an amendment to the Billeting Act itself, directing the civil magistrates to quarter upon private houses, where the Assemblies of America did not fulfil the present requirements. Grenville advised to invest the Governor and Council of each Colony with power to draw on the colonial treasurer, who, in case of refusal to answer such bills out of the first aids in his hands, howsoever appropriated, should be judged guilty of a capital crime and be tried and punished in England. And since the Colonies persisted in the denial of the Parliamentary right of taxation, he offered for consideration, that every American, before entering into office, should subscribe a political Test nearly in the words of the Declaratory Act, acknowledging the unlimited sovereignty of Great Britain.

These several points were discussed till one in the morning, when a question was so framed by Grenville, that the Rockinghams could join him in the division; but their united voices were no more than ninety-eight against one hundred and eighty.

"The new measures for the Colonies," observed Choiseul,[2] "will, no doubt, meet with opposition in both Houses of Parliament; but their execution will encounter still more considerable resistance in America."

On the fifteenth of May, Townshend reported his resolutions to the House, when a strenuous effort was made to have them re-committed; the friends of

[1] Beckford in Chat. Corr. iii. 251.

[2] Choiseul to De Guerchy, 14 May, 1767; Same to De Kalb, May, 1767.

CHAP. XXIX. 1767. May.

Rockingham, pretending to wish a more lenient measure, yet joining with Grenville who spoke for one more severe, effective and general. But Townshend, by surpassing eloquence, brought the House back to his first Resolutions, which were adopted at about nine in the evening without a division.

Grenville then moved that many of the Colonies denied and oppugned the sovereignty of Great Britain; in other words, were in a state of open rebellion; and wished that they might be reduced to submission by force; but a large majority was against him. In the midst of one of his speeches, the implacable man stopped short, and, looking up to the gallery, said, "I hope there are no American Agents present; I must hold such language as I would not have them hear." "I have expressly ordered the sergeant to admit none," said the Speaker, "and you may be assured there are none present." Yet Johnson, of Connecticut, had braved the danger of an arrest, and sat in the gallery to record the incidents of the evening for the warning of his countrymen.[1] The persevering Grenville next moved his Test for America; but the House dreaded to re-produce a union[2] of the Colonies. "At least, then," renewed Grenville, "take some notice of those in America, who have suffered for their loyal support of your sovereignty;" and naming Ingersoll,[3] Hutchinson, Oliver, Howard, and others, he moved an Address in

[1] On the fifteenth, W. S. Johnson, at the risk of imprisonment, was present at the Debate. His report of the Debate is before me; so too is that of Garth, which is very full as to the substance of the debate, though names are omitted. W. S. Johnson to Pitkin, 16 May, 1767; Garth to South Carolina, 17 May, 1767.

[2] W. S. Johnson to his father, 18 May, 1767.

[3] W. S. Johnson to Jared Ingersoll, 16 May, 1767.

CHAP. XXIX. 1767. May.

their favor; and this being seconded by Lord North, passed without dissent.

After ordering the Bill to disfranchise New-York, as well as sanctioning the new system of colonial revenue and administration, the House rose; unconscious that it had taken steps which pride would not allow to be recalled; and which, if not retracted, would force the Colonies to unite for Independence.

The bitterness against America grew with its indulgence. On the twenty-first, news came that Georgia[1] had refused compliance with the Billeting Act; and for a Colony, that had been established at the public expense, to question the will of Parliament was held to be "unexampled insolence." The Secretary at War, therefore, as if to ensure confusion, introduced a Bill, extending the obnoxious law a year beyond the time when it would have expired by its own limitation.

The moment was inviting to the Opposition. Raising some trivial questions on the form in which the amnesty Act of Massachusetts had been disallowed, the united factions of Rockingham, Bedford and Temple on one division left the Ministry a majority of but six, and on another of but three.[2]

On both these occasions the King made two of his brothers vote with the Ministry; of which the dissolution would have left him at the mercy of the coalition. He wished to enforce the absolute authority of Parliament in America, and to consummate his victory over the aristocracy in England. For the one he needed to dismiss Shelburne;[3] for

[1] Prior Documents, 130; Walpole, iii. 40; W. S. Johnson to Gov. of Connecticut, 9 June, 1767.

[2] De Guerchy to Choiseul, 26 May, 1767.

[3] Chatham Corr. iii. 254.

CHAP. XXIX. 1767. May. the other, to employ the name of Chatham. Grafton readily adopted a plan, to lead the aristocracy into disputes among themselves; and then, separating the Bedfords from the rest, to introduce a part of them to power. Keen observers saw the certainty of changes, and predicted a "mosaic" Ministry.[1]

To proceed securely, Grafton required some understanding with Chatham; but Chatham refused to see him, pleading his disability.[2] The King himself intervened by a letter, framed with cool and well considered adroitness, but which seemed an effusion of confidence and affection. In the House of Lords the Earl had given an open defiance to the whole nobility; and the King charged him by his "duty, affection, and honor," not to "truckle" now, when the "hydra" was at the height of its power. For success, nothing was wanted but that he should have "five minutes' conversation" with Grafton.[3]

Chatham yielded to such persuasion; though suffering from a universal tremor, which application to business visibly increased.[4] Grafton was filled with grief at "the sight of his great mind, bowed down and thus weakened by disorder;"[5] but he obtained from him the declaration, that "he would not retire except by his majesty's command."[6]

June. At a second interview in June,[7] Grafton, urged by

[1] Chesterfield to his Son, 1 June, 1767.

[2] Chatham Corr. iii. 255—260.

[3] King to Chatham, 30 May, 1767, 34 m. past 2, and 35 m. past 8, p. m. Chat. Corr. iii. 260—264.

[4] De Guerchy to Choiseul, 10 June, 1767.

[5] Grafton's Autobiography.

[6] Walpole's Memoirs, iii. 53.

[7] The Duke of Grafton in his autobiography, does not carefully discriminate between his two interviews with Lord Chatham. The first must have been inconclusive, since a second was so soon necessary. In part vi. of his work, he speaks of his "interesting and most important conversation with Lord Chatham on the King's birth-

the wishes of the King, complained of Shelburne and intimated, that "he could not be allowed to continue in his office." Chatham summoned spirit to vindicate his friend, and to advise the dismission of Townshend. He was with great difficulty led to believe that a junction was necessary with either the Bedfords or the Rockinghams; but, of the two, Grafton thought him inclined to prefer the former. The interview lasted two full hours, and the Ministers parted with the most cordial professions of good will and mutual attachment.

Grafton was left with the position of Prime Minister; but it was the King, who from this time controlled the Cabinet and managed affairs. His influence was adverse to the cause of European Liberty, which, nevertheless, continued to grow in strength. "Men are opening their eyes," said Voltaire,[1] "from one end of Europe to the other. Fanaticism, which feels its humiliation and implores the arm of authority, makes the involuntary confession of its defeat. Let us bless this happy revolution which has taken place in the minds of men of probity within fifteen or twenty years. It has exceeded my hopes."

That a greater change hung over America could not escape the penetration of Jonathan Trumbull, the Deputy Governor of Connecticut. He was a perfect model of the virtues of a rural magistrate, never weary of business, profoundly religious, grave in his man-

day, 1767, and in the part iv. in which he gives an account of the interview, he adds a note from Lord Camden, dated June 4, which he says he received "as he was stepping into his phaeton to go to North End." The letter of the King to Chatham, in the Chatham Correspondence, iii. 266, dated June 2, is of July 2. The inclosure was written in the evening of July 1, 1767, and was delivered by Grafton to the King, July 2.

[1] Voltaire to d'Alembert, 4 June, 1767.

CHAP. XXIX. 1767. June. ners, calm and discriminating in judgment, fixed in his principles, steadfast in purpose, and by his ability and patriotism enchaining universal respect and the unfailing confidence of the freemen of his Colony. His opinion was formed, that if "methods tending to violence should be taken to maintain the dependence of the Colonies, it would hasten a separation;"[1] that the connection with England could be preserved by "gentle and insensible methods," rather than "by power or force." But not so reasoned Townshend, who, after the Whitsuntide Holidays, "stole"[2] his Bill imperceptibly through both Houses.[3] The Stamp Act had called an American revenue "just and necessary;" and had been repealed as impolitic. Townshend's Preamble to his Bill granting duties in America on glass, red and white lead, painter's colors and paper, and three pence a pound on tea, declared an
July. American revenue "expedient."[4] By another Act[5] a Board of Customs was established at Boston; and general Writs of Assistance were legalized. For New-York the Lords of Trade, avowedly from political reasons, refused to the Presbyterians any immunities, but such as might be derived from the British Law of Toleration;[6] while an Act of Parliament[7] suspended the functions of its Representatives, till they should render obedience to the Imperial Legislature.

On such an alternative, it was thought that that Province would submit without delay; and that the

[1] Jonathan Trumbull to William S. Johnson, 23 June, 1767.

[2] Lord Beauchamp in Cavendish Debates, i. 215.

[3] W. S. Johnson to Dep. Gov. Trumbull, 14 Sept. 1767. Garth to Committee of South Carolina, 6 June, 1767.

[4] 7 Geo. III. c. XLVI.

[5] 7 Geo. III. c. XLI.

[6] Report of the Board of Trade, 10 July, 1767.

[7] Garth, 17 May, 1767; 7 Geo. III. chap. LVI.

Americans, as their tea would now come to them at a less price than to the consumers in England, would pay the impost in their own ports with only seeming reluctance. CHAP. XXIX 1767. July.

But the new measures were, in their character, even more subversive of right than those of Grenville. He had designedly left the civil officers dependent on the local legislators, and consigned the proceeds of the American tax to the Exchequer.[1] Townshend's revenue was to be disposed of under the sign manual at the King's pleasure. This part of the system had no limit as to time or place, and was intended as a perpetual menace. In so far as it provided an independent support for the crown officers, it did away with the necessity of colonial legislatures. Wherever the power should be exercised, Governors would have little inducement to call Assemblies, and an angry Minister might dissolve them without inconvenience to his Administration.[2] Henceforward "no native" of America could hope to receive any lucrative commission under the crown, unless he were one of the martyrs to the Stamp Act. Places would be filled by some Briton-born, who should have exhibited full proof of his readiness to govern so refractory a people as the Americans according to the principle of bringing them to the most exact and implicit obedience to the dictates of England.[3]

Such an one was Tryon, now Governor of North Carolina, a soldier who, in the army, had learned little

[1] Compare Hartley's Letters on the War.

[2] W. S. Johnson to the Gov. of Connecticut, 13 July, 1767; Garth to Committee of South Carolina, 5 July, 1767.

[3] W. S. Johnson to Stuyvesant of New-York, 10 July, 1767.

CHAP. XXIX. 1767. July. but a fondness for display. To mark the boundary which in October, 1765, had been agreed upon between the Carolinas and the Cherokees,[1] he, at the cost of an impoverished and suffering Colony,[2] marched a company of riflemen through the woods,[3] to the banks of Reedy River. The Beloved Men of the Cherokees met him on the way. "The Man above," said their Orator, "is head of all. He made the land and none other, and he told me that the land I stand on is mine, and all that is in it. True it is, the Deer and the Buffaloes and the Turkeys are almost gone. I refer all to him above. The White People eat what they have here; but our food is further off. The land is very good, but I will not love it. The land on this side the line I will not love, I give it to the White People. When they buy land, they give what soon wears out; but land lasts always. Yet the land is given when the line is run."[4] As he spoke, he laid down a string of beads on the course of the border. From the Elm Tree on Reedy River, the frontier was marked as far as to an Oak on the top of the Mountains which rise over the sources of the Pacolet and the Broad; and thence it was agreed that it should run directly to Chiswell's Lead Mines on the New River branch of the Kanawha."[5] The Cherokee Chiefs, who knew well the cruelty and craft of the most pernicious beast of prey in the mountains,

[1] Tryon to Rutherford, &c., Commissioners, 4 June, and 6 June, 1767.

[2] Compare Martin's History of North Carolina, ii. 228.

[3] Tryon to Secretary of State, 8 July, 1767.

[4] Jud's Friend's Talk in reply to Tryon, at Tyger River Camp, 2 June, 1767.

[5] Deed with the Cherokees, 13 June, 1767.

ceremoniously distinguished the Governor by the name of the Great Wolf.[1] CHAP. XXIX.

The Highlands of North Carolina were already the homes of a comely and industrious race.[2] Well might David Hume, in view of the ever expanding settlements of those who spoke the same tongue with himself, invite Gibbon to admire, how "the solid and increasing establishments in America promised superior stability and duration to the English language."[3] 1767. July.

[1] Tryon to the Secretary of State, 14 July, 1767.

[2] Tryon to the Secretary, 8 July.

[3] David Hume to Gibbon, 1767, in Burton.

CHAPTER XXX.

HOW TOWNSHEND'S AMERICAN TAXES WERE RECEIVED BY FRANCE AND AMERICA.—COALITION OF THE KING AND THE ARISTOCRACY.

JULY—NOVEMBER, 1767.

CHAP. XXX. 1767. July. THE anarchy in the Ministry was agreeable to the King, for it enabled him to govern as well as to reign. Grafton made no tedious speeches in the closet, and had approved the late American regulations; persuading himself even that the choice of tea as the subject of taxation was his own;[1] that the law, suspending the legislative functions of New-York, was marked by moderation and dignity;[2] and that abrogating the Charters of the American Colonies would be their emancipation from "fetters."[3]

The King, who wished to retain Conway in office and had looked into his heart to know how to wind and govern him, attached him by the semblance of perfect trust; showing him all Chatham's letters,[4] and

[1] Grafton of himself, in his Autobiography.

[2] Grafton's Autobiography.

[3] Grafton's Autobiography.

[4] Walpole's Memoirs, iii. 61, 62. Here Walpole becomes a leading authority on account of his intimacy with Conway, and for the time, with Grafton. The comparison with the Autobiography of the latter, shows that Walpole was well-informed.

giving him leave to treat with his own old associates, though Grafton desired to effect through Gower a junction with the friends of Bedford.[1]

But Rockingham, who never opened his eyes to the light that was springing from the increased intelligence of the masses, and left out of view that all his glory as a statesman had come from his opposition to Grenville and Bedford, governed himself exclusively by the ancient principle of his party "to fight up against the King and against the people,"[2] and set about forming a Ministry by cementing the shattered fragments of the old Whig aristocracy. He began with Bedford. "Bedford and Grenville are one," said Rigby, by authority; "and neither of them will ever depart from the ground taken, to assert and establish the entire sovereignty of Great Britain over her Colonies."[3] But Rockingham avoided all detail as to measures and as to men, and according to the old fashion, satisfied himself by declaring for a "wide and comprehensive" system. After a week's negotiation,[4] and with no plan but to support privilege against prerogative, he announced to Grafton[5] his readiness to form a new Administration.

The King whom Rockingham had now to encounter, was greatly his superior in sagacity and consistency of conduct. Remaining implacable towards

[1] Grafton to Northington, 18 July, 1767.

[2] Marquis of Lansdowne to Arthur Lee, in Life of Arthur Lee, ii. 357.

[3] Phillimore's Life and Correspondence of Lord Lyttelton, ii. 724.

[4] Numerous Papers illustrating the negotiation are to be found in Bedford's Correspondence, iii. Compare, also, Lyttelton's Life and Correspondence; the Grenville Papers, iv.; and Albemarle's Rockingham, ii.

[5] Grafton to Rockingham, 15 July, 1767; Rockingham to Grafton, 16 July, 1767.

CHAP. XXX. 1767. July. Grenville,[1] he surveyed calmly the condition of the chequered factions, which had been so freshly and so loosely put together; he saw that his own consent to their union would set them at variance among themselves;[2] and he gave Rockingham leave to revive, if he could, the exclusive rule of the great Whig families. He knew that he was master of the field. "The King may make a page first Minister,"[3] said Lord Holland. The day was past when England was to be governed by Privilege alone; but with the decline of the aristocracy, the people not less than the King increased in authority; demanded more and more to know what was passing in Parliament; and prepared to enforce their right to intervene. All that could be done through the press in their support, was done with alacrity.[4] "Power," thought a French observer,[5] "has passed into the hands of the populace and the merchants. The country is exceedingly jealous of its liberty."

While Rockingham, self-deluded as to the purposes of his associates,"[6] summoned his political allies to London, Shelburne was quieting the controversy with America respecting the Billeting Act. New-York had foreseen the storm, and without recognising the binding force of the British Statute, or yet conforming to its provisions, it

[1] Walpole's Memoirs, iii. 67, 68; and compare 86.

[2] Compare Bedford to Rockingham, 16 July, 1767, in Bedford's Corr. iii. 373. Grenville to Temple, 18 July, 1767, in Grenville Papers, iv. 59. Walpole's Memoirs. Temple to Rigby, 17 July, 1767. Bedford to Rockingham, 17 July, 1767, &c. &c. Grenville to Rigby, 16 July, 1767; and Same to Same, 17 July, 1767, 9 o'clock.

[3] Walpole's Memoirs, iii. 66.

[4] Compare T. Hollis to Andrew Eliot, 23 Feb. 1767.

[5] Durand, acting as French minister at London, to Choiseul, 21 July, 1767.

[6] Walpole's Memoirs, iii. 68.

CHAP. XXX. 1767. July.

had made a grant of money[1] for the use of the army, without specifications. This, by the advice of the Attorney General and Solicitor General,[2] Shelburne received as a sufficient compliance,[3] and the Assembly went on as though nothing had happened. The health of Chatham was all the while growing worse; and his life began to be despaired of. His letters were kept from him.[4] Of the transactions that were going forward, he was scarce even a spectator, and seemed to be unconcerned in the event.[5]

About nine o'clock in the evening of the twentieth, the leaders of the two branches of the Oligarchy met at Newcastle House. When Rockingham had explained the purpose of the meeting, Bedford, on behalf of Temple and Grenville,[6] declared their readiness to support a comprehensive administration, provided it adopted the capital measure of asserting and establishing the sovereignty of Great Britain over its Colonies. At this, Rockingham flew into a violent passion, and[7] complained of their calling on him and his friends for a declaration on American affairs; whatever answer he might give, they would throw a construction on his conduct to his disadvantage before the public.[8]

Bedford insisted with firmness on the declaration.

[1] Moore to Shelburne, 18 June, 1767.

[2] Shelburne to Chatham, in Chat. Corr. iv. 325.

[3] Shelburne to Moore, 18 July, 1767. Compare Vote of New-York Assembly of 6 June, 1767. Message of Moore of 18 Nov. 1767. Board of Trade to the King, 7 May, 1768.

[4] Lady Chatham to Grafton, North End, 31 July, 1767.

[5] De Guerchy to Choiseul, 10 June, 16 June, 8 July, 1767. T. Whately to Lord Temple, 30 July, 1767.

[6] Grenville to Rigby, 16 July, 1767; Temple to Rigby, 16 July, 1767. Joint letter of Temple and Grenville, 17 July, 1767.

[7] Bedford's Journal, 20 July, 1767; Durand to Choiseul, 28 July, 1767.

[8] Rockingham to Dowdeswell in

CHAP. XXX. 1767. July.

"We may as well demand one from you," cried Richmond,[1] "that you never will disturb that country again." Sandwich interposed to reconcile the difference[2] by substituting an ambiguity for the explicit language of Grenville.

Yet the same difficulty recurred on discussing the division of employments. In the House of Commons the lead must belong to Conway or Grenville. Against the latter Rockingham was inflexible; and Bedford equally determined against the former. So at one o'clock at night the meeting broke up without any result, though the Duke of New Castle, in his vain entreaties, had been moved to tears.[3]

The next day Newcastle, whom forty years' experience had accomplished as an adept in the art of constructing Ministries by compromise, made an effort to revive the system which had flourished during his long career; and the two parties met once more at his house. But the difficulty about America could not be got over. Rockingham again avowed his distrust of Grenville[4] and Temple, and insisted on Conway's taking the lead in the House of Commons. This left no possibility of agreement; "and we broke up," says Bedford, "with our all declaring ourselves free from all engagements to one another, and to be as before this negotiation began."

During the suspense the King, who had never been in earnest for a change,[5] would not admit Rock-

Cavendish Debates, i. 584. Rockingham to Hardwicke, in Albemarle, ii. 50. This letter has the wrong date, of July 2 for July 20.

[1] Walpole's Memoirs, iii. 80.

[2] Almon's Political Register, I. 204.

[3] Durand to Choiseul, 28 July, 1767.

[4] Compare Lyttelton to Temple, Nov. 1767, in Lyttelton's Life and Corr. ii. 740.

[5] Journal of the second Lord

ingham to an audience; now that he had failed, he was received to make confession, that the country required a strong, united, and permanent administration and that he himself could not form one of any kind. He did not omit to add some reproaches about the past; but the King was in the best humor. He bowed very graciously, and Rockingham bowed, and so they parted. "What did the King say to you?" asked Grafton and Conway eagerly, as Rockingham came out; and the only answer he could make was—"Nothing."

Once more Rockingham was urged to join with the friends of Chatham;[1] but he was unaccommodating and impracticable.[2] "He has managed it ill," thought Hardwicke.[3] Richmond and others were anxious and uneasy.[4] A leader of a party had never done so much to diminish its influence. Very honest, truly liberal, of a merciful and generous nature, his intellect bore no comparison to his virtues, his conduct no analogy to his good intentions. Deceived by his reverence for the past, without ability to plan a system suited to his age, he left the field open to those who wished ill to liberty in America and in England. His enemies were pleased, for he had acted exactly as their interests required; the King was never in better spirits.[5] Aug.

Grafton, too, obtained the credit of moderation by his seeming readiness to retire; and, after the rejection of all his offers to Rockingham, people saw

wicke, in Life of Lord Chancellor Hardwicke, iii. 459.

[1] Compare Durand to Choiseul, 3 August, 1767.

[2] Whately to Temple, 30 July, 1767; in Lyttelton, 729.

[3] Life of Lord Chancellor Hardwicke, iii. 459.

[4] E. Burke to Rockingham, 18 August, 1767.

[5] E. Burke to Rockingham, 1 August, 1767.

CHAP. XXX. 1767. Aug.

him at the head of the Treasury with less dissatisfaction. He retained the confident expectation of an alliance[1] with Bedford, who could not keep his party together without official patronage;[2] but for the moment, he relied on Townshend.[3]

So Charles Townshend remained in the cabinet, treating every thing in jest,[4] scattering ridicule with full hands, and careless on whom it fell. Grafton was apparently the Chief; but the King held the helm, and as the dissolution of Parliament drew near, was the more happy in a dependent Ministry. The patronage of the Crown amounted to an annual disbursement of six millions sterling,[5] and the secret service money was employed to cover the expenses of elections, at a time when less than ten thousand voters chose a majority of the House of Commons. As merchants and adventurers, rich with the profits of trade or the spoils of India,[6] competed for boroughs, the price of votes within twenty years had increased three-fold. The Duke of Newcastle grumbled as usual. Edmund Burke grumbled also, because the moneyed men of his party did not engage more of "the venal boroughs."[7] In the great contest with oppression, he had no better reliance than on the English constitution as it was, and the charitable purchase of venal boroughs by opulent noblemen of his connection.

"May the anarchy in the British government last

[1] Walpole's Memoirs, iii. 99.

[2] Durand to Choiseul, 7 August, 1767.

[3] Grafton's Autobiography.

[4] Durand to Choiseul, 7 August, 1767.

[5] Durand to Choiseul, 12 August, 1767.

[6] Durand to Choiseul, 7 August, 1767.

[7] Burke to Rockingham, 13 August, 1767.

for ages," wrote Choiseul.[1] "Your prayer will be heard," answered Durand, then in London as Minister.[2] "The opposition during this reign will always be strong, for the cabinet will always be divided; but the genius of the nation, concentrating itself on commerce and Colonies, compensates the inferiority of the men in power, and makes great advances without their guidance." "My position," observed Choiseul as he contemplated, alike in Asia and in America, the undisputed ascendency of the nation which he called his "enemy,"[3] "is the most vexatious possible; I see the ill; I do not see the remedy." Anxious to send none but the most accurate accounts, Durand made many inquiries of Franklin, and asked for all his political writings. "That intriguing nation," said Franklin,[4] "would like very well to blow up the coals between Britain and her Colonies; but I hope we shall give them no opportunity."

"In England," observed Durand,[5] "there is no one who does not own that its American Colonies will one day form a separate State. The Americans are jealous of their liberty and will always wish to extend it. The taste for independence must prevail among them. Yet the fears of England will retard its coming, for she will shun whatever can unite them."—"Let her but attempt to establish taxes in them," rejoined Choiseul, "and those countries,

[1] Choiseul to Durand, Compiegne, 4 August, 1767; La minute de cette Dépêche étoit de la main du Duc de Choiseul.

[2] Durand to Choiseul, August, 1767. No date of the day. The P. S. is 22 August.

[3] From the Dispatch of the fourth of August.

[4] Franklin to his son, 28 August, 1767; Writings, vii. 357.

[5] Durand to Choiseul, 11 August, 1767.

CHAP. XXX. 1767. Aug.

greater than England in extent, and perhaps becoming more populous, having fisheries, forests, shipping, corn, iron and the like, will easily and fearlessly separate themselves from the mother country." "Do not calculate," replied Durand,"[1] "on a near revolution in the American Colonies. They aspire not to independence but to equality of rights with the mother country. A plan of union will always be a means in reserve by which England may shun the greater evil.—When the separation comes, the other Colonies of Europe will be the prey of those, whom excessive vigor may have detached from their parent stock. The loss of the Colonies of France and of Spain will be the consequence of the revolution in the Colonies of England."[2]

The idea of emancipating the whole colonial world was alluring to Choiseul; and he judged correctly of the nearness of the conflict. "The die is thrown," said men in Boston, on hearing the Revenue Act had been carried through. "The Rubicon is past."[3]—"We will form one universal combination," it was whispered, "to eat nothing, drink nothing, and wear nothing imported from Great Britain."[4] The Fourteenth of August was commemorated as the Anniversary of the first resistance to the Stamp Act.[5] The intended appropriation of the new revenue, to make the crown officers independent of the people, stung the patriots to madness. "Such counsels," they said, "will de-

[1] Durand to Choiseul, 30 August, 1767.

[2] Durand to Choiseul, 5 Sept. 1767.

[3] Compare the Narrative in Bernard to Shelburne, 14 Sept. 1767.

[4] Compare Letter of Hutchinson, 18 July, 1767.

[5] Memorial of Commissioners of Customs in America, to the Lord of the Treasury, 12 February, 1768.

CHAP. XXX. 1767. Aug.

prive the prince who now sways the British sceptre of millions of free subjects."[1] And when it was considered, that Mansfield and the Ministry declared some of the grants in colonial Charters to be nugatory on the ground of their extent, the press of Boston, in concert with New-York,[2] following the precedent set by Molineux in his argument for Ireland, reasoned the matter through to its logical conclusion.

"Liberty," said the earnest writer,[3] "is the inherent right of all mankind. Ireland has its own Parliament and makes laws; and English statutes do not bind them, says Lord Coke, because they send no knights to Parliament. The same reason holds good as to America. Consent only gives human laws their force. Therefore the Parliament of England cannot extend their jurisdiction beyond their constituents. Advancing the powers of the Parliament of England, by breaking the rights of the Parliaments of America, may in time have its effects." "If this writer succeeds," said Bernard, "a civil war must ensue;"[4] and the prediction was well founded, for the King, on his part, was irrevocably bent on giving effect to the new system.[5]

The Act suspending the legislative functions of New-York increased the discontent. The danger of the example was understood; and while patriots of Boston encouraged one another to justify themselves

[1] Britannus Americanus, in Boston Gazette, 545, 2, 1, of 17 August, 1767.

[2] Bernard to Shelburne, 14 Sept. 1767.

[3] In the Boston Gazette of the 24th of August, appeared a paper taken from Molineux's Case of Ireland, with variations to adapt it to America.

[4] Bernard to Shelburne, 24 August, 1767.

[5] Minute Book, xxxviii. 459. Whitehall Treasury Chambers, 27 August, 1767.

CHAP. XXX. 1767. Aug. in the eye of the present and of coming generations,[1] they added, "Our strength consists in union. Let us, above all, be of one heart and one mind.—Call on our sister Colonies to join with us.—Should our righteous opposition to slavery be named rebellion,[2] yet pursue duty with firmness, and leave the event to Heaven."[3] An intimate correspondence grew up between New-York and Boston. They would nullify Townshend's Revenue Act by consuming nothing on which he had laid a duty; and avenge themselves on England by importing no more British goods.

Sept. At the beginning of this excitement, Charles Townshend was seized with fever, and after a short illness, during which he met danger with the unconcerned levity that had marked his conduct of the most serious affairs,[4] he died at the age of forty-one, famed alike for incomparable talents, and extreme instability.[5] Where were now his gibes?[6] Where his flashes of merriment that set the table in a roar; his brilliant eloquence which made him the wonder of Parliament? If his indiscretion forbade esteem, his good-humor dissipated hate. He had been courted by all parties, but never possessed the confidence of any. He followed no guide, and he had no plan of his own. No one wished him as an adversary; no one trusted him as an associate. He some-

[1] Sui Imperator, in Boston Gazette, 648, 3, 1; 31 August, 1767.

[2] Israel Manduit to Lieut. Gov. Hutchinson, London, 10 Dec. 1767. "That treasonable letter to Edes and Gill, in your Boston Gazette of 31 August last."

[3] A. F. to Edes and Gill, in Boston Gazette, 648, 3, 2.

[4] Walpole's Memoirs of George III. iii. 99.

[5] W. S. Johnson to E. Dyer, 12 Sept. 1767, and other letters of Johnson.

[6] Letters of Lady Hervey, Sept. 1767.

CHAP. XXX. 1767. Sept.

times spoke with boldness; but at heart he was as timid as he was versatile. He had clear conceptions, depth of understanding, great knowledge of every branch of administration,[1] and indefatigable assiduity in business. During the last session of Parliament, his career had been splendid and successful. He had just obtained the Lord Lieutenancy of Ireland for his brother, and a Peerage for his wife, to descend to his children;[2] and with power, fortune, affection, and honors clustering around him, he fell in the bloom of manhood, the most celebrated statesman who has left nothing but errors to account for his fame.

The choice of his successor would decide on the continuance of the Ministry, of which his death seemed to presage the overthrow. Choiseul,[3] a good judge, esteemed Grenville by far the ablest financier in England, and greatly feared his return to office. It was believed, that on the day of Townshend's death, Grafton advised the recall of Grenville; and that the King replied with strong emotion, "Never speak to me again of that man; for I never, my life long, will see him."[4]—"The King himself has the greatest distrust of those who would rule him, so that he never will let any one prevail," said the Princess Amelia; "were Bute and the Princess of Wales no more, Ministers would not be more stable."[5] Following his

[1] Durand to Choiseul, 8 Sept. 1767.

[2] Grafton's Autobiography.

[3] See many of his letters to the embassy at London.

[4] Durand to Choiseul, 11 Sept. 1767. That the King spoke very civilly to Lord Suffolk respecting his enemy Grenville after Grenville's death only illustrates a proverb of two thousand years ago. The letter of Durand is not conclusive, but Walpole had good means of information; Grafton says that Grenville was never liked by the King; and the Grenville Diary for 1765, fully accounts for the King's invincible repugnance to a minister whose stubbornness had made him turn red and even shed tears.

[5] Durand to Choiseul, 16 Sept. 1767.

CHAP. XXX. 1767. Sept.

own sure instinct, he directed that the vacant place should be offered to Lord North. Receiving the summons, North hastened to London, declined the office from fear of his inability to cope with Grenville on questions of finance, returned to the country, and changed his mind just in season to accept[1] before the appointment of another.

At that time Lord North was thirty-five years old, having seen the light in the same year with Washington. While the great Virginian employed himself as a careful planter, or fulfilled his trust as a colonial legislator, or, in his hour of leisure, leaning against the primeval oaks on the lawn at Mount Vernon, in full view of the thickly forested hill which now bears the Capitol, mused on the destinies of his country and resolved to preserve its liberty, Lord North entered the cabinet, in which he was to remain for fifteen of the most eventful years in the history of Britain. He was a Minister after the King's own heart; not brilliant, but of varied and extensive knowledge; good-humored and able; opposed to republicanism, to reform, and to every popular measure. He had voted for the Stamp Act, and against its repeal;[2] and had been foremost in the pursuit of Wilkes. Though choleric, he was of an easy temperament; a friend to peace, yet not fearing war; of great personal courage, which however partook something of apathy; rarely violent; never enterprising; of such moderation in his ambition, his

[1] North to Grafton, 10 Sept. 1767. Charles Lloyd to Lord Lyttelton, 17 Sept. 1767; Lyttelton's Life, 733, 734.

[2] Compare W. S. Johnson to Gov. Pitkin, 1767.

CHAP. XXX. 1767. Sept.

wishes and his demands, that he seemed even disinterested. His judgment was clear and his perceptions quick; but his power of will was feeble; a weakness which only endeared him the more to his royal master, making his presence soothing, not by arts of flattery, but by the qualities of his nature. He took a leading part in the conduct of affairs, just as the people of America were discussing the character of the new Revenue Act, which the King had not suggested; which no living member of the cabinet would own; which Grafton, the Prime Minister, described as "absurd;" but which was left as the fatal bequest of Charles Townshend to his successors and his country.[1]

The new taxes were not to be collected till the twentieth of November; and should the Sons of Liberty effect a universal agreement to send for no more goods from Britain, no customs would, even then, fall due. "But such a confederacy," said Bernard,[2] "will be impracticable without violence;" and he advised a regiment of soldiers as the surest way of "inspiring notions of acquiescence and submission." "Ships of war and a regiment," said Paxton in England,[3] "are needed to ensure tranquillity."

Oct.

Never was a community more distressed or divided by fear and hope, than that of Boston. There the American Board of the Commissioners of the Customs was to be established; and to that town the continent was looking for an example. Rash

[1] Grafton's Autobiography; Compare speeches of Camden, of Grafton, of Shelburne, in the House of Lords, 7 Feb. 1775, and of Camden and Grafton, 5 March, 1776.

[2] Bernard to Shelburne, 31 August, 7 September, 1767.

[3] Compare Bollan to Hutchinson, 11 August, 1767.

CHAP. XXX. 1767. Oct.

words were spoken,[1] rash counsels conceived. "The Commissioners," said the more hasty, "must not be allowed to land."—"Paxton must, like Oliver, be taken to Liberty Tree or the gallows, and obliged to resign."—"Should we be told to perceive our inability to oppose the mother country," cried the youthful Quincy, "we boldly answer, that in defence of our civil and religious rights, with the God of armies on our side, we fear not the hour of trial; though the host of our enemies should cover the field like locusts, yet the sword of the Lord and Gideon shall prevail."[2]

As the lawyers of England all now decided, that American taxation by Parliament was legal and constitutional, the press of Boston sought support in something more firm than human opinion, and more obligatory than the acts of irresponsible legislation. "The law of nature," said they,[3] "is the law of God, irreversible itself and superseding all human law. It perfectly reconciles the true interest and happiness of every individual, with the true interest and happiness of the universal whole. The laws and constitution of the English Government are the best in the world, because they approach nearest to the laws God has established in our nature. Those who have attempted this barbarous violation of the most sacred rights of their country, deserve the name of rebels and traitors, not only against the laws of their country and their King, but against Heaven itself."

[1] Bernard to Shelburne, 21 Sept. 1767.

[2] Boston Gazette of 5 Oct. 1767, 653, 1, 2, Hyperion, by Josiah Quincy.

[3] G. in Boston Gazette of 5 Oct. 1767. 653, 2, 2, Compare N. Rogers to Hutchinson, London, 30 Dec. 1767.

CHAP. XXX. 1767. Oct.

Province called to province. "A revolution must inevitably ensue," said a great student of scripture prophecies,[1] in a village of Connecticut.

"We have discouraging tidings from a mother country," thought Trumbull.[2] "The Americans have been firmly attached to Great Britain; nothing but severity will dissolve the union."

At Boston, revolution was rapidly advancing. Faith in the integrity of Parliament was undermined;[3] men were convinced that arbitrary will might be made the sole rule of government by a concert with Parliament; and they called to mind the words of Locke, that when the constitution is broken by the obstinacy of the Prince, "the people must appeal to Heaven."[4] The nation had the right to resist; and they who deserved to enjoy liberty would find the means.

A petition to the Governor[5] to convene the Legislature having been rejected with "contempt,"[6] the inhabitants of Boston, ever sensitive to "the sound of Liberty,"[7] assembled on the twenty-eighth of October, in Town Meeting, and voted to forbear the importation and use of a great number of articles of British produce and manufacture. They appointed a committee for obtaining a general subscription to such an agreement, and, to extend the confederacy, ordered

[1] B. Gale of Killingworth to Ezra Stiles, 15 Oct. 1767.

[2] The L. Governor of Connecticut to the Agent of Connecticut in London, 17 November, 1767.

[3] From the Craftsman, in the Boston Gazette, 12 October, 1767. 654, 2, 2.

[4] Boston Gazette, 19 Oct. 1767; 655, 1, 1 and 2. Locke on Civil Government, c. xiv.

[5] Cushing and others to Bernard, 7 Oct. 1767.

[6] Bernard to Shelburne, 8 and 15 of October.

[7] Hutchinson to [T. Pownall, probably,] 10 Nov. 1767.

CHAP. XXX. 1767. Oct.

their resolves to be sent to all the towns in the Province and also to the other Colonies.[1]

It was observable that Otis, heretofore so fervid, on this occasion recommended caution, and warned against giving offence to Great Britain.[2] Even the twentieth of November passed away in quiet. Images and placards were exhibited; but they were removed by the friends of the people. A Town Meeting was convened to discountenance riot. Otis, in a long speech, which was said to have been entirely on the side of Government,[3] went so far as to assert the King's right to appoint officers of the customs in what manner and by what denominations he pleased; and he advised the Town to make no opposition to the new duties. But months elapsed before any ship arrived laden with goods that were dutiable. The prospect of having their avarice gratified, blinded Hutchinson and Bernard. The latter reported that the faction "dared not show its face," that "the Province would recover its former reputation" for loyalty. "Our incendiaries seem discouraged," wrote Hutchinson; and as he travelled the Circuit, he spread it through the country, that the New-Yorkers were all for peace, that the people of Boston would be left alone.

Nov.

But on the banks of the Delaware the illustrious Farmer, John Dickinson, of Pennsylvania, who had been taught from his infancy to love humanity and liberty, came forth before the Continent as the cham-

[1] Hutchinson to [T. Pownall,] 10 Nov. 1767. Bernard to Shelburne, 30 Oct. 1767.

[2] Bernard to Shelburne, 30 Oct. 1767.

[3] Bernard to Shelburne, 21 Nov. 1767. Compare also Boston Evening Post of 23 Nov. 1767, and a Card from Otis in Boston Gazette, 30 Nov. 1767.

CHAP. XXX. 1767. Nov.

pion of American rights. He was an enthusiast in his love for England, and accepted the undefined relations of the Parliament to the Colonies as a perpetual compromise, which neither party was to disturb by pursuing an abstract theory to its ultimate conclusions. His words carried the more weight, because he argued against the new Port Duties, only as a conservative.

"If once we are separated from the mother country," he asked in the sincerity of sorrow, "what new form of government shall we adopt? or where shall we find another Britain to supply our loss? Torn from the body to which we were united by religion, liberty, laws, affections, relation, language, and commerce, we must bleed at every vein."[1] He admitted that Parliament possessed a legal authority to regulate the trade of every part of the empire. Examining all the statutes relating to America from its first settlement, he found every one of them based on that principle till the administration of Grenville. Never before did the British Commons think of imposing duties in the Colonies for the purpose of raising a revenue. Grenville first asserted in the Preamble of one Act, that it was "just and necessary" for them to give and grant such duties; and in the Preamble of another, that it was "just and necessary" to raise a further revenue in the same way; while the Preamble of the last Act granting duties upon paper, glass, colors, and tea, disregarding ancient precedents under cover of these modern ones, declared that it was moreover "expedient," that a revenue should be so raised. "This," said the Farmer, "is an INNOVATION and a

[1] Farmer's Letters. Letter iii. in Dickinson's Works, i. 171.

CHAP. XXX. 1767. Nov.

most dangerous innovation. We being obliged to take commodities from Great Britain, special duties on their exportation to us are as much taxes upon us as those imposed by the Stamp Act. Great Britain claims and exercises the right to prohibit manufactures in America. Once admit that she may lay duties upon her exportations to us, for the purpose of levying money on us only, she then will have nothing to do but to lay those duties on the articles which she prohibits us to manufacture, and the tragedy of American liberty is finished. We are in the situation of a besieged city, surrounded in every part but one. If that is closed up, no step can be taken but to surrender at discretion.

"I would persuade the people of these Colonies immediately, vigorously, and unanimously, to exert themselves in the most firm, but the most peaceable manner, for obtaining relief. If an inveterate resolution is formed to annihilate the liberties of the governed, English history affords examples of resistance by force."

The Farmer's Letters carried conviction through the Thirteen Colonies; the men whose fathers came to the wilderness for freedom to say their prayers, would not fear to take up arms against a Preamble which implied their servitude.

CHAPTER XXXI.

MASSACHUSETTS CONSULTS HER SISTER COLONIES.—HILLSBOROUGH'S ADMINISTRATION OF THE COLONIES.

NOVEMBER, 1767—FEBRUARY, 1768.

CHAP. XXXI. 1767. Nov.

ON the twenty-fourth of November, the Twelfth Parliament came together for the last time, previous to its dissolution. Its members were too busy in preparing for the coming elections to interfere with America, about which the King's speech was silent;[1] and when Grenville descanted on two or three papers in the Boston Gazette, as infamous libels on Parliament, the House showed only weariness of his complaints.[2] Bedford himself objected to Grenville's Test for America;[3] and "preferred making an example of some one seditious fellow." The King kept the Ministry from breaking, and proved himself the most efficient man among them. "He makes each of them," said Mansfield,[4] "believe that he is in love with him, and fools them all. They will stand their ground," he added, "unless

[1] Garth to South Carolina, 25 Nov. 1767.

[2] W. S. Johnson to Gov. Pitkin, 26 Dec. 1767. W. S. Johnson to Jared Ingersoll, 30 Nov. 1767. Franklin to Galloway, 1 Dec. 1767, in Works, vii. 369. N. Rogers to Hutchinson, 30 Dec. 1767. Miscellaneous letters ascribed to Junius, x. xxix. and xxxi. in Bohm's edition, ii. 146, 193, 199.

[3] Lyttelton to Temple, in Lyttelton, 741.

[4] Lyttelton to Temple, 25 Nov. 1767; Lyttelton, 737.

CHAP. XXXI. 1767. Nov. that mad man, Lord Chatham, should come and throw a fire-ball in the midst of them." But Chatham's long illness[1] had for the time overthrown his powers. When his health began to give out, it was his passion to appear possessed of the unbounded confidence of the King. A morbid restlessness now led him to great and extravagant expense, in which he vied with those who were no more than his equals in the peerage, but who were besides the inheritors of vast estates. He would drive out with ten outriders, and with two carriages, each drawn by six horses.[2] His vain magnificence deceived no one but himself; and was but the poor relief of humbled pride. "He is allowed to retain office, as a livelihood," observed Bedford. The King complained of him, as "a charlatan, who in difficult times affected ill-health to render himself the more sought after;"[3] and saying that politics was a vile trade, more fit for a hack, than for a gentleman,[4] he proceeded to construct a Ministry that would be disunited and docile.

Dec. On the fifth of December, Bedford, now almost blind and near his end, just before the removal of cataracts from his eyes, told Grenville, that his age, his infirmities and his tastes disinclined him to war on the Court, which was willing[5] to enter into a treaty with him, and each member of the Opposition would do well to exercise a like freedom.[6] "He chooses to give bread to his kinsmen and friends;"

[1] Compare Durand to Choiseul, 23 Nov. 1767.

[2] Durand to Choiseul, 10 Dec. 1767.

[3] Durand to Choiseul, 1 Feb, 1768.

[4] Grenville Papers, iv. 184.

[5] Compare the entry in the Duke's Diary of Oct. 1.

[6] Durand to Choiseul, 13 Dec. 1767.

CHAP. XXXI. 1767. Dec.

said those whom he deserted.[1] Grenville could not conceal his despair.[2] To his junction with Bedford, he had sacrificed the favor of the King. Left to battle alone by the ally for whom he had been a martyr, the famed financier saw "the nothingness of the calculations of party." His health began to fail; the little that remained to him of life became steeped in bitterness; he seemed ready to curse his former associates and to die. At the time when the public indignation was roused by the news of the general agreement which the town of Boston was promoting, and fears were entertained, that Paxton on his arrival would be taken to Liberty Tree and compelled to resign his new commission,[3] the Ministry was revolutionized, but without benefit to Grenville. The Colonies were taken from Shelburne and consigned to a separate department of State, with Lord Hillsborough as its Secretary. Conway made room for Lord Weymouth, a vehement but not forcible speaker; in private life, cold and taciturn; impoverished by gambling, and of such habits that the world[4] said he passed all the day in sleep and all the night in drinking. Gower, who had a better reputation, became President of the Council; the Post Office was assigned to Sandwich, the ablest of them all as well as the most malignant against America; while Rigby was made Vice-Treasurer of Ireland, till he could get the Pay-Office. All five

[1] Durand to Choiseul, 8 Jan. 1768.

[2] Durand to Choiseul, 18 Dec. 1767.

[3] Durand to Choiseul, 10 Dec. 1767.

[4] Durand to the Duke of Choiseul, 19 Jan. 1768. Du Chatelet to the Duke of Choiseul, 20 Feb. 1768.

CHAP. XXXI. 1767. Dec. were friends of the Duke of Bedford, and united respecting America in one opinion, which it was pretended Grafton also had accepted.[1]

Nor be it left unnoticed, that Jenkinson, who took so large a part in framing the Stamp Act, held a place with Lord North at the Treasury Board. "In him," boasted Mauduit to his client, Hutchinson, "we have gained a fresh accession in strength.[2] He is my fast friend, and has never yet failed me in any thing which he undertook for me. He empowered me to tell you he will make your affair one of his first concerns." Jenkinson, whose noiseless industry exercised a prevailing influence over the neglect of Grafton and the ease of Lord North, formed the active and confidential bond between the Treasury and the office holders in Boston. "They of Massachusetts," wrote Mauduit, "may be brought to repent of their insolence."

To assert and maintain the authority of Parliament over America, was the principle on which the friends of Bedford entered the Ministry. Their anger[3] was quickened by the resolutions of Boston to set on foot manufactures and to cease importations.[4] "The Americans," it was said with acrimony, "are determined to have as little connection with Great Britain as possible;[5] and the moment they can, they will renounce dependence."[6] The partisans of the new Ministers professed to think it

[1] Israel Mauduit to Hutchinson, 15 Dec. 1767.

[2] I. Mauduit to Hutchinson, 10 Dec. 1767.

[3] Durand to Choiseul, 11 December, 1767.

[4] W. S. Johnson to R. Temple, 12 Feb. 1767. Franklin to W. Franklin, 19 Dec. 1767.

[5] N. Rogers to Hutchinson, London, 30 Dec. 1766.

[6] W. S. Johnson to Governor Pitkin, 26 Dec, 1766.

CHAP. XXXI. 1767. Dec.

desirable that "the Colonies should forget themselves still further." "Five or six frigates," they clamored, "acting at sea and three regiments on land, will soon bring them to reason and submission."[1] "The waves," replied Franklin,[2] "never rise but when the winds blow;" and addressing the British public, he showed that the new system of politics tended to dissolve the bonds of union between the two countries. "What does England gain by conquests in America," wrote the French Minister, "but the danger of losing her own Colonies? [3]—Things cannot remain as they are; the two nations will become more and more embittered, and their mutual griefs increase.—In four years,[4] the Americans will have nothing to fear from England, and will be prepared for resistance." He thought of Holland as a precedent, yet "America," he observed, "has no recognised chieftain; and without the qualities united in the House of Orange, Holland would never have thrown off the yoke of Spain."[5]

1768. Jan.

The extreme purpose of the Bedford party to abrogate colonial charters and introduce a uniformity of government, appeared immediately on Hillsborough's taking possession of his newly created office. Johnson, the faithful agent of Connecticut, a churchman, and one who from his heart wished to avoid a rupture between the Colonies and England, waited upon him to congratulate him on his advancement.[6]

[1] Durand to Choiseul, 1 Jan. 1768.

[2] Causes &c., Works, iv. 242.

[3] Durand to Choiseul, 21 Dec. 1767.

[4] Durand to Choiseul, Dec. 1767. Compare Andrew Eliot to Thomas Hollis, 15 Dec. 1767.

[5] Durand to Choiseul, 1 Jan. 1768.

[6] W. S. Johnson to W. Pitkin, 13 Feb. 1768.

CHAP. XXXI. 1768. Jan.

"Connecticut," declared Hillsborough, "may always depend upon my friendship and affection."

"Connecticut," said Johnson, "is a loyal Colony." "You are a very free Colony," rejoined Hillsborough; "generally you have used your very extraordinary powers with moderation; but you are very deficient in your correspondence, so that we have too little connection with you."—"That," answered the agent, "is owing to the good order and tranquillity which have so generally prevailed in a quiet Colony, where the government is wisely administered and the people easy and happy. Add to this: from the nature of our constitution fewer occasions arise of troubling the King's Ministers with our affairs than in the Governments immediately under the Crown."

"A request for a copy of your Colony laws," said Hillsborough, "has been repeatedly made; but I cannot find that any obedience has been paid to the requisition."—"The Colony," replied Johnson, "has several times sent over copies of the printed Law Book; there is one or more at the Plantation Office." —"It is the duty of the Government," resumed Hillsborough, "to transmit from time to time, not only the laws that pass, but all the minutes of the proceedings of the Council and Assembly, that we may know what you are about, and rectify whatever may be amiss."—"If your Lordship," rejoined the agent, "wants a copy of our laws for private perusal, for the information of your clerks, or for reference, the Colony will send you one of their Law Books; and you will find it as good a code of laws, almost, as could be devised for such an infant country; and in no respect inferior to any collection of the kind in any of the Colonies. But if your Lordship means to have the laws transmitted for the inspection of the Ministry as such, and for the purpose of approbation or disapprobation by his Majesty in Council, it is what the Colony has never done, and, I am persuaded, will never submit to. By the charter which King Charles the Second granted, the Colony was invested with a power of legislation, not subject to revision. In point of fact, your Lordship well knows, that those laws have never been re-examined here, that the Colony has for more than a century been in the full exercise of those powers, without the least check or interruption, except in a single instance, in such times and under such circumstances, as I believe you will not mention but with detestation, much less consider as a precedent."

"I have read your Charter," said Hillsborough; "it is very full and expressive; and I know what powers you have exercised under it. But there are such things as extravagant grants, which are, therefore, void. You will admit, there are many things which the King cannot grant, as the inseparable incidents of the Crown. Some things which King Charles pretended to grant, may be of that nature, particularly the power of absolute legislation, which tends to the absurdity of creating an independent state."

"Nobody," replied Johnson, "has ever reckoned the power of legislation among the inseparable incidents of the Crown. All lawyers are agreed, that it is an undisputed prerogative of the Crown to create corporations; and the power of law-making is, in some degree at least, incident to every corporation; depending not merely on the words of the grant, but founded in the reason of things, and coextensive with

CHAP. XXXI. 1768. Jan. the purposes for which the body is created. Every corporation in England enjoys it as really, though not as extensively as the Colony of Connecticut. Since, therefore, no question can be made of the right of the Crown to create such bodies and grant such powers in degree, it would be very difficult to limit the bounty of the Prince. The law has not done it, and who can draw the line? Surely not the Ministers of the Prince. The Colony Charters are of a higher nature and founded on a better title than those of the corporations of England. These are mere acts of grace and favor; whereas those in America were granted in consideration of very valuable services done, or to be performed. The services having been abundantly executed at an immense expense by the grantees in the peopling and cultivation of a fine country, the vast extension of his Majesty's dominion, and the prodigious increase of the trade and revenues of the empire, the Charters must now be considered as grants upon valuable considerations, sacred and most inviolable. And even if there might have been a question made upon the validity of such a grant as that to Connecticut in the day of it, yet Parliament as well as the Crown having, for more than a century, acquiesced in the exercise of the power claimed by it, the Colony has now a Parliamentary sanction, as well as a title by prescription added to the royal grant, by all which it must be effectually secured in the full possession of its Charter rights."

"These are matters of nice and curious disquisition," said Hillsborough, evasively; "but at least your laws ought to be regularly transmitted for the inspection of the Privy Council and for disapprobation, if found repugnant to the laws of England."

CHAP. XXXI. 1768. Jan.

"An extra-judicial opinion of the King's Minister," answered Johnson, "or even of the King's Privy Council, cannot determine whether any particular Act is within that proviso or not; this must be decided by a court of law having jurisdiction of the matter, about which the law in question is conversant. If the General Assembly of Connecticut should make a law flatly contradictory to the statute of Great Britain, it may be void; but a declaration of the King in Council would still make it neither more nor less so, but be as void as the law itself, for other words in the Charter clearly and expressly exclude them from deciding about it."

"I have not seen these things," said Hillsborough, "in the light in which you endeavor to place them. You are in danger of being too much a separate, independent State, and of having too little subordination to this country." And then he spoke of the equal affection the King bore his American subjects, and of the great regard of the Ministers for them as Britons, whose rights were not to be injured.

"Upon the repeal of the Stamp Act," said Johnson, "we had hoped these were the principles adopted; but the new duties imposed last winter, and other essential regulations in America, have damped those expectations and given alarm to the Colonies."

"Let neither side," said Hillsborough, "stick at small matters. As to taxes, you are infinitely better off than any of your fellow-subjects in Europe. You are less burdened than even the Irish."

"I hope that England will not add to our burdens," said Johnson; "you would certainly find it redound to your own prejudice."

Thus for two hours together, they reasoned on

CHAP. XXXI. 1768. Jan.

the rights of Connecticut; and Hillsborough showed plainly his opinion, that its Charter must be declared void, not on the pretence that it had been violated or misused, but because the people by the enjoyment of it were too free.

Connecticut so united caution with patriotism, that successive British Ministers were compelled to delay abrogating its Charter, for want of a plausible excuse. Hillsborough on his side, under the exterior of warm professions of tenderness, cherished the fixed purpose of disregarding colonial privileges. His apologists called him honest and well meaning; he was passionate and full of self-conceit;[1] alert in conducting business; wrongheaded in forming his opinions, and pompously stiff in adhering to them. He proposed as his rule of conduct, to join inflexibility of policy with conciliatory language; and in a man of his moderate faculties, this attempt to join firmness with suavity became a mixture of obstinacy and deceit.

His first action respecting Massachusetts was marked by duplicity. Hutchinson, through Mauduit, his agent, and Jenkinson, obtained an annual grant of two hundred pounds sterling. Hillsborough gave to the grant the form of a secret warrant under the King's sign manual on the Commissioners of the Customs at Boston.[2] That a Chief Justice, holding office during pleasure and constantly employing his power for political purposes, should also receive money from the King, was fatal to the independence of the bench;

[1] Franklin's works, vii. 507.

[2] Hutchinson to Hillsborough, 18 April, 1768. "I have good reason to believe I am indebted to your Lordship for the form of the warrant," viz., "warrant for £200 per annum, on the Commissioner of the Customs."

the secrecy of the grant betrayed on the part of the Minister a sense of shame. CHAP. XXXI.

It was this use of the new revenue which the reflecting people in Boston particularly abhorred. 1768. Jan. "We shall be obliged," said they, "to maintain in luxury sycophants, court parasites and hungry dependents, who will be sent over to watch and oppress those who support them.[1] If large salaries are given, needy poor lawyers from England and Scotland, or some tools of power of our own, will be placed on the bench. The Governors will be men rewarded for despicable services, hackneyed in deceit and avarice; or some noble scoundrel who has spent his fortune in every kind of debauchery.

"Unreasonable impositions tend to alienate the hearts of the Colonists. Our growth is so great, in a few years Britain will not be able to compel our submission. Who thought that the four little Provinces of Holland would have been able to throw off the yoke of that powerful kingdom of Spain? —yet they accomplished it by their desperate perseverance." "Liberty is too precious a jewel to be resigned."[2]

Such were the sentiments of the more moderate among the patriots. Still the attempt at concerting an agreement not to import had thus far failed; and unless the Assembly of Massachusetts should devise methods of resistance, the oppressive law would gradually go into effect. The hot spirits in that body

[1] Andrew Eliot to T. Hollis, 10 Dec. 1767; and compare A. Eliot to Archdeacon Blackburne, 15 Dec. 1767.

[2] Compare Andrew Eliot to Rev. William Harris, Dec. 1767.

CHAP. XXXI. 1768. Jan.

were ready to break out into a flame; there were men among them who would not count the consequences.[1] Of the country Members, Hawley, than whom no one was abler, or more sincere, lived far in the interior; and his excitable nature, now vehement, now desponding, unfitted him to guide. The irritability of Otis had so increased, that he rather indulged himself in "rhapsodies"[2] and volcanic "flashes"[3] of eloquence, than framed deliberate plans of conduct. Besides, his mind had early embraced the idea "of a general union of the British Empire, in which every part of its wide dominions should be represented under one equal and uniform direction, and system of laws;" and though the Congress of New-York drew from him a tardy concession,[4] that an American representation was impossible, yet his heart still turned to his original opinion, and in his prevailing mood, he shrunk from the thought of Independence. The ruling passion of Samuel Adams, on the contrary, was the preservation of the distinctive character and institutions of New-England. He thoroughly

[1] Andrew Eliot to T. Hollis, 5 Jan. 1768; and compare Thomas Hollis to A. Eliot, 1 July, 1768.

[2] The word is Bernard's; compare Bernard to Secretary of State, 5 March, 1768.

[3] Letter of Hutchinson, of 17 Feb. 1768.

[4] The curious inquirer may find this paper in which Otis reconciled himself to the position adopted alike by the Legislature of Massachusetts and the General Congress at New-York against an American representation in Parliament, in the Boston Gazette and Country Journal, No. 561, page ii. column 1, of Monday, December 30, 1765. The idea of "a general union of all parts of the British Empire under an equal and uniform direction, and system of laws," seems to me to have been always dear to him. His mind gave way before he came to the conclusion, to which he might have been led, on becoming convinced that such a union was impossible. In 1768 it still had many advocates in England and in America, Otis among the number.

understood the tendency of the measures adopted by Parliament; approved of making the appeal to Heaven, since freedom could not otherwise be preserved; and valued the liberties of his country more than its temporal prosperity, more than his own life, more than the lives of all. The confidence of his townsmen sustained his fortitude; his whole nature was absorbed by care for the public; and his strictly logical mind was led to choose for the defence of the separate liberties of America, a position which offered no weak point for attack. His theory, on which the Colonies were to repose till the dawn of better days, as a small but gallant army waits for aid within its lines, he embodied in the form of a letter from the Assembly of the Province to their Agent.[1] On the sixth of

[1] The papers which I possess or have seen, compel me to say, that the document referred to is the work of Samuel Adams, both in its substance and in its form. The evidence for it is both internal and external. Internal evidence: 1. The paper has the style of Samuel Adams. This has been universally admitted. 2. It conveys the exact political opinions of Samuel Adams. One may see the lineaments of his mind in every sentence; and so true is this, that he who wishes a key to the political career of that statesman, from his coming into political life to his end, needs only to study this production. As to external evidence, 1. Andrew Eliot, a most estimable clergyman of Boston, thoroughly well informed, one of the most sensible men of that day, writing to Thomas Hollis on the twenty-seventh of September, 1768, for the purpose of correcting a mistake that had been made respecting the authorship of a paper which Hollis had reprinted in England, says expressly that this letter of the House to its Agent which Hollis had also reprinted, was written by Samuel Adams. Here is explicit contemporary authority of the most trustworthy kind. 2. The original document is said by the late Samuel Adams Welles (I have myself never seen it), to be in the handwriting of Samuel Adams; and there is no evidence that any part of it exists or ever existed in the handwriting of any one of his contemporaries. 3. Samuel Adams writing to Dennys de Berdt on the 30th of January, 1768, refers to this public letter from the House of Representatives, and describes it as a letter, "in which," to use the very words of S. Adams, "I have the good fortune to have my own private sentiments so exactly expressed, as to make it needless for me to say any thing of them in this letter." This seems to me to approach an ac-

CHAP. XXXI. 1768. Jan. January, and for the evening and morning of many succeeding days, the paper was under severe examination in the House. Seven times it was revised; every word was weighed; every sentence considered; and each seemingly harsh expression tempered and refined. At last on the twelfth of January, the letter was adopted, to be sent to the Agent, communicated to the British Ministry, and published to the world, as expressing the unchangeable opinions of Massachusetts.

knowledgment, that the public letter was his own.

Indirect evidence abounds. Not only do the contemporary letters of Bernard and of Hutchinson, and the History of Hutchinson, and the biography of Eliot, attribute generally many Massachusetts State Papers to the pen of Samuel Adams, but there is also a report of a conversation between Otis and Samuel Adams, in which Otis, on the last day of June or early in July of this very year, blamed the latter for intending to print a public letter; and in the course of the dispute Otis said to S. Adams, "You are so fond of your own draughts that you can't wait for the publication of them to the proper time." This remark which referred to a letter to Lord Hillsborough, defending the letter to De Berdt and its consequences, speaks not of a draught of one letter, but generally of "draughts;" which is in harmony with all the contemporary testimony. See the unpublished part of the letter of Bernard to Hillsborough, 9 July, 1768.

Otis was named first among the representatives of Boston, and placed at the head of Committees long after his powers had failed. It was excusable that his biographer, led by this circumstance, by his reputation as the beginner of the Revolutionary strife, and by the natural inclination of a writer of a life to illustrate his theme, should have readily adopted the opinion that Otis was the author of this and other similar pieces. The papers which prove the reverse have come to light or to notice since he wrote; and no doubt his candor if he still survived, would lead him to revise his opinion. The papers of this session are not in the style of Otis, nor do they contain his opinions; but contain opinions, which he, for himself individually, never made his own. Not one contemporary writer so much as hints at his being the author of them. The inquirer who will put together the papers known to have been written, or speeches uttered by Otis from midsummer 1767 to his retirement, will have no doubt left on his mind. The gradual increase of that irritability which finally mastered the intellect of Otis, began to be apparent before this time. He still continued to make long and perhaps frequent speeches, and still beyond all others manifested his loathing of the corrupt and selfish Crown Officers. But his remarks became more and more personal, and uncertainty hung over his opinions, which varied with his moods of mind. I know of no calmly written paper of any considerable length which can be attributed to him as its author after 1765.

CHAP. XXXI. 1768. Jan.

Disclaiming the most distant thought of independence of the mother country, provided they could have the free enjoyment of their rights, the House affirmed,[1] that "the British constitution hath its foundation in the law of God and nature; that in every free state, the supreme Legislature derives its power from the constitution;" and "is bounded and circumscribed "by its fundamental rules."

That the right to property exists by a law of nature, they asserted, on the one side, against "the visionary and impracticable Utopian schemes of levelling and a community of goods;" on the other, against all Acts of the British Parliament, taxing the Colonists.

"In the time of James II.," they continued, "the Crown, and the Ministers of the Crown, without the intervention of Parliament, demolished Charters and levied taxes in the Colonies at pleasure. Our case is more deplorable and remediless. Our ancestors found relief by the interposition of Parliament; but by the intervention of that very power we are taxed, and can appeal from their decision to no power on earth."

They further set forth the original contract between the King and the first planters, as the Royal promise in behalf of the English nation; their title by the common law and by statute law to all the liberties and privileges of natural born subjects of the realm; and the want of equity in taxing Colonies whose manufactures were prohibited and whose trade was restrained.

[1] Letter from the House of Representatives, to D. de Berdt, Agent for the Province in England, January 12, 1768, in Bradford's Massachusetts State papers, 124.

CHAP. XXXI. 1768. Jan.

Still more they objected to the appropriation of the revenues from the new duties to the support of American civil officers and an American army, as introducing an absolute government. The Judges in the Colonies held their commissions at the pleasure of the Crown; if their salaries were to be independent, a corrupt Governor might employ men who would "deprive a bench of justice of its glory, and the people of their security." Nor need the money be applied by Parliament to protect the Colonists; they were never backward in defending themselves, and when treated as free subjects, they always granted aids of their own accord, to the extent of their ability, and even beyond it. Nor could a standing army among them secure their dependence; they had towards the mother country an English affection, which would for ever keep them connected with her, unless it should be erased by repeated unkind usage.

They objected to the establishment of Commissioners of the Customs, as a needless expense in itself, and dangerous to their liberties from the increase of Crown officers. Still more, they expressed alarm at the Act, conditionally suspending the powers of the Assembly of New-York, and thus annihilating its legislative authority.

"King James and his successors," thus they proceeded, "broke the copartnership of the supreme legislative with the supreme executive, and the latter could not exist without the former. In these remote dominions, there should be a free legislative; otherwise strange effects are to be apprehended, for the laws of God and nature are invariable." [1]

[1] Bradford's Massachusetts State papers, 133.

The House of Representatives, having sanctioned this Remonstrance, next addressed Shelburne,[1] Chatham, Rockingham,[2] Conway, Camden, the Treasury Board, at which sat Grafton, Lord North, and Jenkinson, letters which contained the same sentiments, and especially enforced the impracticability of an American representation in the British Parliament.[3] But no memorial was sent to the Lords; no petition to the House of Commons. The colonial Legislature joined issue with the British Parliament, and adopting the draft of Samuel Adams,[4] approached the King as umpire with their Petition. CHAP. XXXI. 1768. Jan.

To him, in beautifully simple language, they recounted the story of the colonization of Massachusetts; the forfeiture of their first Charter; and the confirmation to them, on the Revolution, of their most essential rights and liberties; the principal of which was that most sacred right of being taxed only by representatives of their own free election. They complained that the Acts of Parliament, "imposing taxes in America, with the express purpose of raising a revenue, left them only the name of free subjects."

The mode of relief by an American representation in Parliament they declare to be "utterly impractica-

[1] The House of Representatives to Shelburne, 15 January, 1768, Bradford's State Papers, 137. Compare the contrary opinions of Otis, in Gordon's Hist. of the Amer. Rev. i. 228, 229.

[2] House to Rockingham, 22 Jan. 1768, in Bradford, 142.

[3] The True Sentiments of America: Contained in a Collection of Letters, &c. &c. Published at the instance of Thomas Hollis.

[4] Of this document, I possess the draft as made by Samuel Adams with his own hand. Handwriting of itself does not prove authorship, but this paper seems to me to be no copy. The letter of Andrew Eliot also attributes the authorship of the Petition to Samuel Adams. Otis, too, used respecting it language of praise, quite inconsistent with his having been concerned in preparing it. See Bernard to Hillsborough, 9 July, 1768, not the printed Letter, which is an extract, but the original.

CHAP. XXXI. 1768. Jan.

ble;" and they referred the consideration of their present circumstances to the wisdom and clemency of the King.

In the several papers which, after a fortnight's anxious deliberation, were adopted by an Assembly, composed for the most part of farmers and delegates from the rural population, the calmness of the language is suited to the earnestness of their purpose; nor is there one line which betrays haste, or hesitation. It remained for the House "to inform the other Governments with its proceedings against the late Acts, that, if they thought fit, they might join [1] therein." But this, it was said in a house of eighty-two Members, would be considered in England, as appointing a second Congress; and the negative prevailed by a vote of two to one. The country members were slow in perceiving the imminence and extent of the public danger.

At this appearance of indecision, Bernard conceived "great hopes." "It will," said he, "make some atonement for their Remonstrance." [2]

The towns in the central Provinces had not as yet seconded the proposal of Boston to import nothing from England. "The British Government will probably pursue the mildest policy," wrote De Kalb to Choiseul from Philadelphia.[3] "The Colonies are but lightly taxed, and could not resist force. Distance from the British Government makes these people more free; but at heart they have little disposition to

[1] Compare Bernard to Shelburne, 18 Feb. 1768.

[2] Bernard to the Secretary of State, 30 January, 1768, in Letter to the Ministry, 7. and Bernard to Shelburne, 2 Feb. 1768.

[3] De Kalb to the Duke de Choiseul, Philadelphia, 15 January, 1768. But compare his letter to Choiseul of 20 January, 1768.

CHAP. XXXI. 1768. Jan. Feb.

throw off their dependence by the aid of foreign powers." The tone of public feeling seemed unprepared for action and averse to a rupture.

But Samuel Adams and the few who shared his courage contended indefatigably[1] against the principle of taxation. The hesitancy in the Assembly had proceeded not from timidity but caution. The Members spoke with one another in private, till their views became clearer. Then on the fourth day of February, a motion was made to reconsider the vote against writing to the other Colonies. The House was counted; eighty-two were again found to be present; the question was put and carried by a large majority, and the former vote erased from the journals.[2]

On the same day, a question, whether the House would appoint a committee to prepare a letter, to be sent to each House of Representatives or Burgesses on the Continent, to inform them of the measure which it had taken, passed in the affirmative after debate. A masterly circular letter which Samuel Adams[3] had drafted, was, on the eleventh of February, read in the House, and accepted almost unanimously.

Expressing a firm confidence that the united supplications of the distressed Americans would meet with the favorable acceptance of the King, they set forth the importance that proper constitutional mea-

[1] Bernard to Hillsborough, 19 May, 1768; and Same to Shelburne, 18 Feb. 1768.

[2] Account by Samuel Adams in the Letter from the House to Hillsborough, 30 June, 1768.

[3] Of this most important paper I possess the draft, in the handwriting of Samuel Adams. Besides that and the evidence of the contemporary letter by Andrew Eliot, the whole conduct of Samuel Adams for the next seven years is a perpetual proof that the measure was his own.

CHAP. XXXI. 1768. Feb. sures respecting the Acts of Parliament, imposing taxes on the Colonies, should be adopted; and that the representatives of the several assemblies upon so delicate a point, should harmonize with each other. They made known their "disposition freely to communicate their mind to a sister Colony, upon a common concern."

They then embody the substance of all their representations to the Ministry; that the legislative power of Parliament is circumscribed by the constitution, and is self-destroyed whenever it overleaps its bounds; that allegiance as well as sovereignty is limited; that the right to property is an essential, unalterable one, engrafted into the British system, and to be asserted, exclusive of any consideration of Charters; that taxation of the Colonies by the British Parliament in which they are not represented, is an infringement of their natural and constitutional rights; that an equal representation of the American people in Parliament is for ever impracticable; that their partial representation would be worse even than taxation without their consent. They further enumerate as grievous the civil list independent of the people for officers holding commissions at the pleasure of the Crown; the Billeting Act; and the large powers of the Commissioners of the Customs appointed to reside at Boston.

"The House," they continued, "is fully satisfied that your Assembly is too generous and liberal in sentiment, to believe that this letter proceeds from an ambition of taking the lead, or dictating to the other Assemblies. They freely submit their opinions to the judgment of others, and shall take it kind in

CHAP. XXXI. 1768. Feb.

you to point out to them any thing further that may be thought necessary."[1]

A fair copy of this Circular was ordered to be transmitted to England, to be produced in proof of its true spirit and design; they drew their system of conduct from reason itself, and despised concealment.

[1] Bradford's Massachusetts State Papers, 134.

CHAPTER XXXII.

AN AMERICAN EMPIRE IS IN THE DIVINE DECREES—HILLSBOROUGH'S ADMINISTRATION OF THE COLONIES CONTINUED.

FEBRUARY—MARCH, 1768.

CHAP. XXXII. 1768. Feb.

THE day after the Circular was adopted, the Board of Commissioners of the Revenue met at Boston, and with the utmost secrecy, addressed to their superiors in England a memorial which, in connection with the reports of Bernard, was designed to effect a fatal change in the policy of England. Expressing apprehensions for their own safety, they complained against the American Press, especially against the seeming moderation, parade of learning, and most mischievous tendency of the Farmer's Letters; against New England Town Meetings, "in which," they said, "the lowest mechanics discussed the most important points of government with the utmost freedom;" against Rhode Island, as if it had even proposed to stop the Revenue money; against Massachusetts, for having invited every Province to discountenance the consumption of British manufactures. "We have every reason," they added, "to expect that we shall find it impracticable to enforce the execution of the Revenue Laws, until the hand of Government is pro-

CHAP. XXXII. 1768. Feb.

perly strengthened. At present there is not a ship of war in the Province, nor a company of soldiers, nearer than New-York."[1]

The alternative was thus presented to the Ministry and the King. On the one side Massachusetts asked relief from taxation without representation, and invited the several Colonies to unite in the petition; the Crown officers, on the other, sent their memorial for a fleet and regiments.

But what could an armed force find to do? The system of opposition was passive. The House left no doubt of its purpose not to arrest the execution of any law; and, on the twenty-sixth of February, by a vote of eighty-one to the one vote of Timothy Ruggles, discouraged the use of superfluities, and gave a preference to American manufactures in Resolves,[2] which, said Bernard, "were so decently and cautiously worded, that at another time they would scarcely have given offence."[3] Could an army compel a colonist to buy a new coat instead of continuing to wear an old one? or force the consumption of tea? or compel any one to purchase what he was resolved to do without? Every one in England, Grafton, North, even Hillsborough, professed to disapprove of Townshend's Revenue Act. Why will they not quiet America by its revocation? Sending regiments into Boston will be a summons for America to make the last appeal.

[1] Memorial of the Commissioner of Customs, 12 Feb. 1768. Compare Treasury Minute Book xxxix. 108. Letter of the Commissioners, of 3 May, 1768.

[2] Memorial of Commissioners of the Customs, 28 March, 1768. Boston Gazette, 29 Feb. 1768.

[3] Bernard to Shelburne, 1768.

CHAP. XXXII. 1768. Feb.

Grenville and his friends[1] insisted on declaring meetings and associations like those of Boston illegal and punishable; and advised some immediate chastisement. "I wish," said he, "every American in the world could hear me. I gave the Americans bounties on their whale fishery, thinking they would obey the Acts of Parliament;" and he now spoke for a prohibition of their fisheries.[2] Some of the Ministry went far beyond him, and were ready to proceed against Massachusetts with immediate and extreme severity.[3] When America was mentioned, nothing could be heard but the bitterest invectives of its enemies. That it must submit, no one questioned.

While Hillsborough was writing[4] encomiums on Bernard, praising his own "justice and lenity," and lauding the King as the tender and affectionate father of all his subjects, the superior discernment of Choiseul was aware of the importance of the rising controversy; and that he might unbosom his thoughts with freedom, he appointed to the place of ambassador in England his own most confidential friend, the Count du Chatelet,[5] son of the celebrated woman with whom Voltaire had been intimately connected. The new diplomatist was a person of quick perceptions, daring courage as a statesman, and perfect knowledge of the world; and he was, also, deeply imbued with the liberal principles of the French philosophy of his age.

[1] W. S. Johnson's Journal, 15 Feb. 1768, and W. S. Johnson to Pitkin, 12 March, 1768.

[2] Nathaniel Rogers to Hutchinson, 27 Feb. 1768.

[3] W. S. Johnson to Pitkin, 12 March, 1768; Journal, 18 Feb. 1768.

[4] Hillsborough to Bernard, 16 February, 1768.

[5] Du Châtelet to Choiseul, 13 Feb. 1768.

CHAP. XXXII. 1768. Feb.

The difficulty respecting taxation was heightened by personal contentions, which exasperated members of the Legislature of Massachusetts. The House [1] discovered that their leaving the Crown officers out of the Council had been misrepresented by Bernard to Shelburne; and in the most temperate language they wisely suggested the recall of the Governor,[2] of whose accusatory letters they requested copies.[3] "It is not in the power of these people to move my temper," wrote Bernard.[4] The indignation of Otis rose almost to a frenzy; a paper in the Boston Gazette, bearing the marks of his excited mind,[5] exposed "the obstinate malice, diabolical thirst for mischief, effrontery, guileful treachery, and wickedness" of Bernard. The Governor called on the House to order a prosecution of the printers. "The Liberty of the Press," they answered,[6] "is the great bulwark of freedom." On occasion of proroguing the Legislature, Bernard [7] chid in public its leading Members. "There are men," said he, "to whose importance everlasting contention is necessary. Time will soon pull the masks off those false patriots, who are sacrificing their country to the gratification of

March

[1] Bradford, 117, 118. Shelburne to Bernard, 17 Sept. 1767, received Feb. 1768. Bernard to Shelburne, 2 Feb. 1768. Resolve of the House, 13 Feb. 1768, in Bradford, 112, 113. Bernard to Shelburne, 20 Feb. 1768. Bernard's message to the House of Representatives, 16 Feb. 1768, in Bradford, 113. Answer of the House of Representatives, 18 Feb. 1768. In Bradford 113—116.

[2] House of Representatives to Shelburne, 22 Feb. 1768.

[3] Compare Bernard to Shelburne, 5 March, 1768.

[4] Bernard to Shelburne, 22 Feb. 1768.

[5] In the supplement to the Boston Gazette, No. 674, 2, 3, of Feb. 29, 1768.

[6] House to Governor, 4 March, 1768.

[7] Bernard's speech on Proroguing the Legislature, 4 March, 1768. Br. 120, 121.

CHAP. XXXII. 1768. March

their own passions. I shall defend this injured country from the evils which threaten it, arising from the machinations of a few, very few, discontented men." "The flagitious libel,"[1] he wrote home, "blasphemes Kingly government itself." But it was only a coarse sketch of his own bad qualities. "I told the Grand Jury," said Hutchinson, "almost in plain words, that they might depend on being damned,[2] if they did not find against the paper, as containing High Treason." The Jury refused. "Oaths and the laws have lost their force,"[3] wrote Hutchinson; while the people were overjoyed,[4] and "the honest and independent Grand Jurors" became the favorite toast of the Sons of Liberty.

On the day on which the General Court was prorogued, merchants of Boston came together, began a subscription to renounce commerce with England, and invited the merchants of the whole Continent to give the world the spectacle of a universal passive resistance.

De Kalb, who was astonished at the prosperity of the Colonies and the immense number of merchant vessels in all the waters from the Chesapeake[5] to Boston, thought for a moment, that if the Provinces could jointly discuss their interests by deputies, an independent State would soon be formed. The people were brave; and their militia not inferior to regular troops. And yet after studying the spirit of

[1] Bernard to Shelburne, 5 March, 1768.

[2] Hutchinson to —— 26 March, 1768.

[3] Hutchinson to the Duke of Grafton, 27 March, 1768. Hutchinson to Richard Jackson, 23 March, 1768.

[4] Compare A. Eliot to T. Hollis, 18 April, 1768. Hutchinson's Hist. of Massachusetts, iii. 184.

[5] De Kalb to Choiseul, 25 Feb. 1768.

1768. March

New England,[1] he was persuaded that all classes sincerely loved their mother country, and, as he believed, would never accept foreign aid. Besides so convinced were they of the justice of their demands and their own importance, they would not hold it possible that they should be driven to the last appeal. "It is my fixed opinion," said he, "that the firebrands will be worsted, and that the Colonies will, in the end, obtain all the satisfaction which they demand. Sooner or later the government must recognise its being in the wrong."

The Crown officers in Boston were resolved that instead of concessions, America should suffer new wrongs. "The annual election of Councillors," wrote Bernard,[2] "is the canker worm of the constitution of this government, whose weight cannot be put in the scale against that of the people." "To keep the balance even," argued Hutchinson, "there is need of aid from the other side of the water."[3]

How to induce the British Government to change the Charter, and send over troops was the constant theme of discussion; and it was concerted that the eighteenth of March, the anniversary of the Repeal of the Stamp Act, should be made to further the design. Reports were industriously spread of an intended insurrection on that day; of danger to the Commissioners of the Customs. The Sons of Liberty, on their part, were anxious to preserve order. At day-break the effigy of Paxton and that of another revenue officer, were found hang-

[1] De Kalb to Choiseul, 2 March, 1768.

[2] Compare also Bernard to the Secretary of State, 12 March, 1768.

[3] Hutchinson to Thos. Pownall, 23 Feb. 1768.

CHAP. XXXII. 1768. March

ing on Liberty Tree; they were instantly taken down by the friends of the people. The Governor endeavored to magnify "the atrociousness of the insult," and to express fears of violence; the Council justly insisted there was no danger of disturbance. The day was celebrated[1] by a temperate festival, at which toasts were drunk to the Freedom of the Press, to Paoli and the Corsicans, to the joint freedom of America and Ireland; to the immortal memory of Brutus, Cassius, Hampden and Sidney. Those who dined together broke up early. There was no bonfire lighted, and "in the evening," these are Hutchinson's[2] words, written within the week of the event, "we had only such a mob as we have long been used to on the Fifth of November, and other holidays." Gage[3] too, who afterwards made careful inquiry in Boston, declared the disturbance to have been "trifling." But Bernard reported a "great disposition to the utmost disorder; hundreds "parading the streets with yells and outcries that were quite terrible." As the mob passed his house, "there was so terrible a yell that it was apprehended they were breaking in. It was not so; however, it caused the same terror as if it had been so."—"The whole made it a very terrible night to those who thought themselves objects of the popular fury." And this was said of a mere usual gathering of men, women, and children at a time of rejoicing, when no harm was done or intended. "I can afford no protection

[1] Boston Gazette of 21 March, 1768; 677, 3, 1.

[2] Hutchinson to Richard Jackson, 23 March, 1768.

[3] Gage to the Secretary of State, 31 October, 1768.

1768. March

to the Commissioners," he continues. "I have not the shadow of authority or power. I am obnoxious to the madness of the people, yet left exposed to their resentment without any possible resort of protection. I am then asked why I do not apply for troops, as well to support the King's Government as to protect the persons of his officers. I answer, His Majesty's Ministers have within these three years been fully acquainted with the defenceless state of this Government, and therefore I leave it entirely to the Administration to determine upon a measure which they are much more able to judge of, and be answerable for, than I can be. I shall have danger and trouble enough when such orders arrive, though I keep ever so clear of advising or promoting them. Those who have the command of the mob can restrain them, and of course let them loose."[1] "Your Lordship may depend upon it, that nothing less than the abolition of all the Acts imposing duties is proposed. When that is done, the transition to all other acts of Parliament will be very short and easy."[2]

Such were Bernard's importunities for troops, while he was giving the strongest assurances that he had not written any thing to get them sent; and he used to protest he wished the people of the Province could have a sight of all his letters to the Ministry, that they might become convinced of his friendship.[3] At the same time he was constantly entreating the Secretary to conceal his correspondence.

[1] Bernard to the Secretary of State, 19 March, 1768.

[2] Bernard to the Secretary of State, 21 March, 1768.

[3] Town of Boston's Appeal to the world, 22.

CHAP. XXXII. 1768. March

To ensure the arrival of an armed force, the Commissioners of the Customs applied directly to the Naval Commander at Halifax,[1] and also sent a second memorial to the Lords of the Treasury. They said that a design had certainly been formed to bring them on the eighteenth of March to Liberty Tree, and oblige them to renounce their commissions. "The Governor and magistracy," they add, "have not the least authority or power in this place. The mob are ready to be assembled on any occasion. Every officer who exerts himself in the execution of his duty will be exposed to their resentment. If the answer from Government to the remonstrances of the Lower House of Assembly should not be agreeable to the people, we are fully persuaded, that they will proceed to violent measures. In the mean time we must depend on the favor of the mob for our protection. We cannot answer for our security for a day, much less will it be in our power to carry the Revenue Laws into effect."[2]

These letters went from Boston to the Ministry in March. The tales of riots were scandalously false. The people were opposed to the revenue system of the British Parliament; and they hoped for redress; if the Ministry should refuse it, they on their part were resolved to avoid every act of violence, to escape paying the taxes by never buying the goods on which they were imposed, and to induce their repeal by ceasing to con-

[1] Commodore Hood to Mr. Grenville, Halifax, July 11, 1768, in Grenville papers, iv. 306.

[2] Memorial from the Commissioners of the Customs at Boston, 28 March, 1768.

CHAP. XXXII. 1768. March

sume English manufactures. England had on her side the general affection of the people, the certainty that the country could not as yet manufacture for itself, and consequently the certainty that the schemes of non-importation would fail. If she refuses to take back the last Revenue Act, there is danger that she will substitute a frank and upright man for Bernard, whose petulance, duplicity, and corruption are now exposed, and patiently await the time when the wants of the colonists will weary them of their self-denial, and lead them to abandon it of themselves.

But the administration of public affairs had degenerated into a system of patronage, which had money for its object; and was supported by the King from the love of authority. The Government of England had more and more ceased to represent the noble spirit of England. The Twelfth Parliament, which had taxed America and was now near its dissolution, has never been rivalled in its bold profligacy. Its predecessors had been corrupt. The men of Bolingbroke's time took bribes more openly than those of Walpole; those of Walpole than those of the Pelhams; and those of the Pelhams, than those since the accession of George the Third; so that direct gifts of money were grown less frequent, as public opinion increased in power. But there never was a Parliament so shameless in its corruption as this Twelfth Parliament which virtually severed America from England. It had its votes ready for any body that was Minister, and for any measure that the Minister of the day might propose. It gave an almost unanimous support to Pitt, when, for the last time in seventy years, the foreign politics of England were on the

CHAP. XXXII. 1768. March

side of liberty. It had a majority for Newcastle after he had ejected Pitt; for Bute when he dismissed Newcastle; for Grenville so long as he was the friend of Bute; for Grenville, when he became Bute's most implacable foe; and for the slender capacity of the inexperienced Rockingham. The shadow of Chatham, after his desertion of the House, could sway its decisions. When Charles Townshend, rebelling in the Cabinet, seemed likely to become Minister, it listened to him. When Townshend died, North easily restored subordination.

Nor was it less impudent as to measures. It promoted the alliance with the King of Prussia and deserted him; it protected the issue of general warrants, and utterly condemned them; it passed the Stamp Act, and it repealed the Stamp Act; it began to treat America with tenderness, then veered about, imposed new taxes, changed essentially American Constitutions, and showed a readiness to suspend and abolish the freedom of the American Legislative. It was corrupt, and it knew itself to be corrupt, and made a jest of its own corruption. While it lasted, it was ready to bestow its favors on any Minister or party; and when it was gone, and had no more chances at prostitution, men wrote its epitaph as of the most scandalously abandoned body that England had ever known.[1]

Up to this time the Colonists had looked to Parliament as the bulwark of their liberties; henceforward they knew it to be their most dangerous enemy. They avowed that they would not pay

[1] W. S. Johnson, 29 April, 1768.

taxes which it assumed to impose.[2] Some still allowed it a right to restrain colonial trade; but the advanced opinion among the patriots was, that each provincial Legislature must be perfectly free; that laws were not valid unless sanctioned by the consent of America herself. Without disputing what the past had established, they were resolved to oppose any Minister that should attempt to "innovate" a single iota in their privileges. "Almighty God himself," wrote Dickinson,[3] "will look down upon your righteous contest with approbation. You will be a band of brothers, strengthened with inconceivable supplies of force and constancy by that sympathetic ardor which animates good men, confederated in a good cause. You are assigned by Divine Providence, in the appointed order of things, the protector of unborn ages, whose fate depends upon your virtue."

CHAP. XXXII
1768. March

The people of Boston responded to this appeal. In a solemn Meeting,[4] Malcom moved their thanks to the ingenious author of the Farmer's Letters; and Hancock, Samuel Adams, and Warren, were of the committee to greet him in the name of the Town as "the Friend of Americans, and the benefactor of mankind."

"They may with equal reason make one step more;" wrote Hutchinson [1] to the Duke of Grafton; "they may deny the regal as well as the parliamentary authority, although no man as yet has that in his thoughts."

[2] Du Châtelet to Choiseul, 12 March, 1768.

[3] Farmer's Letters, xii. Works, i. 282.

[4] Bernard to Hillsborough, 28 March, 1768.

[1] Hutchinson to the Duke of Grafton, 27 March, 1768.

CHAP. XXXII. 1768. March

Du Chatelet,[1] in England, having made his inquiries into the resources of America, was persuaded that even if the detailed statements before him were one half too large, England could not reduce her Colonies should they raise the standard of rebellion. "Their population is so great," said he to Choiseul, "that a breath would scatter the troops sent to enforce obedience. The ever existing attractions of an entire independence and of a free commerce, cannot fail to keep their minds continually in a state of disgust at the national subjection. The English Government may take some false step, which will in a single day set all these springs in activity. A great number of chances can hasten the revolution which all the world foresees without daring to assign its epoch. I please myself with the thought that it is not so far off as some imagine, and that we should spare neither pains nor expense to co-operate with it. We must also nourish his Catholic Majesty's disposition to avenge his wrongs. The ties that bind America to England are three fourths broken. It must soon throw off the yoke. To make themselves independent, the inhabitants want nothing but arms, courage, and a chief. If they had among them a genius equal to Cromwell, this republic would be more easy to establish than the one of which that usurper was the head. Perhaps[2] this man exists; perhaps nothing is wanting but happy circumstances to place him upon a great theatre."

[1] Du Châtelet to Choiseul, 12 March, 1768; and compare other letters.

[2] Peut-être cet homme existe-t-il; peut-être ne manque-t-il plus que de quelques circonstances heureuses pour le placer sur un grand théâtre. Du Châtelet, 12 March.

CHAP XXXII. 1768. March

At Mount Vernon conversation turned at this time on the dangers that overhung the country. "Whenever my country calls upon me," said Washington, "I am ready to take my musket on my shoulder."

April.

"Courage, Americans;"[1] cried one of the famed New-York "Triumvirate" of Presbyterian lawyers, William Livingston,[2] as I believe; "Courage, Americans: liberty, religion and sciences, are on the wing to these shores. The finger of God points out a mighty empire to your sons. The savages of the wilderness were never expelled to make room for idolaters and slaves. The land we possess is the gift of Heaven to our Fathers, and Divine Providence seems to have decreed it to our latest posterity. So legible is this munificent and celestial deed in past events, that we need not be discouraged by the bickerings between us and our parent country. The angry cloud will soon be dispersed, and America advance to felicity and glory, with redoubled rapidity and vigor. The day dawns, in which the foundation of this mighty empire is to be laid, by the establishment of a regular American Constitution. All that has hitherto been done seems to be little beside

[1] American Whig, No. v. Parker's New-York Gazette of 11 April, 1768.

[2] Theodore Sedgwick's Life of William Livingston, 145. Rev. Dr. Johnson to W. S. Johnson, Stratford, 22 April, 1768. "Within this month the wicked Triumvirate of New-York, S. L. and Sc. [William Smith, William Livingston, and John Morin Scott,] have in Parker's paper," &c. &c. &c. Manuscript letter of Thomas B. Chandler to ——, 7 April, 1768. "The first Whig was written by Livingston, the second by Smith, the third by ——, and the fourth by Smith as far as the thundergust, and then Livingston went on in his high prancing style," &c. &c. Unluckily there is no positive mention of the author of No. v. That it was not Smith, appears from the use made of it, after the rupture with England.

CHAP. XXXII. 1768. April. the collection of materials for this glorious fabric. 'Tis time to put them together. The transfer of the European part of the family is so vast, and our growth so swift, that, BEFORE SEVEN YEARS ROLL OVER OUR HEADS, the first stone must be laid."

CHAPTER XXXIII.

AN ARMY AND A FLEET FOR BOSTON.—HILLSBOROUGH'S ADMINISTRATION OF THE COLONIES CONTINUED.

April—June, 1768.

CHAP. XXXIII 1768. April.

"Send over an army and a fleet to reduce the dogs to reason;"[1] such was the cry of those round the court and the public offices in England, at every rumor of colonial discontents. On the fifteenth of April the news of the Circular letter of Massachusetts reached the Ministers. "It is an incentive to rebellion,"[2] said some of them; and their choleric haste dictated the most impolitic measures that could have been devised. To insulate the offending Province, and if possible the town of Boston, a letter was sent by Hillsborough to the Governors of each of the twelve other Colonies, with a copy of the Circular, which was described as "of a most dangerous and factious tendency," calculated "to inflame the minds" of the people, "to promote an unwarrantable combination, and to excite open opposition to the authority of Parliament." "You will there-

[1] Compare Franklin's writings, vii. 256, of 8 May, 1768, and Durand to Choiseul, 1 January, 1768.

[2] De Berdt to the Speaker, 29 July, 1768.

CHAP. XXXIII. 1768. April.

fore," said he,[1] "exert your utmost influence to prevail upon the Assembly of your Province to take no notice of it, which will be treating it with the contempt it deserves.—If they give any countenance to this seditious paper, it will be your duty to prevent any proceedings upon it by an immediate prorogation or dissolution."[2] This order he sent even to the Governor of Pennsylvania, who, by its Charter, had no power to prorogue or dissolve an Assembly. Massachusetts was told, that the King considered "their resolutions contrary to the sense of the Assembly, and procured by surprise. You will, therefore," such was the command to Bernard, "require of the House of Representatives in his Majesty's name to rescind the resolution which gave birth to the Circular letter from the Speaker, and to declare their disapprobation of that rash and hasty proceeding." "If the new Assembly should refuse to comply, it is the King's pleasure that you should immediately dissolve them."[3] In America, the best informed of the Crown Officers attributed the instruction to "the express order of the King."[4]

The Agent of the Assembly of Massachusetts interceded for the Colony. Its Petition was received by Hillsborough for the King's perusal, but was never officially presented. "It has been resolved in Council," said the Secretary, "that Governor Bernard have strict orders to insist upon the Assembly's revoking their Circular letter; and if refused, he is

[1] Hillsborough's Circular Letter, 21 April, 1768, as addressed to Rhode Island, in Prior Documents, 220.

[2] See Hillsborough's letter as sent to Maryland. This clause was omitted from the letter sent to Rhode Island.

[3] Hillsborough to Bernard, 22 April, 1768.

[4] Hutchinson to Bernard, 4 August, 1770.

immediately to dissolve them. Upon their next choice, he is again to insist on it; and, if then refused, he is to do the like; and as often as the case shall happen. I had settled the repeal of these Acts with Lord North; but the opposition of the Colonies, renders it absolutely necessary to support the authority of Parliament."[1]

Here was a colonial system, never before thought of. Townshend had suspended the legislative functions of New-York by Act of Parliament. Now a Secretary of State speaking for the King, offered to Massachusetts the option of forfeiting its representative government, or submitting to his mandate. At the same time the Commander-in-Chief in America, who was responsible to no one on that Continent, and in New-York itself took precedence[2] of the Governor, was ordered to maintain the public tranquillity.[3] But it was characteristic of Massachusetts, that the peace had not been broken. The power of Parliament was denied, but not resisted. "Things are fast hastening to a crisis," said Eliot[4] of Boston. Yet none desponded. The people were persuaded that England had greater cause to fear the loss of their trade, than they the withholding of her protection. "The grand design of God in the settlement of New England,"[5] began to be more clearly discerned. Some enthusiasts saw in this western Continent the wilderness spoken of

[1] De Berdt to the Speaker of Massachusetts Assembly, 29 July, 1768, in Bradford's State Papers.

[2] Moore to Shelburne, 5 March, 1768; Gage to Lord Barrington, 28 March, 1768; Hillsborough to Moore, 14 May, 1768. Moore to Hillsborough, 19 August, 1768, &c.

[3] Hillsborough to Gage, 23 April, 1768.

[4] Andrew Eliot to Thomas Hollis, 18 April, 1768.

[5] Boston Gazette, 25 April, 1768, 682, 1, 3.

CHAP. XXXIII 1768. April. in the vision of the Evangelist John, as the asylum of persecuted multitudes, to whom "the wings of a Great Eagle" had been given to bear them to the "place prepared by God" for their "rest from tribulation."

Meantime, on Saturday, the second day of April, the Assembly of Virginia read the Circular letter from Massachusetts, and referred it to a committee of the whole House.[1] The petitions of freeholders of the counties of Chesterfield, Henrico, Dinwiddie and Amelia, pointed to the Act of Parliament suspending the legislative power of New-York, as of a tendency, fatal to the liberties of a free people. The county of Westmoreland dwelt also on the new Revenue Act, as well as on the Billeting Act. The freeholders of Prince Williams enumerated all three, which, like the Stamp Act, would shackle North America with slavery. On the seventh, the illustrious Bland reported Resolutions, reaffirming the exclusive right of the American Assemblies to tax the American Colonies; and they were unanimously confirmed. A committee of twelve, including Bland and Archibald Cary, prepared a Petition to the King, a Memorial to the House of Lords, and a Remonstrance to the House of Commons, which, after being carefully considered and amended, were unanimously adopted. On Friday, the fifteenth, Bland invited a conference with the Council; and the Council with Blair,[2] as acting President after Fauquier's death, agreed to the papers which the House had prepared, and which were

[1] Journal of Virginia House of Burgesses, from 31 March to 15 April, 1768, p. 55.

[2] Blair to Hillsborough, 18 May, 1768, inclosing the Virginia Petition, Memorial and Remonstrance.

penned in a still bolder style than those from Massachusetts.

CHAP. XXXIII 1768. April.

After this the Burgesses of Virginia, to fulfil all their duty, not only assured Massachusetts of their applause for its attention to American Liberty, but also directed their Speaker to write to the respective Speakers of all the Assemblies on the Continent, to make known their proceedings, and to intimate how necessary they thought it, that the Colonies should unite in a firm but decent opposition to every measure which might affect their rights and liberties.

In the midst of these proceedings of a representative body, which truly reflected the sentiments of a people, the Thirteenth British Parliament, the last which ever legislated for America, was returned. So infamous was the old House in public esteem, that one hundred and seventy of its members failed of being rechosen.[1] But still corruption lost nothing of its effrontery; boroughs were sold openly, and votes purchased at advanced prices. The market value of a seat in Parliament was four thousand pounds; at which rate the whole venal House would have been bought for not much over two millions sterling,[2] and a majority for not much over one million. Yet in some places a contest cost the candidates twenty to thirty thousand pounds apiece, and it was affirmed that in Cumberland one person lavished a hundred thousand pounds. The election was the warmest and most expensive ever known. The number of disputed returns exceeded all precedent; as did the riots, into which a misguided populace,

[1] W. S. Johnson to Gov. Pitkin, 24 April, 1768.

[2] B. Franklin to W. Franklin, 13 March, 1768. Writings, vii. 394.

CHAP. XXXIII indulged once every seven years with the privilege of an election, had been entriced.

1768. April. The first incident in the history of this Parliament, was an unexampled interference of the Court. Wilkes represented Westminster. "I think it highly proper to apprise you that the expulsion of Wilkes appears to be very essential, and must be effected," wrote the King to Lord North,[1] who stood ready to obey the peremptory and unconstitutional mandate.

May. At the opening, the great question was raised, if strangers should be excluded from the debates. "It has always been my opinion," said Barrington, "that strangers should not be allowed to hear them." "Strangers are entitled to hear them," replied Seymour. "I ever wished," said Grenville, "to have what is done here, well known." The people no longer acquiesced in the secrecy of the proceedings of their professed representatives. The decision was postponed; but this is the last Parliament of which the debates are not reported.

The new House was not more just to the Colonies than its predecessor. Out of doors, America was not without those who listened to her complaints. The aged Oglethorpe,[2] founder of the Colony of Georgia, busied himself with distributing pamphlets in her behalf among the most considerable public men. Franklin, in London, collected and printed the Farmer's Letters. "They are very wild,"[3] said Hillsborough of them; many called them treasonable and seditious; yet Burke approved their principle. Trans-

[1] King to Lord North, 25 April, 1768.

[2] Miss De Berdt to Mr. Read.

[3] Franklin, vii. Compare W. S. Johnson to Pitkin, 29 July, 1768.

lated into French, they were much read in Parisian saloons; and their author was compared with Cicero.

"In America the Farmer is adored;" said the Governor of Georgia;[1] "and no mark of honor and respect is thought equal to his merit." At that time Georgia was the most flourishing Colony on the continent.[2] Lands there were cheap and labor dear; it had no manufactures; though, of the poorer families, one in a hundred perhaps might make its own coarse clothing of a mixture of cotton and wool.[3] Out of twenty-five members of the newly elected Legislature at least eighteen were professed "Sons of Liberty," "enthusiasts" for the American cause, zealous for "maintaining their natural rights." They unanimously made choice of Benjamin Franklin, as their agent; and nothing but their prorogation prevented their sending words of sympathy to Massachusetts. New Jersey expressed its desire to correspond and unite with the other Colonies.[4] The Connecticut Assembly in May, after a solemn debate, concluded to petition the King only; "because," said they, "to petition the Parliament would be a tacit confession of its right to lay impositions upon us; which right and authority we publicly disavow." Nor would the Court issue Writs of Assistance, although it was claimed that they were authorized by Townshend's Revenue Act. The times tried men's courage; some grew alarmed for consequences; but others "were carried above fear."[5]

[1] Sir James Wright to Lord Hillsborough, 23 May, 1768.

[2] Wright to Hillsborough, 30 May, 1768.

[3] Wright to Hillsborough, 31 May, 1768.

[4] New Jersey to Massachusetts, 9 May, 1768, in Prior Documents, 216. W. Franklin to Hillsborough, 11 July, 1768.

[5] E. Silliman to W. S. Johnson, 10 Nov. 1768. Wm. Pitkin to W. S. Johnson, 6 June, 1768; Wm. Pitkin to Richard Jackson, 10 June, 1768.

CHAP. XXXIII
1768. May.

At New-York the merchants held a meeting to join with the inhabitants of Boston in the agreement not to import from Great Britain; and against the opinion of the Governor, the royal Council held, that the meetings were legal; that the people did but assemble to establish among themselves certain rules of economy; that as they were masters of their own fortune, they had a right to dispose of it as they pleased.[1]

While Massachusetts received encouragement from its sister Colonies, its Crown officers continued and extended their solicitations in England for large and fixed salaries, as the only way to keep the Americans in their dependence. Grenville's influence was the special resource of Hutchinson and Oliver,[2] who had supported his Stamp Act and suffered as its martyrs; and they relied on Whately to secure for them his attention and favor; which they valued the more, as it seemed to them probable, that he would one day supersede Grafton.

Bernard, on his part, addressed his importunities to Hillsborough; and asked leave to become an informer, under an assurance that no exposure should be made of his letters.[3] Yet how could public measures be properly founded on secret communications, known only to the Minister and the King? Should the right of the humblest individual to confront witnesses against him be held sacred? and should rising nations be exposed to the loss of chartered privileges

[1] Moore to Hillsborough, 10 May, 1768. Compare Rev. Dr. Johnson to the Archbishop Secker, 10 May, 1768.

[2] Oliver to Thomas Whately, 11 May, 1768.

[3] Bernard to Hillsborough, 12 May, 1768.

CHAP. XXXIII. 1768. May.

and natural rights on concealed accusations? With truer loyalty towards the mother country, Samuel Adams,[1] through the Agent, advised the repeal of the Revenue Acts, and the removal of a Governor, in whom the Colonies could never repose confidence.

But Bernard went on, persuading Hillsborough that America had grown refractory[2] in consequence of the feeble administration of the Colonies during the time of Conway and Shelburne; that it required "his Lordship's distinguished abilities"[3] to accomplish the "most arduous task of reducing them into good order." "It only needs," said Hutchinson,[4] "one steady plan, pursued a little while." At that moment the people of Massachusetts, confidently awaiting a favorable result of their appeal to the King, revived their ancient spirit of loyalty. At the opening of the political year on the last Wednesday in May, the new House of Representatives came together with a kindlier disposition towards England than had existed for several years. The two parties were nearer an equality.[5] On the day of election, after hearing a sermon in which Shute of Hingham denied the supreme authority of Parliament and justified resistance to laws not based on equity,[6] the Legislature seemed willing to restore Hutchinson to the Council, and on the first ballot he had sixty-eight votes where he needed but seventy-one.[7]

[1] Samuel Adams to S. de Berdt, 14 May, 1768.

[2] Bernard to Hillsborough, 19 May, 1768.

[3] Bernard to Hillsborough, 12 May, 1768.

[4] Hutchinson to ——, 26 May, 1768.

[5] Hutchinson to Richard Jackson, 14 June, 1768.

[6] Letter of Hutchinson, 21 July, 1768.

[7] Compare Bernard to Hillsborough, 30 May, 1768; Hutchinson to Nathaniel Rogers, 7 June, 1768.

CHAP. XXXIII 1768. May.

He himself was the cause of his defeat. As the Convention were preparing to ballot a second time, Samuel Adams rose to ask whether the Lieutenant-Governor was a pensioner; on which Otis, the other "chief head of the faction," stood up and declared that Hutchinson had received a warrant from the Lords of the Treasury for two hundred pounds a year out of the proceeds of the new duties; and distributing votes for Artemas Ward, he cried out: "Pensioner or no pensioner; surely the House will not think a pensioner of the Crown a fit person to sit in Council." "But for the warrant," confessed Hutchinson, "I should have been elected." "And that," added Bernard, "would have put quite a new face upon public affairs." "I," said Hutchinson, "gave Ward a Lieutenant Colonel's commission in the Provincial Forces, thinking to bring him over;—he is a very sulky fellow."[1] "The Government," repeated Bernard, "should insist upon it, that the Lieutenant Governor and Secretary should have seats and votes at the Council Board without an election."[2] "This annual election of the Council spoils the Constitution," wrote Hutchinson,[3] though he afterwards uttered the falsehood of denying his opinion. "The House," reported Bernard to Hillsborough, "has shown ingratitude, undutifulness and insolence." "They will not come to a right temper," said Hutchinson, "until they find that, at all events, the Parliament will maintain its authority, and that to oppose

[1] Hutchinson to T. Pownal, 7 June, 1768.

[2] Bernard to Hillsborough, 30 May, 1768.

[3] Hutchinson to R. Jackson, 4 June, 1768.

it any longer must prove their ruin."[1] Such were the representations of men, on whom Hillsborough was eager to bestow signal marks of his confidence; having resolved to reward Bernard's zeal with the lucrative post of Lieutenant Governor of Virginia, and to leave the Government of Massachusetts in the hands of Hutchinson.[2]

June.

Just at this time, the Ministry in England received the letters of March from the Commissioners of the Customs and from Bernard, and totally misconceiving the state of things, Hillsborough, on the eighth of June, peremptorily ordered Gage to send a regiment to continue permanently in Boston, for the assistance of the civil magistrates and the officers of the revenue.[3] The Admiralty was also directed to send one frigate, two sloops, and two cutters to remain in Boston harbor;[4] and the little castle of William and Mary was to be occupied and repaired.[5]

This first act of hostility on the part of Great Britain was adopted at a time when America thought of nothing more than peaceable petitioning and passive resistance by a non-importation agreement, which the adverse interests and disinclination of the merchants had as yet rendered void.

[1] Hutchinson to N. Rogers, 30 or 31 May, 1768.

[2] Richard Jackson to Hutchinson, 3 June, 1768.

[3] Hillsborough to Gage, 8 June, 1768.

[4] Hillsborough to the Lords of the Admiralty, 11 June, 1768. Narrative of Facts relative to American Affairs.

[5] Hillsborough to Gage, 8 June, and to Bernard, 11 June, 1768.

CHAPTER XXXIV.

DOES MASSACHUSETTS RESCIND?—HILLSBOROUGH'S COLONIAL ADMINISTRATION CONTINUED.

JUNE—JULY, 1768.

CHAP. XXXIV. 1768. June.

SOME weeks would elapse before these orders would become known in the Colony. Meantime, the Commissioners of the Customs assumed more and more airs of haughtiness, with the strangest superciliousness[1] expressed publicly their hatred to the country, and in executing their office, did not shun to give offence. The Romney, a ship of fifty guns sent from Halifax at their request, had, for about a month, lain at anchor in the harbor, and forcibly and insolently impressed New England men returning from sea. On the morning of the tenth of June, one man

[1] Governor Wentworth of New Hampshire to the Marquis of Rockingham, November 13, 1768; in Albemarle's Rockingham, ii. 88. "More obstructions have arisen to the service in this country, from the servants of Government, than from any other cause. At first the strangest superciliousness and publicly expressed hatred to the country, excited disrespect and apprehensions against them." Compare Mr. John Temple to Mr. Grenville, Boston, New England, November 7, 1768, in Grenville Papers, iv. 396, 397. "I am perfectly of opinion with General Gage, that the King's cause has been more hurt in this country by some of his own servants, than by all the world besides."

CHAP. XXXIV. 1768. June.

who had been impressed, was rescued; and when Nathaniel Waterman went on board the Romney to liberate another by offering a substitute, Conner, the Captain, indulged in a storm of anger. "No man," said he, "shall go out of this vessel. The town is a blackguard town, ruled by mobs; they have begun with me by rescuing a man whom I pressed this morning. By the Eternal God, I will make their hearts ache before I leave it."[1] And he continued his impressments, in violation, as the lawyers and people of Boston believed, of an explicit statute.

The Commissioners had a rankling hatred against John Hancock, partly because he with his company of the Boston Cadets had refused to act as escort,[2] on the day of the General Election, if they were in the procession; and partly because he openly denounced the revenue Acts. His sloop, named "Liberty," had discharged her cargo and had taken in freight for a new voyage; when suddenly, on Friday the tenth of June, near sunset, and just as the laborers were returning home, the officers of the customs, obeying the written directions of the Commissioners,[3] seized her for a false entry, which it was pretended had been made several weeks before. The collector thought she might remain at Hancock's Wharf after she had received the broad arrow;[4] but the Comptroller had concerted to moor her under the guns of the Romney, which lay a quarter of a mile

[1] Affidavit of Nathaniel Waterman. Compare also Hutchinson to R. Jackson, 18 June, 1768.

[2] A. Oliver to Thomas Whately, 11 May, 1768.

[3] Harrison and Hallowell to Commissioners of the Customs, 11 June, 1768.

[4] Hutchinson to R. Jackson, 16 June, 1768.

CHAP. XXXIV. off, and "made a signal for the man of war's boats to come ashore."

1768. June. "You had better let the vessel lie at the wharf," said Malcom, to the officer. "I shall not," answered Hallowell the Comptroller, and gave directions to cut the fasts. "Stop, at least, till the owner comes," said the people who crowded round. "No, damn you," cried Hallowell, "cast her off." "I'll split out the brains of any man, that offers to reeve a fast, or stop the vessel," said the Master of the Romney; and he shouted to the marines, to fire. "What rascal is that, who dares to tell the marines to fire?" cried a Bostoneer; and, turning to Harrison, the Collector, a well-meaning man, who disapproved the violent manner of the seizure, he added, "The owner is sent for; you had better let the vessel lie at the wharf till he comes down." "No, she shall go," insisted the Comptroller; "and show me the man who dares oppose it."[1] "Kill the damned scoundrel," cried the Master. "We will throw the people from the Romney overboard," said Malcom, stung with anger. "By God, she shall go," repeated the Master and he more than once called to the marines, "Why don't you fire?"[2] and "bade them fire."[3] So they cut her moorings, and with ropes in the barges, the sloop was towed away to the Romney.

A crowd "of boys and negroes"[4] gathered at the

[1] See the affidavits of Joseph Piper, William Ross, Caleb Hopkins, Benjamin Goodwin, and others taken in June, 1768, and annexed to the Memorial of de Berdt, of 21 July, 1768.

[2] John Rowe's affidavit.

[3] Benjamin Goodwin's affidavit.

[4] Hutchinson to Whately, Boston, 18 June, 1768.

heels[1] of the Custom House Officers, and threw stones, bricks and dirt at them, alarming them, but doing no serious mischief; and while Samuel Adams, Hancock and Warren, with others, were deliberating what was to be done, a mob broke windows in the house of the Comptroller and of an Inspector, and failing to find a boat belonging to the Romney, seized on the Collector's pleasure-boat, dragged it in triumph to Boston Common and burnt it. After this, at about one o'clock, they dispersed,[2] and the town resumed its quiet.

CHAP. XXXIV. 1768. June.

On Saturday nothing indicated a recurrence of riots; and the Council[3] had only to appoint a committee to ascertain the facts attending the seizure by the examination of witnesses on the following Monday.

The Commissioners had not been harmed, nor approached, nor menaced. But they chose to consider the incident of the last evening an insurrection, and were provoked that their representations were so little heeded. Four of the five, went on board the Romney;[4] perhaps a little from panic, but more to support their own exalted notions of their dignity; terrify the town by fear of revenge on the part of England; and ensure the active interposition of the British Government. Temple, one of their number, refused to take part in the artifice, and remained in full security on shore.

[1] Affidavits of Harrison the Collector, B. Hallowell, Jr., the Comptroller, and R. A. Harrison, Jr. 11 June, 1768. Letters to the Ministry, 122, 125.

[2] Hutchinson to R. Jackson, 16 June, 1768. De Berdt's Memorial to Hillsborough, with the accompanying affidavits. Bernard's Letter to the Ministry.

[3] Hutchinson to T. Whately, Boston, 18 June, 1768. Compare also T. Whately to Grenville, 26 July, 1768, in Grenville Papers, iv. 322.

[4] Proceedings of the Board of Commissioners on board the Romney, 13 June, 1768. Letters &c. &c. 117, 118.

CHAP. XXXIV. 1768. June.

During the usual quiet of Sunday,[1] while all the people were "at meeting," the fugitive officers informed Bernard by letter that they could not, "consistent with the honor of their commission, act in any business of the revenue under such an influence, as prevailed" in Boston, and declared their wish to withdraw to the castle. "They have abdicated," said the people of Boston, and "may they never return." They really were in no danger, and every body knew it. They were playing a game to deceive the Ministry. The Council found that the riot of Friday had been only "a small disturbance." "Dangerous disturbances," reported Gage, whose information came from royalists, "are not to be apprehended."[2]

While the Commissioners stifled their doubts about the wisdom of their conduct, by resolving that "the honor of the Crown would be hazarded by their return to Boston,"[3] its inhabitants on the fourteenth met at Faneuil Hall, in a legal town meeting. The attendance was so great that they adjourned to the Old South Meeting House, where Otis was elected moderator, and welcomed with rapturous applause.

In the course of a debate, one person observed that every captain of a man-of-war, on coming into harbor, should be subordinate to the Legislature of the Colony. William Cooper[4] proposed, "that if any one should promote the bringing troops here, he

[1] Commissioners of the Customs to Bernard, 12 June, 1768; John Robinson to Collector and Comptroller of Boston, 12 June, 1768, Harrison and Hallowell to John Robinson, 12 June, 1768.

[2] See Gage to Hillsborough, 17 June, 1768, and the Report of the Council.

[3] Memorial of Commissioners, in Letters, &c. 120.

[4] Hutchinson to Jackson, 18 June. 1768.

should be deemed a disturber of the peace and a traitor to his country."[1] An address to the Governor was unanimously agreed upon, which twenty-one men were appointed to deliver. CHAP. XXXIV. 1768. June.

On adjourning the meeting to four o'clock the next afternoon, Otis, the moderator, made a speech to the inhabitants, strongly recommending peace and good order; and expressing a hope that their grievances might, in time, be removed. "If not," said he, "and we are called on to defend our liberties and privileges, I hope and believe we shall, one and all, resist even unto blood; but I pray God Almighty, that this may never so happen."[2]

Meantime the committee moved in a procession of eleven chaises to the house of the Governor in the country, to present the Address, in which the Town claimed for the province the sole right of taxing itself, expressed a hope the Board of Customs would never re-assume the exercise of their office, commented on impressment, and demanded the removal of the ship Romney from the harbor. In words which Otis approved and probably assisted to write, they said: "To contend with our parent state is the most shocking and dreadful extremity, but tamely to relinquish the only security we and our posterity retain for the enjoyment of our lives and properties, without one struggle, is so humiliating and base, that we cannot support the reflection. It is at your option to prevent this distressed and justly incensed people

[1] Bernard to Hillsborough, 16 June, 1768.

[2] Anonymous Letter signed G. to the Commissioners of the Customs, 14 June, 1768; Letters, &c. 137.

CHAP. XXXIV. from effecting too much, and from the shame and reproach of attempting too little."[1]

1768. June. Bernard received the address with obsequious courtesy; and the next day gave in writing an inoffensive answer, clearing himself of the responsibility for the measures complained of, and promising not indeed to remove the Romney, but to stop impressments. "I shall think myself," he said, "most highly honored if I can be in the lowest degree an instrument in preserving a perfect conciliation between you and the parent state."[1]

No sooner had he sent this message, than he, and all the officers of the Crown at once busied themselves in concert[3] to get regiments ordered to Boston. The Commissioners of the Customs saw in the disturbances of the tenth of June, "an insurrection rather than a riot."[4] A nameless writer, vouched for by the Commissioners, declared, "that there was certainly a settled scheme to oppose even the King's troops' landing; that the promoters of the present evils were ready to unmask and openly discover their long and latent design to rebel." "He that runs may read," wrote another; "without some speedy interposition, a great storm will arise."[5] The Comptroller and even the worthy Collector reported a "general spirit of insurrection, not only in the town,

[1] Address of the inhabitants of the Town of Boston, in Hutchinson's History, iii., Appendix J. Hutchinson is cautious to omit the Answer of Bernard.

[2] Bernard's Answer to the Town of Boston; Boston Chronicle for 1768, page 253.

[3] Appeal to the World, 19, 20.

[4] Commissioners to Bernard, 13 June, 1768; Letters to the Ministry, 134.

[5] Letter from a Gentleman of Character, 14 June, 1768. Letters to the Ministry, 140--141.

but throughout the province."[1] On the fifteenth of June, the Commissioners of the Customs wrote to Gage and to Hood, demanding further protection; for, said they, "the leaders of the people of Boston will urge them to open revolt."[2]

CHAP. XXXIV. 1768. June.

To the Lords of the Treasury they reported "a long concerted and extensive plan of resistance to the authority of Great Britain," breaking out in "acts of violence sooner than was intended;" and they gave their opinion "that nothing but the immediate exertion of military power would prevent an open revolt of the town of Boston, and probably of the Provinces."[3]

"If there is not a revolt," wrote Bernard to Hillsborough, "the leaders of the Sons of Liberty must falsify their words and change their purposes."[4] Hutchinson sounded the alarm to his various correspondents, especially to Whately,[5] to whom Paxton also sent word, that "unless they should have immediately two or three regiments, it was the opinion of all the friends to government, that Boston would be in open rebellion."[6] To interpret and enforce the correspondence, Hallowell, the comptroller, was despatched as their emissary to London.[7]

To bring troops into Boston, was the surest way of hastening an insurrection; the letters, soliciting them, may have been kept secret, but the town

[1] Harrison and Hallowell to Commissioners, 14 June, 1768; Letters to the Ministry, 136.

[2] The Commissioners to Gen. Gage and Commodore Hood, 15 June, 1768. Letters to the Ministry, 137.

[3] Commissioners to the Lords of the Treasury, 16 June, 1768.

[4] Bernard to Hillsborough, 16--18 June, 1768.

[5] Compare Whately to Grenville, 26 July, 1768; in Grenville Papers, iv. 322. "I now know," &c. &c.

[6] Charles Paxton to T. Whately, in the Letters, &c. 41.

[7] Bernard to Hillsborough, P. S. 18 June, 1768. Hutchinson to Whately, 18 June, 1768.

CHAP. XXXIV. 1768. June. divined their purpose; and at its legal meeting on Friday, the seventeenth, instructing its representatives in words prepared by John Adams,[1] it put its sentiments on record. "After the repeal of the last American Stamp Act," it said, "we were happy in the pleasing prospect of a restoration of tranquillity and harmony. But the principle on which that detestable act was founded continues in full force, and a revenue is still demanded from America, and appropriated to the maintenance of swarms of officers and pensioners in idleness and luxury. It is our fixed resolution to maintain our loyalty and due subordination to the British Parliament, as the Supreme Legislative in all cases of necessity for the preservation of the whole empire. At the same time, it is our unalterable resolution, to assert and vindicate our dear and invaluable rights and liberties, at the utmost hazard of our lives and fortunes; and we have a full and rational confidence that no designs formed against them will ever prosper.

"Every person who shall solicit or promote the importation of troops at this time, is an enemy to this town and Province, and a disturber of the peace and good order of both."[2]

Having given these instructions the Town Meeting broke up. The Assembly, which was in session, had been a spectator of the events; and the very next morning, on motion probably of Otis, a joint committee was raised to inquire "if measures had been taken, or were taking, for the execution of the

[1] J. Adams, Works ii. 215, iii. 501.

[2] Instructions in Appendix Hutchinson, iii. 489--491.

late Revenue Acts of Parliament by a naval or military force."[1]

CHAP. XXXIV. 1768. June.

In the midst of these scenes arrived Hillsborough's letter, directing Massachusetts to rescind its resolutions.[2] After timid[3] consultations between Bernard, Hutchinson and Oliver, after delays till the town meetings were fairly over, and after offers from Bernard to act as a mediator,[4] on Tuesday, the twenty-first of June, the message was delivered. In the afternoon, when it was read a second time to a full house and a gallery crowded with one or two hundred persons,[5] Otis spoke for nearly two hours.

"The King," said he, "appoints none but boys for his Ministers. They have no education but travelling through France, from whence they return full of the slavish principles of that country. They know nothing of business when they come into their offices, and do not stay long enough in them to acquire that little knowledge which is gained by experience; so that all business is really done by the clerks." He passed an encomium on Oliver Cromwell, and extolled the times preceding his advancement, and particularly the sentence pronounced by the people of England on their King, contrasting the days of the Puritans with the present days, when the people of England no longer knew the rights of Englishmen. He praised, in the highest language, "the elegant, pure, and nervous Petition to the King,"

[1] Bernard to Hillsborough, 18 June, 1768.

[2] Compare Franklin's Writings, iv. 531.

[3] Gage to Hillsborough, 17 June, 1768.

[4] Bernard to Hillsborough, 18 June, 1768. Letter 37.

[5] Bernard to Hillsborough, 9 September, 1768.

CHAP. XXXIV. 1768. June.

adopted the last session by the Assembly, but rejected by the Minister. And showing the impossibility of their consenting to rescind measures of an Assembly which had ceased to exist, measures which had already been executed, measures which they more and more approved of, "I hope," said he, "another Congress will take place.[1] When Lord Hillsborough knows that we will not rescind our acts, he should apply to Parliament to rescind theirs. Let Britain rescind their measures or they are lost for ever."[2]

Meantime the Governor became ludicrously panic-struck. At one moment he fancied that the people would rise and take possession of the castle; and, in the next he wished to withdraw to the castle for security.

The Assembly were aware that they were deliberating upon more important subjects than had ever engaged the attention of an American Legislature. They knew that the Ministry was bent on humbling them. The continent was watching to see if they dared be firm. They were consoled by the sympathy of Connecticut,[3] and New Jersey.[4] But when the letter from Virginia[5] was received, it gave courage more than all the rest. "This is a glorious

[1] Bernard to Hillsborough, 28 June, 1768. Letter 42.

[2] MS. postscript to Bernard's Letter to Hillsborough, No. 9 of 25 June to 1 July, 1768.

[3] Connecticut Speaker to Massachusetts, 11 June, 1768; Prior Documents, 216.

[4] New Jersey Speaker to Massachusetts, 9 May, 1768. Governor W. Franklin to Hillsborough, 11 July, 1768.

[5] Peyton Randolph, the Speaker of the House of Burgesses of Virginia, to the Massachusetts Speaker, Prior Documents, 213. Bradford's History of Massachusetts, i. 145. The passage quoted is in Bradford but not in Prior Documents.

day," said Samuel Adams, using words which, seven years later, he was to repeat. "This is the most glorious day ever seen," responded his friend, Samuel Cooper. The merchants of Boston met, and successfully renewed the agreement not to import from England.[1]

CHAP. XXXIV. 1768. June.

The House, employing the pen of Samuel Adams[2] without altering a word, reported a letter[3] to Lord Hillsborough, in which they showed that the Circular Letter of February was, indeed, the declared sense of a large majority of their body; and expressed their reliance on the clemency of the King, that to petition him would not be deemed inconsistent with respect for the British constitution, nor to acquaint their fellow-subjects of their having done so, be discountenanced as an inflammatory proceeding.

Then came the great question, taken in the fullest House ever remembered. The votes were given by word of mouth, and against seventeen that were willing to yield, ninety-two refused to rescind. They finished their work by a message to the Governor, thoroughly affirming the doings from which they had been ordered to dissent. On this Bernard, trembling with fear,[4] prorogued them, and then dissolved the Assembly.

July.

Massachusetts was left without a Legislature. Its people had no intention to begin a rebellion; but only to defend their liberties, which had the

Letter from Hutchinson to Bollas, 14 July, 1768.

[2] Eliot's Biographical Dictionary of New England, sub voce Samuel Adams.

[3] Bradford's Massachusetts State Papers, 151; House to Lord Hillsborough, 30 June, 1768.

[4] Bernard to Hillsborough, 9 July, 1768.

CHAP. XXXIV. 1768. July.

sanction of natural right and of historic tradition. "The Americans," observed the clear-sighted Du Chatelet,[1] "have no longer need of support from the British Crown, and see in the projects of their metropolis measures of tyranny and oppression." "I apprehend a breach between the two countries," owned Franklin.[2] "I was always of opinion since the accession of George the Third, that matters would issue the way you now expect," wrote Hollis[3] to a New England man, who predicted independence; "you are an ungracious people. There is original sin in you. You are assertors of Liberty, and the principles of the Revolution."

"The whole body of the people of New Hampshire were resolved to stand or fall with the Massachusetts." "It is best," counselled the good Langdon[4] of Portsmouth, "for the Americans to let the King know the utmost of their resolutions, and the danger of a violent rending of the Colonies from the mother country." "No Assembly on the Continent," said Roger Sherman[5] of Connecticut, "will ever concede that Parliament has a right to tax the Colonies." "The Parliament of England has no more jurisdiction over us," declared the politicians of that Colony, "than the Parliament of Paris."[6] "We cannot believe," wrote William Williams[7] of Lebanon, "that they will draw the sword on their own children; but

[1] Du Chatelet to Choiseul, 21 June, 1768.

[2] Franklin to his Son, 2 July, 1768. Works, vii. 411. Franklin to Joseph Galloway, 2 July, 1768; Works, vii. 412.

[3] T. Hollis to A. Eliot, 1 July, 1768.

[4] Samuel Langdon to Ezra Stiles, 6 July, 1768.

[5] Quoted in W. S. Johnson to R. Sherman, 28 Sept. 1768.

[6] B. Gale quoted in W. S. Johnson to B. Gale.

[7] W. Williams to W. S. Johnson, Lebanon, Connecticut, 5 July, 1768.

CHAP. XXXIV. 1768. July.

if they do, our blood is more at their service than our liberties."

In New-York, the merchants still held those meetings, which Hillsborough called, "if not illegal and unwarrantable, very unnatural, ungrateful, and unbecoming." "The circumstances of the Colonies demand firmer union,"[1] said men of Pennsylvania. "The Colonies," wrote Chandler,[2] the churchman, "will soon experience worse things than in the time of the late Stamp Act, or I am no prophet." The Assembly of Maryland treated Lord Hillsborough's letter with the contempt he had ordered them to show for the Circular of Massachusetts. "We shall not be intimidated by a few sounding expressions from doing what we think is right," said they in their formal reply;[3] and they sent their thanks to Massachusetts, "their sister Colony, in whose opinion they declared they exactly coincided."[4] As for South Carolina, they could not enough praise the glorious ninety-two who would not rescind; toasting them at banquets, and marching by night through the streets of Charleston, in processions to their honor by the blaze of two and ninety torches.

English statesmen were blindly adopting measures to carry out their restrictive policy;[5] establishing in America Courts of Vice Admiralty at Halifax, Boston, Philadelphia, and Charleston,[6] on the

[1] John Erving to Ezra Stiles, 1 July, 1768.

[2] Thomas B. Chandler to the Rev. D. Johnson, 7 July, 1768.

[3] Maryland House of Delegates to Gov. Sharpe.

[4] Maryland to Massachusetts, 23 June, 1768; received early in July, Prior Documents, 219.

[5] Thomas Bradshaw to John Pownall, 8 July, 1768. Circular of Hillsborough, of 11 July, 1768.

[6] Treasury Minute of 30 June, 1768.

CHAP. XXXIV. 1768. July. system of Grenville; taking an account of the cost to the Exchequer of the Stamp Act, so as to draw on the sinking fund to liquidate the loss;[1] or meditating to offer the Colonies some partial and inadequate representation in Parliament;[2] inattentive to the character of events which were leading to the renovation of the world. Not so the Americans. Village theologians studied the Book of Revelation[3] to see which seal was next to be broken, which angel was next to sound his trumpet. "Is not God preparing the way in his Providence,"[4] thus New England ministers communed together, "for some remarkable revolutions in Christendom, both in polity and religion?" And as they pondered on the prophecies of the New Testament, they were convinced that "the time was drawing very near, when the man of sin would be destroyed, and the Church," which, in the mouth of New England divines, included civil and religious liberty, "would rise and spread through the nations."

Who will deny that the race has a life and progress of its own, swaying its complex mind by the guiding truths which it developes as it advances? While New England was drawing from the Bible proof of the nearness of the overthrow of tyranny, Turgot at Paris, explained to David Hume the perfectibility and onward movement of the race.[5] "The British Government," said he,

[1] Grey Cooper to Auditor of the Revenue, 1 July, 1768. Same to Same, 5 July, 1768.

[2] George Grenville to Gov. Pownall, 17 July, 1768, in Pownall's Administration of the Colonies: ii. 113, in Ed. of 1777.

[3] The Revelation of St. John the Divine, Chap. xvi.

[4] Ezra Stiles's Correspondence, July, 1768.

[5] Turgot to Hume, Paris, 3 July, 1768, in Burton's Hume, iii. 163, 164.

"is very far from being an enlightened one. As yet none is thoroughly so. But tyranny combined with superstition, vainly strives to stifle light and liberty by methods alike atrocious and useless; the world will be conducted through transient disorders to a happier condition." CHAP. XXXIV. 1768. July.

In that progress the emancipation of America was to form a glorious part; and was the great object of the French Minister for Foreign Affairs. "We must put aside projects and attend to facts," wrote Choiseul[1] to Du Chatelet in July, after a conversation of six hours with a person intimately acquainted with America. "My idea, which perhaps is but a reverie, is, to examine the possibility of a treaty of commerce, both of importation and exportation, of which the obvious advantages might attract the Americans. Will it not be possible to present them, at the moment of a rupture, an interest powerful enough to detach them at once from their Metropolis? According to the prognostications of sensible men, who have had opportunity to study the character of the Americans, and to measure their progress from day to day in the spirit of independence, this separation of the American Colonies from the metropolis, sooner or later, must come. The plan I propose hastens its epoch.

"It is the true interest of the Colonies to secure for ever their entire liberty, and establish their direct commerce with France and with the world. The great point will be to secure their neutrality, which will necessarily bring on a treaty of al-

[1] Extrait de la Lettre de 15 Juillet, 1768, à Monsieur le Comte du Chatelet.

CHAP. XXXIV. 1768. July. liance with France and Spain. They may want confidence in the strength of our navy; they may raise suspicions of our fidelity to our engagements; they may fear the English squadrons; they may hope for success against the Spaniards and against ourselves. I see all these difficulties and do not dissemble their extent; but I see also the controlling interest of the Americans to profit by the opportunity of a rupture to establish their independence. This cannot be done without risks; but he that stops at difficulties will never attempt any thing.

"We have every reason to hope, that the Government on this side will conduct itself in a manner to increase the breach, not to close it up. Such is its way. True, some sagacious observers think it not only possible but easy to reconcile the interests of the Colonies and the mother country; but I see many obstacles in the way, I meet too many persons of my way of thinking, and the course pursued thus far by the British Government seems to me completely opposite to what it ought to be to effect this conciliation."

While time and humanity, the principles of English liberty, the impulse of European Philosophy, and the policy of France were all assisting to emancipate America, the British colonial Administration, which was to place itself as a barrier against destiny and stop the natural force of moral causes in their influence on the affairs of men, vibrated in its choice of measures between terror and artifice. From a prevailing opinion of Hillsborough's abilities, American affairs were left by the other Ministers very much to his management;[1] and he took his opinions from Bernard. That favorite Governor was now promising the Council of Massachusetts, that if they would omit to discuss the question of the power of Parliament, he would support their Petition for relief. The Council followed the advice,[2] and Bernard, as a fulfilling of his engagement, wrote a letter which he showed to several of them, recommending that part of the Petition praying relief against such Acts as were made for the purpose of drawing a revenue from the Colonies."[3] Then in a secret letter of the same date, he sent an elaborate argument[4] against the repeal or any mitigation of the late revenue Act; quieting his conscience for the fraud by saying, that "drawing a revenue from the Colonies," meant carrying a revenue out of them; and that he wished to see the revenue from the Port Duties expended on the resident officers of the Crown.[5]

CHAP. XXXIV. 1768. July.

Great Britain at that time had a colonial Secre-

[1] Franklin's Writings, iv. 527. The Rise and Progress of the Differences between Great Britain and her American Colonies.

[2] See Proceedings of the Governor and Council of the Province of Massachusetts Bay, for June 30, 1768, July 7, 1768, and the Petition of the Council to the King. "If it should appear to your majesty, that it is not for the benefit of Great Britain and her colonies (over which your paternal care is conspicuous), that any revenue should be drawn from the colonies, we humbly implore your majesty's gracious recommendation to Parliament, that your American subjects may be relieved from the operation of the several Acts made for that purpose," &c. &c. See Appendix to Letters to Hillsborough, &c. &c.

[3] Bernard to Hillsborough, 16 July, 1768, First Part. Compare Same to Same, 30 Nov. 1768; in Letters to Hillsborough, 27, 28.

[4] Bernard to Hillsborough, No. ii. Second Part; 16 July, 1768. I owed my copy of this second part to my friend, P. Force, of Washington. It was taken from Bernard's own Letter Book. The letter itself is preserved in the British State Paper office also.

[5] Compare Bowdoin to Hillsborough, 15 April, 1769. And Bowdoin did not know of the secret second part of Bernard's Letter of July, 1768.

CHAP. XXXIV. 1768. July. tary who encouraged this duplicity, and wrote an answer to be shown the Council,[1] keeping up the deception, and even using the name of the King, as a partner in the falsehood.[2] Hillsborough greedily drank in the flattery offered him, and affected distress at showing the King the expressions of the partiality of his correspondent.[3] In undertaking the "very arduous task of reducing America into good order," he congratulated himself on having "the aid of a Governor, zealous, able and active," like Bernard, who, having educated Hutchinson for his successor, was now promised the rank of a baronet, and the administration of Virginia.

[1] Bernard to Hillsborough, 30 Nov. 1768.

[2] Hillsborough to Bernard, 14 Sept. 1768.

[3] Hillsborough to Bernard, 11 July, 1768.

CHAPTER XXXV.

THE REGULATORS OF NORTH CAROLINA.—HILLSBOROUGH'S ADMINISTRATION OF THE COLONIES CONTINUED.

July—September, 1768.

CHAP. XXXV. 1768. July.

The people of Boston had gone out of favor with almost every body in England.[1] Even Rockingham had lost all patience, saying the Americans were determined to leave their friends on his side the water, without the power of advancing in their behalf a shadow of excuse.[2] This was the state of public feeling, when, on the nineteenth of July, Hallowell arrived in London with letters giving an exaggerated account of what had happened in Boston on the tenth of June. The news was received with general dismay; London, Liverpool and Bristol grew anxious; stocks fell greatly, and continued falling. Rumors came also of a suspension of commerce, and there was a debt due from America to the merchants and manufacturers of England of four millions sterling.[3]

In the Ministry, anger expelled every other sentiment, and nearly all united in denouncing "ven-

[1] W. S. Johnson to Thaddeus Burr, London, 28 July, 1768.

[2] N. Rogers to Hutchinson, 2 July, 1768.

[3] Francès to Choiseul, 22 July, 1768.

CHAP. XXXV. 1768. July. geance," as they expressed it, "against that insolent town" of Boston.[1] The thought of gaining quiet by repealing or modifying the act, was utterly discountenanced. "If the Government," said they, "now gives way as it did about the Stamp Act, it will be all over with its authority in America." As Grafton had escaped to the country,[2] Hallowell was examined at the Treasury Chambers before Lord North and Jenkinson.[3] He represented that the determination to break the revenue laws was not universal; that the revenue officers who remained there were not insulted; that the spirit displayed in Boston, did not extend beyond its limits; that Salem and Marblehead made no opposition to the payment of the duties; that the people in the country would not join, if Boston were actually to resist Government; and that the four Commissioners at the castle could not return to town, till measures were taken for their protection.

The Memorial of the Commissioners themselves to the Lords of the Treasury announced, that "there had been a long concerted and extensive plan of resistance to the authority of Great Britain; that the people of Boston had hastened to acts of violence sooner than was intended; that nothing but the immediate exertion of military power could prevent an open revolt of the town, which would probably spread throughout the Provinces."[4] The counter memorial in behalf of Boston, proving that the riot had been caused by the imprudent and violent pro-

[1] W. S. Johnson's P. S. to Letter of 23 July, 1768, to W. Pitkin.

[2] Hamilton to Calcraft, 24 July, 1768. Chat. Corr. iii. 385. Francès to Choiseul, 29 July, 1768.

[3] Treasury Chamber, 21 July, 1768. Present, Lord North, Mr. Campbell, and Mr. Jenkinson.

[4] Narration of Facts relative to American Affairs; Thomas Bradshaw to J. Pownall, 22 July, 1768.

ceedings of the officers of the Romney[1] met little notice. At the same time[2] letters arrived from Virginia, with their petitions and memorial, "expressed," said Blair, the President of the Council, "with modesty and dutiful submission;" but under the calmest language, uttering a protest against the right of Parliament to tax America for a revenue. CHAP. XXXV. 1768. July.

The party of Bedford, and the Duke himself, spoke openly of the necessity of employing force to subdue the inhabitants of Boston, and to make a striking example of the most seditious, in order to inspire the other Colonies with terror.[3] This policy, said Weymouth, will be adopted.

Shelburne, on the contrary, observed, that people very much exaggerated the difficulty; that it was understood in its origin, its principles, and its consequences; that it would be absurd to wish to send to America a single additional soldier, or vessel of war, to reduce Colonies, which would return to the mother country of themselves from affection and from interest, when once the form of their contributions should be agreed upon.[4] But his opinions had no effect, except that the King became "daily" more importunate with Grafton, that Shelburne should be dismissed.[5]

The Cabinet were also "much vexed" at Shelburne's reluctance to engage in secret intrigues with Corsica, which resisted its cession by Genoa to France. The subject was, therefore, taken out of his

[1] De Berdt's Memorial, 24 July, 1768. Twelve affidavits sent from Boston in June.

[2] Narrative of Facts relative to American affairs.

[3] Francès to Choiseul, 29 July, 1768.

[4] Francès to Choiseul, 29 July, 1768.

[5] Grafton's Autobiography.

CHAP. XXXV. 1768. July.

hands, and the act of bad faith conducted by his colleagues.[1] Unsolicited by Paoli, the General of the insurgents, they sent to him Dunant, a Genevese, as a British emissary, with written[2] as well as verbal instructions.

Paoli was found wanting every thing, money, artillery, armed vessels, muskets with bayonets, and small field-pieces, such as could be carried on mules;[3] but he gave assurances of the fixed purpose of himself and of the Corsican people to defend their common liberty;[4] and persuaded the British Ministry, that if supplied with what he needed, he could hold out for eighteen months.[5] "A moment was not lost in supplying most of the articles requested by the Corsicans" "in the manner that would least risk a breach with France;" "and indeed many thousand stands of arms were furnished from the stock in the Tower, yet so as to give no indication that they were sent from Government." While British Ministers were enjoying the thought of baffling France, they had the vexation to find Paoli himself obliged to retire by way of Leghorn to England. But their notorious interference was treasured up in memory as a precedent.

When, on the twenty-seventh of July, the Cabinet definitively agreed on the measures to be pursued towards America, it sought to unite all England by resting its policy on Rockingham's Declaratory Act, and to divide America by proceeding severely only against Boston.

[1] Grafton's Autobiography.

[2] Grafton to Dunant in Grafton's Autobiography.

[3] Conference of Dunant with General Paoli, 24 July, 1768.

[4] Pasquali di Paoli to the Duke of Grafton, 24 July, 1768.

[5] Grafton's Autobiography.

For Virginia, it was most properly resolved that the office of its Governor should no longer remain a sinecure, as it had been for three quarters of a century; and Amherst,[1] who would not go out to reside there, was in consequence displaced, and ultimately indemnified.

In selecting a new Governor, the choice fell on Lord Botetourt; and it was a wise one, not merely because he had great affability and a pleasing address, and was attentive to business, but because he was ingenuous and frank, sure to write fearlessly and truly respecting Virginia, and sure never to ask the Secretary to conceal his reports. He was to be conducted to his Government in a seventy-four, and to take with him a splendid coach of state. He was to call a new Legislature, to closet its members, as well as those of the Council;[2] and, to humor them in almost any thing except the explicit denial of the authority of Parliament.[3] It would have been ill for American Independence, if a man like him had been sent to Massachusetts.

But "with Massachusetts," said Camden,[4] "it will not be very difficult to deal, if that is the only disobedient Province." For Boston his voice did not entreat mercy.[5] The cry was, it must be made to

[1] Hillsborough to Amherst, 27 July, 1768; Junius, ii. 216. Francès to Choiseul, 5 August, 1768.

[2] See Narrative of Facts, Hillsborough to Bernard, 30 July, 1758, Francès to Choiseul, 5 August, 1768.

[3] Instructions to Lord Botetourt, dated 21 August, 1768.

[4] See Camden to Grafton, 4 Sept. 1768, in Grafton's Autobiography.

[5] Grafton's Memoirs intimate no dissent on his part or on Camden's. They both joined in driving Shelburne out of the Ministry.

The letter writers from London affirmed their adhesion. Compare Israel Mauduit to Hutchinson, 11 April, 1767, and 15 Dec. 1767, and 19 Feb. 1769, with the extract of a letter in the Boston Chronicle of Oct. 31—Nov. 7, 1768, p. 427, which must be an extract of a letter from Israel Mauduit to Hutchinson,

CHAP. XXXV. 1768. July. repent of its insolence; and its Town Meetings no longer be suffered to threaten and defy the Government of Great Britain.[1] Two additional regiments of five hundred men each, and a frigate were at once to be sent there; the ship of the line, which was to take Botetourt to Virginia, might also remain in those seas. A change in the Charter of Massachusetts was resolved on by Hillsborough; and he also sent over orders to inquire, "if any persons had committed acts which, under the authority of the statute of Henry the Eighth[2] against treason committed abroad, might justify their being brought to England to be tried in the King's Bench."[3]

Salem,[4] a town whose representatives, contrary, however, to the judgment of their constituents, voted in favor of rescinding, was indicated as the future capital of the Province. Now Boston must tremble, "for," said the Secretary, "the Crown will support the laws and the subject must submit to them."

At this time Bernard received from Gage, in consequence of the earlier orders from England, an offer of troops, if he would make a requisition for them. But the Council, after a just analysis of the late events, gave their opinion, that the civil power did

written after this Cabinet meeting of the 27 of July, as appears from Same to Same, 10 Feb. 1769.

"All these are friends to the Duke of Bedford: they all agree in one sentiment about America, and the Duke of Grafton professes now to be of the same opinion." Dec. 15, 1767.

"Lord Camden will go as far as any one in carrying it [the Act declaratory of the power to tax] into execution." Letter of 1768. "The Duke of Grafton is certainly determined to support the King's government." Id.

[1] Israel Mauduit to Hutchinson, in Boston Chronicle, i. 428.

[2] 35 Henry VIII. c. ii.

[3] Hillsborough to Bernard, 30 July, 1768.

[4] Compare Bernard to Hillsborough, 6 August, 1768; and Hallowell's examination.

not need the support of the troops, nor was it for his Majesty's service or the peace of the Province, that any should be required. Bernard dared not avow his own opinion;[1] but, in his spite, he wrote to Hillsborough for "positive orders"[3] not to call "a new Assembly until the people should get truer notions of their rights and interests." CHAP. XXXV. 1768. July.

The advice of the Council was inspired by loyalty. All attempts at a concert to cease importations had hitherto failed; the menace of the arrival of troops revived the design, and early in August, most of the merchants of the town of Boston subscribed an agreement, that they would not send for any kind of merchandise from Great Britain, some few articles of necessity excepted, during the year following the first day of January, 1769; and that they would not import any tea, paper, glass, paints or colors, until the act imposing duties upon them should be repealed.[3] Aug

On the anniversary of the fourteenth of August,[5] the streets of Boston resounded with songs in praise of freedom; and its inhabitants promised themselves that all ages would applaud their courage.

Come, join hand in hand, brave Americans all,
By uniting we stand, by dividing we fall;
To die we can bear, but to serve we disdain;
For shame is to Freedom more dreadful than pain.
  In freedom we're born, in freedom we'll live;

[1] Bernard to Hillsborough, 6 August, 1768.

[2] Bernard to Gage, 30 July, 1768.

[3] State of the Disorders, Confusions, &c. Bernard to Hillsborough, 9 August, 1768; and Hutchinson to T. Whately, 10 August, 1768.

[4] Francès to Choiseul, 29 Sept. 1768; Bernard to Hillsborough, 29 August, 1768.

CHAP. XXXV. 1768. Aug.

Our purses are ready,
Steady, boys, steady,
Not as slaves, but as freemen, our money we'll give.

The British administration was blind to its dangers, and believed union impossible.[1] "You will learn what transpires in America infinitely better in the city than at court;" wrote Choiseul[2] to the French Minister in England. "Never mind what Lord Hillsborough says;" he wrote again; "the private accounts of American merchants to their correspondents in London are more trustworthy."[3]

The obedient official sought information in every direction—especially of Franklin, than whom no man in England uttered more prophetic warnings, or in a more benign or more loyal spirit. "He has for years been predicting to the Ministers the necessary consequences of their American measures," said the French envoy;[4] "he is a man of rare intelligence and well-disposed to England; but, fortunately, is very little consulted." While the British Government neglected the opportunities of becoming well-informed respecting America, Choiseul collected newspapers, documents, resolves, instructions of towns, and even sermons of the Puritan clergy, and with clear sagacity and candid diligence, proceeded to construct his theory.

"The forces of the English in America are scarcely ten thousand men, and they have no cavalry;" thus reasoned the dispassionate statesmen of France; "but

[1] Francès to Choiseul, 5 August, 1768.

[2] Choiseul to Francès, Compiegne, 6 August, 1768.

[3] Choiseul to Francès, 27 August, 1768.

[4] Francès to Choiseul, 12 August, 1768.

the militia of the Colonies numbers four hundred thousand men, and among them several regiments of cavalry. The people are enthusiastic for liberty, and have inherited a republican spirit, which the consciousness of strength and circumstances may push to extremities. They will not be intimidated by the presence of troops, too insignificant to cause alarm." It was, therefore, inferred that it would be hazardous for England to attempt reducing the Colonies by force.

"But why," asked Choiseul,[1] "are not deputies from each Colony admitted into Parliament as members?" And it was answered[2] that "the Americans objected to such a solution, because they could not obtain a representation proportioned to their population, and so would be whelmed by superior numbers; because the distance made their regular attendance in Parliament impossible; and because they knew its venality and corruption too well to be willing to trust it with their affairs. They had no other representatives than agents at London, who kept them so well informed, that no project which would turn to their disadvantage could come upon them by surprise." By this reasoning Choiseul was satisfied,[3] that an American representation in Parliament was not practicable; but also that "no other method of conciliation" would prove less difficult, and that unanimity in America would compel the British Government to risk the most violent measures, or to yield.

[1] Choiseul to Francès, 21 August, 1768.

[2] Francès to Choiseul, 26 August, 1768.

[3] Choiseul to Francès, 7 Sept. 1768.

CHAP. XXXV. 1768. Aug. When, on the nineteenth of August, England heard that Massachusetts had, by a vast majority of its representatives, refused to rescind the resolutions of the preceding winter, Lord Mansfield was of the opinion that all the members of the late Legislative Assembly at Boston should be sent for, to give an account of their conduct, and that all the rigors of the law should be exercised against those who should persist in refusing to submit to Parliament.[1] "Where rebellion begins," said he, "the laws cease, and they can invoke none in their favor."[2]

Sept. To the ambassador of Spain, he expressed the opinion that the affair of the Colonies was the gravest and most momentous that England had had since 1688, and saw in America the beginning of a long and even infinite series of revolutions. "The Americans," he insisted, "must first be compelled to submit to the authority of Parliament; it is only after having reduced them to the most entire obedience that an inquiry can be made into their real or pretended grievances."[3] The subject interested every court in Europe, was watched in Madrid, and was the general theme of conversation in Paris, where Fuentes, the Spanish Minister, expressed the hope that "the English might master their Colonies, lest the Spanish Colonies also should catch the flame."[4]

"I dread the event," said Camden; "because the Colonies are more sober and consequently more determined in their present opposition than they were upon the Stamp Act." "What is to be done?" asked

[1] Francès to Choiseul, 29 Sept. 1768.

[2] Francès to Choiseul, 16 Sept. 1768.

[3] Francès to Choiseul, 23 Sept. 1768.

[4] Walpole's George III., iii. 253.

CHAP. XXXV. 1768. Sept.

Grafton; and Camden answered, "Indeed, my dear Lord, I do not know. The Parliament cannot repeal the Act in question, because that would admit the American principle to be right, and their own doctrine erroneous. Therefore it must execute the law. How to execute it, I am at a loss. Boston is the ringleading Province; and if any country is to be chastised, the punishment ought to be levelled there."[1]

But the system which made government subordinate to the gains of patronage, was every where producing its natural results. In South Carolina, the profits of the place of Provost-Marshal were enjoyed under a patent as a sinecure by a resident in England,[2] whose deputy had the monopoly of serving processes throughout the Province, and yet was bound to attend courts nowhere but at Charleston. As a consequence the herdsmen near the frontier adjudicated their own disputes and REGULATED their own police, even at the risk of a civil war.[3]

The blood of "rebels" against oppression was first shed among the settlers on the branches of the Cape Fear River. The emigrants to the upland glades of North Carolina, though occupying rich lands, had little coin or currency; yet as the revenue of the Province was raised by a poll-tax,[4] the poorest laborer among them must contribute towards it as much as the richest merchant. The

[1] Grafton's Autobiography, Camden to Grafton, 4 Sept. 1768. Campbell, v. 279, dates the Letter 4 Oct.

[2] See the Letters on the subject between the Committee of Correspondence of South Carolina and its Agent in England.

[3] Ramsay's History of South Carolina, i. 214, ii. 125.

[4] Boston Chronicle for Nov. 7–14, 1768. Tax in Orange for 1768, as stated by Edward Fanning.

CHAP. XXXV. 1768. Sept.

sheriffs were grown insolent and arbitrary; often distraining even quadruple the value of the tax, and avoiding the owner, till it was too late for him to redeem his property. All this was the more hateful, as a part of the amount was expended by the Governor in building himself an extravagantly costly palace; and a part was notoriously embezzled. The collecting officers and all others, encouraged by the imperious example of Fanning,[1] who loaded the titles to estates with doubts,[2] and charged illegal fees for recording new deeds, continued their extortions;[3] sure of support from the whole hierarchy of men in place. Juries were packed; and the Grand Jury was almost the agent of the extortioners. The cost of suits at-law, under any circumstances exorbitant, was enhanced by an unprecedented extent of the right of appeal from the county court to the remote superior court; where a farmer of small means would be ruined by the expense of attendance with his witnesses. "We tell you in the anguish of our souls," said they to the Governor, "we cannot, dare not go to law with our powerful antagonists; that step, whenever taken, will terminate in the ruin of ourselves and families."[4] Besides, the Chief Justice was Martin Howard,[5] a profligate time-server, raised to the bench as a convenient reward for having suffered in the time of the Stamp Act, and ever ready to use his place as a screen for the dishonest profits of men in office, and

[1] Record of the court at Hillsborough in Husband's Petition signed by near five hundred of Orange County, 30 April, 1768. Address of the inhabitants of Anson County, to Gov. Tryon, 1768.

[2] Compare Sabine's Loyalists under Fanning.

[3] Cases of Extortion &c. substantiated by Testimony, MS.

[4] Regulators to Gov. Tryon, 1768.

[5] Compare Sabine's Loyalists.

CHAP. XXXV. 1768. Sept.

the instrument of political power. Never yet had the tribunal of justice been so mocked.

Goaded[1] by oppression and an intuitive jealousy of frauds, men associated as "Regulators,"[2] binding themselves to avoid if possible all payment of taxes,[3] except such as were levied, and were to be applied according to law; and "to pay no more fees than the law allows, unless under compulsion, and then to bear open testimony against it." They proposed to hold a General Meeting quarterly;[4] but they rested their hopes of redress on the independent use of their elective franchise; being resolved to know and enjoy the liberties which they had inherited, without turning pale at the name of "rebellion." "An officer," said the inhabitants of the west side of Haw River,[5] "is a servant to the public; and we are determined to have the officers of this country under a better and honester regulation."

It was easy to foresee that the rashness of ignorant, though well-meaning husbandmen, maddened by oppression, would soon expose them to the inexorable vengeance of their adversaries. As one of the Regulators rode to Hillsborough, his horse was, in mere wantonness, seized for his levy, but was soon rescued by a party, armed with clubs and eleven muskets. Some one at Fanning's door showed pistols, and threatened to fire among them; upon which four or

[1] Tyree Harris's Advertisement.

[2] A plain, simple Narrative of Facts, signed in behalf of the Regulators, by a Committee of eight. MS.

[3] Association Paper agreed upon, &c. &c. 1768, probably of 4 April, MS. I have a very full collection of papers on the subject of the Regulators.

[4] Vote at a General Meeting of the Regulators, 4 April, 1768.

[5] Request of the Inhabitants of the West Side of Haw River to the Assemblymen and Vestrymen of Orange County, 1768.

CHAP. XXXV. 1768. Sept.

five heated, unruly persons in the crowd discharged their guns into the roof of the house, making two or three holes, and breaking two panes of glass without further damage.[1] At Fanning's instance, a warrant was issued by the Chief Justice to arrest three of the rioters, and bring them all the way to Halifax.[2]

Raising a clamor against the odiousness of rebellion, Fanning himself, as military Commander in Orange, called out seven companies of militia;[3] but not above one hundred and twenty men appeared with arms, and of these, all but a few stood neutral or declared in favor of the Regulators.[4] In Anson County[5] on the twenty-first of April, a mob interrupted the inferior court; and, moreover,[6] bound themselves by oath[7] to pay no taxes, and to protect each other against warrants of distress or imprisonment.

In Orange County the discontented did not harbor a thought of violence,[8] and were only preparing a Petition to the Governor and Council. "They call themselves Regulators," said Fanning, "but by lawyers they must be termed rebels and traitors;" and he calumniated them as plotting to take his life, and lay Hillsborough in ashes.[9] Meantime Tryon, who as the King's Representative, should have joined impartiality with lenity, made himself an open volunteer

[1] Committee of Regulators to Governor Tryon, 30 May, 1768. Lieut. Col. Gray to Colonel Fanning, 9 April, 1768.

[2] Memorandum preceding Gray's Letter.

[3] Col. Fanning to Col. Gray, 13 April, 1768.

[4] F. Nash and T. Hart to Col. Fanning, 17 April, 1768.

[5] Col. Spencer to Gov. Tryon, 28 April, 1768.

[6] Address from the Inhabitants of Anson County to Tryon.

[7] The Oath, in Rules and Resolves of the Anson Mob.

[8] Compare the Letter of the Regulators to Tryon, 30 May, 1768.

[9] Fanning to Tryon, 23 April, 1768.

on the side of Fanning,[1] and while he advised the people to petition the Provincial Legislature,[2] he empowered Fanning to call out the militia of eight counties besides Orange, and suppress insurrections by force. CHAP. XXXV. 1768. Sept.

The people of Orange, and equally of Anson, Rowan and Mecklenburg, were unanimous in their resolution to claim relief of the Governor. Flattery was, therefore, mixed with menaces, to allure the Regulators to sign a Petition which Fanning had artfully drafted,[3] and which rather invoked pardon than demanded redress.[4] "You may assure yourself from my knowledge of things," wrote Fanning's agent to Herman Husbands, "one couched in any other terms cannot go down with the Governor. The hands and the feet, should not run in mutiny against the head." But he vainly sought to terrify the rustic patriot by threats of confiscation of property, perpetual imprisonment, and even the penalties for High Treason.[5]

On the last day of April, the Regulators of Orange County, peacefully assembled on Rocky River, appointed twelve men on their behalf, "to settle the several matters of which they complained;[6] instructed "the Settlers" to procure a table of the taxables, taxes, and legal fees of public officers;[7]

[1] Governor Tryon to Fanning, 27 April, 1768.

[2] Governor Tryon's Proclamation.

[3] Plain and Simple Narration of Facts, 1768.

[4] Paper offered for Signature at the Council of Regulators, 25 April, 1768. Petition to his Excellency, William Tryon, Esq. &c. &c., inclosed in the letter of Ralph McNair to Herman Husbands, without date, but about 25 April, 1768.

[5] McNair to Herman Husbands, April, 1768.

[6] General meeting of the Regulators, 30 April, 1768.

[7] Instructions to the Settlers appointed by the County.

CHAP. XXXV. 1768. Sept.

and framed a Petition to the General Assembly, to secure them a fair hearing, and redress where they had been wronged.[1]

Fanning, on his side, unable to induce the Regulators to heed the offer[2] of his services, advertised their union as a daring insurrection, announced his authority to employ against them the militia of eight counties, and bade them expect "no mitigation of punishment for their crimes;" at the same time twenty-seven armed men of his procuring, chiefly Sheriffs and their dependents, and officers, were suddenly despatched on secret service, and after travelling all night, arrived near break of day, on Monday the second of May, at Sandy Creek, where they made prisoners of Herman Husbands and William Butler.[3]

Against Husbands there was no just charge whatever. He had never so much as joined "the Regulation;" had never been concerned in any tumult; and was seized at home on his own land. The "astonishing news," therefore, of his captivity, set the County in a ferment. Regulators and their opponents, judging that none were safe, prepared alike to go down to his rescue, but were turned back[4] by "the glad tidings," that the Governor himself had promised to receive their complaints.

Hurried to gaol, insulted, tied with cords, and threatened with the gallows, Husbands succeeded by partial concessions, the use of money, and by giving bonds, to obtain his liberty. But it seemed to him,

[1] Petition of the Regulators to the Governor, Council and Assembly.

[2] Col. Fanning to Jacob Fudge, 1 May, 1768.

[3] A plain simple Narrative of Facts.

[4] Doings of a General Meeting of Regulators and Inhabitants of Orange County, 21 May, 1768.

CHAP. XXXV. 1768. Sept.

that "he was left alone;" and how could an unlettered farmer contend against so many? In his despair he thought to leave his home and every thing he loved most dearly, and exile himself into some new land. With this purpose he "took the woods;"[1] but hearing that the Governor had promised that the extortioners might be brought to trial, he resolved to impeach Fanning, and to show before the world whether he was a principal in riots, or whether he had done no more than prosecute every lawful method for justice and redress.[2]

The Regulators, on their part, prepared their Petition, which was signed by about five hundred men; fortified it with a precise specification of acts of extortion, confirmed in each instance by oath; and presented[3] it to the Governor with their plain and simple Narrative, in the hope that "naked truth," though offered by the ignorant, might weigh as much as the artful representations of their "powerful adversary." Their language was that of loyalty to the King, and, with a rankling sense of their wrongs, breathed affection to the British Government, "as the wholesomest Constitution in being."[4] It is Tryon himself who relates that "in their commotions no mischief had been done," and that "the disturbances in Anson and Orange had subsided."[5] The Regulators awaited the result of the suits at law. But Tryon would not wait.[6] He repaired to Hillsbo-

[1] Husbands' Impartial Relation, &c. &c.

[2] Compare Letter from North Carolina in Boston Gazette, of 12 August, 1771; 853, 2, 1.

[3] Copy of the Petition and Signatures in my possession.

[4] Meeting of the Committee at Thomas Coxe's Mill, in a movement from Herman Coxe's.

[5] Tryon to Hillsborough, 16 June, 1768.

[6] Martin's North Carolina, ii. 237, 238.

CHAP XXXV. 1768. Sept. rough, threw himself entirely against the Regulators, and demanded of them unconditional and immediate submission,[1] and that twelve of them should give bonds in a thousand pounds each, for the peaceful conduct of them all. An alarm went abroad, the first of the kind, that Indians[2] as well as men from the lower counties, were to be raised to cut off the inhabitants of Orange County as "Rebels." About fifteen hundred men[3] were actually in arms; and yet when in September, the causes came on for trial in the presence of Tryon, and with such a display of troops, Husbands was acquitted on every charge; and Fanning who had been a volunteer witness against him, was convicted on six several indictments.[4] A verdict was also given against three Regulators. The court punished Fanning by a fine of one penny on each of his convictions; the Regulators were sentenced to pay fifty pounds each, and be imprisoned for six months.

Tryon would have sent troops to reduce the Regulators to submission by fire and sword; but his sanguinary disposition was overruled by the Council of War.[5] The Regulators remained quiet at their own homes, brooding over the failure of their efforts for redress. They resolved at the next election to

[1] Tryon to Inhabitants of Orange County, &c. 1 August, 1768. Depositions of Tyree Harris and of R. Sutherland, 3 August. Regulators to Gov. Tryon, delivered 5 August. Order in Council at Hillsborough, 13 August, and Letter of Tryon to the Regulators.

[2] Letter of James Hunter, Thos. Welburn, and Peter Julian, in behalf of the Regulators, 19 August, 1768.

[3] A General Return of the troops assembled under His Excellency's command, Hillsborough Camp, 22 September, 1768.

[4] Copy of the Docket, relating to the Indictments, in Herman Husbands' Impartial Account. See Wheeler's History of North Carolina, ii. 321, 322.

[5] Proceedings and Resolutions of the Council of War, held at Hillsborough, 22–23 Sept. 1768.

choose trustworthy men for their representatives; and when the time came, so general was the discontent, North Carolina changed thirty[1] of its delegates. Yet its people desponded, and saw no way for their extrication. CHAP. XXXV. 1768. Sept.

[1] Husband's Impartial Relation.

CHAPTER XXXVI.

THE TOWNS OF MASSACHUSETTS MEET IN CONVENTION.—HILLSBOROUGH'S ADMINISTRATION OF THE COLONIES CONTINUED.

SEPTEMBER—1768.

CHAP. XXXVI. 1768. Sept.

THE approach of military rule convinced Samuel Adams of the necessity of American Independence. From this moment,[1] he struggled for it deliberately and unremittingly as became one who delighted in the stern creed of Calvin, which, wherever it has prevailed, in Geneva, Holland, Scotland, Puritan England, New England, has spread intelligence, severity of morals, love of freedom, and courage. He gave himself to his glorious work, as devotedly as though he had in his keeping the liberties of mankind, and was a chosen instrument for fulfilling what had been decreed by the Divine counsels from all eternity. Such a cause left no room for fear. "He was," said Bernard, "one of the principal and most desperate of the chiefs of the faction;" "the all in all"[2] wrote Hutch-

[1] S. Adams's own statement to a friend in 1775. MS.

[2] "Instar omnium;" the phrase is taken from a later letter of Hutchinson's.

CHAP. XXXVI. 1768. Sept.

inson, who wished him "taken off," and who has left on record, that his purity was always above all price. Henceforward, one high service absorbed his soul—the independence of his country. To promote that end, he was ready to serve, and never claim a reward for service; to efface himself and put forward others; seeking the greatest things for his country, and content with the humblest for himself. Boston gathered about him. From a town of merchants and mechanics, it grew with him to be the hope of the world; and the sons of toil, as they took courage to peril fortune and life for the liberties they inherited, rose to be and to feel that they were the champions of human freedom.

With the people of Boston, in the street, at public meetings, at the ship-yards, wherever he met them, he reasoned on the subject that engrossed his affections. His clear sagacity discerned that Bernard, and Hutchinson, and the Commissioners of the Customs, had solicited the aid of an army; and he exclaimed against their treachery with bitterness. He held that it would be just to destroy every soldier whose foot should touch the shore. "The King," he would say, "has no right to send troops here to invade the country; if they come, they will come as foreign enemies."

"We will not submit to any tax," he spoke out, "nor become slaves. We will take up arms and spend our last drop of blood, before the King and Parliament shall impose on us, or settle Crown officers

[1] Affidavit of Richard Silvester, sworn to before Chief Justice Hutchinson, and sent to the Secretary of State at the time the Ministry designed to take off the principal incendiaries. The words of S. Adams are known to have been uttered at or near this time.

CHAP. XXXVI. 1768. Sept. independent of the colonial Legislature to dragoon us." He openly denied the superiority of the existing forms of government. It was not reverence for Kings, he would say, that brought the ancestors of New England to America. They fled from Kings and bishops, and looked up to the King of Kings. "We are free, therefore," he concluded, "and want no King."[1] "The times were never better in Rome, than when they had no King and were a free State." As he reflected on the extent of the Colonies in America, he saw the vast empire that was forming, and was conscious it must fashion its own institutions, and reform those of England.

But at this time Massachusetts had no representative body. Bernard had hinted, that instructions might be given to forbid the calling of the Assembly even at the annual period in May; and to reduce the Province to submission by the indefinite suspension of its Legislature. Was there no remedy? The men of Boston and the villages round about it were ready to spring to arms. But of what use were "unconnected" movements? Ten thousand men had assembled suddenly in 1746 on the rumor of the approach of a French expedition; thirty thousand could at a signal come forth, with gun in hand, to drive the British troops into the sea; but was there the steady courage to keep passion in check, and restrain disorder?

On the fifth of September, there appeared in the Boston Gazette, a paper in the form of Queries,[2]

[1] Affidavits in the State-paper Office London.

[2] Queries in Boston Gazette, 5 Sept. 1768; 701, 31, signed Clericus Americanus. Bernard to Hillsborough, 16 Sept. 1768, Letters to Hillsborough, &c. 70.

CHAP. XXXVI. 1768. Sept.

designed to persuade the people that the Acts of Parliament and the measures of the British Government for their execution, necessarily implied a leaping over all those covenants and compacts which were the basis of the political union with Great Britain; that, therefore, it was expedient for the inhabitants of every town in the Province, to choose representatives for a General Assembly with instructions, on their coming together, to pray for the enlargement of their privileges to the extent of that first original Charter[1] of the Colony, which left to the people the choice of their Governor, and reserved to the Crown no negative on their laws. "If," continued the writer, "an army should be sent to reduce us to slavery, we will put our lives in our hands and cry to the Judge of all the earth, who will do right, saying: Behold—how they come to cast us out of this possession which thou hast given us to inherit. Help us, O Lord, our God; for we rest on Thee, and in Thy name we go against this multitude."

Wednesday, the seventh, early in the morning, the Senegal left the port.[2] The next day, the Duke of Cumberland, a large ship, sailed for Nova Scotia. On the eighth of September, Bernard let it be known that both vessels of war were gone to fetch three regiments. Sullen discontent appeared on almost every brow.[3] On the ninth a Petition was signed for a Town Meeting "to consider of the most wise, constitutional, loyal, and salutary

[1] "The old Charter which had nothing of royalty in it." Bernard to Hillsborough, 16 September, 1768; Letters to Hillsborough, 74.

[2] Compare Gage to Hillsborough, 7 Sept. 1768.

[3] Bernard to Gage, 16 Sept, 1768. Captain Corner's Diary, Thursday, 8 Sept.

CHAP. XXXVI. 1768. Sept. measures"[1] in reference to the expected arrival of troops.

Union was the heart's desire of Boston; union first with all the towns of the Province, and next with the sister Colonies; and the confidence which must precede union could be established only by consummate prudence and self-control. On Saturday, Otis, Samuel Adams, and Warren met at the house of Warren,[2] and drew up the plan for the Town Meeting, the Resolves, and the order of the debates. The subject was not wholly new; Otis had long before pointed out the proper mode of redress in the contingency[3] which had now occurred. It must be ascertained if the Colony in the midst of excitement could preserve the self-possession necessary for instituting government.[4]

All day Sunday Bernard suffered from "false alarms and threats as usual;" insisted, that a rising was agreed upon;[5] and in his fright at an empty barrel placed on the beacon, actually called a meeting of the Council."[6]

On Monday the twelfth, the inhabitants of Boston gathered in a Town Meeting at Faneuil Hall, where the arms belonging to the town, to the number of four hundred muskets, lay in boxes on the floor. After a prayer from the fervid and eloquent Cooper, minister of the Congregation in Brattle Street, and the election of Otis as moderator, a committee in-

[1] Words of the Petition to the Selectmen.

[2] Bernard to Hillsborough, 16 September, 1768, Letters to the Ministry, 70. Corner's Diary, 10 September, 1768.

[3] Diary of John Adams, in Works, ii. 161, 162.

[4] Captain Corner's Diary, Sunday, 11 Sept. 1768.

[5] Bernard to Gage, 16 Sept.

[6] Bernard to Hillsborough, Letters to the Ministry, 71.

CHAP. XXXVI. 1768. Sept.

quired of the Governor the grounds of his apprehensions that regiments of his majesty's troops were daily to be expected; and he was also requested "in the precarious situation of their invaluable rights and privileges, civil and religious, to issue precepts for a General Assembly." On the next morning at ten o'clock, report was made, that troops were expected to arrive; and that Bernard refused to call an Assembly. Rashness on the part of the people of Boston would have forfeited the confidence of their own Province, and the sympathies of the rest; while feebleness would have overwhelmed their cause with ridicule. It was necessary for them to halt; but to find a position where it was safe to do so; and they began with the declaration that "It is the first principle in civil society, founded in nature and reason, that no law of the society can be binding on any individual, without his consent, given by himself in person, or by his representative of his own free election." They further appealed not to natural rights only, but to the precedents of the revolution of 1688; to the conditions on which the House of Hanover received the throne; to the bill of rights of William and Mary; and to their own Charter; and then they proceeded to resolve, "That the inhabitants of the town of Boston will, at the utmost peril of their lives and fortunes, maintain and defend their rights, liberties, privileges, and immunities." To remove uncertainty respecting these rights, they voted, "that money could not be levied, nor a standing army be kept up in the Province but by their own free consent."

This report was divers times distinctly read and

CHAP. XXXVI. 1768. Sept.

considered, and it was unanimously voted that it be accepted and recorded. The record remains to the honor of Boston among all posterity.

"There are the arms," said Otis, pointing to the chests in which they lay. "When an attempt is made against your liberties, they will be delivered." One man, impatient to offer resistance, cried out, that they wanted a head; another, an old man, was ready to rise and resume all power; a third reasoned, that liberty is as precious as life, and may equally be defended against the aggressor; that when a people's liberties are threatened, they are in a state of war and have a right to defend themselves.

But every excessive opinion was overruled or restrained, so that the country might the more cheerfully respond to the town of Boston. The Bill of Rights declared that for the redress of grievances, Parliaments ought to be held frequently; the Assembly of Massachusetts had been arbitrarily dissolved; and Bernard refused to issue writs for a new one; so that the legislative rights of the Colony were suspended. The Town therefore, following the precedent of 1688, proposed a Convention in Faneuil Hall. To this body they elected Cushing, Otis, Samuel Adams, and Hancock, a committee to represent them; and directed their Selectmen to inform the several towns of the Province of their design.[1] It was also voted by a very great majority

[1] Compare Edmund Burke's Speech, 8 Nov. 1768, in Cavendish, i. 89. "Such an order to a Governor was an annihilation of the Assembly; and when the Assembly was dissolved, an usurped Assembly met."

CHAP. XXXVI. 1768. Sept.

that every one of the inhabitants should provide himself with fire-arms and ammunition; and this vote was grounded partly on the prevailing rumor of a war with France, but more on the precedent of the Revolution of King William and Queen Mary. A cordial letter was read from the merchants of New-York, communicating the agreement[1] of themselves and the mechanics, to cease importing British goods.

It was also unanimously voted, that the selectmen wait on the several ministers of the Gospel within the town to desire that the next Tuesday might be set apart as a day of fasting and prayer; and it was so kept by all the Congregational churches.

On the fourteenth of September, just after a vessel had arrived in forty days from Falmouth, bringing news how angry people in England were with the Americans,[2] that three regiments were coming over, that fifty State prisoners were to be sent home, the Selectmen issued a circular, repeating the history of their grievances, and inviting every town in the Province to send a Committee to the Convention, to give "sound and wholesome advice," and "prevent any sudden and unconnected measures." The city of London had never done the like in the great rebellion.[3]

The proceedings of the Meeting in Boston had a greater tendency towards a revolution, than any previous measures in any of the Colonies. "They

[1] New-York Resolves subscribed by merchants, dated 27 August, 1768, and Resolves by the tradesmen of New-York, dated 5 Sept. 1768, referring to the salutary measures entered into by the people of Boston. In supplement to Boston Gazette of 19 Sept. 1768.

[2] Captain Corner's Diary, 14 Sept. 1768.

[3] Hutchinson's History, iii. 205.

CHAP. XXXVI. 1768. Sept.

have delivered their sentiments in the style of a ruling and sovereign nation, who acknowledge no dependence;" wrote Gage. "Sedition," he feared, "might be catching, and show itself in New-York."[1] "Your life is in danger from those Catilines, the Sons of Liberty," said Auchmuty[2] to Hutchinson. Bernard was sure that but for the Romney, a rebellion would have broken out; he reported a design against the Castle, and talked of discovering the very names of five hundred men enrolled for the service; he acknowledged what he called "the melancholick truth, that his government was subdued;" he trembled for his own safety; two regiments would not be sufficient for his protection. "I dare not," said he, "publish a proclamation against the Convention,[3] without first securing my retreat." "I wish I were away,"[4] he owned to those around him; the offer of a baronetcy and the Vice-Government of Virginia coming to hand, he accepted them "most thankfully," and hoped to embark for England in a fortnight.[5] He had hardly indulged in this day-dream for twenty-four hours, when his expectations were dashed by the account of Botetourt's appointment, and he began to quake, lest he should lose[6] Massachusetts also. Of a sudden he was become the most anxious and unhappy man in Boston.

[1] Gage to Hillsborough, 26 Sept. 1768.

[2] Robert Auchmuty to Hutchinson, 14 Sept. 1768.

[3] Bernard to Hillsborough, 9 Sept. and 16 Sept. 1768. Letters to the Ministry, 70, 74.

[4] Compare Hillsborough to Gage, 16 Sept. 1768, and Captain Corner's Diary, Thursday, 15 Sept. "Threats and panic as usual. The Governor wishes himself away; says he believes the Romney prevented rebellion."

[5] Bernard to Hillsborough, 17 September, 1768.

[6] Bernard to Hillsborough, 18 September, 1768.

CHAP. XXXVI. 1768. Sept.

On Monday, the nineteenth, Bernard announced to the Council, that two regiments were expected from Ireland, that two others were coming at once from Halifax, and desired that for one of them quarters might be prepared[1] within the town. "The process in quartering," replied the Council,[2] "must be regulated by the Act of Parliament;" and that required the civil officers to "quarter and billet the officers and soldiers in his Majesty's service in the barracks; and only in case there was not sufficient room in the barracks to find other quarters for the residue of them."[3] The Council, therefore, after an adjournment of three days, during which "the militia were under arms,[4] exercising and firing," spoke out plainly, that as the barracks at Castle William were sufficient to accommodate both regiments ordered from Halifax, the Act of Parliament required that they should be quartered there. Upon this, Bernard produced the letter of General Gage, by which it appeared, that one only of the coming regiments was ordered for the present to Castle William, and one to the town of Boston. "It is no disrespect to the General" answered the Council, "to say that no order whatsoever, coming from a General or a Secretary of War, or any less authority than his Majesty and Parliament, can supersede an Act of Parliament;" and they insisted, that General Gage could not have intended otherwise, for the Act provided, "that if any military officer should take upon himself to quarter

[1] Bernard to Hillsborough, 23 September, 1768.

[2] See Note to the Letter of the Major part of the Council to Lord Hillsborough, 15 April, 1769, in Letters to Hillsborough.

[3] Major part of the Council to Hillsborough, 15 April, 1769.

[4] Captain Corner's Diary.

CHAP. XXXVI. 1768. Sept.

soldiers in any of his Majesty's dominions in America otherwise than was limited and allowed by the Act, he should be *ipso facto* cashiered and disabled to hold any military employment in his Majesty's service."[1] Besides it was urged that quartering troops in the body of the town was inconsistent with its peace.

The Council, who were conducted in their opposition by James Bowdoin, one of the most heartily loyal men in the King's dominions, was in the right in the interpretation of the law, and equally so on the question of prudence; for why irritate the people of the town unnecessarily by the presence of soldiers? At the Castle they would be serviceable on the shortest notice.

Bernard, with no ground of complaint against the Council, but that they respected the law and gave good and prudent advice, only wrote to Hillsborough:[2] "The Council are desirous to lend a hand to the Convention, to bring about a forfeiture of the Charter.[3] The Government is entirely subdued. If the three regiments ordered to Boston, were now quietly in their quarters, it would not follow that it could renew its functions. The forfeiture of the Charter is an event most devoutly to be wished."[4]

On the appointed day, Thursday, the twenty-second of September, the anniversary of the King's coronation, about seventy persons, from sixty-six

[1] Bernard to Hillsborough, 23 Sept. 1768, and answer of the Council, 26 Sept. 1768.

[2] Compare Bernard to Hillsborough, 24 Sept. 1768, and S. Adams to De Berdt, Oct. 1768.

[3] Bernard to Hillsborough, 26 September, 1768.

[4] Bernard to Hillsborough, 27 September, 1768.

CHAP. XXXVI. 1768. Sept.

towns, came together in Faneuil Hall in Convention,[1] and their number increased, till ninety-six towns and eight districts, nearly every settlement in the Colony, were represented. By the mere act of assembling, the object of the Convention was accomplished. It was a bold and successful attempt to show, that f the policy of suppressing the Legislature should be persisted in, a way was discovered by which legislative government could still be instituted, and a general expression of opinion and concentration of power be obtained. And though at first Otis was unaccountably absent,[2] they marked their own sense of the character of this meeting by electing the Speaker and Clerk of the late House of Representatives to the same offices in their own body.

"They have committed treason," shouted all the Crown officers in America. "At least the selectmen, in issuing the Circular for a Convention, have done so;" and pains were taken to obtain and preserve some of their original letters with their signatures. "Boston," said Gage, "is mutinous,"[3] "its resolves treasonable and desperate." "Mad people procured them; mad people govern the town and influence the Province."[4]

The Convention, soon after it was organized, requested the Governor to summon the Constitutional Assembly of the Province, in order to consider of measures for preventing an unconstitutional encroach-

[1] Compare Francès of the French Embassy at London to Choiseul, 28 October, 1768.

[2] "Mr. Otis in the country much disconcerts them." Captain Corner's Diary for 22 Sept. "the Coronation."

[3] Compare Paper of Intelligence, inclosed in Gage's, No. 15, of 26 September, 1768.

[4] Letters, &c. &c. 41.

CHAP. XXXVI.

1768. Sept.

ment of military power on the civil establishment. The Governor[1] refused to receive this petition; and he admonished "the gentlemen assembled at Faneuil Hall, under the name of a Convention,"[2] to break up instantly and separate themselves, or they should be made to "repent of their rashness." The message was received with derision.

In the same spirit, the Council, adhering to their purpose of conforming strictly to the Billeting Act, reduced to writing the reasons for their decision to provide no quarters in town till the barracks at the Castle should be full; and on the twenty-sixth of September communicated it to Bernard, published it in the Boston Gazette, and sent a copy to Lord Hillsborough. The law was explicit and unambiguous; and not only sanctioned but required the decision which they had taken.

The paper of the Council proved a disregard for an Act of Parliament by the very persons who set up to enforce Parliamentary authority. On the side of the Province, no law was violated;[3] only men would not buy tea, glass, colors, or paper; on the side of Hillsborough, Bernard and Gage, requisitions were made contrary to the words and the indisputable intent of the Statute. In the very beginning of the coercive measures, Boston gained a moral victory; it placed itself on the side of law; and proved its enemies to be lawbreakers. The immediate effect of the publication was, says Bernard,[3] "the greatest

[1] Bernard's Message, to Gentlemen assembled at Faneuil Hall.

[2] Compare the Report on this subject of Francès to Choiseul, 4 November, 1768.

[3] Samuel Adams to De Berdt, Oct. 1768.

[4] Supplement to Bernard to Hillsborough, No. 24, of 27 Sept. 1768.

CHAP. XXXVI. 1768. Sept.

blow that had been given to the King's Government." "Nine tenths of the people considered the declaration of the Council just."[1] "Throughout the Province they were ripe for almost any thing."[2] The British Ministry, never dared seriously to insist on the provision for the troops required by the Billeting Act.

The Convention, which remained but six days in session, repeated the Protest of Massachusetts against taxation of the Colonies by the British Parliament; against a standing army; against the danger to "the liberties of America from a united body of pensioners and soldiers."[3] They renewed their Petition to the King, which they enjoined their Agent to deliver in person as speedily as possible. They resolved to preserve good order, by the aid of the civil magistrate alone. "While the people," said they, "wisely observe the medium between an abject submission under grievous oppression on the one hand, and irrational attempts to obtain redress on the other, they may promise themselves success in recovering the exercise of their just rights, relying on Him who ruleth according to his pleasure, with unerring wisdom and irresistible influence, in the hearts of the children of men."[4] They then dissolved themselves, leaving the care for the public to the Council.

This was the first great example in America of

[1] Hutchinson to T. Whately, Boston, 4 Oct. 1768.

[2] Andrew Eliot to T. Hollis, 27 Sept. 1768.

[3] Boston Gazette, 10 October, 1768, contains the letter from the Convention to De Berdt, dated Boston, 27 September, 1768, and signed, Thomas Cushing, Chairman.

[4] Compare Francès to Choiseul, 21 Sept. 1768; and Same to Same, 23 Sept. 1768. Also A. Eliot, to T. Hollis, 27 Sept, 1768, and Same to Same, 17 Oct. 1768.

CHAP. XXXVI. 1768. Sept.

the Fabian policy; the first restoration of affairs by delay. Indiscreet men murmured; but the intelligent perceived the greatness of the result. When the Attorney and Solicitor-General of England were called upon to find traces of high treason in what had been done, De Grey as well as Dunning declared, none[1] had been committed. "Look into the papers," said De Grey, "and see how well these Americans are versed in the crown law; I doubt whether they have been guilty of an overt act of treason, but I am sure they have come within a hair's breadth of it."[2]

[1] Opinion of De Grey and Dunning on the Papers submitted to them, Nov. 1768.

[2] The Attorney General in the Debate of 26 Jan. 1769; Cavendish, i. 196.

CHAPTER XXXVII.

THE CELTIC-AMERICAN REPUBLIC ON THE BANKS OF THE MISSISSIPPI.

SEPTEMBER—OCTOBER, 1768.

CHAP. XXXVII. 1768. Sept.

ON Wednesday the twenty-eighth of September, just after the Convention broke up, the squadron from Halifax arrived, and anchored at noon in Nantasket Bay. It brought not two regiments only, but artillery also, which Bernard, by a verbal message, had specially requested. Dalrymple, the commander of the troops, "expressed infinite surprise that no quarters had been prepared." On Thursday, the twenty-ninth, a Council was summoned, at which Smith, the commanding officer of the fleet, and Dalrymple, were present. After much altercation, the Council adhered to the law; and the Governor to his declaration of a total want of power to do any thing in his province.[1] "Since that resolution was taken to rise in arms in open rebellion," wrote Gage,[2] "I don't see any cause to be scrupulous." On the following day the whole squadron was anchored near the

[1] Dalrymple to Gage, 2 Oct. 1768.

[2] Gage to Bernard, 2 Oct. 1768.

CHAP. XXXVII. 1768. Sept. Romney,[1] off Castle William, in the hope to intimidate the Council; but without success. At that moment Montresor, the engineer, arrived express from General Gage, to assist in recovering the Castle, if he should find it in the hands of the rebels; and he brought an order to land not one but both the regiments within the settled part of the town of Boston itself.[2]

Oct. The first of October, the order was to be executed. The Governor on the occasion stole away into the country, leaving Dalrymple to despise "his want of spirit,"[3] and "to take the whole upon himself," without the presence of a civil officer. As if they were come to an enemy's country,[4] eight ships of war with tenders were placed off the wharves, with loaded cannon, and springs on their cables, so that they commanded the town; after this, the fourteenth and twenty-ninth regiments and a part of the fifty-ninth, with a train of artillery and two pieces of cannon, effected their landing[5] on the Long Wharf. Each soldier having received sixteen round of shot, they marched with drums beating, fifes playing, and colors flying, through the streets of the defenceless, unarmed, quiet town, which made not the least show of resistance, and by four in the afternoon they paraded on Boston Common.

"All their bravadoes ended as may be imagined," said an officer. "Men are not easily brought to

[1] Captain Smith to Commodore Hood, 5 Oct. 1768.

[2] Bernard to Hillsborough, 1 Oct. 1768. Letters to the Ministry, 92. Proceedings of Council, Number v. 3 Oct. 1768, in Letters to Hillsborough, 126.

[3] Lieut. Colonel Dalrymple to Commodore Hood, 4--5 Oct. 1768.

[4] Council of Massachusetts Bay to Hillsborough, 15 April, 1769. Letters, &c.

[5] Captain Smith to Commodore Hood, 5 Oct. 1768. L. Col. Dalrymple to Gage, Bernard to Hillsborough.

fight," wrote Hutchinson,[1] "when they know death by the sword, or the halter will be the consequence." "Great Britain," remarked a wise observer, "will sooner or later repent her mistaken policy."[2]

Dalrymple encamped the twenty-ninth regiment, which had field equipage; for the rest, he demanded quarters of the Selectmen. They knew the law too well to comply; but as the night was cold, the compassion of the inhabitants was moved for the soldiers, and about nine o'clock the Sons of Liberty allowed them to sleep in Faneuil Hall.[3] "By management," said he, "I got possession of the School of Liberty, and thereby secured all their arms."[4]

"I will keep possession of this town, where faction seems to prevail beyond conception," he blustered;[5] we shall see how he redeemed his word. For the present, the passive resistance which he encountered compelled him to ask aid of the Commander of the fleet. The troops were in a miserable condition, having neither quarters nor any means to dress their provisions.

On Monday, the third, Bernard laid before the Council Dalrymple's requisition for the enumerated allowances to troops in barracks. "We," answered the Council, "are ready, on our part, to comply with the Act of Parliament, if the Colonel will on his."[6]

After two days reflection, the Council consented to the appointment of a commissary, if he would

[1] Letter of Hutchinson to———, 8 Dec. 1768.

[2] A Eliot to T. Hollis, 17 Oct. 1768.

[3] Dalrymple to Gage, 2 Oct. 1768.

[4] Dalrymple to Hood, 4 Oct. 1768.

[5] Dalrymple to Gage, 2 Oct. 1768.

[6] Bernard to Hillsborough. Letters to the Ministry, 94, 5 October, 1768; Dalrymple to Commodore Hood, 4 October, 1768; Captain Smith to Commodore Hood, 5 October, 1768.

CHAP. XXXVII. 1768. Oct. "take the risk of the Province's paying" the charge of his office. The condition was strictly right; for to appropriate money, was the attribute of the Assembly. Since there was no Assembly, no power in the Province could pledge its credit.[1]

"Tyranny begins," said Samuel Adams,[2] "if the law is transgressed to another's harm. It behoves the public to avail themselves of the remedy of the law. It is always safe to adhere to the law. We must not give up the law and the Constitution, which is fixed and stable, and is the collected and long digested sentiment of the whole, and substitute in its room the opinion of individuals, than which nothing can be more uncertain."

While Hood meditated embarking for Boston to winter there,[3] Gage came from New-York to demand, in person, quarters for the regiments in the town. The Council would grant none till the barracks at the Castle were filled.[4]

The Governor and the Sheriff attempted, at least, to get possession of a ruinous building, belonging to the Province; but its occupants had taken the opinion of the best lawyer, and kept them at bay.[5]

Bernard next summoned all the acting justices to meet him, and renewed the General's demand for quarters. "Not till the barracks are filled," they answered, conforming to the law.[6] "How absurd

[1] Bernard to Hillsborough, 5 Oct. 1768. Major part of Council to Hillsborough, 15 April, 1769.

[2] Samuel Adams in Boston Gazette, 10 October, 1768.

[3] Commodore Hood to Mr. Stephens, Secretary of the Admiralty; Halifax, 12 Oct. 1768.

[4] Gage to Commodore Hood, 18 Oct. 1768.

[5] Bernard to Hillsborough, 18 Oct. 1768.

[6] Compare Samuel Adams to Dennys De Berdt, Esq., Boston, 3 October, 1768.

CHAP. XXXVII. 1768. Oct.

and ungrateful," cried Hutchinson.[1] "The clause" wrote Gage, "is by no means calculated for this country, where every man studies law."[2] "I am now at the end of my tether," said Bernard to his Council, and he asked them to join him in naming a commissary. "To join in such appointment," answered the Council, "would be an admission that the Province ought to be charged with the expense." The officers themselves could not put the troops into quarters, for they would, under the Act, be cashiered, on being convicted of the fact before two justices of the peace. "Before two justices," exclaimed Gage, "the best of them the keeper of a paltry tavern."[3]

At last, the weather growing so severe that the troops could not remain in tents, "the commanding officer[4] was obliged to hire houses at very dear rates," as well as procure, at the expense of the Crown, all the articles required by Act of Parliament of the Colony. The Main Guard was established opposite the State House, and cannon were pointed towards the rooms in which the Legislature was accustomed to sit. But as the town gave an example of respect for law, there was nothing for the troops to do. Two regiments were there as idle lookers-on, and two more were coming to share the same inactivity. Every one knew that they could not be employed except on a requisition from a civil officer; and there was not a magistrate in the Colony that saw any reason for calling in their aid, nor a person in town

[1] Hutchinson to T. Pownall, 8 Nov. 1768.

[2] Bernard to Hillsborough, 1 Nov. 1768; Gage to Hillsborough, 31 October, 1768.

[3] Gage to Hillsborough, 31 Oct. 1768.

[4] Hutchinson to ——, 8 Dec. 1768.

CHAP. XXXVII. 1768. Oct.

disposed to act in a way to warrant it. So that after all that had been done, the spirit of the Colonies was as intractable as ever.

The Commissioners of the Customs, whose false alarms had brought troops to the Province, having received orders to return to Boston, wished to get from the Council some excuse for their departure, as well as for their return. "They had no just reason for absconding from their duty," said Bowdoin;[1] and the Council left them to return of themselves; but in an Address to Gage, adopted by a vote of fifteen out of nineteen,[2] they explained how trivial had been the disorders on which the request for troops had been grounded. Gage became convinced by his inquiries, that the disturbance in March was trifling; that on the tenth of June the Commissioners were neither attacked nor menaced; that more obstructions had arisen to the service from the servants of Government, than from any other cause.[3] But purblind in the light, he adopted the sentiments and language of Bernard; and advised barracks and a fort on Fort Hill to command the town; while the Governor urged anew a forfeiture of the Charter, and owned that "troops would not restore the authority of Government."[4]

[1] Votes of the Council, inclosed in Gov. Bernard's Letter, No 31. 5 Nov. 1768. Major part of the Council to Hillsborough, 59,60.

[2] Address to General Gage from fifteen members of the Council, 27 Dec. 1768; Letters to Hillsborough, 129, 134.

[3] Governor Wentworth to the Marquis of Rockingham, New Hampshire, November 12, 1768. "It gives me great pleasure to find the General, since his arrival in Boston, has entirely the same sentiments." In Albemarle's Rockingham, ii. 88. It is to be borne in mind that Wentworth was as loyal to Great Britain as any of them all.

[4] Gage to Hillsborough, 31 Oct. 1768; Letters to Hillsborough, 33, 34. Bernard to Hillsborough, 12 Nov. 1768; Bernard to Secretary Pownall, 7 Nov. 1768.

It was on every one's lips, that the die was thrown, that they must wait for the event; but the parties who waited, were each in a different frame of mind. A troublesome anxiety took possession of Bernard, who began to fear his recall, and intercede to be spared.[1] "These red coats make a formidable appearance," said Hutchinson, with an exulting countenance, and an air of complacency, buoyant with the prospect of rising one step higher. The soldiers liked the country they were come to, and, sure that none would betray them, soon deserted in numbers.[2] The Commissioners were more haughty than before, and gratified their malignity by arresting Hancock and Malcom on charges, confidently made but never established.[3] All were anxious to know the decision of the King and the New Parliament, respecting the great question between Government by consent and Government by authority.

But the determination of the King was evident from the first. "Chatham, even if he is crazed, is the person who most merits to be observed," wrote Choiseul;[4] but the British Ministry had less discernment. Yielding to the "daily"[5] importunities of the King, Grafton prepared to dismiss Shelburne.[6] The assent of Camden was desired. "You are my pole star," Camden[7] was accustomed to say to Chatham; "I have sworn an oath, I will go, I will go where you

[1] Hutchinson to T. Whately, Boston, 17 Oct. 1768.

[2] Andrew Eliot to Thomas Hollis, 17 Oct. 1768.

[3] Gage to Hillsborough, No. 19 and No. 28, 5 March, 1769.

[4] Choiseul to the French Embassy at London, 21 August, 1768.

[5] Grafton's Autobiography.

[6] Compare Francès to Choiseul, 7 Oct. 1768.

[7] Camden to Chatham, 20 March, 1768. Chatham's Correspondence, iii. 325.

CHAP. XXXVII. 1768. Oct.

lead." But now he encouraged Grafton to slight their justly dissatisfied benefactor, as "brooding over his own suspicions and discontent."[1] "I will never retire upon a scanty income," he added, "unless I should be forced by something more compelling than the Earl of Shelburne's removal. You are my pole star, Chatham being eclipsed."[2]

Grafton wished earnestly to gain Chatham's acquiescence in the proposed change, and repaired to Hayes to give assurances, that no new "bias" swayed him from the connection, to which his faith was pledged. "My Lord's health," answered the Countess, "is too weak to admit of any communication of business; but I am able to tell your Grace, from my Lord himself, that Lord Shelburne's removal will never have his consent." The King awaited anxiously the result of the interview;[3] and notwithstanding the warning, Shelburne was removed. To Camden's surprise,[4] the resignation of Chatham instantly followed. Grafton and the King interposed with solicitations;[5] but even the hope of triumphing over the aristocracy had lost its seductive power; and the Earl remained inflexible. Camden knew that he ought to have retired also;[6] he hushed his scruples by the thought that

[1] Lord Camden to the Duke of Grafton, 29 Sept. 1768; in Campbell's Chancellors, v. 277.

[2] Camden to Grafton, 4 September, 1768. The date of 4 Sept. seems to me the correct one.

[3] Lady Chatham's Memorandum of a conversation with the Duke of Grafton, 9 Oct. 1768. Chatham Corr. iii. 337.

[4] Camden to the Duke of Grafton, 14 Oct. 1768. "Though I was apprehensive that Lord Shelburne's dismissal would make a deep impression upon Lord Chatham's mind, yet I did not expect this sudden resignation."

[5] King to Chatham, 4 Oct. 1768 Chatham Corr. iii. 343.

[6] Camden to Chatham, 20 March, 1768. "Indeed, my dear Lord, our seals ought to go together," &c. Chat. Corr. iii. 325.

his illustrious friend had not asked him to do it; and continued saying "He shall still be my pole star,"[1] even while the emoluments of office were for a time attracting him to advise a public declaration from the King, that Townshend's revenue Act should be executed, and "Boston," "the ringleading Province," be "chastised."[2]

CHAP. XXXVII. 1768. Oct.

The removal of Shelburne opened the Cabinet to the ignorant and incapable Earl of Rochford, who owed his selection to the mediocrity of his talents and the impossibility of finding a Secretary of State more thoroughly submissive.[3] He needed money, being so poor as to have once told Choiseul with tears in his eyes, that if he lost the embassy which he then filled, he should be without resources.[4] He had a passion also to play a part, and in his moments of glorying, would boast of his intention to rival not Chatham, he would say, but Pitt;[5] though he could not even for a day adhere steadily to one idea. "His meddlesome disposition," said Choiseul, "makes him a worse man to deal with than one of greater ability." "You," answered Du Chatelet,[6] "may turn his foibles and defects to the advantage of the King." After his accession, the Administration was the weakest and the worst which England has known since its Revolution.

It had no sanction in public opinion, and the subservient Parliament was itself losing its authority and

[1] Camden to the Countess of Chatham, 22 October, 1768.

[2] Camden to Grafton, 4 Sept. or 4 Oct. 1768.

[3] Francès to Choiseul, 29 Sept. 1768.

[4] Choiseul to Francès, 21 Sept. 1768.

[5] Choiseul to Francès, 12 Oct. 1768.

[6] Du Chatelet to Choiseul, 18 Nov. 1768; Same to Same, 28 Nov. 1768.

CHAP. XXXVII. 1768. Oct.

the reverence of the nation. A reform was henceforward advocated by Grenville. "The number of electors," such was his declared[1] opinion, "is become too small in proportion to the whole people, and the Colonies ought to be allowed to send members to Parliament."[2]

"What other reason than an attempt to raise discontent," replied Edmund Burke as the organ of the Rockingham Whigs, "can he have for suggesting, that we are not happy enough to enjoy a sufficient number of voters in England? Our fault is on the other side." And he mocked at an American Representation and union with America as the vision of a lunatic.[3]

The opinions of Grenville were obtaining universal circulation, just as intelligence was received of the proceedings of the town of Boston relative to the proposed convention. From their votes, it was inferred that the troops would be opposed, should they attempt to land; that Massachusetts Bay, if not all the Colonies, must henceforward be considered as in a state of actual rebellion, and measures were concerting to rely upon superiority in arms, and to support authority in America, at all hazards. "Depend upon it," said Hillsborough to the Agent of Connecticut, who had presented him the Petition of that Colony, "Parliament will not suffer their authority to be trampled upon. We wish to avoid severities towards you, but if you refuse obedience to our

[1] Grenville to William Knox, October, 1768, in Appendix to vol. ii. of Extra Official State Papers, 23.

[2] The State of the Nation, published in October, 1768.

[3] Edmund Burke's Observations on a State of the Nation; Works, i. 295, 296, 298, Am. Ed.

laws, the whole fleet and army of England shall enforce it."[1] CHAP. XXXVII. 1768. Oct.

The inhabitants of Boston, on their part, resolved not to pay their money without their own consent,[2] and were more than ever determined to relinquish every article that came from Britain, till the obnoxious acts should be repealed and the troops removed. With no hysteric weakness, or feverish excitement, they preserved their peace and patience, leaving the event to God.

It was on the banks of the Mississippi, that uncontrolled impulses first unfurled the flag of a Republic. The treaty of Paris left two European Powers sole sovereigns of the continent of North America. Spain, accepting Louisiana with some hesitation, lost France as the bulwark of her possessions, and assumed new expenses and new dangers, with only the negative advantage of keeping the territory from England.[3] Its inhabitants were of French origin, and loved the land of their ancestry; by every law of nature and human freedom, they had the right to protest against the transfer of their allegiance. No sooner did they hear of the cession of their country to the Catholic King, than, in the spirit of independence, an Assembly sprang into being, representing every parish in the Colony; and at the instance of Lafrénière, they resolved unanimously to entreat the King of France to be touched with their affliction and their loyalty, and not to sever them from his dominions.[4]

[1] W. S. Johnson to the Governor of Connecticut, 18 Nov. 1768.

[2] Samuel Adams to Dennys De Berdt, 3 Oct. 1768.

[3] Grimaldi to Fuentes, 11 May, 1767; in Gayarré, ii. 160.

[4] Gayarré : Histoire de la Louisiane, ii. 134, 135. Louisiana as a French Colony, by the Same, iii. 127, 128.

CHAP. XXXVII. 1768. Oct.

At Paris, their envoy, John Milhet, the wealthiest merchant of New Orleans, met with a friend in Bienville, the time-honored founder of New Orleans, and assisted by the gushing tears and the memory of the early services of the venerable octogenarian, he appealed to the heart of Choiseul. "It may not be," answered Choiseul; "France cannot bear the charge of supporting the Colony's precarious existence."

On the tenth of July 1765, the austere and unamiable[1] Antonio De Ulloa, by a letter from Havana, announced to the Superior Council at New Orleans, that he had received orders to take possession of that city for the Catholic King; but the flag of France was still left flying, and continued to attract Acadian exiles. At last, on the fifth of March 1766, during a violent thunder-gust and rain,[2] Ulloa landed, with civil officers, three Capucine monks, and eighty soldiers.[3] His reception by the turbulent colonists, already allured to republicanism, was cold and gloomy. He brought no orders to redeem the seven millions livres of French paper money, which weighed down a Colony of less than six thousand white men. The French garrison of three hundred refused to enter the Spanish service; the people to give up their nationality. Ulloa could only direct a Spanish Commissary to defray the cost of Government, and was obliged to administer it in New Orleans under the French flag by the old French officers.

[1] Aubry to Lieut. Gov. Brown, 11 Nov. 1768. Aubry to the French Minister, 30 March, 1766, in Gayarré, ii. 157.

[2] Mémoire des Habitans, Gayarré, ii. 182, 216. "La pluie, le tonnerre et le vent, l'introduisirent à la Nouvelle Orléans, le cinq Mars, à Midi. Le temps le plus affreux," &c. &c.

[3] Compare letter of Choiseul to Du Chatelet, 23 May, 1768.

CHAP. XXXVII.
1768. Oct.

In May of the same year, the Spanish restrictive system was applied to Louisiana; in September, an ordinance compelled French vessels having special permits to accept the paper currency in pay for their cargoes, at an arbitrary tariff of prices. "The extension and freedom of trade," remonstrated the merchants, "far from injuring States and Colonies, are their strength and support." The ordinance was suspended; but not till the alarm had destroyed all commerce. Unable to take possession of his office, Ulloa in September retired from New Orleans, to reside at the Balise.[1] It was only there and in Missouri, opposite Natchez, and at the river Iberville, that Spanish jurisdiction was directly exercised.

This state of things continued for a little more than two years. But the arbitrary and passionate conduct of Ulloa, the depreciation of the currency with the prospect of its becoming an almost total loss, the disputes respecting the expenses of the Colony since the cession in 1762, the interruption of commerce, a captious ordinance which made a private monopoly of the traffic with the Indians, uncertainty of jurisdiction and allegiance, agitated the Colony from one end to the other.

It was proposed to make of New Orleans a republic, like Amsterdam or Venice; with a legislative body of forty men, and a single executive. The people in the country parishes met together; crowded in a mass into the city; joined those of New Orleans; and formed a numerous assembly, in which Lafré-

[1] Gage to Shelburne, 17 January, 1767. Compare Aubry to Gage, 17 June, 1767.

CHAP. XXXVII. 1768. Oct.

nière, John Milhet, Joseph Milhet, and the lawyer Doucet were conspicuous. "Why," said they, "should the two sovereigns form agreements which can have no result but our misery without advantage to either?" On the twenty-fifth of October they adopted an Address to the Superior Council, written by Lafrénière and Caresse, rehearsing their griefs, and in their Petition of Rights, they claimed freedom of commerce with the ports of France and America, and the expulsion of Ulloa from the Colony. The Address, sustained by the signatures of five or six hundred persons, was adopted the next day by the Council, in spite of the protest of Aubry; and when the French flag was displayed on the public square, children and women ran up to kiss its folds; and it was raised by nine hundred men, amidst shouts of "Long live the King of France; we will have no King but him."[1] Ulloa retreated to Havana, and sent his representations to Spain; while the inhabitants of Louisiana took up the idea of a republic, as the alternative to their renewed connection with France. They elected their own Treasurer, and syndics to represent the mass of the Colony; sent their envoys to Paris with supplicatory letters to the Duke of Orleans and the Prince of Conti; and memorialized the French Monarch to stand as intercessor between them and the Catholic King. Their hope was to be a Colony of France or a free Commonwealth.[2]

[1] Aubry to Lieut. Gov. Brown at Pensacola, 11 November, 1768. Compare Foucault to the Minister, 22 Nov. 1768, and the Paper published by Denis Braud, reprinted in Pittman's Mississippi: Appendix.

[2] Ulloa to the Spanish Minister, Dec. 1768; Aubry to O'Reilly, 20 August, 1769; Gayarré, ii. 281, 302. There is little need of looking beyond Gayarré, who rests his narrative on authentic documents.

CHAP. XXXVII. 1768. Oct.

"The success of the people of New Orleans in driving away the Spaniards," wrote Du Châtelet to Choiseul, on hearing the news, "is at least a good example for the English Colonies; may they set about following it."[1]

[1] Du Chatelet to Choiseul, 24 Feb. 1769.

CHAPTER XXXVIII.

THE KING AND THE BRITISH PARLIAMENT AGAINST THE TOWN OF BOSTON.—HILLSBOROUGH'S ADMINISTRATION OF THE COLONIES CONTINUED.

OCTOBER—DECEMBER, 1768.

CHAP. XXXVIII. 1768. Oct.

SPAIN valued Louisiana as a screen for Mexico; and England, in her turn, held the valley of the Mississippi from jealousy of France, not to colonize it. To the great joy of Spain,[1] and in conformity to a policy,[2] against which the advice[3] of Shelburne could not prevail, every idea of settling the country was opposed; and every post between Mobile and Fort Chartres was abandoned; John Finley, a backwoodsman of North Carolina, who this year passed through Kentucky,[4] found not one white man's cabin in all the enchanting wilderness. Gage would have even given up Fort Chartres, and as a consequence the intermediate Pittsburg.[5]

It was Hillsborough's purpose to prevent coloni-

[1] D'Ossun, French Ambassador at Madrid, to Choiseul, 6 Dec. 1768.

[2] Compare the elaborate Narrative of Lord Barrington, Secretary of War, of May, 1766.

[3] Shelburne to Gage, 14 Nov 1767.

[4] James T. Morehead's Address, &c. &c. 15, 16.

[5] Gage to Hillsborough, 16 June, 1768.

zation,[1] and to hold the territory through the friendship of the savages. But this design was obstructed by the actual settlements in Illinois and on the Wabash; the roving disposition of the Americans; and the avarice of British officers who coveted profit from concessions of lands. In this conflict of interests, the office of the Colonial Secretary was swayed by wavering opinions,[2] producing only inconclusive correspondence, references, and reports on the questions, how to regulate trade with the Indians; how to "reform" the excess in expenses; how to keep off settlers; how to restrain the cupidity of British Governors and agents.

The Spanish town of Saint Louis, on the west of the Mississippi, was fast rising into importance,[3] as the centre of the fur trade with the Indian nations on the Missouri; but the population of Illinois had declined, and scarcely amounted to more than one thousand three hundred and fifty-eight, of whom rather more than three hundred were Africans. Kaskaskias counted six hundred white persons, and three hundred and three negroes. At Kahokia there were about three hundred persons; at Prairie Du Rocher, one hundred and twenty-five; at St. Philip fifteen; and not more at Fort Chartres,[4] which the floods of Spring

[1] Representation of the Board of Trade, 7 March, 1768. A copy is among the Broadhead Papers, vol. xli. Hillsborough to Gage, 14 March, 1768. W. S. Johnson to Gov. Pitkin, 12 March, 1768.

[2] W. S. Johnson to Gov. Pitkin, 12 Feb. 1767; Same to Same, 13 Nov. 1767. Same to E. Dyer, 12 Sept. 1767. Compare the Papers of the Board of Trade when Clare was its President, with those of Hillsborough. Compare also the Correspondence of Shelburne with that of Hillsborough.

[3] Ensign Hutchins' Remarks on the Illinois Country, MS. Pittman's Mississippi, 49.

[4] State of the Settlements in the Illinois Country; in Gage to Hillsborough, 6 Jan. 1769.

CHAP. XXXVIII 1768. Oct. were threatening to wear away.[1] To Hillsborough's great alarm,[2] the adult men had been formed into military companies.[3] Vincennes, the only settlement in Indiana, claimed to be within a year as old as Detroit,[4] and had rapidly and surprisingly increased.[5] Its own population, consisting of two hundred and thirty-two white persons, ten negro and seventeen Indian slaves, was recruited by one hundred and sixty-eight "strangers."[6] Detroit had now about six hundred souls.[7] All the western villages abounded in wheat, Indian corn, and swine; of beeves there was more than one to each human being; and more than one horse to every two, counting slaves and children.

The course of the rivers inclined the French inhabitants of the West, in disregard of the British Navigation Acts, to send their furs to New Orleans;[8] or across the river by night to St. Louis where they could be exchanged for French goods. All English merchandise came burdened with the cost of land carriage from Philadelphia to Fort Pitt.[9] The British Navigation Acts spread their baleful influence over the western Prairies. In November, Wilkins, the new Commandant in Illinois, following suggestions from Gage, appointed seven civil Judges to decide local con-

[1] Gage to Hillsborough, 16 June, 1768.

[2] Hillsborough to Gage, 12 Oct. 1768, and Gage to Hillsborough, 5 March, 1769.

[3] Gage to Hillsborough, 17 August, 1768.

[4] Remonstrances to General Gage from the old French Inhabitants.

[5] Gage to Hillsborough, 6 January, 1769.

[6] State of the Settlement at St. Vincent on the Ouabache; sent to England by Gage, 6 Jan. 1769; the account, like that of Illinois, was taken in 1768.

[7] See Papers in Gage to Hillsborough, 15 May, 1768.

[8] Captain Forbes to Gen. Gage, Fort Chartres, 15 April, 1768.

[9] Information of the State of Commerce in the Illinois Country, given by Captain Forbes.

troversies;[1] yet without abdicating his own overruling authority.[2] This plan which could be but temporary, led the people under his rule themselves to reflect on the best forms of Government.

But Wilkins was chiefly intent on enriching some Philadelphia fur traders, who were notorious for their willingness to bribe;[3] he reported favorably of their zeal for British commerce,[4] and, in less than a year after his arrival, executed at their request inchoate grants of large tracts of land, of which one sixth part was reserved for himself.

The procedure contravened the explicit orders of Hillsborough, who wished to diminish, and, if possible, to extirpate the Western Settlements, and extend an unbroken line of Indian frontier from Georgia to Canada, as an impassable barrier to emigration. Repeated instructions[5] had been issued for the completion of this boundary; and they were imperatively renewed.[6] At the South, Stuart, who desired to fulfil his trust with fidelity, had already carried the line to the northern limit of North Carolina, and was now to continue it from Chiswell's mine to the mouth of the Kanawha. In this manner all Kentucky, as well as the entire Territory North West of the Ohio, would

[1] Peck's Gazetteer of Illinois, 107. Brown's History of Illinois, 213. Monette's Mississippi Valley, i. 411.

[2] Pittman's Present State of the European Settlements on the Mississippi, &c. 43.

[3] Compare Messrs. Baynton, Wharton, and Morgan, to L. Macleane, Esq., Philadelphia, 9 January, 1767. In Lansdowne House Papers.

[4] Lieut. Col. Wilkins to General Gage, Fort Chartres, 13 September 1768.

[5] See the Record in American State Papers, Class viii. Public Lands, ii. 208.

[6] Circular of 13 Sept. 1766; Shelburne to Stuart, 13 Sept. 1766. Same to Same, 11 Dec. 1766, &c. &c. Compare Shelburne to Gage, 14 Nov. 1767; Board to Shelburne, 23 Dec. 1767; Shelburne to Sir William Johnson, 5 Jan. 1768.

CHAP. XXXVIII. be severed from the jurisdiction of Virginia and confirmed to the savages by solemn treaties.

1768. Oct. This purpose was strenuously opposed by the Province which was to be curtailed. From its ancient Charter, the discoveries of its people, the authorized grants of its Governors since 1746, the encouragement of its Legislature to settlers in 1752 and 1753, the promise of lands as Bounty to officers and soldiers who served in the French war, the continued emigration of its inhabitants,—the Ancient Dominion derived its title to occupy the Great West. Carolina stopped at the line of 36° 30′; on the North, New-York could at most extend to Lake Erie; Maryland and Pennsylvania were each limited by definitive boundaries. None but Virginia claimed the valley of the Ohio.

But in spite of her objections[1] Stuart was not only ordered to complete the demarkation with the Indians, but he was expressly enjoined not to accept any new cession of territory from the Cherokees.[2]

The honest Agent, without regarding the discontent of Virginia, which, though notified,[3] declined co-operating with him, met the Chiefs of the Upper and Lower Cherokees in Council at Hard Labor in Western South Carolina; and on the fourteenth of October, concluded a treaty conforming to the instructions

[1] Fauquier to Shelburne, 2 Feb. 1767; Shelburne to Gage, 14 Nov. 1767; Hillsborough to the Board of Trade, 17 May, 1768; Representation of the Board of Trade, 10 June, 1768, &c.

[2] Hillsborough to Stuart, 15 September, 1768.

[3] Stuart to Blair, President of the Virginia Council, 4 April, 1768. Same to Same, 7 July, 1768, and again, Same to Same, 19 August, 1768.

of the Board of Trade.[1] The Cherokees ratified all their former grants of lands, and established as the western boundary of Virginia, a straight line drawn from Chiswell's mine, on the Eastern Bank of the Great Kanawha, in a northerly course to the confluence of that river with the Ohio.[2]

To thwart the negotiation of Stuart, Virginia had appointed Thomas Walker its Commissioner to the Congress held at Fort Stanwix with the Six Nations. Sir William Johnson, who, as the Indian Agent for the Northern District, had the management of the business, was thoroughly versed in the methods of making profit by his office. William Franklin of New Jersey was present also, ready to assist in obtaining the largest cessions of lands, which might become the foundation for new provincial grants. The number[3] of Indians present was but little short of three thousand. Every art was used to conciliate the chiefs of the Six Nations; and gifts were lavished on them with unusual generosity. They, in turn, complied with the solicitations of the several agents. The line that was established began at the North, where Canada Creek joins Wood Creek;[4] on leaving New-York, it passed from the nearest fork of the West Branch of the Susquehannah to Kittaning on the Alleghany, whence it followed that river and the Ohio. At the mouth of the Kanawha, it met the line

Nov.

[1] John Stuart to Mr. President Blair; Hard Labor, 17 Oct. 1768.

[2] Treaty of 14 Oct. 1768, at Hard Labor, with the chiefs of the Upper and Lower Cherokees. Stuart to Mr. President Blair, Hard Labor, 17 Oct. 1768. Letter from Charles Town, 23 January, 1769.

[3] William Franklin to Hillsborough, 17 Dec. 1768.

[4] Johnson to Hillsborough, 23 Oct. and 18 Nov. 1768.

CHAP. XXXVIII 1768. Nov. of Stuart's treaty. Had it stopped there, the Indian frontier would have been marked all the way from northern New-York to Florida. But instead of following his instructions, Sir William Johnson, pretending to recognise a right of the Six Nations to the largest part of Kentucky, continued the line down the Ohio to the Tennessee River, which was thus constituted the western boundary of Virginia.[1]

While the Congress of Fort Stanwix was in session, Botetourt, the new Governor of Virginia, arrived on the James River, just in the delicious season of the Fall of the Leaf, when that region enjoys a clear but many-tinted sky, and a soft but invigorating air. Bringing a love of rural life, he was charmed with the scenes on which he entered; his house seemed admirable; the grounds around it, well planted and watered by beautiful rills. Every thing was just as he could have wished.[2] Hospitality is the hereditary common law of Virginia; the new Governor, who came up without state to an unprovided residence, was asked abroad every day; and being welcomed as a guest, gave pleasure and was pleased. He thought nothing could be better than the present disposition of the Colony; and he augured well of every thing that was to happen. Received with frankness, he dealt frankly with the people to whom he was deputed. He did not flatter Hillsborough that they would ever willingly submit to being taxed by the mother country; the reverse he

[1] Treaty at Fort Stanwix, 5 Nov. 1768; in the Appendix to Butler's History of Kentucky; and in the Documentary History of New-York, i. 587; I have a manuscript copy.

[2] Botetourt to Hillsborough, 1 Nov. 1769.

said, was their creed; but he justified them by reporting the universal avowal of a most ardent desire to assist upon every occasion, if they might do it as formerly in consequence of requisition.[1] Yet the laws were obeyed, and the duties complained of were collected in every part of the Colony, without a shadow of resistance. He was persuaded that the new Assembly would come together in good humor,[2] which he was resolved not wantonly to disturb. His letters to the Ministry, written with candor, required no concealment.

The Western Boundary was the engrossing subject, which invited the immediate attention of the new Governor. Botetourt entered heartily into the wishes of Virginia, and exerted all his influence, and even put in pledge his life and fortune,[3] to carry its jurisdiction to the Tennessee River on the parallel of thirty-six and a half degrees. "This boundary," it was said, "will give some room to extend our settlements for ten or twelve years."[4]

Nov.

While Virginia was engaged in stretching its dominion over the West, England began to think reconciliation with Massachusetts hopeless, and to prepare for desolating war.[5] Such was the public temper, when news arrived that the troops had landed at Boston without opposition, that the Convention had dissolved, and that all thoughts of resistance were at an end. A very few perceived, that the power of moderation which the people of Boston had dis-

[1] Botetourt to Hillsborough, 17 Feb. 1769.

[2] Botetourt to Hillsborough, 30 March, 1769.

[3] Compare Botetourt to Hillsborough, 24 December, 1768.

[4] Letter from Andrew Lewis and Thomas Walker to Lord Botetourt, inclosed in Lord Botetourt to Hillsborough, 11 Feb. 1769.

[5] W. S. Johnson to Gov. of Connecticut, 18 Nov. 1768.

CHAP. XXXVIII 1768. Nov.

played, was like the fortitude of veteran troops, who wait unmoved by danger, till the word is given. "They act with highest wisdom and spirit," said Thomas Hollis;[1] "they will extricate themselves with firmness and magnanimity." But most men expressed contempt for them, as having made a vain bluster. The apparent success, of which the account reached London just four days before the meeting of Parliament, was regarded as a victory. Americans in London were told with a sneer that they should soon have the company of Otis and others.[2] No one doubted but that, on the arrival of the additional regiments sent from Ireland, he and Cushing, and sixteen other members of the late political assemblies, would be arrested.[3] Hillsborough hastened to send Bernard's dispatches to the Attorney and Solicitor General, asking what crimes had been committed, and if the guilty were to be impeached by Parliament.[4]

The King, in his Speech[5] on the eighth of November, railed at "the spirit of faction breaking out afresh in some of the Colonies." "Boston," said he, "appears to be in a state of disobedience to all law and government, and has proceeded to measures subversive of the constitution, and attended with circumstances that might manifest a disposition to throw off its dependence on Great Britain. With your concurrence and support, I shall be able to defeat the mischievous designs of those turbulent and seditious per

[1] T. Hollis to A. Eliot.

[2] Letter from London, 20 Nov. 1768; in Boston Gazette, 721, 3, 3, of 23 Jan. 1769.

[3] Francès to Choiseul, 4 Nov. 1768.

[4] Hillsborough to the Attorney and Solicitor General, 6 Nov 1768.

[5] Parliamentary History, xvi. 469.

sons, who, under false pretences, have but too successfully deluded numbers of my subjects in America."

In the House of Commons Lord Henly,[1] son of Northington, in moving the Address, signalized the people of Boston for their "defiance of all legal authority."

"I gave my vote to the revenue Act of Charles Townshend," thus he was seconded by Hans Stanley, "that we might test the obedience of the Americans to the Declaratory Law of 1766. Troops have been drawn together in America to enforce it, and have commenced the operation in Boston. Men so unsusceptible of all middle terms of accommodation, call loudly for our correction. What, Sir, will become of this insolent town when we deprive its inhabitants of the power of sending out their rums and molasses to the coast of Africa? For they must be treated like aliens, as they have treated us upon this occasion. The difficulties in governing Massachusetts are insurmountable, unless its Charter and laws shall be so changed as to give to the King the appointment of the Council, and to the Sheriffs the sole power of returning juries." Samuel Adams at Boston, weighed well the meaning of these words,[2] uttered by an organ of the Ministry; but England hardly noticed the presumptuous menace of a violation of chartered rights and the subversion of the independence of juries.

Edmund Burke poured out a torrent of invective against Camden, for the inconsistency of his former

[1] Arthur Lee in Life of R. H. Lee, 261, 262. The Letter is dated erroneously, Oct. 9, for Nov. 9, 1768. I have several reports of this debate. Cavendish, i. 32, &c. William S. Johnson to Gov. Pitkin, 18 November, 1768.

[2] Papers of Samuel Adams.

CHAP. XXXVIII 1768. Nov. opposition to the Declaratory Act with his present support of the plan of the Ministry. "My astonishment at the folly of his opinions," he said, "is lost in indignation at the baseness of his conduct."[1] The order, he insisted, requiring the Massachusetts Assembly to rescind a vote under a penalty, was absolutely illegal and unconstitutional; and in this Grenville agreed with him. "I wish the Stamp Act had never been passed," said Barrington in reply; "but the Americans are traitors; worse than traitors against the Crown; they are traitors against the Legislature. The troops are to bring rioters to justice." Wedderburne, who at that moment belonged to himself and spoke in opposition to enhance his price, declaimed against governing by files of musketeers and terror; and he, too, condemned the Ministerial mandate as illegal.[2] "Though it were considered wiser," said Rigby, "to alter the American tax, than to continue it, I would not alter it, so long as the Colony of the Massachusetts Bay continues in its present state." "Let the nation return to its old good nature and its old good humor," were the words of Alderman Beckford,[3] whom nobody minded, and who spoke more wisely than they all; "it were best to repeal the late act, and conciliate the Colonies by moderation and kindness."

Lord North, the recognised leader of the Ministry and the Friend of the King, made reply: "America must fear you, before she can love you. If America

[1] From the Report of Edmund Burke's Speech, of 8 November, 1768; in the Boston Gazette of 23 January, 1769; 721, 3, 2 and 3.

[2] Arthur Lee's Report of the Debate, in Appendix to Life of R. H. Lee, 262. W. S. Johnson to W. Pitkin, 18 Nov. 1768; and W. S. Johnson's Diary, for 8 Nov. 1768, Cavendish Debates.

[3] W. S Johnson to Pitkin, 15 Nov. 1768.

is to be the judge, you may tax in no instance; you may regulate in no instance. Punishment will not be extended beyond the really guilty; and if rewards shall be found necessary, rewards shall be given. But what we do, we will do firmly; we shall go through our plan, now that we have brought it so near success.[1] I am against repealing the last Act of Parliament, securing to us a revenue out of America; I will never think of repealing it, until I see America prostrate at my feet."[2] The irrevocable words spoke the feeling of Parliament. The Address was carried in the Commons without a division; the Peers seemed unanimous; and though some judged the conduct of the Ministry unwise, there were scarcely more than five or six in both Houses, who defended the Americans from principle. Every body expected "that Boston would meet with chastisement."

But now came the difficulty. There were on the tenth of November more than four regiments in Boston; what could be given them to do? They had been sent over to bring "to justice" those, whom Barrington called "rioters," whom the King had solemnly described as "turbulent and mischievous persons." But after long consideration, De Grey and Dunning, the Attorney and Solicitor General, joined in the opinion,[3] that the Statute of the Thirty-fifth of Henry the Eighth, was the only one by which criminals could be tried in England for offences committed

Cavendish, i. 43.

[2] These words are in W. S. Johnson's Report, and are in the Report in the Boston Gazette. That he, Johnson, reported them correctly, appears from Barre in Cavendish, i. 90, and Lord North himself in Cavendish i. 91.

[3] Attorney and Solicitor Gen. to Hillsborough, 25 Nov. 1768.

CHAP. XXXVIII 1768. Nov. in America; that its provisions extended only to treasons; and that there was no sufficient ground to fix the charge of high treason upon any persons named in the papers laid before them. The law in England was more humane and just than the Colonial Office. The troops found no rebellion at Boston; could they make one? They found a town of which the merchants refused to import goods of British manufacture, or to buy tea brought by way of Great Britain. How could armed men change this disposition? Massachusetts would not even pay for their quarters, because they had not been quartered according to law; so that they were left to make a useless parade up and down the streets of Boston at the cost of the British Exchequer; sharpening the sullen discontent of the townsmen. The employment of soldiery failed from the beginning. "No force on earth," wrote the Governor of New Jersey, "is sufficient to make the Assemblies acknowledge, by any act of theirs, that the Parliament has a right to impose taxes on America."[1]

Each American Assembly, as it came together, denied that right, and embodied its denial in Petitions to the King. Yet the Ministry were pledged to enforce the absolute supremacy of the British Legislature; the King, therefore, instead of hearing the Petitions, disapproved and rejected them; Virginia was soothingly reprimanded; Pennsylvania, whose loyalty had but a fortnight before been confidently extolled by Hillsborough, Rhode Island, whose reverence for the laws he had officially set

[1] W. Franklin to Hillsborough, 23 November, 1768.

forth, Connecticut, which had combined loyalty with love of its liberties, Maryland, which acted strictly in conformity to law in refusing to be overawed by a Secretary's letter,[1] received, as their answer, copies of the Addresses of the two Houses of Parliament, and assurances that the King would not listen to "the views of wicked men," who questioned the supreme authority of that body.

While Hillsborough was setting his name to these papers, Montagu, the Governor of South Carolina,[2] invited its Assembly to treat the letters of Massachusetts and Virginia "with the contempt they deserved;" a committee, composed of Parsons, Gadsden, Pinkney, Lloyd, Lynch, Laurens, Rutledge, Elliott and Dart, reported them to be "founded upon undeniable, constitutional principles;"[3] and the House, sitting with its doors locked, unanimously directed its Speaker to signify to both Provinces its entire approbation.[4] Provoked at what he had had no means to prevent, the Governor, that same evening, dissolved the Assembly by beat of drum; while the general toast at Charleston remained, "The UNANIMOUS TWENTY-SIX, who would not rescind from the Massachusetts Circular." The Assembly of New-York was also in session, fully resolved to follow and to go beyond the common example;[5] and Hillsborough, who expressed his confi-

[1] Hillsborough to the Governor of New-York, to Botetourt of Virginia, to W. Franklin of New Jersey, to Deputy Gov. of Pennsylvania, to Governor of Connecticut, to Governor of Rhode Island, to Governor of Maryland, 15 November, 1768.

[2] Lord Charles Montagu to the Secretary of State, 21 Nov. 1768.

[3] Boston Gazette, 2 Jan. 1769; 718, 2, 2.

[4] Letter of P. Manigault, Speaker, to Massachusetts Speaker, 21 Nov. 1768. In Boston Gazette, 9 Jan. 1769, 719, 3, 2.

[5] W. Franklin to Hillsborough, 23 Nov. 1768.

CHAP. XXXVIII. 1768. Nov.

dence that his letters and the King's firmness would "bring back the misled colonists to a just sense of their duty,"[1] only opened the way to a new complaint, that the King would not even receive from the Colonies their Petitions.

Meantime as the refusal of America to draw supplies from England, was an invitation to other Powers[2] to devise the means of sharing her commerce, the three[3] Secretaries of State were called upon to issue orders to the ministers, consuls, and agents of the British Government in the ports of Europe, Madeira and the Azores, to watch the coming in of an American ship, or the sailing of any ship for the continent of America. The Navigation Acts of which the total repeal would only have increased the trade of the Colonies with their mother country, reduced England to playing the humble and helpless part of a spy in the harbors of independent nations;[4] while the maritime powers of Europe were eagerly watching the progress of the contest, and speculating on its conclusion.

"Can the Ministry reduce the Colonies?" asked Du Chatelet? "Of what avail is an army in so vast a country? The Americans have made these reflections, and they will not give way."[5]

"To the menace of rigor" replied Choiseul, "they will never give way, except in appearance and for a time. The fire will be but imperfectly extinguished,

[1] Hillsborough to Gage, 15 Nov. 1768.

[2] Commissioners of the Customs in America, to Lords of the Treasury, 15 Sept. 1768.

[3] Treasury Minutes, Whitehall, Treasury Chambers, 7 Nov. 1768.

[4] Treasury Minutes, 15 December, 1768. Minute Book, xxxix, 268.

[5] Du Chatelet to Choiseul, No. 4, 11 November, 1768.

CHAP. XXXVIII 1768. Nov.

unless other means than those of force conciliate the interests of the Metropolis and its Colonies. The Americans will not lose out of their view their rights and their privileges; and next to fanaticism for religion, the fanaticism for liberty is the most daring in its measures and the most dangerous in its consequences."[1]

It was obvious that the simplest mode of taking part with the colonists would be by a commerce between the French and Spanish Colonies and the British Colonies on the continent of North America; and on this subject Choiseul sent to Du Chatelet[2] an elaborate digest of all the materials he had collected. But the simple-hearted King of Spain, though he enjoyed the perplexity of England, "because it created embarrassments to the natural enemy[3] of the two Crowns, and secured to France and Spain more time to prepare for contingent events," showed no disposition to interfere.

"What a pity," resumed Du Chatelet to Choiseul, "that neither Spain nor France is in a condition to take advantage of so critical a conjuncture; and that we must regard it as a passive benefit. The moment is not yet come; and precipitate measures on our part might reconcile the Colonies to the metropolis. But if the quarrel goes on as far as it seems likely to do, a thousand opportunities cannot fail to offer of which decisive advantage may be taken. The objects presented to you, to the King, and to his Council, demand the most profound combinations, the most

[1] Choiseul to Du Chatelet, 22 Nov. 1768.

[2] Du Chatelet to Choiseul, 18 Nov. 1768.

[3] D'Ossun to Choiseul at the Escurial, 21 November, 1768.

CHAP. XXXVIII. 1768. Nov. inviolable secrecy. A plan which shall be applicable to every circumstance of change, should be concerted in advance with Spain."[1]

At the same time Du Chatelet gave the utmost attention to the subject of intercolonial commerce; and succeeded in obtaining the opinions of all the American Agents, particularly of Franklin. And Franklin, whom he described as "one of the most upright and enlightened men that ever came from that part of the world, one of the wisest and most sagacious that could be found in any country," agreed in the exact correctness of the memoir which had been prepared under the eye of Choiseul.[2]

Dec. The Agents had repeatedly but separately waited on Lord Hillsborough. On the sixth of December, he met them in a body, to communicate the result of a Cabinet Council. "Administration," said he, "will enforce the authority of the Legislature of Great Britain over the Colonies in the most effectual manner, but with moderation and lenity.[3] All the Petitions we have received are very offensive, for they contain a denial of the authority of Parliament. We have no fondness for the acts complained of; particularly, the late Duty Act is so anti-commercial, that I wish it had never existed; and it would certainly have been repealed, had the Colonies said nothing about it, or petitioned against it only on the ground of its expediency; but the principle you proceed upon extends to all laws; and we cannot, therefore, think of repealing it at least this session of Parlia-

[1] Du Chatelet to the Duke de Choiseul, 18 Nov. 1768.

[2] Du Chatelet to Choiseul, 18 Nov. 1768. Compare Franklin's Writings, vii. 357.

[3] W. S. Johnson to the Governor of Connecticut, 3 January, 1769.

ment, or until the Colonies shall have dropped the point of right. Nor can the conduct of the people of Boston pass without a severe censure." A very long discussion ensued; but he was inflexible.

CHAP. XXXVIII 1768. Dec.

It became evident that the attention of Parliament was to be confined to the Colony of the Massachusetts Bay; for the Memorial and the Remonstrance from Virginia were kept back; and a Petition from the Assembly of Pennsylvania to the House of Commons was put aside. The next day Beckford[2] and Trecothick, as friends to America, demanded rather such general inquiry, as might lead to measures of relief.

"The question of taxation is not before us;" interposed Lord North; "but the question is, whether we are to lay a tax one year, when America is at peace, and take it off the next, when America is in arms against us. I am against the repeal of the Act; it would spread an alarm, as if we did it from fear. The extraordinary appearance this would have in America, the encouragement it would give our enemies and the discouragement it would give our friends, the impossibility of acting with authority, if our authority should receive another wound,—all bind us not to take that question into consideration again." He, therefore, demanded the expression of the united opinion of Great Britain, so that Boston might be awed into obedience.

"The Americans believe," rejoined Beckford, "that there is a settled design in this country to rule them

[1] See Account of the Day in Garth to Committee of South Carolina, 10 Dec. 1768. Also in W. S. Johnson to Gov. of Connecticut, 3 Jan. 1769, and in Cavendish Debates.

CHAP. XXXVIII 1768. Dec. with a military force." "I never wish for dominion, unless accompanied by the affection of the people governed;" said Lord John Cavendish. "Want of knowledge, as well as want of temper," said Lord Beauchamp, "has gradually led us to the brink of a precipice, on which we look down with horror."—Phipps, a captain in the army, added, "My heart will bleed for every drop of American blood that shall be shed, whilst their grievances are unredressed. I wish to see the Americans in our arms as friends—not to meet them as enemies." "Dare you not trust yourselves with a general inquiry?" asked Grenville. "How do we know, parliamentarily, that Boston is the most guilty of the Colonies?" "I would have the Americans obey the laws of the country whether they like them or no;" said Lord Barrington.

The house divided, and out of two hundred who were present, one hundred and twenty-seven voted with the Government to confine the inquiry. The King set himself, and his Ministry, and Parliament, and all Great Britain, to subdue to his will one stubborn little town on the sterile coast of the Massachusetts Bay. The odds against it were fearful; but it showed a life inextinguishable, and had been chosen to keep guard over the liberties of mankind.

The old world had not its parallel. It counted about sixteen thousand inhabitants of European origin, all of whom learned to read and write. Good public schools were the foundation of its political system; and Benjamin Franklin, one of their pupils, in his youth apprenticed to the art which makes knowledge the common property of mankind, had gone forth from them to stand before the nations as the representative of the modern plebeian class.

CHAP. XXXVIII 1768. Dec.

As its schools were for all its children, so the great body of its male inhabitants of twenty-one years of age, when assembled in a Hall which Faneuil, of Huguenot ancestry, had built for them, was the source of all municipal authority. In the Meeting of the Town, its taxes were voted, its affairs discussed and settled; its agents and public servants annually elected by ballot; and abstract political principles freely debated. A small property qualification was attached to the right of suffrage, but did not exclude enough to change the character of the institution. There had never existed a considerable municipality, approaching so nearly to a pure democracy; and, for so populous a place, it was undoubtedly the most orderly and best governed in the world.

Its ecclesiastical polity was in like manner republican. The great mass were congregationalists; each church was an assembly formed by voluntary agreement; self-constituted, self-supported and independent. They were clear that no person or church had power over another church. There was not a Roman Catholic altar in the place; the usages of "papists" were looked upon as worn-out superstitions, fit only for the ignorant. But the people were not merely the fiercest enemies of "popery and slavery;" they were Protestants even against Protestantism; and though the English church was tolerated, Boston kept up its exasperation against prelacy. Its Ministers were still its prophets and its guides; its pulpit, in which, now that Mayhew was no more, Cooper was admired above all others for eloquence and patriotism, by weekly appeals inflamed alike the fervor of piety and of liberty. In the Boston Gazette, it enjoyed a free Press, which gave cur-

CHAP. XXXVIII. rency to its conclusions on the natural right of man to self-government.

1768. Dec. Its citizens were inquisitive; seeking to know the causes of things, and to search for the reason of existing institutions in the laws of nature. Yet they controlled their speculative turn by practical judgment; exhibiting the seeming contradiction of susceptibility to enthusiasm, and calculating shrewdness. They were fond of gain, and adventurous, penetrating and keen in their pursuit of it; yet their avidity was tempered by a well-considered and continuing liberality. Nearly every man was struggling to make his own way in the world and his own fortune; and yet individually and as a body they were public-spirited. In the seventeenth century the community had been distracted by those who were thought to pursue the great truth of justification by faith to Antinomian absurdities; the philosophy of the eighteenth century had not been without an influence on theological opinion; and though the larger number still acknowledged the fixedness of the divine decrees, and the resistless certainty from all eternity of election and of reprobation, there were not wanting, even among the clergy, some who had modified the sternness of the ancient doctrine by making the self-direction of the active powers of man with freedom of inquiry and private judgment the central idea of a protest against Calvinism. Still more were they boldly speculative on questions respecting their constitution. Every house was a school of politics; every man was a little statesman, discussed the affairs of the world, studied more or less the laws of his own land, and was sure of his ability to ascertain and to make good his rights. The ministers, whose prayers, being from no book, were colored with the hue of the times; the merchants, cramped in their enterprise by legal restrictions; the mechanics, who, by their skill in ship-building bore away the palm from all other nations, and by their numbers were the rulers of the town; all alike, clergy and laity, in the pulpit or closet, on the wharf or in the counting-room, at their ship-yards or in their social gatherings, reasoned upon government. They had not acquired estates by a feudal tenure, nor had lived under feudal institutions; and as the true descendants of the Puritans of England, they had not much more of superstitious veneration for monarchy than for priestcraft. Such was their power of analysis, that they almost unconsciously developed the theory of an independent representative commonwealth; and such their instinctive capacity for organization, that they had actually seen a Convention of the people of the Province start into life at their bidding. While the earth was still wrapt in gloom, they welcomed the daybreak of popular freedom, and like the young eagle in his upward soarings, looked undazzled into the beams of the morning.

CHAPTER XXXIX.

A WAY TO TAKE OFF THE INCENDIARIES.—HILLSBOROUGH'S ADMINISTRATION OF THE COLONIES CONTINUED.

DECEMBER, 1768—FEBRUARY, 1769.

CHAP. XXXIX. 1768. Dec.

THE opinion of Parliament was hardly pronounced, when Du Chatelet again pressed America on the attention of Choiseul. "Without exaggerating the projects or the union of the Colonies," said he, "the time of their independence is very near. Their prudent men believe the moment not yet come; but if the English government undertakes vigorous measures, who can tell how far the fanaticism for liberty may carry an immense people, dwelling for the most part in the interior of a continent, remote from imminent danger? And if the metropolis should persevere, can the union, which is now their strength, be maintained without succor from abroad? Even if the rupture should be premature, can France and Spain neglect to profit by the opportunity which they may never find again?

"Three years ago the separation of the English Colonies was looked upon as an object of attention for the next generation; the germs were observed, but no one could foresee that they would be so speedily developed. This new order of things, this

CHAP. XXXIX. 1768. Dec.

event which will necessarily have the greatest influence on the whole political system of Europe, will probably be brought about within a very few years."[1]

"Your views," replied Choiseul, are as subtle as they are comprehensive and well considered. The King is perfectly aware of their sagacity and solidity; and I will communicate them to the Court of Madrid."[2]

The statesmen of France had their best allies in the British Ministry, who hoped to control America by menace and terror. "The matter is now brought to a point;" said Hillsborough in the House of Lords.[3] "Parliament must give up its authority over the Colonies, or bring them to effectual submission. Your Lordships will see it absolutely necessary not to recede an ace; for my part, I cannot entertain a thought of repealing the late Acts, and hope nobody will even move it, or so much as wish for it. Not the amount of the duties, which will not be more than ten thousand pounds per annum in all North America, but the principle upon which the laws are founded, is complained of. Legislation and taxation will stand or fall together. The notion of the Americans is a polytheism in politics, absurd, fatal to the constitution, and never to be admitted. The North Americans, in general, are a very good set of people, and only misled by a few wicked, factious and designing men. I will, therefore, for the present only pro-

[1] Du Chatelet to Choiseul, 9 November, 1768.

[2] Choiseul to Du Chatelet, 20 December, 1768.

[3] Parliamentary History, xvi. 476, 477, Note. W. S. Johnson to the Governor of Connecticut, 3 Jan. 1769. Compare Du Chatelet to Choiseul, 16 Dec. 1768.

CHAP. XXXIX. 1768. Dec. pose several Resolutions which may show the sense of the Legislature. If this is not sufficient, the hand of power must be lifted up, and the whole force of this country exerted to bring the Colonies into subjection." The Resolutions condemned the Assembly of Massachusetts, its Council, and still more its Convention; approved of sending a military force to Boston; and foreshadowed the abrogation of the municipal liberties of that town, and the intended change in the Charter of the Province.

Hillsborough was seconded by Bedford, who also moved an Address to the King,[1] to bring to "condign punishment the chief authors and instigators of the late disorders;" and if sufficient ground should be seen, to put them on trial for "treason" before a special Commission in England, "pursuant to the provisions of the statute of the Thirty-fifth year of King Henry the Eighth." The Resolutions and Address were readily adopted, with no opposition except from Richmond and Shelburne.

The policy of the Administration deceived neither France nor America. "Under the semblance of vigor," said Choiseul, "it covers pusillanimity and fear. If those who are threatened with a trial for High Treason, are not alarmed, the terror and discouragement will affect nobody but the British Ministers. And after all, the main question of taxing the Colonies is as far from a solution as ever."[2]

At Boston the attempt was made to spread terror by threats of seizing the popular leaders. "They expect a voyage to England against their inclina-

[1] Parliamentary Hist. xvi. 479, 480.

[2] Choiseul to Du Chatelet, Versailles, 24 Dec. 1768.

tion;" wrote Hood,[1] who had the chief command of the ships in the harbor. But Samuel Adams, whom it was especially desired to "take off" for treason, "unawed by the menaces of arbitrary power,"[2] pursued his system without fear or faltering. "I must," said he,[2] "tell the men, who on both sides of the Atlantic charge America with rebellion, that military power will never prevail on an American to surrender his liberty;" and through the press he taught the public that a standing army,[3] kept up in the Colonies in time of peace without their consent, was as flagrant a violation of the Constitution as the laying a tax on paper, glass, painters' colors and tea. To effect the removal of the troops from Boston was his unremitting care. In the mean time he sought in the common law the means to curb their insolence; and called upon the magistrates of Boston to govern, restrain, and punish "soldiers of all ranks," according to the laws of the land.[4] The Justices of the Peace for Suffolk at their Quarter Sessions, and the Grand Jury, over which the Crown had no control, never failed to find indictments against soldiers and officers, for their frequent transgressions;[5] and if they escaped the penalties of conviction, it was through the favoritism of a higher Court.

Every where the British claims of power were denied. Georgia approved the conduct and correspondence of Massachusetts and Virginia.[6] New-York completed the expression of American opinion, by

[1] Hood to Stephens, 12 Dec. 1768. In Letters to the Ministry, 113.

[2] Boston Gazette, 5 Dec. 1768.

[3] Vindex, in Boston Gazette, 19 Dec. 1768.

[4] Vindex, Samuel Adams, in Boston Gazette, 12 Dec. 1768.

[5] See the many indictments of officers as well as of soldiers.

[6] Boston Gazette of 13 Feb. 1769; 734, 1, 1.

CHAP. XXXIX. 1769. Jan.

unanimously asserting its legislative rights[1] with unsurpassed distinctness,[2] and appointing an intercolonial committee of correspondence.[3]

The New Year brought a dissolution[4] of its Assembly; and in the new elections, the Government party employed every art to create confusion. It excused the violence of recent disputes; concealing the extremes of difference between the British Parliament and the American people. It sought to gratify the cravings of every interest. It evaded conflicts with the merchants, and connived at importations from Saint Eustatia and Holland. The family of the Delanceys, which had long seemingly led the Opposition in the Province, was secretly won over to the side of authority. One of the Livingstons could no longer sit in the Assembly, for a law made the office of Judge and Representative incompatible; another who was to be returned from the Manor, was held to be ineligible because he resided in the city. The men of business desired an increase of the paper currency, and the Government gave support to the measure. The tenantry wished to vote not by word of mouth on the nomination of their landlords, but as in New England, and the royalists professed to favor the introduction of the ballot. Above all; in New-York the old cry of "No Presbyterian," gave place to that of "No Lawyer."[5] Add to this, that all parties still hoped

[1] Journal of New-York Assembly for 31 Dec. 1768, p. 70. Governor Moore to Hillsborough, 4 January, 1769; Compare Same to Same, 30 March, 1769, and Same to Same, 3 June, 1769.

[2] Andrew Eliot to T. Hollis, 29 January, 1769. Hutchinson to Richard Jackson, Jan. 1769.

[3] Compare R. R. Livingston to R. Livingston, 12 Dec. 1768.

[4] Moore to Hillsborough, 24 Jan. 1769.

[5] John Jay to R. R. Livingston Jr. Jan. 1769.

for an escape from strife by some Plan of Union; that Grafton, who was much connected with New-York, was believed to be well disposed; that the population was not homogeneous in religion, language, customs, or origin; that the Government and the churchmen acted together; that the city was a corporation in which the mayor was appointed by the king; and the reasons appear why at the hotly[1] contested election, which was the last ever held in New-York under the Crown, the coalition gained success over John Morin Scott,[2] and the ardent Sons of Liberty.

In Massachusetts Bernard kept up the ferment. He knew it to be a part of Lord Hillsborough's[3] system that there never should be another election of Councillors, and he[4] and Hutchinson[5] also, most secretly[6] furnished lists of persons whose appointment they advised. They both importuned the Ministry to remove Temple,[7] who would not conceal his opinion,[8] that the affections of the colonists were wasting away from the mother country, from the incapacity and "avarice"[9] of his associates. The wily Hutchinson opposed with all his influence the repeal of the

[1] Moore to Hillsborough, 20 Jan. 1769.

[2] Daniel Colden to his brother, 31 January, 1769.

[3] "It is certainly a part of Lord Hillsborough's plan," &c., Hutchinson to Israel Williams, 26 Jan. 1769; and compare Bernard to Hillsborough, 4 Feb. 1769, "This opinion is so sanguinely entertained," &c. &c.

[4] Postscript, Supplement to No. 4, Private; Bernard to Hillsborough, 14 Feb. 1769.

[5] Hutchinson to Richard Jackson, 28 January, 1769.

[6] See the whole of Bernard to Hillsborough, 26 January, 1769.

[7] Bernard to Hillsborough, 21 Feb. 1769. Hutchinson to the Duke of Grafton.

[8] Boston Gazette of 6 Feb. 1769; 723, 1 and 2. The notes to the Letter from London are by Temple.

[9] Temple to Grenville, 7 November, 1768; in Grenville Papers, iv. 396, and compare 460.

CHAP. XXXIX. 1769. Jan.

Revenue Act;[1] recommended to remove the main objection to Parliamentary authority, by the offer to the colonists of such "a plan of representation" in the British Parliament, as he knew they must reject;[2] informed against the free constitutions of Massachusetts, Connecticut and Rhode Island as tending to produce another Congress;[3] and advised and solicited and importunately demanded such an extension of the laws of Treason as would have rendered every considerable man in Boston liable to its penalties. In letters to a member of that Parliament,[4] whose authority he wished it made treasonable to deny,—written for public purposes,[5] and communicated to Grenville[6] himself, to Temple,[7] and to others,—he declared that "measures which he could not think of without pain were necessary for the peace and good of the Colony." "There must be," said he, "an abridgment of what are called English Liberties."[8] He avowed his desire to see some further restraint, lest otherwise the connection with Great Britain should be broken; and he consoled himself for his advice, by declaring it impossible for so distant a Colony to "enjoy all the lib-

[1] Hutchinson to Richard Jackson, 24 Jan. 1769.

[2] Hutchinson to Richard Jackson, 24 Jan. 1769, and to Gov. Pownall, 29 Jan. 1769.

[3] From the Draft by Hutchinson.

[4] Thos. Hutchinson to T. Whately, 20 Jan. 1769.

[5] Of a previous Letter Whately writes, "I have not been wanting to signify through proper channels," &c. &c. Whately to Hutchinson, London, 11 Feb. 1769.

[6] Compare for example, Whately to Grenville, 3 Dec. 1769. "Another Correspondent, the same gentleman, one of whose letters I lately sent you," &c. &c. The gentleman was Hutchinson. This confirms Almon's statement.

[7] Almon's Biographical anecdotes of Eminent Men; ii. 105. Biog. of Thomas Whately. "Mr. Whately showed them to Mr. Grenville, who showed them to Lord Temple, and they were seen by other gentlemen." This refers to the very letter of Hutchinson above cited. Almon is good authority for what relates to Temple.

[8] The Letters of Gov. Hutchinson and Lieut Gov. Oliver 16 17.

erty of the Parent State." He had put many suggestions on paper, but behind all he had further "thoughts, which he dared not trust to pen and ink."[1]

"Poison will continue to be instilled into the minds of the people," wrote Hutchinson's brother-in-law, Oliver,[2] "if there be no way found to take off the original incendiaries." The Bedford Address for shipping American traitors to England having come to hand, a way was open for "taking them off;" and Bernard and Oliver and Hutchinson, the three relentness enemies to Colonial freedom, with the Attorney-General, were very busy[3] in getting evidence especially against Samuel Adams; and affidavits, sworn to before Hutchinson,[4] were sent to England, to prove him fit to be transported under the Act of Henry the Eighth. Nor was he alone to be called to account; but Edes and Gill, also, "the trumpeters of sedition," and through them "all the chiefs of the Faction, all the authors of numberless treasonable and seditious writings."[5] "A few individuals stigmatized," wrote one of Hutchinson's underlings,[6] "would cause us to reform."

"I sometimes wish," said one of a neighboring Colony, "that two thirds of the gentlemen of the law, and as great a number of the printers, had been shipped to some sandy spot on the African shore for at least seven years."[7]

[1] From the Letter Book; where the person to whom the letter is addressed is not named.

[2] Andrew Oliver to Thomas Whately, Boston, 13 Feb. 1769; in Letters, &c., 30, 31.

[3] Bernard to Hillsborough, 24 January, 1769.

[4] Copies of the Affidavits in my possession.

[5] Bernard to Hillsborough, 25 January, 1769.

[6] N. Rogers [connected with Hutchinson and Oliver], to W. S. Johnson, Jan. 1769.

[7] J Chew of New London, Conn.

CHAP. XXXIX. 1769. Jan.

While Hutchinson, eager to find "proceedings[1] amounting to treason," was taking depositions, so that "the principal actors might be called to account," those whom he sought to arraign as traitors were aware of his designs, publicly[2] reproached him for his baseness in performing "the office of an informer" while he held the post of Chief Justice, and avowed their opinions more boldly than ever. "Parliament will offer you a share in the representative body," said the royalists; and the suggestion was always indignantly spurned, since a true representation was impossible.[3] "Boston may be deprived of its trade," thus they foreshadowed the policy adopted five years later. "What then?" it was asked. "Will the decline of British credit be remedied by turning our sea-ports into villages?" "Governor Bernard has been spoken of with great respect;" reported the official journal. "And so has Otis," rejoined the Boston Gazette; "and has been compared to the Pyms, the Hampdens, the Shippens of Britain." "Bernard has had some very uncommon difficulties to contend with," said royalists in his excuse. "And Otis and his compatriots," retorted Samuel Adams, "have doubtless had none! no toils, no self-denials, no threatenings, no tempting baits! All the virtue is on one side; virtue was never known to be separated from power or profit."[4] "We should have been ruined by this time, had not the troops arrived,"[5] wrote one who was grasping at a lucrative

[1] Hutchinson to Israel Williams, 26 Jan. 1769.

[2] Boston Gazette, 20 Feb. 1769, 725, 3, 1.

[3] Compare A. Eliot to T. Hollis, 29 Jan. 1769.

[4] Samuel Adams under the signature of Shippen, in the Boston Gazette of 30 January, 1769; 722, 2, 1, 2 and 3.

[5] N. Rogers to W. S. Johnson, 12 Jan. 1769.

CHAP. XXXIX. 1769. Jan.

office. "Military power," repeated the people, "is the last resource of ignorant despotism." "The opposition to government is faction;" said the friends to Government. "As well," answered Samuel Adams, "might the general uneasiness that introduced the revolution by William the Third, or that settled the succession in the House of Hanover, be called a Faction." The patriot was in earnest. Since Great Britain persisted in enforcing her Revenue Act, he knew no remedy but American Independence.

Lord North, though he feared to strike, wished to intimidate. He would not allow a Petition from the Council of Massachusetts[1] for the Repeal of Townshend's Act to be referred with the other American papers; nor would he receive a Petition which denied that the Act of Henry the Eighth extended to the Colonies; and on the twenty-sixth of January after a delay of many weeks, he asked the House of Commons to agree with the Resolves and Address of the House of Lords.[2] "No lawyer," said Dowdeswell, "will justify them; none but the House of Lords who think only of their dignity, could have originated them." "Suppose," said Edmund Burke, "you do call over two or three of these unfortunate men; what will become of the rest? *Let me have the heads of the principal leaders*, exclaimed the Duke of Alva; these heads proved Hydra's heads. Suppose a man brought over for High Treason; if his witnesses do not appear, he cannot have a fair trial. God and nature oppose you." Grenville spoke against the Ad-

[1] Cavendish Debates, i. 185, &c.

[2] Parliamentary History, xvi. 485, &c. MS. Letters and Diary of W. S. Johnson; Cavendish Debates, i. 191 &c. Thomas Pownall to S. Cooper, 30 Jan. 1769. T. Whately to Hutchinson, 11 Feb. 1769.

CHAP. XXXIX. 1769. Jan.

dress, and scoffed at the whole plan, as no more than "angry words," and "the wisdom fools put on." Lord North, in reply, assumed the responsibility of the measure; refused "ever to give up an iota of the authority of Great Britain;" and promised good results in America from the refusal to repeal the Revenue Act.

"It is not a question of one refractory Colony," cried Barré; "the whole country is ripe for revolt. Let us come to the point. Are the Americans proper objects of taxation? I think they are not. I solemnly declare, I think they will not submit to any law imposed upon them for the purpose of revenue.

"On a former occasion, the noble Lord told us, that he would listen to no proposition for repeal, until he saw America prostrate at his feet. To effect this is not so easy as some imagine; the Americans are a numerous, a respectable, a hardy, a free people. But were it ever so easy, does any friend to his country really wish to see America thus humbled? In such a situation, she would serve only as a monument of your vengeance and your folly. For my part, the America I wish to see, is America increasing and prosperous, raising her head in graceful dignity, with freedom and firmness asserting her rights at your bar, vindicating her liberties, pleading her services and conscious of her merit. This is the America that will have spirit to fight your battles, to sustain you when hard pushed by some prevailing foe, and by her industry will be able to consume your manufactures, support your trade, and pour wealth and splendor into your towns and cities. If we do not change our conduct towards her, America will be torn from our side. I repeat it; unless you repeal this law, you run the risk of losing America."

CHAP. XXXIX. 1769. Jan.

His reasoning was just; his language flowing and forcible; his voice and action animated; warmed by the nobleness of his subject, he charmed all that heard him; yet the Resolutions were adopted in committee by nearly three votes to one; and the Address was carried by a decided majority.[1]

This adoption of a vengeful and impracticable policy renewed the wakefulness of France. "An attempt to seize the defenders of American Liberties," said its ambassador to Choiseul, "would precipitate the revolution. How great will be the indignation of the Americans, when they learn that Britain, without receiving their representations, without hearing their agents, treats them as slaves, and condemns them as rebels. They never will recognise the right claimed by Parliament; even if they bear with it, their hearts will breathe nothing but independence, and will own no other country than the wilderness which their industry has fertilized. Henceforward, the Colonies are divided from the Metropolis in interests and in principles; and the bonds of their dependence will be severed on the first opportunity. Spain and France should adopt towards them general principles, entirely different from those which have been practised till now; and, even at the risk of transient inconveniences, should depart from the ancient prohibitory laws of commerce. The two courts must consider whether it is for their interest to second the revolution which menaces England, at the risk of the consequences which may a little later result from it for

[1] W. S. Johnson to Governor Pitkin, 9 Feb. 1769. Diary of W. S. Johnson, for Friday 27 Jan. 1769.

CHAP. XXXIX. 1769. Jan. the totality of the New World; and whether the weakening of a common enemy can compensate the risk of such an example to their own Colonies.

"If this question is answered in the affirmative, no precautions must be omitted, to profit by the favorable circumstances, which imprudence alone could have created, and which human wisdom could hardly have foreseen. The inflammatory remedies applied by the Parliament of England, the spirit of revolt, and still more the spirit of contempt shown by a factious people for a vacillating and humiliated Administration, the disunion and indecision which reign in the British cabinet, the acknowledged weakness and instability of the principles of the King's government, all presage coming calamities to England; the only man whose genius might still be feared, is removed from affairs, and enfeebled by gout; and his state of mind is a problem. The others whom birth, credit, wealth or eloquence, may destine to high places, are known to us, and not one of them appears likely to become a formidable enemy."[1]

Feb. This letter from Du Chatelet to Choiseul, was inspired neither by the Courtiers, nor the Parliaments, nor the Aristocracy, nor even by the Burgesses of France; it was the philosophy of the Eighteenth Century, the ripened wisdom of the ages from Descartes to Turgot, uttering its oracles and its counsels in the palaces of absolute monarchs. It excited the most attentive curiosity of Louis the Fifteenth and of every one of his council. An extract of it

[1] Du Chatelet to Choiseul, London, 28 January, 1769.

CHAP. XXXIX. 1769. Feb.

was sent to Madrid, to ascertain the sentiments and intentions of the Catholic King; the Minister of the marine and the Minister of finance were directed to consult the Chambers of Commerce of the Kingdom; while Choiseul, aware of the novelty of a system founded on the principle of a free trade, looked about him on every side for prevailing arguments and motives against hereditary prepossessions.[1]

While the proposals were under consideration, the state of America was again the theme of conversation in the House of Commons;[2] where once more on the eighth of February, strenuous efforts were made to prove the illegality and cruelty of fetching Americans across the Atlantic for trial.

"They may save themselves," said Rose Fuller, "by going still further, and bringing the question to the point of arms."—"You have no right to tax the Colonies," repeated Beckford; "the system has not produced a single shilling to the exchequer; the money is all eaten up by the officers who collect it."—"Your measures," cried Phipps after an admirable statement, "are more calculated to raise than to quell a rebellion. It is our duty to stand between the victim and the altar."—"The statute of the thirty-fifth year of Henry the Eighth," observed Frederic Montagu, "was passed in the worst times of the worst reign, when the taste of blood had inflamed the savage disposition of Henry." "The Act," declared Sir William Meredith, "does not extend to America; and were I an American I

Choiseul to Du Chatelet, 6 Feb. 1769. W. S. Johnson to Gov. Pitkin, 9 Feb. 1769.

[2] Cavendish Debates, i. 207, &c.

CHAP. XXXIX. 1769. Feb.

would not submit to it." On the other side little was urged, except that concession would endanger the Act of Navigation; and the British Parliament after long deliberation, by a great majority, refusing to consider the redress of American grievances, requested the King to make inquisition at Boston for Treason, and to bring over the accused for trial before a Special Commission, away from their country, their relations, friends, and witnesses. It was hoped to make Boston tremble, and terrify the zealous Americans with the apprehension of being arraigned in Westminster Hall and hanged at Tyburn.

The press also gave to the world an elaborate reply [1] to the Farmer's Letters, for which the Board of Trade furnished the materials,[2] and Grenville himself wrote the constitutional argument.[3] "I am tempted," confessed Knox, the champion of the Ministry, "to deny that there is any such thing as Representation at all in the British Constitution; until this notion of Representation is overthrown, it will be very difficult to convince, either the Colonies or the people of England, that wrong is not done the Colonies." [4] The question of British and of American Liberty was identical. The zeal against America was ready to sacrifice the principle of Representative Government in England; where the love of order began to find apologists for "absolute Government." [5]

[1] The Controversy between Great Britain and her Colonies reviewed, &c. &c., 1769.

[2] I. Mauduit to Hutchinson, 10 Feb. 1769.

[3] Grenville wrote from page 67 to page 86 inclusive. Knox's extra official State Papers, Appendix to Part ii. page 15.

[4] Knox in Grenville Papers, iv. 336, 337.

[5] Whately to Grenville, 25 March, 1769; in Grenville Papers, iv. 417.

CHAP. XXXIX. 1769. Feb.

While England was enforcing its restrictive commercial system with the most jealous vigilance,[1] Du Chatelet continued his intercession with Choiseul, to employ Free Trade as the great liberator of Colonies. "The question," he pleaded, "cannot be submitted to the decision of the Chambers of Commerce. We know their principles. They regard every thing in colonial commerce which does not turn exclusively to the benefit of the Kingdom, as contrary to the end for which Colonies were established, and as a theft from the State. To practise on these maxims is impossible. The wants of trade are stronger than the laws of trade. The North of America can alone furnish supplies to its South. This is the only point of view under which the cession of Canada can be regarded as a loss for France; but that cession will one day be amply compensated for, if it shall cause the rebellion and independence of the English Colonies, which become every day more probable and more near."[2] At the same time the Parisian world was alive with enthusiasm for the Americans, and with admiration for their illustrious advocates.[3]

But Spain had been the parent of the protective system, and remained the steadfast supporter of that restrictive policy, by which, in the midst of every resource of wealth, she had been impoverished. From the first proposal of throwing colonial commerce open, she feared the contraband exportation of gold and silver. "Besides;" thus Grimaldi, the

[1] T. Bradshaw to R. Sutton, Esq. 25 Feb. 1769; Treasury Letter Book, xxiv. 106.

[2] Du Chatelet to Choiseul, 17 February, 1769.

[3] Extract of a Letter from London, of 5 April, 1769.

CHAP. XXXIX. 1769. Feb. Spanish Minister, gave his definitive answer; "the position and strength of the countries occupied by the Americans, excite a just alarm for the rich Spanish possessions on their borders. They have already introduced their grain and rice into our Colonies by a commerce of interlopers. If this introduction should be legalized and extended to other objects of commerce, it would effectually increase the power and prosperity of a neighbor, already too formidable. Moreover; it is probable, that if this neighbor should separate from its metropolis, it would assume the republican form of Government; and a republic is a government dangerous from the wisdom, the consistency, and the solidity of the measures which it would adopt for executing such projects of conquests as it would naturally form."[1]

The opinion of Spain was deliberately pronounced and sternly adhered to. She divided the continent of North America with England, and loved to see "her enemy" embarrassed by war with its Colonies; but while she feared England much, she at that early day feared America more; she preferred as a neighbor a dependent Colony to an independent Republic; and Spain was later than Great Britain itself to confess our national existence.

[1] D'Ossun to Choiseul, Madrid, 20 Feb. 1769. A copy of this letter is in the French Archives, Angleterre, T. 485, p. 473. The original is in the series marked Espagne, T. 556. Compare Choiseul to Du Chatelet, 14 March, 1769.

CHAPTER XL.

VIRGINIA COMES TO THE AID OF MASSACHUSETTS.—HILLSBOROUGH'S ADMINISTRATION OF THE COLONIES CONTINUED.

MARCH—MAY, 1769.

CHAP. XL. 1769. March

THE decision of the King of Spain had been hastened by tidings of the rebellion in New Orleans, which engaged the most earnest attention of his Council.[1] The Cabinet, with but one dissentient, agreed that Louisiana must be retained, as a granary for Havana and Port Rico, a precaution against the contraband trade of France, and a barrier to keep off English encroachments by the indisputable line of a great river.

"Still more," said the Duke of Alba, "the world and especially America must see that the King can and will crush even an intention of disrespect." "If France should recover Louisiana," said Masones de Lima, "she would annex it to the English Colonies, or would establish its independence."[2] "A republic in Louisiana," such was D'Aranda's carefully prepared opinion, "would be independent of the European powers, who would all cultivate her friendship and support her ex-

[1] Grimaldi to Fuentes in Gayarré.

[2] Gayarré's Louisiana, iii. 248, 249.

CHAP. XL. 1769. March istence. She would increase her population, enlarge her limits, and grow into a rich, flourishing and free State, contrasting with our exhausted Provinces. From the example before them, the inhabitants of our vast Mexican domain would be led to consider their total want of commerce, the extortions of their Governors, the little esteem in which they themselves are held, the few offices which they are permitted to fill; they would hate still more the Spanish rule, and would think to brave it with security. If by improving the government of the Mexican Provinces and the condition of their inhabitants, we should avoid the fatal revolution, Louisiana would still trade with the harbors on our coast, and also by land with Texas and New Mexico, and through them with Old Mexico. Between Louisiana and Mexico, there are no established limits; the rebels, if they remain as they are, will have a pretext for claiming an arbitrary extension of territory."[1] He therefore advised to reduce the colony, but to keep New Orleans in such insignificance as to tempt no attack.

The King accepted the decision of his Cabinet; adding his fear lest the example of Louisiana should influence the colonies "of other powers," in which he already discerned the rising "spirit of sedition and independence."[2] A different train of reasoning engaged the Cabinet of France.

"Here," said one of its advisers, "is the happy opportunity of dividing the British Empire, by placing before its Colonies the interesting spectacle of two potentates who pardon, who protect, and who deign

[1] Gayarré's Louisiana, iii. 255, 256.

[2] Gayarré's Hist. de la Louisiane, ii. 266.

in concert to utter the powerful word of liberty. War between France and England would bind these countries more firmly to their metropolis. The example of happiness will allure them to the independence towards which they tend. By leading them to confide in France and Spain, they will dare more and dare sooner. Nothing can better persuade to this confidence than to establish liberty in Louisiana,[1] and to open the port of New Orleans to men of all nations and all religions.[2]

CHAP. XL. 1769. March

"The passion for extended dominion must not hide from Spain, that a discontented and ill guarded Colony cannot arrest the march of the English, and will prove an unprofitable expense. Were we to take back Louisiana, our best efforts could effect less than the charm of liberty. Without the magic of liberty, the territory will never become more than a simple line of demarkation. Severity would throw it into despair and into the arms of the English. To give voluntarily what the British Parliament haughtily refuses, to assimilate New Orleans in its form to the freest of the British Colonies, to adopt for it from each of them whatever is the dearest to them, to do more, to enfranchise it and maintain invariably privileges capable of intoxicating the English and the Americans, this is to arm their America against themselves, by risking no more than what would otherwise be neglected." Every Frenchman had in his heart an excuse for the insurgents, and was ready to applaud their delirium of nationality and

[1] Idée sur l'opposition trouvée par les Espagnols à la Louisiane. Archives Françaises, Angleterre.

[2] "La Nouvelle Orleans seroit ouverte à toutes les Nations, et à toutes les religions."

CHAP. XL. 1769. March

courage. Choiseul allowed their deputies to live at Paris, and to publish their griefs; and he communicated to the Ambassador in England the project of the republic on the banks of the Mississippi.[1]

The idea and the reasoning in its support pleased Du Chatelet infinitely. "Spain," said he, "can never derive benefit from Louisiana. She neither will nor can take effective measures for its colonization and culture. She has not inhabitants enough to furnish emigrants, and the religious and political principles of her Government will always keep away foreigners and even Frenchmen. Under Spanish dominion, the vast extent of territory ceded by France to Spain on the banks of the Mississippi will soon become a desert.

"The expense of Colonies is requited only by commerce; and the commerce of Louisiana, under the rigor of the Spanish prohibitive laws, will every day become more and more a nullity. Spain then will make an excellent bargain, if she accords Liberty to the inhabitants of Louisiana, and permits them to form themselves into a republic. Nothing can so surely keep them from falling under English rule, as making them cherish the protection of Spain and the sweetness of independence.

"The example of a free and happy nation, under the guardianship of two powerful monarchs, without restraint on its commerce, without any taxes but those which the wants of the State and of the common defence would require, without any dependence on Europe but for necessary protection, would be a

[1] Choiseul to Du Chatelet, 14 March, 1769.

tempting spectacle for the English Colonies; and exhibited at their very gates, will hasten the epoch of their revolution."[1]

CHAP. XL. 1769. March

But while the statesmen of France were pleasing themselves with the thought of founding at New Orleans a commercial republic like Venice or Amsterdam, as a place of refuge for the discontented of every creed and tongue, Spain took counsel only of her pride. "The world must see that I," said the Catholic King, "unaided, can crush the audacity of sedition."[2] Aware of the wishes of the French Min isters, he concealed his purpose by making no military preparations at Cadiz, and dispatched Alexander O'Reilly in all haste for Cuba, with orders to extirpate the sentiment of independence at New Orleans.

England had proved herself superior in war not to Spain only, but to the combined power of Spain and France. Her navy was the best in the world; her army respectable. Could not she, in her turn, crush the insolent town of Boston, suppress its free schools, shut up its Town Hall, sequester its liberties, drag its patriots to the gallows, and for the life, restless enterprise, fervid charities and liberal spirit of that moral and industrious town, substitute the quiet monotony of obsequious obedience? England could not do what a feebler despotism might undertake without misgivings. She stood self-restrained. A part of the Ministry wished the Charter of Massachusetts

[1] Du Chatelet to Choiseul, 17 March, 1769. "Idée sur l'opposition trouvée par les Espagnols à la Louisiane.

[2] Grimaldi to Fuentes, 1769; Gayarré, ii. 267.

CHAP. XL. 1769. March

abrogated; and the lawyers declared that nothing had been done to forfeit it. They clamored for judicial victims; and the lawyers said Treason had not been committed. They thought to proceed by the hand of power; and were restrained by the necessity of debates in Parliament. Feeble and fluctuating as was the Opposition in numbers, it uttered the language of the British Constitution and the sentiment of the British people, when it spoke for freedom; and it divided the Ministry, when it counselled moderation. England was a land of liberty and law, and the question between her and her Colonies must be argued at the bar of reason. Spain could send an army and a special tribunal to sequester estates and execute patriots. England must arraign its accused before a jury; and the very necessity of hunting through the Statute Books for an old Enactment of Henry the Eighth, while it presented a measure too absurd, as well as too tyrannical to be carried into effect, showed the supremacy of law of which the petulant Ministry must respect the bounds.

The patriots of Boston never wavered in their confidence, that they should recover their rights with the consent of England, or obtain independence. "The resolves" of Parliament fell upon them like so many thunderbolts; but they stood unmoved. "These Oliverians," said a royalist, "begin to think themselves Corsicans, and will resist unto blood."[1] John Adams,[2] though anxious for advancement in his profession, scorned the service of the King; and his associates at the bar rendered "themselves unfit for

[1] Dr. Johnson of Connecticut to his son, 7 March, 1769.

[2] Compare John Adams's Autobiography, Works, ii.

the favor of Government," by "abetting" "the popular party."[1] The people of the near town of Lexington, at their annual meeting, came into a resolution to drink no more tea, till the unconstitutional Revenue Act should be repealed.[2] On the anniversary of the repeal of the Stamp Act, Samuel Adams held up to public view the grievances inflicted on Americans, by combining the power of taxation with a commercial monopoly, and enforcing them both by fleets, armies, commissioners, guarda-costas, judges of the Admiralty, and a host of petty officers whose insolence and rapacity were become intolerable. He pointed out, on the one hand, the weakness of Great Britain, arising from its corruption, its debt, its intestine divisions, its scarcity of food, its want of alliances; and, on the other, the state of the American Colonies, their various climates, soils, produce, rapid increase of population, and the virtue of their inhabitants, and he publicly expressed his conviction that the conduct of Old England was "permitted and ordained by the unsearchable wisdom of the Almighty for hastening" American Independence.[3]

The intrepid Calvinist knew the end at which he aimed; but the British Ministry had no system. "We have but one word, that is, our sovereignty," wrote Thomas Pownall, describing the opinion of all parties;[4] "and it is like some word to a madman, which whenever mentioned throws him into his rav-

[1] Bernard to Hillsborough, 5 March, 1769.

[2] Boston Gazette, 27 March, 1769.

[3] Providence Gazette, 18 March; Boston Gazette, 27 March, 1769. Bernard to Hillsborough, 27 March, 1769. Compare W. S. Johnson to Dr. Benjamin Gale, 10 April, 1769.

[4] T. Pownall to Cooper, 22 March, 1769.

CHAP. XI. 1769. March ings and brings on a paroxysm." The Representation, therefore, of New-York, though carefully written, was rejected by the House of Commons, because it questioned the right of Parliament to tax America. But this sovereignty being asserted, the Ministry, terrified by the recovery of Chatham which alarmed Camden and Grafton, and by the complaints of the merchants at the diminution of exports, were content with the Parliamentary sanction of their measures, wished the controversy with the Colonies well over, and sought to lull them into acquiescence. The plan for altering the Charter of Massachusetts on which Hillsborough had been definitively resolved,[1] was for the present, laid aside; discretionary orders were transmitted to Gage to "send back to Halifax the two regiments, which were brought from that station, and to restore the regular rotation by sending two other regiments to Ireland."[2] Bernard was given up and recalled with a promise to the London merchants that he should not be employed in the Colonies again; and the government of Massachusetts was to be confided to Hutchinson, a town-born citizen of Boston. New-York was to be secured by a confirmation of its jurisdiction over Vermont, and the permission to issue paper-money; and Virginia, by a more extended boundary at the West.

At the same time England professed to seek a good understanding with France. But Choiseul remembered too well the incidents of the last Seven Years' War. "Hatred and jealousy," thus he instructed the French Ambassador, "inspire the English with

[1] Hutchinson to J. Williams of Hatfield, 29 January, 1769.

[2] Hillsborough to Gage, 24 March, 1769.

the desire to weaken and humiliate the power of France, of which they are the most impassioned rivals and the most implacable enemies. Recall, Sir, the events of 1755. At the time when the Court of London professed sentiments of the utmost moderation, and negotiated with us to conciliate amicably our differences about Acadia, it had shamelessly and without a declaration of war, sent out a squadron with orders to attack the ships which we were sending to America under the guaranty of treaties, and under the safeguard of natural right and of public faith. This odious epoch can be renewed; and the English Ministry has given proofs of ability in the art of masking under the professed love of peace a settled purpose of making war."[1]

CHAP. XI. 1769. March

He witnessed, also, the avowed and persevering effort of England, to counterbalance the influence of France by a Northern Alliance. To the British Secretary of State, Du Chatelet. endeavored to convey an adequate idea of the policy of Russia; but it was Rochford's fixed desire that the Empress should derive advantage from the war against the Turks, should be able to dispose of the whole North by main strength, or by predominant influence, and should then sanction an alliance with the Court of London.

April.

"The English Secretary of State is in the wrong," answered Choiseul; "he does not look at these objects from the higher point of view, which should engage the attention of a great Minister. Nothing can be more dangerous for the happiness and repose of hu-

[1] Choiseul to Du Chatelet, 14 March, 1769.

CHAP. XL. 1769. April. manity, nor more to be feared for the principal powers of Europe than the success of the arms and the ambitious projects of Russia. Far from seeking, on such a supposition, the alliance and the friendship of the Empress, it would become their most essential interest to unite to diminish her strength and destroy her preponderance. If the balance of power, that unmeaning word, invented by William the Third, on becoming King of England, to raise all Europe against France, could have a just application, and if this pretended balance of power could be annihilated, it would be by the prodigious increase of the material and moral strength of Russia. She is now laboring to enslave the North; and she will next encroach on the liberty of the South; unless an effective check is seasonably put to her inordinate passion of despotism.

"Instead of contributing to the aggrandizement of Russia, the principal courts ought jointly to restrain her ambition and her cupidity, which may in some respects realize the chimerical idea, once attributed to France, of aiming at universal Monarchy."[1]

Thus the rivalry of England and France met at every point; yet how changed were their relations! The Cabinet of France desired to loosen the bonds that shackled trade; that of England to hold them close. France aspired to protect the liberties of Europe against danger from the Russian Monarchy; England encouraged Russia in her conquests, and invited her to become the arbiter for Europe and the world. France desired the independence of all

[1] Choiseul to Du Chatelet, 16 April, 1769.

colonial possessions; England to retain her own in more complete dependence than before. Both desired and both needed peace; but Choiseul regarded the British proffers of confidence as an unmeaning jargon, and fearing a rupture at any moment, when it should assist to change a Ministry or secure a majority, he told the English plainly, "that the King of France and his Ministry applied themselves unremittingly to maintain peace, but never lost out of sight, that to preserve peace it was necessary to be in a condition to sustain a war."[1] England and France grew more and more distrustful of one another; and while the latter was yielding to the liberal ideas to which free inquiry had given circulation, England more and more forgot that her greatness sprung from her liberty.

CHAP. XL. 1769. April.

The publication of some of the American letters, which had been laid before Parliament and copied for Beckford,[2] unmasked Bernard's duplicity. The town of Boston repelled the allegation, that they were held to their allegiance only by the "band of terror and force of arms." In their representation to the King, which Barré himself presented, they entreated the removal of the troops, a communication of the charges against them, and an opportunity to defend themselves, for justice and law forbade that they should be condemned unheard.

The Council, too, without delay, calmly and unanimously vindicated the Province and themselves. They proved their own undeviating respect for law; they set in a strong light Bernard's unmanly

[1] Choiseul to Du Chatelet, 16 April, 1769.

[2] Hutchinson to Mauduit, 16 April, 1769.

CHAP. XL. 1769. April. duplicity and petty malice; his disposition to overreach; his notoriously false assertions; his retailing of anecdotes both trifling and untrue; his attempts to obtain by Act of Parliament exorbitant and uncontrollable power; and his perpetual conspiracy for "the destruction of their constitution."[1]

While the people of Massachusetts were filled with grief and indignation at the combination against their Charter, which was dearer to them than fortune and life, they and all the Colonies one after another matured their agreements for passive resistance to Parliamentary taxation.

On Monday, the tenth of April, the General Assembly of New-York, at the motion of Philip Livingston, thanked the merchants of the city and Colony, for suspending trade with Great Britain.[2] The same intrepid leader of the patriot party, would next have renewed the resolves, which had occasioned the dissolution of the last Assembly; but he was himself ousted from the present one, because he did not reside within the manor for which he had been returned. Yet amidst the conflict of factions, the system of non-importation was rigorously carried out. The merchants of Philadelphia, now unanimously adopted the agreement, which a few months before they had declined.

The movement spread steadily towards the South. At Mount Vernon, Washington tempered yet cheered and animated those around him. "Our lordly masters in Great Britain," said he, "will be satisfied

[1] Council to Hillsborough, 15 April, 1769. Bowdoin to Hillsborough, same date.

[2] Journals of the General Assembly of New-York, 21, 22. Hillsborough to Moore, 15 July, 1769. Board of Trade's Representation to the King on the Resolves.

CHAP. XL. 1769. April.

with nothing less than the deprivation of American freedom. Something should be done to maintain the liberty which we have derived from our ancestors. No man should hesitate a moment, to use arms in defence of so valuable a blessing. Yet arms should be the last resource. We have already proved the inefficacy of addresses to the throne and remonstrances to Parliament. How far their attention to our rights and privileges is to be awakened or alarmed by starving their trade and manufactures, remains to be tried."[1] And counselling with George Mason, his bosom friend, he prepared a scheme to be offered at the coming session of the Virginia House of Burgesses.

While the British Ministry was palsied by indecision, Thomas Pownall, the predecessor of Bernard as Governor of Massachusetts, stepped forward in the House of Commons to propose that repeal, by which harmony could be restored. "So favorable an opportunity will never recur," said he with perfect truth. "The Colonies are combining against our trade and manufactures; new provocations will be given; British honor will be more deeply engaged. Let Parliament then at once, in advance of new difficulties, repeal the Act, end the controversy, and give peace to the two countries." Trecothick seconded the motion, dwelling on commercial reasons, and recounting the various steps in America to prevent the consumption of British manufactures, and to promote their own. "We will not consent," replied Lord North, "to go into the question, on account of the combinations in America. To do so would be to furnish a fresh instance of haste,

[1] Washington to George Mason, 5 April, 1769; Writings, ii. 351.

CHAP. XL. 1769. April. impatience, levity, and fickleness. I see nothing uncommercial, in making the Americans pay a duty upon tea."

No one would defend the Act, yet few urged its repeal. The Rockingham party were willing that it should remain as a source of embarrassment to the Ministers. Conway next proposed as a middle course, to agree to take it into consideration the next session. "I approve the middle course," said Beckford. "I was the first man who said you ought not tax America for the purpose of revenue. The duty upon tea, with a great army to collect it, has produced in the Southern part of America, only two hundred and ninety-four pounds, fourteen shillings; in the Northern part it has produced nothing." "For the sake of a paltry revenue," cried Lord Beauchamp, "we lose the affection of two millions of people." "We have trusted to terror too long," observed Jackson. "Washing my hands of the charge of severity," said Lord North, "I will not vote for holding out hopes, that may not be realized." "If you are ready to repeal this Act," retorted Grenville, in answer to Lord North, "why keep it in force for a single hour? You ought not to do so, from anger or ill-humor. Why dally and delay in a business of such infinite importance? Why pretend that it is too late in the session, that this is not the time, when the difficulty is every day increasing? If the Act is wrong, or you cannot maintain it, give it up like men. If you do not mean to bind the Colonies by your laws in cases of taxation, tell the Americans so fairly, and conciliate their affections."

Lord North put an end to the conversation, by moving the previous question for the order of the day.[1] "The British Administration will come to no decision," such was Du Chatelet's report to Choiseul. "They will push time by the shoulder, till the Americans consolidate their union, and form a general plan of resistance."[2] CHAP. XL. 1769. April

The question turned on the reality of the principle of representation. America was not alone in asserting representative liberty; the principle was at the same time violated in England. The freeholders of Middlesex elected Wilkes to represent their shire in Parliament. The King wished him expelled; and the House of Commons expelled him. The people rallied to his support; the City of London made him one of its magistrates; by the unanimous vote of Middlesex he was again returned. The House of Commons voted the return to be null and void. The public mind was profoundly agitated; men united as "Supporters of the Bill of Rights," to pay the debts of Wilkes and his election expenses. A third time he was returned and unanimously; for his intended competitor proved too much of a craven to appear. Once more his election was voted to be null. At a fourth trial he was opposed by Luttrell, but polled nearly three fourths of all the votes. The House of Commons, this time, treated him as a person incapacitated to be a candidate, and received Luttrell in his stead. Their disfranchisement of Wilkes had no authority in law, and violated the vital principle of representative Government; by admitting Luttrell, they sequestered and usurped the elective franchise of Middlesex; and Wilkes, who, if he had been left

[1] W. S. Johnson to Governor Trumbull, 26 April, 1769.

[2] Du Chatelet to Choiseul, 21 April, 1769.

CHAP. XL. 1769. April. to himself, would have fallen into insignificance, became the most conspicuous man in England. This subserviency of the body, once esteemed the most august assembly in Europe, exhibited it to the world as a collection of pensioners and office-holders, and the property of the Minister.[1] Yet the Administration, with Parliament as its obedient instrument, heard with alarm how widely the American plan of passive resistance was extending. Besides: Chatham might reappear; and those Ministers who had been of his selection, stood in constant dread of his rebuke. Grafton and Camden, therefore, silent in the House of Lords, insisted in Council, that some attempt should be made to conciliate the Colonies.

May. Accordingly on the first day of May, just on the eve of the prorogation of Parliament, the Cabinet discussed the policy which it should definitively adopt.

All agreed that the duties on the British manufactures of glass, paper, and painters' colors, were contrary to the true principles of commerce, and should be repealed; there remained of Charles Townshend's Revenue Act nothing but the duty on tea; and this, evaded by smuggling or by abstinence from its use, yielded in all America not fifteen hundred dollars, not three hundred pounds a year. Why should such a duty be retained, at the cost of the affections of thirteen Provinces and two millions of people? Grafton spoke first and earnestly for its repeal; Camden seconded him with equal vigor. Granby and Conway gave their voice and their vote on the same side,

[1] W. S. Johnson to Robert Temple, ii. 69.

CHAP. XI. 1769. May.

and Sir Edward Hawke, whom illness detained from the meeting, was of their opinion. Had not Grafton and Camden consented to remove Shelburne, the measure would have been carried, and American independence indefinitely postponed. But Rochford, the new Secretary, with Gower and Weymouth adhered to Hillsborough. The fearful responsibility of deciding fell to Lord North. Of a merciful disposition and of rare intelligence, he was known to be at heart for the repeal of the tax on tea.[1] He wished, and at that time intended, to extend the proposal to the repeal of the other duties,[2] and he never surrendered himself to the party of the Bedfords. But it was the King's fixed rule, never to redress a grievance, unless the prayer for it was made in the spirit of obedience; and then and for years after, he held that "there must always be one tax to keep up the right."[3] He was so much dissatisfied with Grafton's vote on this occasion, that "from that time he was more forward to dictate his will to the Duke, than to inquire first the Duke's opinion on any measure;"[4] and "Lord Camden also sank much in the royal estimation."[5] The most questionable acts of Lord North's public career, proceeded from "an amiable weakness, which followed him through life,[6] the want of power to resist the influence of those he loved." It was the King, who swayed Lord North,

[1] Franklin's Letters of 18 March, 1770, and 8 June, 1770; in Franklin's Writings, vii. 467, 475.

[2] Lord North in Cavendish Debates, i. 485.

[3] King to Lord North, communicated to me by Lady Charlotte Lindsay.

[4] Grafton's Autobiography, iii. 34.

[5] Grafton's Autobiography, iii. 34.

[6] Lady Charlotte Lindsay to Lord Brougham, 8 February, 1839.

CHAP. XL. 1769. May. a junior Lord of the Treasury, contrary, as he himself with the utmost solemnity declared, to his most earnest wish, and his intention at that very time,[1] to give his deciding vote in the Cabinet against the repeal, which the Duke of Grafton, the head of his Board, had proposed and advocated.[2]

Now, indeed, the die was cast. Neither the Bedford party, nor the King meant to give up the right to tax; and they clung to the duty on tea, as an evidence of their lordly superiority. "We can grant nothing to the Americans," said Hillsborough," "except what they may ask with a halter round their necks."[3] "They are a race of convicts," said the famous moralist, the pensioned Samuel Johnson, "and ought to be thankful for any thing we allow them short of hanging."[4] A Circular letter was sent forthwith to all the Colonies, promising on the part of the Ministry to lay no more taxes on America for revenue, and to repeal those on paper, glass, and colors. Camden found fault with the paper as not couched in terms so conciliatory as those in the minute of the Cabinet. The complaint was pitiful, for the substance of the decision had been truly given. More honied words would have been useless hypocrisy. Camden should have blamed himself. When he acquiesced in the removal of Shelburne, he gave his assent to his own humiliation.

[1] Lord North, Cavendish Debates, i. 485.

[2] Besides the Autobiography of the Duke of Grafton, compare the speeches of the Duke of Grafton and of Weymouth in the House of Lords, 5 March, 1776; in Force, vi. 312.

[3] Du Chatelet to Choiseul, 12 May, 1769.

[4] Boswell's Life of Johnson, 435.

The day on which Parliament was prorogued, saw the Legislature of Virginia assembled at Williamsburgh. Great men were there; some who were among the greatest; Washington, Patrick Henry, and for the first time, Jefferson. Botetourt, the only Governor who had appeared in Virginia within memory, proceeded to open the session, drawn in a state coach by six white horses; he was in perfect harmony with the Council; the House of Burgesses voted him a most dutiful address; two and fifty guests were entertained at his table on the first day, and as many more on the second.[1] He took care also to make "a judicious use" of the permission which he had received to negotiate an extended boundary with the Cherokees.

CHAP. XI. 1769. May.

The strife in America had begun on a demand by the Custom House officers for Writs of Assistance. Connecticut had refused them;[2] the Governor and Council, who constituted the highest court in Virginia, heard arguments on their legality, and he concurred with the Council that they were illegal.[3]

Between Botetourt and the Legislature all was courtesy. But the Assembly did not forget its duty; and taking into consideration the Resolutions and Address which Hillsborough and Bedford had proposed, and which both Houses of Parliament had voted by large majorities, on the sixteenth of May, it devised a measure which became the example for the continent.

[1] Botetourt to Hillsborough, 10 May, 1769.

[2] Roger Sherman to Dr. W. S. Johnson, 25 June, 1768.

[3] Botetourt to Secretary of State, 16 May, 1769.

CHAP. XL. 1769. May. Meeting the declaration of Parliament by a direct negative of its own, it claimed the sole right of imposing taxes on the inhabitants of Virginia. With equal unanimity, it asserted the lawfulness and expediency of procuring a concert of the Colonies in care for the violated rights of America. It laid bare the flagrant tyranny of applying to America the obsolete statute of Henry the Eighth; and it warned the King of "the dangers that would ensue," if any person in any part of America should be seized and carried beyond sea for trial. It consummated its work by communicating its Resolutions and asking the concurrence of every Legislature in America.[1]

The Resolves were calm in manner, concise, simple, and effective; so perfect in substance and in form, that time finds no omission to regret, no improvement to suggest. The menace of arresting patriots, which was to have been a formidable instrument of vengeful malignity, lost all its terrors; and Virginia's declaration and action consolidated Union.

Is it asked who was the adviser of the measure? None can tell. Great things were done, and were done tranquilly and modestly, without a thought of the glory that was their due.[2] Had the Ancient Dominion been silent, I will not say that Massachusetts might have faltered; but mutual trust would have been wanting. American freedom was more prepared by courageous counsel than by successful war. The Assembly had but one mind, and their Resolves were the Act of Virginia. Had they been framed by the leaders in Massachusetts Bay them-

[1] Hutchinson's Hist. of Massachusetts, iii. 494.

[2] Jefferson's Autobiography in his Writings, i. 4.

selves, "they could not have been better adapted to vindicate their past proceedings, and to encourage them to perseverance."[1] CHAP. XI. 1769. May.

The next morning the Assembly had just time to adopt an Address to the King, when the Governor, having heard of what he called "the abominable measure,"[2] summoned them and said: "I have heard of your Resolves, and augur ill of their effects; you have made it my duty to dissolve you, and you are dissolved accordingly."[3]

The Burgesses of Virginia, having finished what they could do in their official capacity, met together as patriots and friends, with their Speaker as Moderator. They adopted the Resolves which Washington had brought with him from Mount Vernon; and which formed a well digested, stringent and practicable scheme of non-importation, until all the "unconstitutional" revenue acts should be repealed. Such too was their zeal against the Slave-trade, they made a special covenant with one another, not to import any slaves, nor purchase any imported. These associations were signed by Peyton Randolph, Richard Bland, Archibald Cary, Robert Carter Nicholas, Richard Henry Lee, Washington, Carter Braxton, Henry, Jefferson, Nelson, and all the Burgesses of Virginia there assembled;[4] and were then sent throughout the country for the signature of every man in the Colony.[5]

The voice of the Old Dominion roused the "most

[1] Hutchinson's Hist. of Massachusetts, iii. 233.

[2] Botetourt to Hillsborough, 19 May, 1769.

[3] Wirt's Life of Patrick Henry, 104.

[4] Burk's History of Virginia, iii. 348, 349.

[5] Compare Washington to Colonel Bassett, Mount Vernon, 18 June, 1769; in Maxwell's Virginia Historical Register, iii. 220.

CHAP. XL. 1769. May. temperate Province" of Pennsylvania, from its slumbers to express through its merchants their approval of what had been done. Delaware did still better. Her Assembly adopted the Virginia Resolves word for word,[1] and every Colony South of Virginia in due time followed the example.

[1] John Dickinson to Richard Henry Lee, 22 June, 1769. Life of R. H. Lee, i. 76, 77. Francis Alison to Ezra Stiles, 1 August, 1769.

CHAPTER XLI.

REPUBLICANISM IN THE EAST AND THE WEST.—HILLSBOROUGH'S ADMINISTRATION OF THE COLONIES CONTINUED.

MAY—AUGUST, 1769.

CHAP. XLI. 1769. May.

MASSACHUSETTS had not only like Virginia to assert the rights of America, but also to effect the removal of the troops from Boston, into whose "very streets and lanes" about two thousand men had been sent, in equal disregard of good policy[1] and of an Act of Parliament. For more than ten months, the Colony remained without an Assembly.

Feb.

The servants of the Crown who had placed their hopes on the plan for transporting to England the principal Sons of Liberty, became irresolute and timid.[2] The secret Councils which Bernard now held with Hutchinson[3] and Oliver and Auchmuty, ended only in "despair." They had furnished "ample information;"[4] they had got ready to apply the statute of Henry the Eighth; and had persuaded themselves that inferior offenders would have consulted

[1] Mahon's England, v. 406.
[2] Hutchinson's Hist. iii. 223.
[3] Bernard to Hillsborough, 25 May, 1769.
[4] Hutchinson's History.

CHAP. XLI. 1769. May. safety by betraying their leaders.[1] Since the proposal to ship Samuel Adams, Otis, and their chief supporters across the water had come to naught, the cabal were left without a plan of conduct. The Regiments which had been sent at their suggestion were pronounced to be useless, because they were inactive. Disheartened by the appearance of moderation in the British Government, they complained that their accusations which had, as they thought, "been fully certified, had not been noticed at Westminster for Treason."

The choice of Representatives showed the sense of the people. The town of Boston, on coming together, demanded the withdrawal of the soldiery during the election; but they were only confined within the barracks while the ballot was taken. Of five hundred and eight votes that were cast, the four old representatives, Otis, Cushing, Samuel Adams, and Hancock, received more than five hundred. They were instructed to insist on the departure of the army from the town and Province; and not to pay any thing towards its support.[2]

Of the ninety-two who voted not to rescind, eighty-one, probably all who were candidates, were re-elected; of the seventeen rescinders, only five. Especially Salem condemned the conduct of its former representatives and substituted two Sons of Liberty in their stead. Cambridge charged Thomas Gardner, its representative, "to use his best endeavors, that all their rights might be transmitted inviolable to the latest posterity;" and the excellent man proved

[1] Bernard to Hillsborough, 25 May, 1769.

[2] Bradford's Hist of Mass. i. 180.

CHAP. XLI. 1769. May.

true to his New England town. Nor let history speak the praise only of those who win glory in the field or high honors in the State; a place should be reserved for a husbandman like him, rich in the virtues of daily life, of calm and modest courage, of a character trustworthy and unassuming, who was sent from cultivating his fields to take part in legislation, and carried to his task a discerning mind and an intrepid and guileless heart.—The town of Roxbury recommended a correspondence between the House of Representatives in Massachusetts, and the Assemblies of other Provinces.[1]

Meantime, Bernard received letters, destroying his hope of an appointment in Virginia, and calling him to England. The blow came on him unexpectedly; as he was procuring settlers for his wild lands, and promising himself a long and secure enjoyment of the emoluments of office under military protection. True to his character, he remained to get if he could an appropriation for his own salary for a year, and to bequeathe confusion to his successor.

On the last day of May, the Legislature, before even electing a clerk or a speaker, complained to the Governor of the presence of "the armament by sea and land, in the port, and the gates of the city, during the session of the Assembly."[2]

"Gentlemen," said Bernard, in reply to what he thought insolent terms, "I have no authority over his Majesty's ships in this port, or his troops in this town; nor can I give any orders for the removal of the

[1] Bradford's Hist. of Mass. i. 181.

[2] Message from the House of Representatives to the Governor, 31 May, 1769, the day of general election.

CHAP. XLI. 1769. May.

same." On the election of Councillors, he disapproved of no less than eleven; among them of Brattle and Bowdoin, who had been chosen by a unanimous vote.[1] The House then considered the presence among them of troops, over whom the Governor avowed that the civil power in the Province did not extend. At that very time Gage, who had been intrusted with discretionary authority to withdraw the forces from Boston, ordered two regiments to Halifax, and required Bernard's written opinion respecting the proper disposition of the rest.[2]

After some hesitation,[3] and after conferring with his associates, Bernard reported it to be "the opinion of all that the removal of the troops at that time would have very dangerous consequences;[4] and that it would be quite ruinous to the cause of the Crown to draw them all out of the town of Boston. Two regiments, one in the town, the other at the castle, might be sufficient."[5]

During this secret discussion, the Assembly,[6] in a message to the Governor, represented that the use of the military to enforce the laws was inconsistent with the spirit of a free Constitution, and that a standing army, in so far as it was uncontrollable by the civil authority of the Province, was an absolute power.

Bernard, whose chief anxiety was to get a grant

[1] Bradford's History of Massachusetts, i. 185..

[2] Gage to Mackay, 4 June, 1769; Mackay to Gov. Gage, 12 June. 1769.

[3] Bernard to Gage, 12 June, 1769.

[4] Bernard to Gage, 19 June, 1769.

[5] Bernard to Gage, 26 June, 1769; Gage to Hillsborough, No. 32.

[6] Answer of the House of Representatives to the Governor's Message of May 31, 1769, June 13; in Bradford's Massachusetts State Papers, 169, 171.

CHAP XLI. 1769. May.

of a year's salary,[1] and who, for the moment, mixed some distrust of Hutchinson[2] with his sudden recall, met their complaint of the presence of troops by adjourning the Legislature to Cambridge; and insisting that by the King's instruction the grant of salaries must be the first Act of the Session, he chid the House for "a fortnight's non-activity," and a consequent waste of "time and treasure."[3]

"No time," replied the House, "can be better employed, than in the preservation of the rights derived from the British Constitution; no treasure better expended, than in securing that true old English liberty which gives a relish to every enjoyment;"[4] and in earnest and distinct resolves, they iterated their opinions.[5]

The impatient Governor, eager for his salary, again places before them his own support as their first object.[6] The House paid no heed to his entreaties; but by a unanimous vote, one hundred and nine members being present, petitioned the King to remove him for ever from the Government, enumerating many and just grounds of complaint.[7] All this while Bernard, sure of the royal protection and blinded by avarice, was mainly intent on getting a year's salary. Another week passes. Contrary to the advice of all about him, he communicated to the As-

[1] Hutchinson to Bollan, 13 June, 1769.

[2] I. Williams of Hatfield to Hutchinson, 3 May, 1769.

[3] Message of Governor Bernard, 15 June, 1769. Bernard to Hutchinson, 17 June.

[4] Message from the House of Representatives to the Governor, 19 June, 1769. Bradford, 172, 173.

[5] Resolution of the House of Representatives, 21 June, 1769; Bradford, 174.

[6] Message of Governor Bernard to the House of Representatives, June 21, 1769, Bradford, 175.

[7] Petition of the House of Representatives to the King, 27 June, 1769; Bradford, 188 and 195. Samuel Adams to Dennys De Berdt, 13 July, 1769.

CHAP. XLI. 1769. June. sembly[1] his order to repair to England, and, citing a royal instruction on the subject of provincial grants for the support of Government, coupled his new demand of a year's salary with an intimation, that he should give his assent to no Act, which the grant did not precede.

July. The House, having disdainfully rejected his demand,[2] adopted nearly word for word the three Resolutions of Virginia[3] on taxation,[4] intercolonial correspondence, and trial by a jury of the vicinage. They also enumerated their grievances, and declared the "establishment of a standing army in the Colony, in a time of peace, without consent of its General Assembly, an invasion of the natural and chartered rights of the people."

For the troops thus quartered in Boston against the will of the Province, Bernard demanded[5] the appropriations which the Billeting Act required. "Be explicit and distinct," said he, in a second Message, "that there may be no mistake."[6] The Act of Parliament thus formally referred to, was that, on account of which the legislative powers of New-York had been suspended; it was one to which other Colonies had partially yielded. The troops had been sent to Boston to enforce the laws; their coming had been the deliberate order of the King and his Ministry, and had been specially commended by Parliament. It was well known in what body the hatred of America had

[1] Message from the Governor, 28 June, 1769; Bradford, 175, 176.

[2] Answer of the House of Representatives, 4 July, 1769; in Bradford, 180, 181.

[3] Bradford's State Papers, 176, 177, and 180.

[4] Compare S. Cooper to T. Pownall, 12 July, 1769.

[5] Message of Bernard, 6 July, 1769; Bradford, 183.

[6] Message of Bernard, 12 July, 1769; Bradford, 183, 184.

its strong hold; and an issue was made up between the hereditary Senate of the modern Imperial Rome, and the lawyers and farmers to whom the annual election of Massachusetts entrusted legislative power. One or the other must give way. CHAP. XLI. 1769. July.

After grave deliberation in a most unusually numerous House of one hundred and seven, and as it were, in the presence of the human race and ages to come, they made answer:[1] "As Representatives, by the royal Charter and the nature of our trust, we are only empowered to grant such aids as are reasonable, of which we are free and independent judges, at liberty to follow the dictates of our own understanding, without regard to the mandates of another.—Your Excellency must, therefore, excuse us in this express declaration, that, as we cannot, consistently with our honor, or interest, and much less with the duty we owe our constituents, so we shall NEVER[2] make provision for the purposes mentioned in your messages."

"To his Majesty," rejoined Bernard in his last words, "and if he pleases, to his Parliament, must be referred your invasion of the rights of the Imperial Sovereignty. By your own acts you will be judged. Your publications are plain and explicit, and need no comment." And he prorogued the General Court to the tenth of January. "Their last message," he wrote to Hillsborough, "exceeds every thing."

Newport, Rhode Island, witnessed still bolder resistance. A vessel with a cargo of prohibited goods

[1] Answer of the House of Representatives to the Governor's Messages of July 6 and July 12, 1769;—15 July, 1769.

[2] Bradford's Massachusetts State Papers, 187.

CHAP. XLI. 1769. July.

was rescued from the revenue officers, whose ship named Liberty, was destroyed.[1]

Just as this was heard of at Boston, Hillsborough's Circular promising relief from all "real" grievances and a repeal of the duties on glass, paper and colors, as contrary to the true principles of commerce, was received by Bernard, and was immediately made public. At once the merchants, assembling on the twenty-seventh of July, voted unanimously, that this partial repeal was insufficient, since the duty on tea was to be retained to save "the right" of taxing; and it was resolved to send for no more goods from Great Britain, a few specified articles excepted, unless the revenue Acts should be repealed. The inhabitants of the town were to purchase nothing from violators of this engagement; the names of recusant importers were to be published;[2] and the Acts of Trade themselves came under the consideration of a committee,[3] appointed to prepare a statement of the embarrassments to commerce, growing out of the late regulations.[4]

In the midst of this commotion Bernard, having completed his pecuniary arrangements with Hutchinson to his own satisfaction,[5] on the evening of the last day of July left Boston to sail for Europe. "He was

[1] Hulton, Temple, Paxton, to Gov. Pitkin, 7 Aug. 1769. William Reid's Affidavit. Representation to the King of Commissioners of Inquiry, 22 June, 1773.

[2] See Vote in Boston Gazette, 31 July, 1769; 747, 1, 2.

[3] Francès to the Duke of Choiseul, 8 September, 1769, gives a very good account. Hutchinson's History, iii. 252, 253.

[4] Observations on Several Acts of Parliament, passed in the 4th, 6th and 7th years of his present Majesty's reign, &c. &c.; published by the Merchants of Boston, 1769.

[5] For the preceding jealousy of Bernard, see Andrew Oliver to Hutchinson, 22 June, 1769. Letters passed between Hutchinson and Bernard. Compare I. Williams of Hatfield to T. Hutchinson, 3 May, 1769.

CHAP. XLI. 1769. July.

to have sent home whom he pleased," said the Bostoneers; "but the die being thrown, poor Sir Francis Bernard was the rogue to go first."[1]

Trained as a wrangling proctor in an ecclesiastical court, he had been a quarrelsome disputant rather than a statesman. His parsimony went to the extreme of meanness; his avarice was insatiable and restless. So long as he connived at smuggling, he reaped a harvest in that way; when Grenville's sternness inspired alarm, it was his study to make the most money out of forfeitures and penalties. Professing to respect the Charter, he was unwearied in zeal for its subversion; declaring his opposition to taxation by Parliament, he urged it with all his power. Asserting most solemnly that he had never asked for troops, his letters reveal his perpetual importunities for ships of war and an armed force. His reports were often false, partly with design, partly from the credulity of panic. He placed every thing in the most unfavorable light, and was ready to tell every tale and magnify trivial rumors into acts of Treason. He desponded when conciliation prevailed in England. The officers of the army and the navy despised him for his cowardice and duplicity, and did not conceal their contempt. "He has essentially served us," said the patriot clergyman Cooper;[2] "had he been wise, our liberties might have been lost."

As he departed from Boston, the bells were rung, and cannon fired from the wharves; Liberty Tree was gay with flags; and at night a great bonfire was kindled upon Fort Hill. When he reached

[1] Boston Gazette, 748, 2, 3; of 7 August, 1769.

[2] Cooper to Gov. Pownall, 11 May, 1769.

CHAP. XLI. 1769. July.

England, he found that the Ministry had promised the London merchants never to employ him in America again.[1] And yet he was the Governor whom they had most trusted; for bad men fit bad ends; and the selfish oligarchy by which England was then governed, feeling themselves rebuked by the noble and the free, hated them as dangerous to their rule.[2]

While Boston was advancing steadily towards Republicanism, the enthusiasm which had made the revolution at New Orleans, could not shape for that Colony a secure and tranquil existence. A new petition to France expressed the inflexible resolve of the inhabitants to preserve the dear and inviolable name of French citizens at the greatest peril of their lives and fortunes. They sought communication with the English;[3] but the Governor at Pensacola abstained from offending powers with which his Sovereign was at peace. The dread of Spain and its Government occasioned the daring design of founding a Republic with a Council of forty, to be elected by the people, and an executive chief to be called a protector.[4] It was even proposed, if Louisiana was to be given up to his Catholic Majesty, to burn New Orleans to the ground, and leave to an unwelcome master, nothing but a desert. When near the end of July, it was told that O'Reilly had arrived at the Balise with an overwhelming force, despair prevailed for a moment; and white cockades were dis-

[1] Francès to Choiseul, 11 August, 1769.

[2] Aristotle's Politics, v. c. ix.

[3] Brown to Secretary of State, Pensacola, 1 Dec. 1768. "I am told the whole province of Louisiana have deputed fifty of the principal inhabitants to make a representation to me of their grievances, which is now preparing for the press, demanding to become English subjects, and to settle at the Natchez."

[4] Gayarré, Hist. ii. 337.

CHAP. XLI. 1769. July.

tributed by the Republicans.[1] "O'Reilly is not come to ruin the Colony," said Aubry, who had received instructions to feign ingenuous candor.[2] "If you submit," he repeated publicly and by authority, "the General will treat you with kindness, and you may have full confidence in the clemency of his Catholic Majesty."[3] These promises won faith; and with Aubry's concurrence a committee of three, Lafrênière for the Council, Marquis for the colonists, and Milhet for the merchants, waited on O'Reilly at the Balise, to recognise his authority and implore his mercy.

Aug. O'Reilly, who had no fear except lest the leading insurgents should escape into the English territory,[4] welcomed the deputies with treacherous politeness and the fairest promises,[5] detained them to dine, and dismissed them full of admiration for his talents and confident of a perfect amnesty. So general was the persuasion of security, that Villerê who had escaped upon the Mississippi and was on his way to an English post, returned to the city.

On the morning of the eighth of August, the Spanish squadron of four and twenty vessels, bearing three thousand chosen troops, anchored in front of New Orleans; and before the day was over, possession was taken in behalf of the Catholic King, and the Span-

[1] Acte d'Accusation in Gayarré.

[2] J'avais prévenu cet officier des observations qu'il devait faire et de certaines choses sur lesquelles il devait se lâcher avec une espèce de candeur et d'ingénuité pour exagerer les forces que j'avais à mes ordres, et ranimer l' espérance du public. Il s'acquittat parfaitement de sa commission. O'Reilly to Grimaldi, N. O. 31 Aug. 1769.

[3] Aubry to the Minister; Gayarré, ii. 292.

[4] Don Alexander O'Reilly to the Marquis of Grimaldi, New Orleans 31 August, 1769.

[5] 1 August, 1769, in a second Postscript to the Letter from J. Campbell to Lieut. Gov. Brown of 30 July, 1769.

CHAP. XLI. 1769. Aug. ish flag was raised at every post in the city. On the twentieth, Aubry made a full report of the events of the revolution, and named the chiefs in the enterprise.[1] "It was not easy to arrest them," wrote O'Reilly; "but I contrived to cheat their vigilance." On the twenty-first he received at his home the principal inhabitants; and he invited the people's syndics, one by one, to pass into his private apartment. The invitation was regarded as a special honor, till finding themselves all assembled and alone, they showed signs of anxiety. "For me," says O'Reilly, "I now had none for the success of my plan." Entering his cabinet with Aubry and three Spanish civil officers, he spoke to those who were thus caught in his toils: "Gentlemen, the Spanish nation is venerated throughout the Globe. Louisiana is then the only country in the universe, where it fails to meet with the respect which is its due. His Catholic Majesty is greatly provoked at the violence to his Governor, and at the publications outraging his government and the Spanish nation. You are charged with being the chiefs of this revolt; I arrest you in his name." The accused were conducted with ostentation from O'Reilly's presence to separate places of confinement; Villerē was conveyed on board the frigate that lay at the levee. It is the tradition, that his wife vainly entreated admission to him; that Villerē, hearing her voice, demanded to see her; became frantic with love, anger and grief, struggled with his guard, and fell dead from passion or from their bayo-

[1] Aubry to O'Reilly, 20 August. O' Reilly to Grimaldi, 31 August, 1769.

CHAP. XLI. 1769. Aug.

nets.[1] The official report only declares, that he did not survive the first day of bondage.[2]

The blow fell unexpectedly, and spread consternation. An amnesty for the people reserved the right of making further arrests. Provisional decrees settled the government. On the twenty-sixth and the following days, the inhabitants of New Orleans and its vicinity took the oath of allegiance to the Catholic King.

Nearly two months passed in collecting evidence against the twelve selected victims. They denied the jurisdiction of the Spanish tribunal over actions done under the flag of France and during the prevalence of French laws. But the tribunal was inexorable. The estates of the twelve, who were the richest and most considerable men in the Province, were confiscated in whole or in part for the benefit of the officers employed in the trial; six were sentenced to imprisonment for six, or ten years, or for life; the memory of Villeré was declared infamous; the remaining five, Lafrénière, his young son-in-law, Noyau, Caresse, Marquis, and Joseph Milhet, were condemned to be hanged.

The citizens of New Orleans entreated time for a petition to Charles the Third; the wives, daughters, and sisters of those who had not shared in the revolution, appealed to O'Reilly for mercy; but without effect. Tradition will have it, that the young and gallant Noyau, newly married, might have escaped; but he refused to fly from the doom of his associates.[3] On

[1] Martin's History of Louisiana; Gayarré's Hist. de la Louisiane, ii. 305.

[2] Note at page 303 of Gayarré's Lectures, Third Series.

[3] Gayarré's Louisiana, iii. 338, 339.

CHAP. XLI. 1769. the twenty-fifth of October, the five martyrs to their love of France and liberty, were brought forth pinioned, and in presence of the troops and the people, for want of an executioner, were shot. "At length," said O'Reilly, "the insult done to the King's dignity and authority in this Province is repaired. The example now given can never be effaced."[1]

Spaniards as well as men of other nations, censured the sanguinary revenge. In the several parishes of Louisiana O'Reilly was received with silence and submission. The King of Spain approved his acts; and the Council for the Indies found in his administration "nothing but evidence of the immensity and sublimity of his genius."[2] Aubry perished on his voyage to France, in a ship which foundered in the Garonne. The son of Masan, one of those condemned to imprisonment, made his way to Madrid, offering himself as his father's substitute; by the aid of France the six prisoners were set free.

The census of the city of New Orleans showed a population of eighteen hundred and one white persons, thirty-one free blacks, sixty-eight free persons of mixed blood; sixty domiciliated Indians; and twelve hundred and twenty-five slaves; in all three thousand one hundred and ninety souls. The whole population in the valley of the Mississippi, then subject to the Spanish sway, is estimated at thirteen thousand five hundred. The privileges which France had granted, were abolished, and the Colony was organized like other colonial possessions of Spain. But Spain willingly kept New Orleans depressed, that it might

[1] Gayarré's Hist. ii. 350, 351.

[2] Gayarré's Hist. ii. 378.

not attract too strongly the cupidity of England. Its system of restriction struck its victim to the heart. CHAP. XLI. 1769.

The settlement of the wilderness, of which France had reserved no portion and Spain and England feared to develope the resources, was promoted by native Pioneers. Jonathan Carver of Connecticut, had in three former years explored the borders of Lake Superior, and the country of the Sioux beyond it;[1] had obtained more accurate accounts of that Great River, which bore, as he reported, the name of Oregon[2] and flowed into the Pacific; and he now returned to claim reward for his discoveries, to celebrate the richness of the copper mines of the Northwest; to recommend English settlements on the western extremity of the continent; and to propose opening, by aid of Lakes and Rivers, a passage across the continent, as the best route for communicating with China and the East Indies.[3]

Illinois invited emigrants more than ever; for its aboriginal inhabitants were fast disappearing from the earth. In April, 1769, Pontiac, so long the dreaded enemy of the English, had been assassinated by an Illinois[4] Indian without provocation and in time of peace;[5] the Indians of the Northwest sent round belts to all the Nations to avenge the murder of their Chief. In vain did five or six hundred of the Illinois

[1] Bernard to the Earl of Hillsborough; Same to Lord Barrington and to Fitzherbert, 21 February, 1769.

[2] The Oregon or the River of the West. Carver's Travels, 76.

[3] Carver's Travels through the interior parts of North America, in the years 1766, 1767, and 1768. Introduction, v. vi.

[4] J. Campbell to Lieut. Governor Brown, 30 July, 1769.

[5] Gage to Sir William Johnson, 20 August, 1769. Gage to Hillsborough, 12 August, 1769.

CHAP. XLI. 1769.

crowd for protection round the walls of Fort Chartres; the ruthless spirit of reciprocal murder was not appeased, till the Illinois tribes were nearly all exterminated,[1] and their beautiful and fertile plains, cooled during the summer by the ever blowing West wind, were left vacant for the white man.

Connecticut which at this time was exercising a disputed jurisdiction in the valley of Wyoming,[2] did not forget that by its Charter, its possessions extended indefinitely to the West; and a company of "military Adventurers," headed by one of its most intelligent sons,[3] was also soliciting leave from the Government in England to lead forth a Colony to the south-western banks of the Mississippi.[4]

In his peaceful habitation on the banks of the Yadkin River, in North Carolina, Daniel Boone,[5] the illustrious hunter, had heard Finley, a trader, so memorable[6] as the Pioneer, describe a tract of land west of Virginia, as the richest in North America or in the world.[7] In May 1769, leaving his wife and off-

[1] John F. Schermerhorn's Report concerning the Indians inhabiting the Western Parts of the United States; Mass. Hist. Coll. xii. 8.

[2] Compare Minutes of the Provincial Council, in Pennsylvania Colonial Records, ix. 606–609. Pennsylvania Archives, iv. 342–344. Miner's History of Wyoming.

[3] Timothy Dwight's Travels in New England and New-York, i. 308.

[4] W. S. Johnson to Jos. Trumbull, 15 April, 1769. Compare Martin's Louisiana, ii. 35; Monette's Valley of the Mississippi, i. 407, 408.

[5] "Boone was born in Virginia," McLung, 49. "Boone was born in Bucks County, Pennsylvania, on the right bank of the Delaware river," Collins, 182. Boone "was born in Maryland," Marshall, i. 17. "The advancing settlements of Schuylkill," Morehead, 17. "Bridgeworth, Somersetshire, England," Niles, iv. 33, confounding perhaps the birth-place of his father, with that of Daniel Boone himself. Daniel himself does not seem to have thought about where or when he was born. Filson writes the name Boon.

[6] Compare J. T. Morehead's Address in commemoration, &c. 16, and Marshall's History of Kentucky, i. 7, 8.

[7] Filson's Discovery, Settlement and Present State of Kentucky, published in 1784, and authenticated by a certificate from Boone and Todd and Harrod.

CHAP. XLI. 1769.

spring, having Finley as his pilot, and four others as companions, the[1] young man, of about three and twenty, wandered forth through the wilderness of America, "in quest of the country of Kentucky,"[2] known to the Savages as "the Dark and Bloody Ground," "the Middle Ground" between the subjects of the Five Nations and the Cherokees.[3] After a long and fatiguing journey through mountain ranges, the party found themselves in June on the Red River, a tributary of the Kentucky, and from the top of an eminence surveyed with delight the beautiful plain that stretched to the Northwest. Here they built their shelter and began to reconnoitre the country and to hunt. All the kinds of wild beasts that were natural to America, the stately elk, the timid deer, the antlered stag, the wild-cat, the bear, the panther and the wolf, couched among the canes, or roamed over the rich grasses, which even beneath the thickest shades sprung luxuriantly out of the generous soil. The buffaloes cropped fearlessly the herbage, or browsed on the leaves of the reed, and were more frequent than cattle in the settlements of Carolina herdsmen. Sometimes there were hundreds in a drove, and round the salt-licks their numbers were amazing.[4]

The summer in which for the first time, a party of white men enjoyed the brilliancy of nature near, and

[1] Marshall's History of Kentucky, i. 17. Morehead's Address, 17; compare J. M. Peck in the American Pioneers, i. 243. Boone died in 1820; Niles' Register, iv. 33, brings him into the world in 1730. Monette, i. 363, gives him a son of "nearly twenty years old" in 1773. Boone in his Narrative does not give the age of the son.

[2] The Adventures of Col. Daniel Boon, formerly a Hunter, &c. &c. dictated by himself to John Filson.

[3] Filson in Imlay's Topographical Description of the Western Territory; Third Ed. 308.

[4] Boone's Autobiography.

CHAP. XLI. in the valley of the Elkhorn, passed away in the occupations of exploring parties and the chase. But one by one, Boone's companions dropped off, till he was left alone with John Stewart. They jointly found unceasing delight in the wonders of the forest, till, one evening near Kentucky River, they were taken prisoners by a band of Indians, wanderers like themselves. They escaped; and were joined by Boone's brother; so that when Stewart was soon after killed by savages, the first victim among the hecatombs of white men, slain by them in their desperate battling for the lovely hunting ground,[1] Boone still had his brother to share with him the dangers and the attractions of the wilderness; the building and occupying the first cottage in Kentucky.

In the Spring of 1770, that brother returned to the settlements for horses and supplies of ammunition, leaving the renowned hunter "by himself, without bread, or salt, or sugar, or even a horse or dog." "The idea of a beloved wife"[2] anxious for his safety, tinged his thoughts with sadness; but otherwise the cheerful, meditative man, careless of wealth, knowing the use of the rifle, not the plough, of a strong robust frame, in the vigorous health of early manhood, ignorant of books, but versed in the forest and forest life, ever fond of tracking the deer on foot, away from men, yet in his disposition humane, generous and gentle, was happy in the uninterrupted succession "of sylvan pleasures."

He held unconscious intercourse with beauty
Old as creation.

[1] Butler's History of Kentucky, Second Ed. 19.

[2] Boone's Autobiography in Imlay, 341.

One calm summer's evening, as he climbed a commanding ridge, and looked out upon the remote "venerable mountains" and the nearer ample plains, and caught a glimpse in the distance of the Ohio, which bounded the land of his affections with majestic grandeur, his heart exulted in the region he had discovered. "All things were still."[1] Not a breeze so much as shook a leaf. He kindled a fire near a fountain of sweet water, and feasted on the loin of a buck. He was no more alone than a bee among flowers, but communed familiarly with the whole universe of life. Nature was his intimate, and as the roving woodsman leaned confidingly on her bosom, she responded to his intelligence.

For him the rocks and the fountains, the leaf and the blade of grass had life; the cooling air laden with the wild perfume, came to him as a friend; the dewy morning wrapped him in its embrace; the trees stood up gloriously round about him as so many myriads of companions. All forms wore the character of desire or peril. But how could he be afraid? Triumphing over danger, he knew no fear. The perpetual howling of the wolves by night round his cottage or his bivouac in the brake, was his diversion;[2] and by day he had joy in surveying the various species of animals that surrounded him. He loved the solitude better than the towered city or the hum of business.[3]

[1] "All things were still.—Not a breeze shook the most tremulous leaf.—I kindled a fire," &c. &c. Boone's Autobiography in Imlay, 342.

[2] "The prowling wolves diverted," &c. &c. Boone, 342.

[3] "No populous cities, with all the varieties of commerce and stately structures, could afford so much pleasure to my mind, as the beauties of nature I found here." Boone.

CHAP. XLI.

Near the end of July 1770, his faithful brother came back to meet him at the old camp. Shortly after they proceeded together to Cumberland River, giving names to the different waters; and he then returned to his wife and children; fixed in his purpose at the risk of life and fortune to bring them as soon as possible to live in Kentucky, which he esteemed a second Paradise.[1]

[1] For the authentication of the whole of this account of Boone, compare his Autobiography dictated by him in 1784, and first published by John Filson. It is the source of the historian, the orator and the biographer. It is a pity that the amanuensis and editor garnished the Hunter's Narrative with bits of learning of his own.

CHAPTER XLII.

THE NON-IMPORTATION AGREEMENT ENFORCED.—THE NEW TORY PARTY INSTALLED IN POWER.

AUGUST 1769,—JANUARY 1770.

CHAP. XLII. 1769. Aug.

"THE Lieutenant Governor well understands my system,"[1] said Bernard, as he transferred the Government. Hutchinson was descended from one of the earliest settlers of Massachusetts and loved the land of his birth. A native of Boston, he was its representative for ten years, during three of which he was Speaker of the Assembly; for more than ten other years, he was a member of the Council, as well as Judge of Probate; since June 1758,[2] he had been Lieutenant Governor, and since September 1760, Chief Justice also; and twice he had been chosen Colonial Agent. No man was so experienced in the public affairs of the Colony; and no one was so familiar with its history, usages and laws. In the Legislature he had assisted to raise the credit of Massachusetts by substituting hard money for a paper currency. As a Judge, though he decided political questions

[1] Bernard to Hillsborough, 29 April, 1769.

[2] Hutchinson's History, iii. 75.

CHAP. XLII. 1769. Aug. with the subserviency of a courtier, yet in approving wills, he was considerate towards the orphan and the widow, and he heard private suits with unblemished integrity. In adjusting points of difference with a neighboring jurisdiction, he was faithful to the Province by which he was employed. His advancement to administrative power was fatal to England and to himself. The love of money, which was his ruling passion in youth, had grown with his years; and avarice in an old man is cowardly and mean; knows that its time is short, and clutches with eagerness at immediate gains.

A nervous timidity which was natural to him, had been increased by age as well as by his adverse experience during the riots on account of the Stamp Act; and in the conduct of public affairs made him as false to his employers as to his own honor. While he cringed to the minister, he trembled before the people.

At Boston, Hutchinson professed zeal for the interests and liberties of the Province. With fawning treachery he claimed to be its friend; had at one time courted its favor by denying the right[1] of Parliament to tax America either internally or externally; and had argued with conclusive ability against the expediency and the equity of that measure.[2] He now redoubled his attempts to deceive; wrote favorable letters which he never[3] sent, but read to those about him as evidence of his good will; and professed even to have braved hostility

[1] John Adams in Novanglus.

[2] The Argument still exists in manuscript, and assisted to deceive the Rockingham whigs as well as unsuspecting men in the Colony.

[3] Letters in Letter Book to Bollan, 16 Feb. 1769. Boston Gazette, 4 March, 1776; 1085, 2, 3.

CHAP. XLII. 1769. Aug.

in England for his attachment to colonial liberties.[1] At Boston he wished not to be thought to have been very closely connected with his predecessor.[2] At the same moment, "I have lived in perfect harmony with Governor Bernard," was the time-server's first message to the Colonial Office;[3] "I flatter myself, he will when he arrives in England give a favorable opinion of me;" and expressing his adhesion to the highest system of metropolitan authority, and retaining the services of Israel Mauduit as his agent, he devoted his rare ability and his intimate acquaintance with the history and constitution of the Province to suggest for its thorough "subjection"[4] a system of coercive measures, which England gradually and reluctantly adopted.

Wherever the Colony had a friend, he would artfully set before him such hints as might incline him to harsh judgments.[5] Even to Franklin he vouched for the tales of Bernard as "most just and candid."[6] He paid court to the enemies of American liberty by stimulating them to the full indulgence of their malignity. He sought out great men, and those who stood at the door of great men, the underlings of present Ministers or prospective Ministers, of Grenville, or Hillsborough, or Jenkinson, or the King; urged them incessantly to bring on the crisis by the immediate intervention of Parliament;[7] and advised the change of the

[1] Hutchinson to Lyman.

[2] Cooper to Gov. Pownall, 8 Sept. 1769.

[3] Hutchinson to John Pownall, 25 July, 1769.

[4] Hutchinson to Israel Mauduit.

[5] In proof note the whole tenor of his correspondence with Bollan, whom he could not deceive; with Richard Jackson, whose good opinion he for a time won, and with Gov. Pownall and others.

[6] T. Hutchinson to B Franklin, Boston, 29 July, 1769.

[7] To go no further back than 1769; Hutchinson to T. Whately, 20 Jan. 1769; to R. Jackson, 18 August, 1769; to T. Whately, 24 August, 1769; to Maj. Gen. Mackay, 11

CHAP. XLII. 1769. Aug. Charter of the Province,[1] as well as those of Rhode-Island and Connecticut; the dismemberment of Massachusetts;[2] the diminution of the liberties of New England Towns;[3] the establishment of a citadel[4] within the town of Boston; the stationing of a fleet in its harbor;[5] the experiment of martial law;[6]

Sept. 1769; to Sir Francis Bernard, 6 Oct. 1769; to person not named, 17 October, 1769; to Sir Francis Bernard, 19 October, 1769; to the Earl of Hillsborough, 20 October, 1769; to T. Whately, 20 or 26 Oct. 1769. [Compare Grenville Papers, iv. 481.] To John Pownall, Secretary of the Board of Trade, a private channel for communicating with the Ministry, 23 Oct. 1769; to Israel Mauduit, 27 Oct. 1769; to John Pownall, for Hillsborough's eye, 14 Nov. 1769; to a person not named, 9 Jan. 1770. This is merely a beginning of references to letters of which I have authentic abstracts or copies, and which urge the extreme interposition of Parliament, against the province, or against individuals.

[1] Hutchinson to R. Jackson, 14 June, 1768. "This annual election of the Council spoils the Constitution;" to R. Jackson, 28 January, 1769, acting simultaneously with Bernard, and inclosing a list of persons to be appointed Mandamus Councillors. To John Pownall, 25 July, 1769, "I have lived in perfect harmony with Governor Bernard," which is an avowal of complicity. To Hillsborough, 9 Oct. 1770, compared with the letter to Sir Francis Bernard, 26 Dec. 1770; very strong and decided, as well as artful; and compare the letter to I. Mauduit, Dec. 1770. "Improvements in the Constitution." "It will be best that I should not be suspected by the people here of having suggested any alteration." And again to Sir F. Bernard, 23 January, 1771; "I wished for a delay, rather than to lay the design aside," &c. &c.

[2] Besides earlier letters; see for example, Hutchinson to Secretary Pownall, 5 Dec. 1770; to Sir Francis Bernard, Jan. 1771; to Secretary Pownall, 24 Jan. 1771; to ——, 5 June, 1771; to Secretary Pownall, July, 1773, &c. &c.

[3] Hutchinson to ——, 9 Jan. 1770; a mere hint for a close corporation for Boston. Again to Sec. Pownall, 21 March, 1770; to Hillsborough, 26 July, 1770; a hint, "If the town were a corporation as New-York;" to Sec. Pownall, 20 Nov. 1770; "Endeavor that the letter to which you refer, hinting advantages from the constitution of the City of New-York, may not be laid before the House of Commons," &c. To Secretary Pownall, 3 April, 1771; "It must show to Parliament the necessity of such an alteration in the constitution of the town, as some time ago you gave me a hint of, and will be sufficient to render an act for that purpose unexceptionable." Again 18 April, 1771, to Sec. Pownall, and so on, till the Act of Parliament for the change. Hutchinson liked to make his correspondent seem to have originated the advice. So Feb. 1773, to Sec. Pownall, "In some way or other towns must be restrained."

[4] Hutchinson to Sir Francis Bernard, 12 April, 1770, a hint; to ——, 22 October, 1770, open advice; and other letters.

[5] Many letters.

[6] Hutchinson to T. Whately, 24

CHAP. XLII. 1769. Aug.

the transportation of "incendiaries"[1] to England; the prohibition of the New England fisheries;[2] with other measures, which he dared not trust to paper,[3] and recommended only by insinuations and verbal messages. At the same time he entreated the concealment of his solicitations. "Keep secret every thing I write,"[4] said he to Whately, his channel for communicating with Grenville. "I have never yet seen any rational plan for a partial subjection;" he writes to Jenkinson's influential friend Mauduit; "my sentiments upon these points should be concealed."[5] Though he kept back part of his thoughts, he begged Bernard to burn his letters. "It will be happy if, in the next Session, Parliament make thorough work,"[6] he would write to John Pownall, the Secretary of the Board of Trade; and then "caution" him to "suffer no parts of his letters to transpire."

"I humbly entreat your Lordship, that my letters may not be made public," was his ever-renewed prayer to successive Secretaries of State, so that he conducted the Government like one engaged in a

August, 1769. To person unnamed, 8 Sept. 1769, and other letters—for example, to Sir F. Bernard, 20 Oct. 1770.

[1] See the Affidavits taken by Hutchinson, in 1769, and compare Hutchinson to Sir F. Bernard, 20 Oct. 1770. "I wish you would read the story of the 30 colonies in the 27th and 29th books of Livy." This cunning way of hinting advice is characteristic. See Livy, xxvii. Secs. ix. x., and xxix. Sec. xv. Compare other letters.

[2] Hutchinson to Sir Francis Bernard, 20 October, 1770. "Exclude them from the fishery, and the like;" "they cannot long subsist without trade."

[3] For example, Hutchinson to Sir Francis Bernard, 19 April, 1770. "If besides a penal Act of Parliament, something is not done, which I dare not trust to a letter," &c. &c. Same in other letters.

[4] Hutchinson to Whately, 20 or 26 Oct. 1769.

[5] Hutchinson to I. Mauduit, 27 Oct. 1769.

[6] Hutchinson to J. Pownall, 27 July, 1770, and 26 Nov. 1773.

CHAP. XLII. 1769. Aug. conspiracy or an intrigue. But some of his letters could hardly fail to be discovered; and then it would be disclosed that he had laid snares for the life of patriots, and had urged the "thorough" overthrow of English liberty in America.

The agreement of non-importation originated in New-York, where it was rigidly carried into effect. No acrimony appeared; every one, without so much as a single dissentient, approved the combination as wise and legal; persons in the highest stations declared against the Revenue Acts;[1] and the Governor wished their repeal.[2] His acquiescence in the associations for coercing that repeal, led the moderate men among the patriots of New-York to plan a Union of the Colonies in an American Parliament, preserving the Governments of the several Colonies, and having the members of the general Parliament chosen by their respective Legislatures.[3] They were preparing the greatest work of their generation, to be matured at a later day; their confidence of immediate success assisted to make them alike disinclined to independence, and firm in their expectation of bringing England to reason by suspending their mutual trade.

The people of Boston,[4] stimulated by the unanimity and scrupulous fidelity of New-York, were impatient that a son of Bernard, two sons of Hutchinson, and about five others, would not accede to the

[1] Andrew Oliver to Whately, New-York, 12 August, 1769.

[2] Same to Hutchinson, New-York, 7 August, 1769.

[3] Dr. Cooper to Gov. Pownall, 1 January, 1770. Compare Hutchinson to Sir Francis Bernard, 18 Feb. 1770.

[4] Hutchinson to Hillsborough, Boston, 8 Aug. 1769; Same to Sir Francis Bernard, 8 Aug. 1769.

agreement. At a great and public Meeting of Merchants[1] in Faneuil Hall, Hancock proposed to send for Hutchinson's two sons, hinting what was true, that the Lieutenant Governor was himself a partner[2] with them in their late extraordinary importations of tea. As the best means of coercion, it was voted not to purchase any thing of the recusants; subscription papers to that effect were carried round from house to house, and every body complied.[3]

The Anniversary of the Fourteenth of August was commemorated with unusual solemnity. Three or four hundred dined together in the open field at Dorchester; and since the Ministry had threatened the leading patriots with death for treason, the last of their Forty-Five Toasts was: "Strong halters, firm blocks, and sharp axes, to such as deserve them."[4] The famous Liberty Song was sung, and all the company with one heart joined in the chorus. At five in the afternoon, they returned in a procession a mile and a half long, entered the town before dark, marched round the State-House, and quietly retired each to his own home.[5]

Massachusetts was sustained by South Carolina, whose Assembly, imperfectly imitated by New Jersey,[6] refused compliance with the Billeting Act,[7] and

[1] Boston Gazette, 749, 2, 1, of 14 August, 1769.

[2] Boston Gazette, 4 Sept. 1769; 752, 3, 1.

[3] Hutchinson to Sir Francis Bernard, Boston, 8 August, 1769.

[4] Boston Gazette, 21 August, 1769; 750, 1, 1 and 2.

[5] J. Adams's Works, ii. 219.

[6] Gov. Wm. Franklin to Hillsborough, 27 September, 1769. Hillsborough to Gov. Franklin, December, 1769. Colden to Lord Hillsborough, 4 October, 1769. Hillsborough to Gage, 9 Dec. 1769.

[7] Lieut. Gov. Bull to Gen. Gage, 24 August, 1769.

CHAP. XLII. 1769. Sept. whose people enforced the agreement of not importing, by publishing the names of the few enemies to America, who kept aloof from the Association.[1]

In Europe, France studied with care the news from the Colonies, and was convinced of "their intrepidity"[2] and "their animated and persevering zeal;"[3] while the British Ministry gave no steady attention to American affairs;[4] and defeated the hope of conciliatory measures which all parties seemed to desire,[5] by taking the advice of Bernard.[6]

The ferment in the Colonies went on increasing. Copies having just then been received of the many letters from the public officers in Boston which had been laid before Parliament, Otis, who was become almost irresponsible from his nearness to frenzy,[7] grew wild with rage at having been aspersed as a demagogue, and provoked[8] an affray, in which he, being quite alone, was set upon by one of the Commissioners of the Customs, aided by bystanders, and received "much hurt"[9] from a very severe blow on the head.[10] This affair multiplied quarrels between the people and the King's officers, and mixed per-

[1] Bull to Sec. of State, 25 Sept. 1769, and Hillsborough to Bull, 30 Nov. 1769.

[2] Choiseul to Du Chatelet, Versailles, 8 Sept. 1769.

[3] Choiseul, 15 Sept. 1769.

[4] Hugh Hammersley to Sharpe, 14 Sept. 1769.

[5] Hugh Hammersley to Sharpe, 30 Nov. 1769.

[6] Francés to the Duc de Choiseul, London, 8 Sept. 1769.

[7] Compare John Adams's Diary, Works, ii. 219, 220.

[8] See the Boston Gazette of 4 September, 1769, for publications by Otis.

[9] From a letter of Hutchinson. Compare the Diary of John Adams, which shows that Otis was not so much hurt but that he was abroad the next day.

[10] For an account of the fray see Boston Gazette, 11 Sept. 1769. Compare Tudor's Life of Otis, 362; John Robinson in Boston Gazette, 11 Sept. 1769; Otis in Boston Gazette, 18 Sept.; John Gridley's Affidavit, 13 Sept. 1769.

CHAP. XLII. 1769. Oct.

sonal bitterness with the struggle for suspending the trade with England.

Early in October a vessel, laden with goods shipped by English houses themselves, arrived at Boston. The military officers had been speculating on what would be done, and Dalrymple stood ready[1] to protect the factors. But his assistance was not demanded; Hutchinson permitted the merchants to reduce the consignees to submission, and even to compel an English adventurer to re-embark his goods.[3] One and another of the Boston recusants yielded; even the two sons of Hutchinson himself by their father's direction, gave up eighteen chests of tea and entered fully into the agreement. Four still held out, and their names, with those of the two sons of Hutchinson, whose sincerity was questioned, stand recorded as infamous on the journals of the town of Boston.[3] On the fifteenth another ship arrived; again the troops looked on as bystanders, and witnessed the complete victory of the people.[4]

A letter from New-York next invited Boston to extend the agreement against importing indefinitely until every Act imposing duties should be repealed; and on the seventeenth, by the great influence of Molineux, Otis, Samuel Adams and William Cooper, this new form was adopted.[5]

On the eighteenth of October, the town, sum-

[1] Dalrymple to Gage, 1 October, 1769.

[2] New-York Gazette, No. 1398, 16 Oct. 1769. Dalrymple to Gage, October, 1769. Votes at the Meeting of the Merchants, 4 Oct. 1769. Boston Gazette, 9 Oct. 1769: 757, 1, 1 and 2, and 3.

[3] Hutchinson to Sir Francis Bernard, 19 Oct. 1769.

[4] Dalrymple to Gage, 16 October, 1769.

[5] Hutchinson to ——, 17 Oct. 1769. Dalrymple to Gage, 22 October, 1769.

CHAP. XLII. 1769. Oct. moned together by lawful authority, made their "Appeal to the World." They refuted and covered with ridicule "the false and malicious aspersions" of Bernard, Gage, Hood, and the Revenue Officers; and making the language and the intrepidity of Samuel Adams[1] their own, they avowed their character and proclaimed their decision, with a boldness that would have seemed arrogance, had not events proved it to have been magnanimity. "A legal meeting of the Town of Boston," such were their words, "is an Assembly where a noble freedom of speech is ever expected and maintained; where men think as they please and speak as they think. Such an Assembly has ever been the dread, often the scourge of tyrants.[2]

"We should yet be glad that the ancient and happy union between Great Britain and this country might be restored. The taking off the duties on paper, glass and painters' colors, upon commercial principles only, will not give satisfaction. Discontent runs through the continent upon much higher principles. Our rights are invaded by the Revenue Acts; therefore until they are ALL repealed," "and the troops recalled," "the cause of our just complaints cannot be removed."

The declaration of the town of Boston[3] was fearless and candid; Hutchinson, through secret channels, sent word to Grenville, to Jenkinson and Hillsbo-

[1] Large fragments of his draft have been preserved and are in my possession. I believe no doubt is entertained of the authorship of the Appeal.

[2] An Appeal to the World, or a Vindication of the Town of Boston, p. 18.

[3] Appeal to the World by the people of the Town of Boston, 18 October, 1769; pp. 32, 33.

CHAP. XLII. 1769. Oct.

rough, that all would be set right if Parliament,[1] within the first week of its session,[2] would change the municipal government of Boston,[3] incapacitate its patriots to hold any public office,[4] and restore the vigor of authority by decisive action. He would abolish the existing "vague, uncertain sort of government;" he would have no "partial subjection."[5] But he prepared also for the inaction of Parliament; writing orders for a new and large supply of teas for his sons' shop; and instructing his correspondent how to send them to market, so as to elude the vigilance of the Boston committees.[6]

Meantime languor crept over all the servants of Government. Two regiments remained to preserve order; "I consider myself to be without support,"[7] said their Commander; who could get no leave to employ his little army. On Saturday the twenty-eighth, a great multitude of people laid hold of an informer,[8] besmeared him with tar and feathers, and with the troops under arms as spectators, carted him through the town which was illuminated for the occasion. Mein, a printer, whose caricatures of leading patriots had given offence, engaged in a quarrel, fired pistols, and fled for shelter to the main guard, whence he was obliged to escape in dis-

[1] Hutchinson to Sir Francis Bernard, 19 Oct. 1769.

[2] Hutchinson to Whately, 20 Oct. 1769; and see Whately to Grenville, 3 Dec. 1769; in Grenville Papers, iv. 486.

[3] Hutchinson to John Pownall Secretary of the Board of Trade, at which Hillsborough presided, 23 Oct. 1769.

[4] Same letter.

[5] Hutchinson to Israel Mauduit, 27 Oct. 1769.

[6] Hutchinson to William Palmer, 24 October, 1769. Compare Same to Same, 5 Oct. 1769.

[7] Dalrymple to Gage, 28 October, 1769.

[8] Hutchinson to Hillsborough, 31 Oct. 1769. Dalrymple to Gage, 29 October, 1769. Hutchinson to Sir Francis Bernard, 30 Oct. 1769.

CHAP. XLII. 1769. Oct. guise, only to abscond from the town. Terrified by the commotions, the only two importers who had continued to stand out, capitulated.[1]

To the military, its inactivity was humiliating. Soldiers and officers spoke of the people angrily as rebels. "The men were rendered desperate" by the firmness with which the local magistrates put them on trial for every transgression of the provincial laws.[2] Arrests provoked resistance. "If they touch you, run them through the bodies," said a Captain in the twenty-ninth regiment to his soldiers, and was indicted for the speech.[3] The magistrates continued their efforts to check the insolence of offenders by the civil authority, although soldiers were repeatedly rescued from peace officers, and contrived to evade legal punishments.[4]

Nov. In November, a true Bill was found by the Grand Jury against Thomas Gage, as well as many others, "for slandering the town of Boston."[5] Dalrymple was so "continually engaged in disagreeable broils," that he and other officers longed to leave the town. Martial Law not having been proclaimed, "a military force," Hutchinson owned, "was of no sort of use," and was "perfectly despised."[6] "Troops," said Samuel Adams, "which have heretofore been the terror of the enemies to liberty, parade the streets, to become the objects of the contempt even of women and children."[7]

The menace that he and his friends should

[1] Dalrymple to Gage, 6 November, 1769.

[2] Dalrymple to Gage, 28 Oct. 1769.

[3] The Bill of Indictment found against Parmely Molesworth in the Superior Court, in Nov. 1769. Original papers of S. Adams.

[4] Paper by James Bowdoin.

[5] Indictment found and Presented by the Grand Jury at Boston. I have the originals of some of them.

[6] Hutchinson's Hist. iii. 263.

[7] Samuel Adams to D. De Berdt, 6 Nov. 1769.

CHAP. XLII. 1769. Nov.

be arrested and shipped to England, was no more heeded than idle words. The Assembly of North Carolina, in November, unanimously[1] adopted the protest of Virginia against the proposal, and thus provoked a dissolution, which opened to the Regulators some hope of relief through new elections.

But a different turn was given to public thought, when Botetourt, the King's own Friend, communicated to the Assembly of Virginia the ministerial promises of a partial repeal, and with the most solemn asseverations abdicated in the King's name all further intentions of taxing America. The Council, in its reply, advised the entire repeal of the existing taxes; the Burgesses expressed their gratitude for "information sanctified by the royal word;" and considered the King's influence to be pledged "towards perfecting the happiness of all his people."[2] Botetourt was so pleased with their Address, that he found his prospect brighten, and praising their loyalty, wished them freedom and happiness, "till time should be no more."

The flowing and confident assurances of Botetourt encouraged the expectation that the unproductive tax on tea would also be given up. Such was his wish; and such the advice of Eden, the new Lieutenant Governor of Maryland.[3] To the Legislature of New-York, Colden, who, on account of the death of Moore, now administered the Government, announced unequivocally "the greatest probability that the late duties imposed by the authority of Parliament, so much to the dissatisfaction of the Colo-

[1] Tryon to Hillsborough, 22 Nov. 1769.

[2] Burk's Virginia, iii. 352.

[3] Eden to Hillsborough, 23 Nov. 1769.

CHAP. XLII. 1769. Nov. nies, would be taken off in the ensuing session."[1] The confident promise confirmed the loyalty of the House, though by way of caution they adopted and put upon their journals the resolves of Virginia.[2]

Dec. The cardinal policy of New-York was the security and development of colonial liberty through an American Constitution, based upon a union of the Colonies in one general Congress. This purpose, it was believed, might be accomplished, without dissolving the connection with Great Britain. "They are jealous of the scheme in England," said William Smith; "yet they will find the spirit of Democracy so persevering, that they will be under the necessity of coming into it."[3] Under the pretext of framing common regulations of trade with the Indians, the Assembly of New-York at its present session, with the concurrence of its Lieutenant Governor,[4] invited each Province to elect representatives to a body which should exercise legislative power for them all. It was a great step towards the American Union. Virginia, when she heard of the proposal, made choice of Patrick Henry and Richard Bland, to appear as her Representatives.[5] But the cherished scheme was defeated for the time by the British Ministry, who saw in Union the certain forerunner of independence.

[1] Journal of the General Assembly, 4, Speech of the Lieutenant Governor, 22 November, 1769. Compare Hillsborough to Colden, 18 January, 1770.

[2] Colden to Hillsborough, 4 Dec. 1769, and 16 Dec. 1769.

[3] Letter from William Smith, the historian of New-York, quoted in Hutchinson to Sir Francis Bernard, 18 February, 1770. Compare the narrative of William Smith Jr., in the Biographical Sketch of his father, prefixed to the New-York Historical Society's edition of Smith's History of New-York. See the Journals of the New-York Assembly for 30 Nov. 1769, pages 18 and 95, 98, 103, 105, &c. &c.

[4] Colden to Hillsborough, 21 Feb. 1770, and Hillsborough to Colden, 14 April, 1770.

[5] Henry and Bland to Colden, 1770.

A general tendency to conciliation prevailed. Since the merchants of Philadelphia chose to confine their agreement for non-importation to the repeal of Townshend's Act,[1] the merchants of Boston for the sake of Union gave up their more extensive covenant, and reverted to their first stipulations.[2] The dispute about the Billeting Act had ceased in New Jersey and Pennsylvania; the Legislature of New-York, pleased with the permission to issue colonial bills of credit,[3] disregarded the appeal from MacDougall, "to the betrayed inhabitants of the city and Colony, and sanctioned a compromise by a majority of one. CHAP. XLII. 1769. Dec.

South Carolina[4] was commercially the most closely connected with England. A Colony of planters, it numbered about forty-five thousand whites; of negroes more than eighty thousand. The annual exports from Charleston reached in value about two and a quarter millions of dollars, of which three fourths went directly or indirectly to England. Unhappily its laws restraining the importation of negroes had expired on the first of January, and their renewal was prohibited. In consequence, five thousand five hundred negroes, chiefly adults, for immediate service, were sent there within eleven months, and, were sold upon an average at near forty pounds sterling each, amounting in the aggregate to a million of dollars. But however closely the ties of interest

[1] Letter of Robert Morris, Charles Thompson, and Thomas Mifflin to the Merchants of London.

[2] Cooper to Gov. Pownall, 1 Jan. 1770. Hutchinson to Hillsborough, P. S. 5 Dec. 1769.

[3] Compare Colden to Hillsborough, 4 Oct. 1769; and Same to Same, 6 January, 1770.

[4] Bull to Hillsborough, 6 Dec. 1769.

CHAP. XLII. 1769. Dec. bound Carolina to England, the people were high-spirited; and notwithstanding the great inconvenience to their trade, they persevered in the strict observance of their association; looking with impatient anxiety for the desired repeal of the Act complained of.[1]

Thus all America confined its issue with Great Britain to the single question of the Act imposing a duty on tea. "Will not a repeal of all other duties satisfy the colonists?"[2] asked one of the ministerial party of Franklin in London. And he frankly answered: "I think not; it is not the sum paid in the duty on tea, that is complained of as a burden, but the principle of the Act, expressed in the Preamble." The faithful advice was communicated to the Ministry; but what effect could it produce, where Hillsborough administered the Colonies with Bernard for his Counsellor?

Men felt that a crisis[3] was near which would affect every part of the British empire. Hutchinson saw no prospect of establishing such a government as he desired, until free speech in the mother country should be restrained; and Otis, who was bowed to the ground with the sorrow of despair, had no hope for America, but "from some grand revolution in England."[4] The question was not a narrow colonial one respecting three pence a pound duty on tea; it involved the reality of representative Government, and its decision would show, whether the feudal monarchy of the

[1] Bull to Hillsborough, 6 Dec. 1769.

[2] Strahan to Franklin, 21 Nov. 1769, and Franklin to Strahan, 29 Nov. 1769; in Franklin iv. 258, 261. Compare Franklin's Works, vii. 478.

[3] Compare Israel Williams to Hutchinson, 20 Nov. 1769.

[4] Compare Hutchinson to Sir Francis Bernard, 4 Oct. 1769.

Middle Ages was to make way for authority resting on centralized power, or for government resting on the consent of the public reason. The colonists had friends in the friends of liberty in England. As the cause of the people was every where the same, South Carolina in December remitted to London ten thousand five hundred pounds currency, to the Society for supporting the Bill of Rights, that the liberties of Great Britain and America might alike be protected.[1]

Many of the patriots of Ireland[2] saw that their hopes were bound up with those of the Colonies; and Bushe, the friend of Grattan, in imitation of Molineux, published "the case of Great Britain and America," with a vehement invective against Grenville. "Hate him," said he to Grattan; "I hope you hate him." And it was Grenville's speeches and Grenville's doctrine, "that roused Grattan to enter on his great career in Ireland."[3]

The laboring people of England, also, in the manufacturing districts, especially in Birmingham, longed to enjoy the abundance and freedom of America, and the ships which refused to take English merchandise might have returned full freighted with skilful artisans.[4] In the history of the English people, this year marks the establishment of Public Meetings,[5] under the lead of Yorkshire. The principle of representation, trampled upon by a venal Parliament, was to be renovated by the influence of voluntary assemblies.

[1] Vote of the Assembly of South Carolina, 8 Dec. 1769. Letter of Manigault, Gadsden, &c. to Hanbery & Co. London, 9 December, 1769. Order in Council, 5 April, 1770; Hillsborough to Lieut. Gov. Bull, 12 June, 1770.

[2] Gov. Pownall to S. Cooper, 25 Sept. 1769, and S. Cooper to Gov. Pownall, 1 Jan. 1770.

[3] Grattan's Life of Grattan, i. 135, 136.

[4] T. Pownall to S. Cooper, 25 Sept. 1769.

[5] Albemarle's Rockingham, ii. 93.

CHAP. XLII. 1769. Dec. The Press, too, came forward with unwonted boldness, as the interpreter of public opinion and a legitimate power in the state. "Can you conceive," wrote the anonymous Junius[1] to the King, "that the people of this country will long submit to be governed by so flexible a House of Commons? The oppressed people of Ireland give you every day fresh marks of their resentment. The Colonies left their native land for freedom and found it in a desert. Looking forward to independence, they equally detest the pageantry of a King and the supercilious hypocrisy of a bishop."

1770. Jan. The meeting of Parliament in January, 1770, would decide, whether the British Empire was to escape dismemberment. Chatham recommended to the more liberal aristocracy[2] that junction with the people, which, after sixty years, achieved the Reform of the British Constitution; but in that day it was opposed by the passionate impulses of Burke,[3] and the inherent reluctance of the high-born.

The debate on the ninth turned on the capacity and rights of the people, and involved the complaints of America and of Ireland, not less than the discontent of England at the disfranchisement of Wilkes.

"It is vain and idle to found the authority of this House upon the popular voice," said Charles Jenkinson, pleading for the absolute independence of Parliament. "The discontents that are held up as spectres," said Thomas de Grey, brother of the Attorney General, "are the senseless clamors of the thoughtless,

[1] Junius to the King, 19 Dec. 1769.

[2] Fitzwilliam to Rockingham, 1769; in Albemarle, ii. 142. Chatham to Rockingham, Id. 193.

[3] Burke in Albemarle, ii. 195.

and the ignorant, the lowest of the rabble. The Westminster petition was obtained by a few despicable mechanics, headed by base-born people." "The privileges of the people of this country," interposed Serjeant Glynn, "do not depend upon birth and fortune; they hold their rights as Englishmen, and cannot be divested of them but by the subversion of the Constitution." "Were it not for petition-hunters and incendiaries," said Rigby, "the farmers of Yorkshire could not possibly take an interest in the Middlesex election of representatives in Parliament. But supposing that a majority of the freeholders had signed these petitions without influence and solicitation; the majority, even of this class, is no better than an ignorant multitude."

Up rose the representative of the Yorkshire weavers and freeholders, "the spotless" Sir George Saville. "The greatest evil," said he, "that can befall this nation, is the invasion of the people's rights by the authority of this House. I do not say that the majority have sold the rights of their constituents; but I do say, I have said, and I shall always say, that they have betrayed them. The people understand their own rights and know their own interests as well as we do; for a large paternal estate, a pension, and support in the treasury, are greater recommendations to a seat in this Assembly, than either the honesty of the heart or the clearness of the head."

Gilmour invited censure on such unprecedented expressions. Conway excused them as uttered in heat. "I am not conscious," resumed Saville, "that I have spoken in heat; if I did, I have had time to cool, and I again say, as I said before, that

CHAP. XLII. 1770. Jan. this House has betrayed the rights of its constituents." "In times of less licentiousness," rejoined Gilmour, "members have been sent to the Tower for words of less offence." "The mean consideration of my own safety," continued Saville, "shall never be put in the balance against my duty to my constituents. I will own no superior but the laws; nor bend the knee to any but to Him who made me."

The accusation which Saville brought against the House of Commons, was the gravest that could be presented; if false, was an outrage in comparison with which that of Wilkes was a trifle. But Lord North[1] bore the reproach meekly and soothed the majority into quietude. The debate proceeded, and presently Barré spoke. "The people of England know, the people of Ireland know, and the American people feel, that the iron hand of ministerial despotism is lifted up against them; but it is not less formidable against the prince, than against the people."—"The trumpeters of sedition have produced the disaffection;" replied Lord North, speaking at great length. "The drunken ragamuffins of a vociferous mob are exalted into equal importance with men of judgment, morals, and property. I can never acquiesce in the absurd opinion that all men are equal. The contest in America which at first might easily have been ended, is now for no less than sovereignty on one side, and independence on the other." The Ministry who were crushed in the argument, carried the House by a very large majority.

In the House of Lords, Chatham, whose voice had

[1] H. Walpole, iii. 39.

not been heard for three years, proposed to consider the causes of the discontent which prevailed in so many parts of the British dominions. "I have not," said he, "altered my ideas with regard to the principles upon which America should be governed. I own I have a natural leaning towards that country; I herish liberty wherever it is planted. America was settled upon ideas of liberty, and the vine has taken deep root and spread throughout the land. Long may it flourish.[1] Call the combinations of the Americans dangerous; yet not unwarrantable. The discontent of two millions of people should be treated candidly; and its foundation removed." "Let us save," he continued, "this Constitution, dangerously invaded at home; and let us extend its benefits to the remotest corners of the empire. Let slavery exist nowhere among us; for whether it be in America, or in Ireland, or here at home, you will find it a disease which spreads by contact, and soon reaches from the extremity to the heart."

Camden, whom Chatham's presence awed more than office attracted, awoke to his old friendship for America, and by implication accused his colleagues of conspiring against the liberties of the country.

Lord Mansfield, in his reply to Chatham, "which was a masterpiece of art and address,"[2] declined giving an opinion on the legality of the proceedings

[1] W. S. Johnson's Report of Chatham's Speech, in his letter to Gov. Trumbull of Connecticut, 10 January, 1770; and in a letter to the Rev. Dr. W. S. Johnson, of the same date. The report of the American on America is the safest guide. The American understood the figure of the vine to refer to liberty in America. Chatham never meant to say it had embraced whole nations.

[2] W. S. Johnson's Report of the Debate. H. Walpole in Memoirs, iii. 35.

CHAP. XLII. 1770. Jan.

of the House of Commons in reference to the Middlesex election, but contended, that whether they were right or wrong, the jurisdiction in the case belonged to them and from their decision there was no appeal. "I distrust," rejoined Chatham, "the refinements of learning," which fall to the share of so small a number of men. Providence has taken better care of our happiness, and given us in the simplicity of Common Sense a rule for our direction by which we shall never be misled." The words were revolutionary; Scotland, in unconscious harmony with Kant and the ablest minds in Germany, was renovating philosophy by the aid of Common Sense and Reason; Chatham transplanted the theory, so favorable to democracy, into the Halls of legislation. "Power without right," he continued, aiming his invective at the venal House of Commons, "is a thing hateful in itself and ever inclining to its fall. Tyranny is detestable in every shape; but in none so formidable, as when it is assumed and exercised by a number of tyrants."

Though the House of Lords opposed him by a vote of more than two to one, the actual Ministry was shattered; and Chatham, feeble and emaciated as he was, sprang forward with the party of Rockingham, to beat down the tottering system, and raise on its ruins a Government more friendly to liberty.

But the King was the best politician among them all. Dismissing Camden, he sent an offer of the Chancellor's place to Charles Yorke, who was of the Rockingham connection. He had long coveted the high dignity beyond any thing on earth. Now that it was within his reach, he vacillated, wished delay, put the temptation aside; and formally announced his refusal, hoping a recurrence of the opportunity at a later day.

"If you will not comply," said the King, "it must make an eternal breach between us." Yorke gave way, was reproached by Hardwicke his brother, and by Rockingham; begged his brother's forgiveness, kissed him and parted friends; and then with a fatal sensibility to fame[1] went home to die by his own hand. His appalling fate scattered dismay among the Ministry, and encouraged the opposition to put forth its utmost energies.

On the twenty-second of January, Rockingham, overcoming his nervous weakness, summoned resolution to make a long speech in the House of Lords. He turned his eyes, however, only towards the past, condemning the policy of George the Third, and defending the old system of English government, which restrained the royal prerogative by privilege. While the leader of the great Whig party cherished no hope of improvement from any change in the forms of the Constitution, the aged and enfeebled Chatham, once more the man of the people, rose to do service to succeeding generations. "Whoever," said he, "understands the theory of the English Constitution and will compare it with the fact, must see at once how widely they differ. We must reconcile them to each other, if we wish to save the liberties of this country. The Constitution intended that there should be a permanent relation between the constituent and representative body of the people. As the House of Commons is now formed, that relation is not preserved, it is destroyed;" and he proceeded to open before the House of

[1] Burke, i. 303.

CHAP. XLII. 1770. Jan.

Lords, as the mature result of his long reflection, a most cautious beginning of Parliamentary reform. The Reform of the English Parliament! How much must take place before that event can come about.

Shrinking from the storm, Grafton threw up his office. The King affected regret, but had foreseen and provided against the contingency, being at this moment equally tranquil and resolved.[1] Conway hinted at trying Rockingham and his friends. "I know their disposition," said the King, "and I will not hear of them. As for Chatham, I will abdicate the crown sooner than consent to his requirements." Before the world knew of the impending change, he sent Weymouth and Gower, of the Bedford party, "to press Lord North in the most earnest manner to accept the office of First Lord Commissioner of the Treasury;"[2] and he preceded their visit by a friendly autograph note of his own. Lord North did not hesitate; and the King exerted all his ability and his ten years' experience to establish the Minister of his choice, teaching him how to flatter Conway,[3] and "how to prevent desertion.'

On the last day of January, the new Prime Minister, amidst great excitement and the sanguine hopes of the opposition, appeared in the House of Commons. "The ship of state," said Barré, "tossed on a stormy sea, is scudding under a jury-mast, and hangs out signals for pilots from the other side." "The pilots

[1] In the King's letter to Lord North of the 23 January, the King writes, "My mind is more and more strengthened in the rightness of the measure." That implies previous consideration of the measure.

[2] King to Lord North, 23 Jan. 1770.

[3] King to Lord North, 29 Jan. 1770.

CHAP. XLII. 1770. Jan.

on board," answered North, "are very capable of conducting her into port." All agreed that he spoke admirably well; inspiring such confidence that he prevailed by a majority of forty. "A very handsome majority,"[1] said the King; "a very favorable auspice on your taking the lead in administration. A little spirit will soon restore order in my service."[2] From that night, the new Tory Party held possession of the Cabinet. Its opponents were divided between those who looked back to privilege as their old harbor of refuge, and those who saw beyond the abasement of the aristocracy a desirable increase of popular power.

[1] King to Lord North, 3 February, 1770.

[2] King to Lord North, 1 February, 1770.

CHAPTER XLIII.

THE BOSTON MASSACRE.—HILLSBOROUGH'S ADMINISTRATION OF THE COLONIES CONTINUED.

JANUARY—MARCH, 1770.

CHAP. XLIII. 1770. Jan.

"THE troops must move to the castle," said Samuel Adams;[1] "it must be the first business of the General Court to move them out of town."[2] Otis went about declaiming that "the Governor had power to do it by the Constitution."[3] "We consider this metropolis, and indeed the whole Province under duress," wrote Cooper, the minister. "The troops greatly corrupt our morals, and are in every sense an oppression;" and his New Year's prayer to Heaven asked deliverance from their presence.[4]

The Massachusetts Assembly was to meet on the tenth of January, and distant members were already on their journey;[5] when Hutchinson most unwisely for himself, and still more so for England, prorogued

[1] Hutchinson to Sir Francis Bernard, 20 Dec. 1769.

[2] Hutchinson to Hillsborough, 20 Dec. 1769.

[3] Hutchinson to person unnamed, 10 January, 1770.

[4] Rev. S. Cooper to Gov. Thomas Pownall, 1 Jan. 1770.

[5] Hutchinson to Sir Francis Bernard, 10 Jan. 1770.

it to the middle of March. The delay prevented any support to its Petition against Bernard; and any Representation during the session of Parliament in which the last revenue Act was to be modified or repealed. The reason assigned for the prorogation was neither the good of the Colony, nor the judgment of the Lieutenant Governor, but an arbitrary instruction [1] from Hillsborough, and of such an instruction Samuel Adams denied the validity.[2]

The spirit of non-importation rather rose than abated. Yet as tea had advanced one hundred per cent.,[3] Hutchinson, who was himself a very large importer of it,[4] could no longer restrain his covetousness. His two oldest sons, therefore, who were his agents, violating their engagement, broke open the lock, of which they had given the key to the Committee of merchants, and secretly made sales.[5] "Do they imagine," cried Samuel Adams, "they can still weary the patience of an injured country with impunity?" and avowing that in the present case, the will of society was not declared in its laws, he called not on the merchants only, but on every individual of every class in city and country, to compel the strictest adherence to the agreement.[6]

The merchants,[7] in pursuance of a vote at a very full meeting, went in a body to the house of the

[1] Hillsborough to Hutchinson, 4 Nov. 1769.

[2] Vindex in Boston Gazette, Monday, 8 Jan. 1770.

[3] So stated by Lord North in the House of Commons. Cavendish Debates, i. 488.

[4] See Hutchinson's orders to Wm. Palmer of London, 1769. MS.

[5] He that will read Hutchinson's many letters on this subject will learn his art of concealment and false representation. Or compare his History, iii. 266–268.

[6] Determinatus, in Boston Gazette, of 8 January, 1770.

[7] Dr. Cooper to Gov. Pownall, 30 January, 1770.

CHAP. XLIII. 1770. Jan.

Hutchinsons.[1] None of them were allowed to enter; the Lieutenant Governor himself threw up a window and pretended to charge them with a tumultuous and menacing application to him as Chief Magistrate. "We come," they answered, "to treat with your sons, who have dishonorably violated their own contract, to which they had pledged their honor." "A contract," answered Hutchinson from the window, "without a valuable consideration is not valid in law." But he remained in great perplexity, fearing loss of property by riot. Early the next morning, he sent for the upright William Phillips, the moderator of the meeting, and engaged for his sons, that a sum of money should be deposited in the room of the tea that had been sold, and that the rest should be returned. The capitulation was immediately reported to the meeting and accepted.[2]

"This," said Bernard's friends, "was as good a time as any to have called out the troops;" and they thought it best to bring matters "to extremities."[3] Dalrymple was ready; and ordered his men to equip themselves with twelve rounds for an attack.[4] "He has now thrown down the reins into the hands of the people," cried the Customs' Commissioners of Hutchinson, "and he can never recover them."[5] "I am a ruined man," said he despondingly to Phillips. "I humbly hope," thus he wrote to those who dealt out offices in London, "that a single error in judg-

[1] Hutchinson to Hillsborough, 24 January, 1770.

[2] Dr. Cooper to Gov Pownall. Hutchinson to Sir Francis Bernard, and several letters in January.

[3] Hutchinson to Sir Francis Bernard, 21 January, 1770.

[4] Gov. Jona. Trumbull to W. S. Johnson, 29 January, 1770.

[5] Dr. Cooper to Gov. Pownall, 30 January, 1770.

ment will not cancel more than thirty years' laborious and disinterested services in support of government." He looked to his Council; and they would take no part in breaking up the system of non-importation. He called in all the justices who lived within fifteen miles; and they thought it not incumbent on them to interrupt the proceedings. He sent the sheriff into the adjourned meeting of the merchants with a letter to the moderator, requiring them in his Majesty's name to disperse; and the meeting, of which justices of peace, selectmen, representatives, constables and other officers made a part, sent him an answer, that their Assembly was warranted by law. He saw that the answer was in Hancock's handwriting,[1] and he treasured up the autograph to be produced one day, when Hancock should be put on trial.

The news from Boston spread through the country. "It is hard," said Trumbull, now Governor of Connecticut, "to break connections with our mother country; but when she strives to enslave us, the strictest union must be dissolved."[2] And as he looked through the world, he exclaimed: "The Lord reigneth, let the earth rejoice, and the multitude of the isles be glad thereof; the accomplishment of some notable prophecies is at hand."[3]

"If the people of New-York are more restrained," wrote Hutchinson, "it is owing to the form of government of their city."[4] Their Liberty Pole had stood safely in the Park for nearly three years. The

[1] Hutchinson to ———, January, 1770.

[2] Gov. Jona. Trumbull to W. S. Johnson, 29 January, 1770.

[3] Gov. Jona. Trumbull to W. S. Johnson, 3 March, 1770.

[4] Hutchinson to ———, 10 January, 1770.

CHAP. XLIII. 1770. Feb. soldiery who had become, as at Boston, exasperated against the citizens, resolved to cut it down, and after three repulses, they succeeded.

On the seventeenth, the indignant people assembled in the fields to the number of three thousand, and without planning retaliation, expressed abhorrence and contempt of the soldiers as enemies to the Constitution, and to the peace of the city.[1] The soldiers replied by an insulting placard; and on two successive days engaged in an affray with the citizens, in which wounds and bruises were received on both sides,[2] but the latter had the advantage. The newspapers loudly celebrated the victory; and the Sons of Liberty, purchasing a piece of land near the junction of Broadway and the Bowery, erected a Liberty Pole, strongly guarded by iron bands and bars, deeply sunk into the earth, and inscribed "Liberty and Property." At the same time, the brave MacDougall, son of a devout Presbyterian of the Scottish isle of Ila, a man who had made a fortune as a sailor, and had himself carefully cultivated his mind, courageous and fiery, yet methodical and self-possessed,[3] was persecuted by the Government. In consequence of his appeal to the people against the concessions of the Assembly, which voted supplies to the troops, he was indicted for a libel; and refusing to give bail, this "first Son of Liberty in bonds for the glorious cause" was visited by such throngs in his prison, that he was obliged to appoint hours for their reception.[4]

[1] Hutchinson, iii. 270.

[2] Lieut. Gov. Colden to Hillsborough, 21 Feb. 1770.

[3] Extract of a Letter from New-York, of 24 Feb. 1770, printed at Philadelphia in March, copied into the Boston Gazette of 16 April, 1770; 784, 2, 182.

[4] Leake's Life of Lamb, 61. Holt's Gazette.

Intelligence of these events, especially of the conflict of the citizens with the soldiers, was transmitted to Boston,[1] where the townsmen emulously applauded the spirit of the "Yorkers." The determination to keep clear of paying the Parliament's taxes spread into every social circle. One week three hundred wives of Boston, the next a hundred and ten more, with one hundred and twenty-six of the young and unmarried of their sex, renounced the use of tea till the Revenue Acts should be repealed.[2] How could the troops interfere? Every body knew, that it was against the law for them to fire without the special authority of a civil magistrate; and the more they paraded with their muskets and twelve rounds of ball, the more they were despised, as men who desired to terrify and had no power to harm. Hutchinson, too, was taunted with wishing to destroy town meetings, through which he himself had risen; and the Press, calling to mind his days of shop-keeping, was cruel enough to jeer him for his old frauds, as a notorious smuggler.[3]

Theophilus Lillie, who had begun to sell contrary to the agreement, found a post planted before his door, with a hand pointed towards his house in derision. One of his neighbors, Richardson, an informer, asked a countryman to break the post down by driving the wheel of his cart against it. A crowd interposed; a number of boys chased Richardson to his own house and threw stones. Provoked but not endangered, he fired among them, and killed one of

[1] Supplement of the Boston Gazette of 19 Feb. 1770.

[2] Boston Gazette, 12 Feb. 1770, and the next number.

[3] Boston Gazette, 19 Feb. 1770; 776, 2, 2.

CHAP. XLIII. 1770. Feb. eleven years old, the son of a poor German. At his funeral five hundred children walked in front of the bier; six of his school-fellows held the pall; and men of all ranks moved in procession from Liberty Tree to the Town House, and thence to the "burying place." Soldiers and officers looked on, with wounded pride. Dalrymple was impatient to be set to work[1] in Boston, or to be ordered elsewhere.[2] The common soldiers of the twenty-ninth regiment were notoriously bad fellows;[3] licentious and overbearing. "I never will miss an opportunity of firing upon the inhabitants," said one of them, Kilroi by name; "I have wanted such an opportunity ever since I have been in the country;"[4] and he repeated the threat several times. It was a common feeling in the regiment. On the other hand, a year and a half's training had perfected the people in their part. It was no breach of the law for them to express contempt for the soldiery; they were ready enough to confront them; but they were taught never to do it, except to repel an attack. If any of the soldiers broke the law, which they often did, complaints were made to the local magistrates, who were ready to afford redress.[5] On the other hand, the officers screened their men from legal punishment, and sometimes even rescued them from the constables.

March On Friday the second day of March, a soldier of the twenty-ninth, asked to be employed at Gray's Ropewalk, and was repulsed in the coarsest words.

[1] Compare Dalrymple to Gage.

[2] Hutchinson ——, March, 1770; in Letter Book, i. 374.

[3] Hutchinson's Letter Book.

[4] Testimony of Samuel Hemmingway; Hutchinson to ——, 6 Dec. 1770; and to Hillsborough, 3 Dec. 1770.

[5] Boston Account, 10.

He then defied the ropemakers to a boxing match; and, one of them accepting his challenge, he was beaten off. Returning with several of his companions, they too were driven away. A larger number came down to renew the fight with clubs and cutlasses, and in their turn encountered defeat. By this time Gray and others interposed, and for that day prevented further disturbance.[1]

There was an end of the affair at the Ropewalk, but not at the barracks, where the soldiers inflamed each other's passions, as if the honor of the regiment were tarnished.[2] On Saturday they prepared bludgeons;[3] and being resolved to brave the citizens on Monday night,[4] they forewarned their particular acquaintance not to be abroad. Without duly restraining his men, Carr, the Lieutenant Colonel of the twenty-ninth, made complaint to the Lieutenant Governor of the insult they had received.[5]

The Council, deliberating on Monday, seemed of opinion, that the town would never be safe from quarrels between the people and the soldiers, as long as soldiers should be quartered among them. In the present case the owner of the Ropewalk gave satisfaction by dismissing the workman complained of.

The officers should, on their part, have kept their men within the barracks after night-fall. Instead of it they left them to roam the streets. Hutchinson should have insisted on measures of precaution;[6] but

[1] Boston Narrative, 14, 15.

[2] James Bowdoin in the Boston Narrative.

[3] John Fisher's Deposition in Boston Narrative, 40; S. Adams in Boston Gazette of 31 Dec. 1770.

[4] S. Adams, in Boston Gazette, 24 Dec. 1770.

[5] Hutchinson's Hist. iii. 270, 271.

[6] Gordon's Hist. of American Revolution, i. 281.

CHAP. XLIII. 1770. March

he too much wished the favor of all who had influence at Westminster.

Evening came on. The young moon was shining brightly in a cloudless winter sky, and its light was increased by a new fallen snow.[1] Parties of soldiers were driving about the streets,[2] making a parade of valor, challenging resistance, and striking the inhabitants indiscriminately with sticks or sheathed cutlasses.

A band which rushed out from Murray's Barracks,[3] in Brattle Street, armed with clubs, cutlasses and bayonets, provoked resistance, and an affray ensued. Ensign Maul, at the gate of the barrack-yard, cried to the soldiers, "Turn out, and I will stand by you; kill them; stick them; knock them down; run your bayonets through them;"[4] and one soldier after another levelled a firelock and threatened to "make a lane" through the crowd. Just before nine, as an officer crossed King Street, now State Street, a barber's lad cried after him, "There goes a mean fellow who hath not paid my master for dressing his hair;" on which the sentinel stationed at the westerly end of the Custom House, on the corner of King Street and Exchange Lane, left his post, and with his musket gave the boy a stroke on the head, which made him stagger and cry for pain.[5]

The street soon became clear,[6] and nobody troubled

[1] R. Treat Paine's Trial of the Soldiers, 121.

[2] Hutchinson's History, iii. 271.

[3] Jeremiah Belknap's Testimony, Boston Narrative, 65.

[4] James Kirkwood, Boston Narrative, 70, and 19 20. Dr. Richard Hiron's Trial of the Soldiers, 61, 62.

[5] Boston Narrative, 23, Note Boy's Evidence, given on Preston's Trial; quoted by Vindex in Boston Gazette, of 24 Dec. 1770.

[6] Lieut. Col. Marshall, in Trial of the British Soldiers, 31. Boston Narrative, 77.

the sentry, when a party of soldiers issued violently from the main guard,[1] their arms glittering in the moonlight, and passed on hallooing, "Where are they? where are they? let them come." Presently twelve or fifteen[2] more, uttering the same cries, rushed from the South into King Street, and so by way of Cornhill, towards Murray's Barracks. "Pray, soldiers, spare my life," cried a boy of twelve, whom they met; "No, no, I'll kill you all," answered one of them, and knocked him down with his cutlass. They abused and insulted several persons at their doors and others in the street, "running about like madmen in a fury,"[3] crying, "Fire," which seemed their watchword, and, "Where are they? knock them down." Their outrageous behavior occasioned the ringing of the bell at the head of King Street.

The citizens whom the alarm set in motion, came out with canes and clubs; and partly by the interference of well-disposed officers, partly by the courage of Crispus Attucks, a mulatto, and some others, the fray at the Barracks was soon over. Of the citizens, the prudent shouted "Home, Home; " others, it was said, called out, "Huzza for the main guard, there is the nest; " but the main guard was not molested the whole evening.

A body of soldiers came up Royal Exchange Lane, crying "Where are the cowards?" and brandishing their arms, passed through King Street.

[1] Lieut. Col. Thomas Marshall, in Trial, 31, 32.

[2] Nathaniel Appleton in Boston Narrative, 63, and in Trial of Soldiers, 30, 31. John Appleton in Trial, 31.

[3] Nathaniel Appleton, 31.

CHAP. XLIII. 1770. March

From ten to twenty boys came after them, asking, "Where are they, where are they?" "There is the soldier who knocked me down," said the barber's boy,[1] and they began pushing one another towards the sentinel.[2] He primed and loaded his musket.[3] "The lobster[4] is going to fire," cried a boy. Waving his piece about, the sentinel pulled the trigger.[5] "If you fire you must die for it," said Henry Knox, who was passing by. "I don't care," replied the sentry; "damn them, if they touch me I'll fire." "Fire and be damned," shouted the boys, for they were persuaded he could not do it without leave from a civil officer; and a young fellow spoke out, "We will knock him down for snapping;" while they whistled through their fingers and huzzaed.[6] "Stand off," said the sentry, and shouted aloud, "Turn out, main guard."[7] "They are killing the sentinel," reported a servant from the Custom House, running to the main guard. "Turn out, why don't you turn out?" cried Preston,[8] who was Captain of the day, to the guard. "He appeared in a great flutter of spirits," and "spoke to them roughly." A party of six, two of whom, Kilroi and Montgomery, had been worsted at the Ropewalk,[9] formed with a corporal in front, and Preston following.[10] With bayonets fixed, they haughtily "rushed through the people,"[11] upon the trot, cursing them, and pushing them as they went

[1] Edward Payne, Boston Narrative, 103; B. Lee, Trial, 69.

[2] William Parker, Trial, 77.

[3] Benjamin Lee, Trial, 69.

[4] Alexander Cruikshank's Trial, 65, "lobster and rascal."

[5] Henry Knox, Boston Narrative, 101; and in Trial, 68, 69.

[6] Benjamin Lee, Trial, 69.

[7] Benjamin Lee, Trial, 69.

[8] John Bulkely, Trial 69.

[9] Boston Gazette, 31 Dec, 1770.

[10] William Whittington, Trial, 74; Preston's Case.

[11] Samuel Adams in Boston Gazette, 10 Dec. 1770.

1770. March

along. They found about ten persons round the sentry, while about fifty or sixty came down with them. "For God's sake," said Knox, holding Preston by the coat, "take your men back again; if they fire, your life must answer for the consequences." "I know what I am about," said he, hastily, and much agitated. None pressed on them or provoked them, till they began loading, when a party of about twelve in number, with sticks in their hands, moved from the middle of the street where they had been standing, gave three cheers, and passed along the front of the soldiers, whose muskets some of them struck as they went by. "You are cowardly rascals," they said, "for bringing arms against naked men;" "lay aside your guns,[1] and we are ready for you." "Are the soldiers loaded?" inquired Palmes of Preston. "Yes," he answered, "with powder and ball."[2] "Are they going to fire upon the inhabitants?" asked Theodore Bliss. "They cannot, without my orders;" replied Preston;[3] while "the town-born" called out, "Come on, you rascals, you bloody backs, you lobster scoundrels, fire if you dare. We know you dare not."[4] Just then Montgomery received a blow from a stick thrown which hit his musket; and the word "Fire," being given, he stepped a little on one side, and shot Attucks, who at the time was quietly leaning on a long stick. The people immediately began to move off. "Don't fire," said Langford, the watchman, to Kilroi, looking him full in the face; but yet he did so, and Samuel Gray, who was standing next Langford with

[1] Ebenezer Bridgham, 8, 9.

[2] Richard Palmes, in the Trial, 18.

[3] Theodore Bliss, Trial, 82.

[4] Preston's Case.

CHAP. XLIII. 1770. March

his hands in his bosom, fell lifeless. The rest fired slowly and in succession on the people, who were dispersing. One aimed deliberately at a boy, who was running for safety. Montgomery then pushed at Palmes to stab him; on which the latter knocked his gun out of his hand, and levelling a blow at him hit Preston.[1] Three persons were killed, among them Attucks the mulatto; eight were wounded, two of them mortally. Of all the eleven not more than one had had any share in the disturbance.

So infuriated were the soldiers, that, when the men returned to take up the dead, they prepared to fire again, but were checked by Preston, while the Twenty-Ninth Regiment appeared under arms in King Street, as if bent on a further massacre. "This is our time,"[2] cried soldiers of the Fourteenth; and dogs were never seen more greedy for their prey.[3]

The bells rung in all the churches; the town drums beat. "To arms, to arms," was the cry. And now was to be tested the true character of Boston. All its sons came forth, excited almost to madness; many were absolutely distracted by the sight of the dead bodies, and of the blood, which ran plentifully in the street, and was imprinted in all directions by the foot-tracks on the snow. "Our hearts," says Warren, "beat to arms; almost resolved by one stroke to avenge the death of our slaughtered brethren."[4] But they stood self-possessed and irresistible, demanding justice according to the law. "Did you not know,

[1] See the Note at the end of the Chapter.

[2] Mrs. Mary Gardner, B. N. 25. Deposition, 144. Of her credibility, see Samuel Adams in Boston Gazette, 31 Dec. 1770.

[3] William Fallass, Boston Narrative, 143. Compare those of Allman, of Matthias King, and of Robert Twelves Hewes.

[4] Warren's Oration, 5 March, 1772.

that you should not have fired without the order of a civil Magistrate?" asked Hutchinson on meeting Preston. "I did it," answered Preston, "to save my men."[1]

The people would not be pacified, till the regiment was confined to the guard-room and the barracks; and Hutchinson himself gave assurances that instant inquiries should be made by the County Magistrates. The body of them then retired, leaving about one hundred persons to keep watch on the examination, which lasted till three hours after midnight.[2] A warrant was issued against Preston, who surrendered himself to the Sheriff; and the soldiers who composed the party were delivered up and committed to prison."[3]

The next morning the Selectmen of the Town and the Justices of the County spoke with Hutchinson at the Council Chamber. "The inhabitants," said the former, "will presently meet, and cannot be appeased while the troops are among them." Quincy of Braintree, on behalf of the Justices, pointed out the danger of "the most terrible consequences." "I have no power to remove the troops," said Hutchinson, "nor to direct where they shall be placed;" but he sent to invite Dalrymple and Carr, the Commanding Officers, to be present in Council. They attended, and the subject was "largely discussed."

At eleven, the Town Meeting was opened in Faneuil Hall by prayer from Cooper; then Samuel Adams and fourteen others, among them, Hancock

[1] Vindex, Samuel Adams, in Boston Gazette, 10 Dec. 1770, and 14 Jan. 1771.

[2] Hutchinson to Gage, 6 March, 1770. "I was up till three o'clock." Hutchinson to Sir Francis Bernard, 12 March, 1770.

[3] Dalrymple's Narrative of the Late Transactions at Boston.

CHAP. XLIII. 1770. March

and Molineux, were chosen to proceed to the Council Chamber, where in the name of the Town they delivered this message: "The inhabitants and soldiery can no longer live together in safety; nothing can restore peace and prevent further carnage, but the immediate removal of the troops."[1] To effect this, they asked the exertion of his power and influence.

Hutchinson desired to parley with them.[2] "The people," they answered, "not only in this town, but in all the neighboring towns, are determined that the troops shall be removed." "An attack on the King's troops," replied Hutchinson, "would be High Treason, and every man concerned would forfeit his life and estate." The Committee unmoved, recalled his attention to their peremptory demand and withdrew.

My readers will remember, that the instructions from the King which placed the army above the civil power in America, contained a clause, that where there was no officer of the rank of Brigadier, the Governor of the Colony or Province might give the word. Dalrymple, accordingly, offered to obey the Lieutenant Governor, who, on his part, neither dared to bid the troops remain, nor order their withdrawal. So the opinion which had been expressed by Bernard during the last summer, and at the time had been approved by Dalrymple, was called to mind as the

[1] Hutchinson to Gage.

[2] We have the account of what passed in Council, by Hutchinson to Gage, to Hillsborough, and to Sir Francis Bernard; by Dalrymple, in his Narrative sent to Hillsborough; by the Affidavit of Andrew Oliver, Secretary, in his Narrative sent through Hutchinson and Bernard to Hillsborough; by the Report of the Committee of the Council, respecting the Representation made by Secretary Oliver, in Bradford, 264. Compare also Private Letters of Cooper, Hutchinson, and others.

rule for the occasion. The Lieutenant Governor, therefore, acquainted the Town's Committee, that the Twenty-Ninth Regiment, which was particularly concerned in the late differences, should without delay be placed at the Castle, and the Fourteenth only be retained in town under efficient restraint.[1] Saying this, he adjourned the Council to the afternoon.

The vigorous will of Samuel Adams now burst forth in its majesty. As Faneuil Hall could not hold the throng from the surrounding country, the Town had adjourned to the Old South Meeting House. The street between the State House and that church was filled with people. "Make way for the Committee," was the shout of the multitude, as Adams came out from the Council Chamber, and baring his head, which was already becoming gray, moved through their ranks, inspiring heroic confidence.

To the people who crowded even the gallery and aisles of the spacious Meeting House, he made his report, and pronounced the answer insufficient. On ordinary occasions he seemed like ordinary men; but in moments of crisis, he rose naturally and unaffectedly into the attitude of highest dignity, and spoke as if the hopes of humanity were dependent on his words. The Town, after deliberation, raised a new and smaller Committee, composed of Samuel Adams, Hancock, Molineux, William Phillips, Warren, Henshaw and Pemberton, to bear their final message. They found the Lieutenant Governor surrounded by the Council.

[1] Reply of the Lieut. Gov. to the Town of Boston.

CHAP. XLIII. 1770. March

and by the highest officers of the British Army and Navy on the Station.

Hutchinson had done his utmost to get Samuel Adams shipped to England as a traitor; at this most important moment in their lives, the patriot and the courtier stood face to face. "It is the unanimous opinion of the Meeting," said Samuel Adams to him in the name of all, "that the reply made to the vote of the inhabitants in the morning, is unsatisfactory; nothing less will satisfy than a total and immediate removal of all the troops." "The troops are not subject to my authority," repeated Hutchinson; "I have no power to remove them." Stretching forth his arm which slightly shook as if "his frame trembled at the energy of his soul,"[1] in tones not loud, but clear and distinctly audible, Adams rejoined: "If you have power to remove one regiment, you have power to remove both.[2] It is at your peril if you do not.[3] The meeting is composed of three thousand people. They are become very impatient. A thousand men are already arrived from the neighborhood, and the country is in general motion. Night is approaching; an immediate answer is expected." As he spoke, he gazed intently on his irresolute adversary. "Then," said Adams who not long afterwards described the scene, "at the appearance of the de-

[1] John Adams to Jedediah Morse, and Same to Tudor.

[2] These are the words as I received them traditionally from John Quincy Adams, and they agree with Hutchinson to Bernard of the 18th of March, except that Hutchinson represented them as addressed to Dalrymple who stood at his side. But the Town and S. Adams addressed Hutchinson himself, and would not release him from his responsibility.

[3] Andrew Oliver's Narrative.

[4] Dalrymple's Narrative of the Late Transactions at Boston.

termined citizens, peremptorily demanding the redress of grievances, I observed his knees to tremble; I saw his face grow pale; and I enjoyed the sight."[1] As the Committee left the Council Chamber, Hutchinson's memory was going back in his reverie to the days of the Revolution of 1688.[2] He saw in his mind, Andros seized and imprisoned, and the people instituting a new government; he reflected that the citizens of Boston and the country about it were become four times as numerous as in those days, and their "spirit full as high." He fancied them insurgent, and himself their captive; and he turned to the Council for advice. "It is not such people as formerly pulled down your House, who conduct the present measures;" said Tyler, "but they are people of the best characters among us, men of estates, and men of religion. It is impossible for the troops to remain in town; there will be ten thousand men to effect their removal, be the consequence what it may."

Russell of Charlestown, and Dexter of Dedham, a man of admirable qualities, confirmed what was said. They spoke truly; men were ready to come down from the hills of Worcester County, and from the vale of the Connecticut. The Council unanimously advised sending the troops to the Castle forthwith. "It is impossible for me," said Dalrymple again and again, weakening the force of what he said by frequently repeating it, "to go any further lengths in this matter. The information given of the intended rebellion is a

[1] Samuel Adams to James Warren, of Plymouth, 25 March, 1771.

[2] Hutchinson to Lord Hillsborough, 12 March, 1770.

CHAP. XLIII. 1770. March

sufficient reason against the removal of his Majesty's forces."[1]

"You have asked the advice of the Council," said Gray to the Lieutenant Governor; "they have given it unanimously; you are bound to conform to it." "If mischief should come, by means of your not joining with us," pursued Irving, "the whole blame must fall upon you; but if you join with us, and the commanding officer after that should refuse to remove the troops, the blame will then be at his door."[2] Hutchinson finally agreed with the Council, and Dalrymple assured him of his obedience. The Town's Committee, being informed of this decision, left the State House to make their welcome report to the Meeting. The inhabitants listened with the highest satisfaction; but, ever vigilant, they provided measures for keeping up a strong military watch of their own, until the Regiments should leave the town.[3]

It was a humiliation to the officers and soldiers to witness the public funeral of the victims of the fifth of March; but they complained most of the watch set over them. The Colonel of the town militia had, however, taken good legal advice, and showed the old Province Law under which he kept it; and the Justices of the Peace in their turns attended every night during its continuance.[4] The British officers gnashed their teeth in anger at the contempt into which they had been brought. The troops came to overawe the people, and maintain the laws;

[1] Dalrymple's Narrative.

[2] Andrew Oliver's Narrative. Report of a Committee of Council, reporting March 6, 7.

[3] Boston Narrative.

[4] Boston Narrative.

and they were sent as law-breakers to a prison rather than to a garrison. "There," said Edmund Burke, "was an end of the spirited way we took, when the question was, whether Great Britain should or should not govern America."[1]

[1] E. Burke's Speech, Monday, 7 March, 1774.

NOTE.

The questions that the inquirer, on examining the evidence, may raise, are three. I. Were the soldiers or the townsmen the aggressors? II. Did Preston give the order to fire? III. Were the soldiers pelted and struck before firing?

There would never have been any difficulty in answering these questions, but for the trials which followed. The lawyers employed were skilful in constructing hypotheses to suit their purpose. "The Case" of Preston is confessedly false. It was written by some royalist lawyer, and was published for purposes to be answered in England. The *ex parte* affidavits secretly taken and sent to England, are not trustworthy. The Depositions published in the Boston Narrative, were taken openly and in the presence of persons representing all parties. The evidence taken on Preston's trial, has, I believe, never been fairly or fully printed. I have seen only parts of it. The report of the soldiers' trial is valuable though imperfect. In using it, care must be taken to separate the evidence of known and responsible persons from that of the feeble-minded, the biassed, and those who evidently spoke falsely. I have seen many unpublished private letters of persons in the interest of the officers, as well as the official papers on the subject.

I. As to the first question, all the evidence agrees that the townspeople acted on the defensive, and made no resistance till attacked. On this point we have also the emphatic statement of James Bowdoin, Samuel Pemberton, and Joseph Warren, as well as the uncontroverted reasoning of Samuel Adams.

II. Did Preston give the order to fire? I think he did.

1. Disciplined men in the regular army were not likely to fire without orders. Preston himself said to T. Bliss, "They cannot fire without my orders." See the Testimony of T. Bliss.

2. The men said positively they had his orders to fire.

3. There were many witnesses to his giving the word to fire.

CHAP. XLIII. 1770. March

4. He himself owned it to Hutchinson when he said "I did it to save my men."

5. Afterwards he was obliged to confess he said Fire, yet pretending that he preceded the word by Don't; but first, this is not the word an officer would give to men whose guns were levelled, and whom he wished to prevent firing. Second, there was time between the first gun and the last to have stopped the procedure, which he did not do.

6. Hutchinson in his first report, does not clear him of the order to fire.

7. Gage does not clear him of the order.

8. His counsel, a determined royalist, was convinced he gave the order. "I am afraid poor Preston has but little chance. Mr. Auchmuty who is his counsel, tells me the evidence is very strong to prove, the firing upon the inhabitants was by his order, and he doubts whether the assault would be an excuse for it." Hutchinson to Sir Francis Bernard, 30 March, 1770. Considering the relations of the parties this is most significant language. The opposite views were the hypothesis for the trial.

9. As Auchmuty before the trial believed that Preston gave the order, so Josiah Quincy, Jr. has left on record his opinion that the verdict of the jury was an unjust one. Callisthenes, in Boston Gazette, 28 Sept. 1772; 912, 3, 1; and again, Edward Sexby, 12 Oct. 1772; Boston Gazette, 914, 1, 2. But this is not so decisive as the opinion, at the time, of Auchmuty and Hutchinson.

10. The monstrously false insinuations in the "Case of Captain Preston." If Preston had given no orders, the offensive falsehoods would have been superfluous.

III. Were the soldiers pelted and struck while on duty before firing? The necessities of the defence naturally exaggerated the provocation, and the statements respecting it are contradictory. When were boys together after a newly fallen snow without throwing snowballs? A little discrimination as to the character of the witnesses and the effect of the testimony on those best able to judge, will show whether the soldiers were endangered.

1. Auchmuty's opinion of the insufficiency of the assault to justify the soldiers has already been cited.

2. Hutchinson, whose testimony as given at the time, is of the highest importance, writes of the firing:—

"I think, admitting every thing in favor of it, that the action was too hasty, though the great provocation may be some excuse." Hutchinson to Sir Francis Bernard, 12 March, 1770. "How far the affronts and the abuse offered by the inhabitants may avail to excuse this action, is uncertain." Hutchinson to Lord Hillsborough, 12 March, 1770.

3. Rev. Dr. Cooper's opinion is worthy of great attention. "Soldiers &c. fired without the least reason to justify so desperate a step." Dr. S. Cooper to Gov. Pownall, 26 March, 1770.

4. No one of the soldiers was hurt, nor was there any of the things said to have been thrown at them, to be found on the place next morning. Boston Gazette, 830, 2, 2.

5. Look at the testimony of trustworthy men. Edward Paine, cited in Boston Gazette, of 7 Jan. 1771, "perceived nothing but the talk that he thought would have induced the sentry or any of the soldiers to fire." Henry Knox, afterwards General and Secretary at War, was close by and saw nothing thrown. His testimony is very strong. Among others, Langford the watchman, says, "The boys were swearing and using bad words, but they threw nothing." Trial, 11. "I saw nobody strike a blow, nor offer a blow." Trial, 12. Brown saw nothing thrown at the soldiers. Trial 14. Testimony of Richard Palmes on Preston's Trial. He was standing close by Preston and Montgomery. Question. At the time the soldiers fired, did you see a number of things thrown at them? Answer. I saw nothing thrown or touch them, except that which struck Montgomery.

6. Compare on the other hand the testimony to prove the pelting. The chief witness was Andrew, a negro servant, famed for his "lively imagination." James Bailey, a friend of the sentry, swore, "the boys were throwing pieces of ice at him." Q. Did you see the pieces of ice thrown? A. Yes; they were hard and large enough to hurt any man. Q. Did you see any of the pieces of ice hit him? A. There was nothing thrown after I went to him; if any thing was thrown, it was before.

This same witness was used to countenance the story, which Hutchinson gives in his History, iii. 272.

Q. Did you see any thing thrown before the firing? A. Yes; Montgomery was knocked down with a stick, and his gun flew out of his hand, and when he recovered he discharged his gun.

Against this, weigh the evidence of Bass, Fosdick, and Palmes. Jedediah Bass. Q. Was you looking at Montgomery all the time before he fired? A. Yes. Q. Are you certain he did not fall before he fired? A. Yes. Q. Are you sure if he had fallen, you must have seen him? Yes. Nathaniel Fosdick being asked when Montgomery fell, answered, "It was after he had fired."

Richard Palmes. Q. Are you sure Montgomery did not fall just before he discharged his gun? A. Yes. After the trial Palmes persisted in his statement. "I assure the world upon the oath I then took, that Montgomery did not fall, till he attempted to push his bayonet through my body; which was about the time the last gun went off."

CHAPTER XLIV.

THE NON-IMPORTATION AGREEMENTS FAIL.—HILLSBOROUGH'S ADMINISTRATION OF THE COLONIES CONTINUED.

MARCH—JULY, 1770.

CHAP. XLIV. 1770. March

AT the cry of innocent blood shed by the soldiery, the continent heaved like a troubled ocean. But in Boston itself, the removal of the troops to the barracks at Castle William, however offensive to the pride of the army, smoothed the way for conciliation. The Town was resolved on bringing the party who had fired to trial, that the supremacy of the civil authority might be vindicated; at the same time, it wished that every opportunity of defence should be furnished the prisoners; and with the very general approbation of the people,[1] and at the urgent[2] solicitations of Samuel Adams and his associates, John Adams and the younger Quincy consented to be retained as their Counsel.

It was for England to remove the cause of the

[1] Gov. Wentworth of New Hampshire to Hillsborough.

[2] It is an error to suppose that the Town of Boston did not consistently wish every proper assistance to be rendered the prisoners. It took care publicly to mark its confidence in Quincy in May, and in John Adams in June.

[3] Advised and *urged* by an Adams, [S. Adams,] a Hancock, a Molineux, &c. &c. Quincy, 27.

CHAP. XLIV. 1770. March

strife. In the House of Lords, Chatham, affirming as he had done four years before, the subordination of the Colonies and the right of Parliament to bind their trade and industry, disclaimed the American policy, adopted by his former colleagues when he himself was nominally the Minister. "In this," said he, as in all the rest, I have been disappointed and deceived."[1] "The idea of drawing money from the Americans by taxes was ill judged; trade is your object with them. They should be encouraged; those millions are the industrious hive who keep you em ployed;" and he invited the entire repeal of the Revenue Act of Charles Townshend.

On the evening of the fifth of March, the House of Commons entered seriously upon the consideration of the question. Lord North founded a motion for a partial relief, not on the Petitions of America, because they were marked by a denial of the right; but on one from merchants and traders of London. "The subject," said he,[2] "is of the highest importance. The combinations and associations of the Americans for the temporary interruption of trade, have already been called unwarrantable in an Address of this House; I will call them insolent and illegal.[3] The duties upon paper, glass, and painters' colors bear upon the manufactures of this country, are uncommercial, and ought to be taken off. It was my intention to have extended the proposal to the removal of the other duties; but the Americans have not deserved indulgence. The Preamble to the Act and the duty on

[1] W. S. Johnson to Gov. Trumbull, 6 March, 1770.

[2] Debates of the Fifth of March, 1770, in Cavendish, ii. 484.

[3] W. S. Johnson's report of the Debate.

CHAP. XLIV. 1770. March tea must be retained as a mark of the Supremacy of Parliament and the efficient declaration of its right to govern the Colonies.[1]

"I saw nothing unjust, uncommercial or unreasonable in the Stamp Act; nothing but what Great Britain might fairly demand of her Colonies; America took flame and united against it. If there had been a permanence of Ministers, if there had been a union of Englishmen in the cause of England, that Act would at this moment have been subsisting.

"I was much inclined to yield to the wishes of many, who desire that the duty upon tea should be repealed. But tea is not a manufacture of Great Britain. Of all commodities it is the properest for taxation. The duty is an external tax such as the Americans had admitted the right of Parliament to impose. It is one of the best of all the port duties. When the revenue is well established, it will go a great way towards giving additional support to our Government and judicatures in America. If we are to run after America in search of reconciliation, I do not know a single Act of Parliament, that will remain. Are we to make concessions to these people, because they have the hardihood to set us at defiance? No authority was ever confirmed by the concession of any point of honor or of right. Shall I give up my right? No, not in the first step. I will strengthen my water-guard: I will do any thing before I will buy off contraband trade. New-York has kept strictly to its agreements; but the infractions of them by the people of Boston, show that they will soon come to nothing. The necessities of the Colonies and their want of union

[1] W. S. Johnson's Report.

CHAP. XLIV. 1770. March

will open trade. There is an impossibility of their manufacturing to supply any considerable part of their wants. If they should attempt it and be likely to succeed, it is in our power to make laws, and so to check the manufactures in America for many years to come. This method I will try, before I will give up my right. Gentlemen talk of the harsh measures pursued by this country towards America. Every session has produced some mark of affection towards her; bounty after bounty; importation of flax; permission to export rice. We are treated as hard task-masters, because we will not give up an undoubted right of the Legislature."

Thomas Pownall moved the repeal of the duty on tea also. The House of Commons, like Lord North in his heart,[1] was disposed to do the work of conciliation thoroughly. It was known that Grenville would not give an adverse vote.[2] "It is the sober opinion of the Americans," said Mackay, fresh from the military Command in Boston, "that you have no right to tax them. When beaten out of every argument, they adduce the authority of the first man of the law, and the first man of the State." Grenville assumed fully the responsibility of the Stamp Act; but he revealed to the House that the measure of taxing America had been the wish of the King. On the present occasion, had the King's friends remained neutral, the duty on tea would have been repealed; with all their exertions, in a full House, the majority for retaining it was but sixty-two.[3] Lord

[1] Franklin to Dr. Cooper, 8 June, 1770; Franklin's Works, vii. 475. And compare vii. 467.

[2] Compare Du Chatelet to the Duke of Choiseul, No. 38; 27 Feb. 1770.

[3] Franklin to a Friend in America, 18 March, 1770; Writings, vii. 466.

CHAP. XLIV. 1770. March North seemed hardly satisfied with his success; and reserved to himself liberty to accede to the repeal on some agreement with the East India Company;[1] with fatal weakness of purpose, delaying the measure which his good sense and humanity approved.

The decision came from the King who was the master of the House of Commons, and the soul of the Ministry, busying himself even with the details of all important affairs. He had many qualities that become a sovereign,—temperance, regularity, and industry; decorous manners, and unaffected piety; frugality in his personal expenses, so that his pleasures laid no burden on his people; a moderation which made him ever averse to wars of conquest; courage, which dared to assume responsibility, and could even contemplate death serenely; a fortitude that met accumulated dangers without flinching and rose with adversity.

But his mind was bigoted, narrow, and without comprehensiveness, morbidly impatient of being ruled, and yet himself incapable of reconciling the demands of civilization with the establishments of the past. He was the great founder and head of the New Tory or Conservative party, which had become dominant through his support. To that cause all his instincts were blindly true; so that throughout his career, he was consistent in his zeal for authority, his hatred of reform, and his antipathy to philosophical freedom of inquiry and to popular power. On these points he was inflexibly obstinate and undisguised; nor could he be justly censured for dissimulation, except for that

[1] Garth to South Carolina Committee, 6 March, 1770. W. S. Johnson to Gov. Trumbull, 6 March, 1770.

disingenuousness which studies the secret characters of men in order to use them as its instruments. No one could tell whether the king really liked him. He could flatter, cajole, and humor, or frown and threaten; he could conceal the sense of injuries and forget good service; bribe the corrupt by favors, or terrify deserters by punishment. In bestowing rewards, it was his rule, as far as possible, to preserve the dependence of his favorites by making none but revocable grants; and he required of his friends an implicit obedience. He was willing to govern through Parliament, yet did not conceal his readiness to stand by his Ministers, even though they should find themselves in a minority; and was sure that one day the Government must disregard majorities.

CHAP. XLIV. 1770. March

With a strong physical frame, he had also a nervous susceptibility which made him rapid in his utterance; and so impatient of contradiction, that he never could bear the presence of a Minister who resolutely differed from him, and was easily thrown into a state of high excitement, bordering upon madness. Anger which changed Chatham into a seer, pouring floods of light upon his mind, and quickening his discernment, served only to cloud or disturb the mind of George the Third, so that he could not hide his thoughts from those about him, and, if using the pen, could neither spell correctly nor write coherently. Hence the proud, unbending Grenville was his aversion; and his years with the compliant Lord North, though full of public disasters, were the happiest of his life. Conscious of his devotion to the cause of legitimate authority, and viewing with complacency his own correctness of morals, he identified himself with the cause which he venerated.

CHAP. XLIV. 1770. March

His eye did not rest on Colonial liberty or a people struggling towards more intelligence and happiness; the Crown was to him the emblem of all rightful power. He had that worst quality of evil, that he, as it were, adored himself; and regarded opposition to his designs as an offence against integrity and patriotism. He thought no exertions too great to crush the spirit of revolution, and no sufferings or punishment too cruel or too severe for those whom he esteemed as rebels.

The chaotic state of parties in England at this period of transition from their ancient forms, favored the King's purposes. The liberal branch of the aristocracy had accomplished the duty it had undertaken; and had not yet discovered the service on which humanity would employ it next. After the revolution of 1688, the defeated cause, whose followers clung to the traditions of the Middle Age, had its strongest support in the inhabitants of the rural districts. Through them only could the tory, who retained the implicit reverence for Monarchy and for the Church, hope to succeed against the friends of the new political system; and the more frequent and the more complete the opportunity of the appeal, the greater was his prospect of a victory. The Tory faction, therefore, in its warfare against actual progress, addressed itself to the sympathies of the common people. It would have annual Parliaments; it would have democratic supremacy; it led the van of patriotism, and its speeches even savored of republicanism. The party of the past sought to win a triumph over those in power, by making an alliance with the party of the future. In this manner it came about that the Whigs for half a century stood between the tendency of Monarchy towards absolute power on the one hand, and the hereditary superstitions and tender affection of the country for the old social hierarchy on the other; fighting strenuously alike against the prerogative and against the people. But time which is the greatest of all innovators had changed their political relations. The present King found the Whig aristocracy divided; and he readily formed a coalition with that part of it which respected the established forms more than the principles of the Revolution. No combination could rise against this organized conservatism of England, but one which should revive "Revolution principles," and insist on a nearer harmony between them and the forms of the Constitution. As yet Rockingham and his adherents avowed the same political creed with the clan of Bedford, and were less friendly to reform than Grenville. When Burke and Wedderburne were allies, the opposition wore the aspect of a selfish struggle of the discontented for place; and the Whig aristocracy, continuing its war against the people as well as against the King, fell more and more into disrepute. A few feeble voices among the Commoners, Chatham and Shelburne and Stanhope among the Peers, cried out for Parliamentary reform; they were opposed by the members of the great Whig connection, who may have had a good will to advocate public liberty, but, like hounds which have lost the scent and wander this way and that, were ignorant in what direction to go, and too haughty to be taught by men of humble birth. The King, therefore, was strengthened by the divisions among those who really wished to practise a policy of liberty, and had nothing to fear from an opposition. The changing

CHAP. XLIV. 1770. March politicians were eager to join his standard; and while the great seal was for a time put in commission, Thurlow superseded the liberal Dunning.

The new Solicitor General whose "majestic sense" and capacity of mind[1] have been greatly overrated, was a man of a coarse nature and a bad heart. The mother of his children was a kept mistress; he himself was strangely profane, and unmindful of social decorum. His manners were so rough that he enjoyed among the people the credit of being fearless of the aristocracy; but no man was in reality more subservient to their interests. Lord North, who timidly conformed to precedents, governed himself on questions of law by his advice;[2] and Thurlow proved the evil genius of that Minister and of England. Towards America no man was more sullenly unrelenting; and his influence went far towards rendering a crisis unavoidable.[3]

Schemes were revived for admitting representatives from the American Colonies into the British House of Commons;[4] but they attracted little attention. The Government would not change its system; the well-founded Petition of Massachusetts against Bernard was dismissed by the Privy Council, as "groundless, vexatious and scandalous."[5] At the same time, his interference had involved his successor in needless embarrassments. By his advice, Hutchinson,

[1] Henley's Northington, 59.

[2] Compare Francès to Choiseul, 20 July, 1770.

[3] Grafton in his Autobiography.

[4] Considerations on the Expediency of admitting representatives from the American Colonies in the British House of Commons, 1770. See Tucker's Four tracts, 164; and The Monthly Review, xliii. 161.

[5] Report of Council, 7 March, and Orders in Council, 14 March, 1770; in appendix to Bernard's Select Letters.

against his own judgment,[1] convened the Legislature at Cambridge.[2] For this display of resentment he could give no plausible reason. To the Assembly he excused himself by saying that his instructions had 'made it necessary;" but he produced no such intructions; the plea, moreover, was false, for Hillsborough had left him discretionary power.[3] The House and the Council remonstrated, insisting that even though he were instructed[4] to meet the Assembly at Cambridge, yet it was his duty under the Charter to adjourn the session to the Court-house in Boston. "I am a servant of the King," replied Hutchinson, "to be governed by his Majesty's pleasure."[5] Thus a new question arose respecting the proper use of the prerogative; while the Assembly proceeded to business "only from absolute necessity."[6]

Yet in spite of appearances and of the adverse influence of the Government, popular liberty was constantly gaining ground in England as well as in America. The last public act of Grenville's life was a step towards representative reform by establishing a more impartial method of deciding controverted elections.

[1] Hutchinson to Gage, 25 Feb. 1770.

[2] Hutchinson to Hillsborough, 28 Feb. 1770. First draft in the Remembrancer, 1775, p. 95. Same to Same, Second draft, written in March, but dated 23 Feb. 1770.

[3] Hillsborough to Hutchinson, 9 December, 1769. Hutchinson to Gage, 25 Feb. 1770. "I am left to my discretion."

[4] Address of the Council to Hutchinson, 20 March, 1770; Bradford, 197.

[5] Message from the Governor to the Council, 21 March, 1770, Bradford.

[6] Bradford's State Papers, 202. Suppose a petulant or angry minister were to be displeased with the two Houses of Parliament, and to mark his resentment, were to summon them to meet at Wolverton or Rye, instead of Westminster; in what temper would he find them? Yet that would be analogous to the act of Hutchinson.

CHAP. XLIV. It was perhaps the most honorable trophy of his long career.

1770. April. On the ninth of April, four days after Grenville had carried his bill triumphantly to the House of Lords, one more attempt was made to conciliate America; and Trecothick of London, supported by Beckford and Lord Beauchamp, by Dowdeswell, Conway, Dunning the late Solicitor General, and Sir George Saville, proposed[1] the repeal of the duty on tea. The King who watched Parliament closely, was indignant at this "debate in the teeth of a standing order,"[2] on a proposal which had already been voted down. "I wish to conciliate the Americans, and to restore harmony to the two countries," said Lord North; "but I will never be intimidated by the threats nor compelled by the combinations of the Colonies to make unreasonable or impolitic concessions." So the next order of the day was called for by a vote of eighty to fifty-two.

The news of the Boston Massacre[3] reached England at a time when the Legislature of Massachusetts was solemnly declaring, that the keeping a standing army in the Colony, in a time of peace, without its consent, was against law. "God forbid," said Grenville in the House of Commons,[3] on the twenty-sixth of April, "we should send soldiers to act without civil authority."—"Let us have no more angry votes against the people of America," cried Lord Beauchamp. "The officers" observed Barré, "agreed in

[1] Garth to Committee of South Carolina, 11 April, 1770. W. S. Johnson to Gov. Trumbull of Connecticut, 14 April, 1770.

[2] King to Lord North, 9 April, 1770; from the papers of Lord North, communicated to me by his daughter.

[3] Sir Philip Francis to Calcraft, 21 April, 1770.

[4] Cavendish Debates, i. 551.

1770. April.

sending the soldiers to Castle William; what Minister will dare to send them back to Boston?" "The very idea of a military establishment in America," cried William Burke, "is wrong." In a different spirit, Lord Barrington proposed a change in the too democratical Charter of Massachusetts.[1]

The American question became more and more complicated with the history and the hopes of freedom in England. The country was suffering from the excess of aristocracy in its constitution; Burke, writing with the authority of the great whig party, prescribed more aristocracy as the cure of the evil. But English liberty was like the lofty forest tree which begins to decay at its top; it needed a renewal of the soil round its root. Chatham saw the futility of the plan; and unable to obtain from Rockingham the acceptance of his far reaching views, he stepped forward himself as the champion of the people. "I pledge myself to their cause," said he in the House of Lords on the first of May, "for I know it is the cause of truth and justice." "I trust the people of this country," said Camden, "will renew their claims to true and free and equal representation as their inherent and unalienable right." Shelburne insisted that Lord North, for his agency with regard to the Middlesex elections, deserved impeachment. Stanhope pledged himself to the support of liberty, if necessary, at the cost of his life.

May.

On the ninth of May, Edmund Burke,[2] acting in thorough conjunction with Grenville, brought the

[1] Report of the Debate in the Boston Gazette of 25 June, 1770; 794, 4, 2.

[2] Cavendish Debates, ii. 14; Boston Gazette, 9 July, 1770; 796, 2, 2.

CHAP. XLIV. 1770. May. affairs of America before the House of Commons in Resolutions, condemning the contradictory measures that had been pursued since his friends had been dismissed, but carefully avoiding any indication of the policy which the party in power should adopt.[1] Burke was supported by Wedderburn, who equally had no measures to propose. "Nothing," said he, "offers itself but despair. Lord Hillsborough is unfit for his office. The nation suffers by his continuance. The people have a right to say, they will not be under the authority of the sword. If you drive men to desperation, they will act upon the principles of human nature; principles to be supported; principles to be honored. At the close of the last reign, you had the continent of America in one compact country. Not quite ten years have passed over, and you have lost those Provinces by domestic mismanagement. All America, the fruit of so many years' settlement, nurtured by this country at the price of so much blood and treasure—is lost to the Crown of Great Britain in the reign of George the Third." Lord North, in his reply, declared himself the only man of the Ministry, who was decidedly for the repeal of the Revenue Act of 1767; defended the partial repeal, because he wished to see the American associations defeat themselves; questioned the veracity of Wedderburn; and treated the ill-cemented coalition, as having no plan beyond the removal of the present Ministers. "God forgive the noble Lord for the idea of there being a plan to remove him," retorted Wedderburn; "I know no man

[1] W. S. Johnson to Gov. Trumbull, 21 May, 1770.

of honor and respectability, who would undertake to do the duties of the situation." CHAP. XLIV. 1770. May.

The Opposition was plainly factious; and the resolutions which only censured the past were defeated by a vote of more than two to one. Chatham would not attend the debate, when they were brought forward in the House of Lords; but spurning the lukewarm temper of the Rockingham Whigs, he placed himself before the nation as the guide of the future, zealous for introducing "a more full and equal representation."[1] His patriotism was fruitless for that generation; light on representative reform was not to break on England from the House of Lords. But America was an essential part of the English world. To New England the men of the days preceding the ill-starred Commonwealth had borne their ideas of government, and there the system of an adequate, uncorrupt and equal representation existed in undimmed lustre. There the people annually came together in their towns, annually elected their representatives, and gave them instructions which were sacredly obeyed.

The instructions which the town of Boston, adopting the language of the younger Quincy, this year addressed to the faithful representatives of its choice, cited the Journals of the House of Lords in evidence of "a desperate plan of imperial despotism," which was to be resisted if necessary, "even unto the uttermost;" and therefore recommended martial virtues, valor, intrepidity, military emulation, and, above all, the firm and lasting union of the Colonies.

[1] Vote of the Common Council of London, 14 May, 1770. Motion of Lord Chatham, 14 May, 1770; in Chat. Corr. iii. 457. Chatham to the London Deputation, 1 June, 1770.

CHAP. XLIV. 1770. May. The document could not increase the zeal of the patriots of Boston; Hutchinson made an effective use of it to quicken the apprehensions of the Ministry; and its reception contributed to produce that new set of measures, which hastened American Independence by seeking to crush its spirit.[1] England assumed, that there existed a design for a general revolt, when there only existed a desire to resist "innovations;" but the inference was a just one, that between the opinions of the House of Lords and those of the Town of Boston, the difference was irreconcilable.

The eagerness of Hutchinson to keep Bernard's favor and ingratiate himself with Hillsborough, induced him to call the newly elected Legislature, as he had done the last, to Cambridge. "Not the least shadow of necessity," said the House in its remonstrance, "exists for it. Prerogative is a discretionary power vested in the King only for the
June. good of the subject." Hutchinson had over-acted his part; and now found himself embarrassed by his own arbitrary act, for which he dared not assign the true reason and could not assign a good one. The House censured his conduct by a vote of ninety-six against six, and refused to proceed to any other business than that of organizing the Government. Thus Hutchinson opened his administration with a foolish strife, wantonly provoked, and promising no advantage whatever to British authority.

Meantime a most elaborate paper on the disorders in America, was laid before the British Council.

[1] Hutchinson's History, iii. 290.

Long and earnest deliberations ensued. On the one side, Hillsborough pressed impetuously for the execution of his plans, as the only means of arresting the progress of America towards Independence; while Lord North, with better judgment, was willing to wait, being persuaded that the associations for non-importation would fall asunder of themselves. CHAP XLIV. 1770. June.

Canada, Carolina and Georgia, and even Maryland and Virginia had increased their importations; and New England and Pennsylvania had imported nearly one half as much as usual; New-York alone had been perfectly true to its engagement; and its imports had fallen off more than five parts in six. It was impatient of a system of voluntary renunciation, which was so unequally kept; and the belief was common, that if the others had adhered to it as strictly, all the grievances would have been redressed.[1] July.

Merchants of New-York, therefore, consulted those of Philadelphia on agreeing to a general importation of all articles except of tea; the Philadelphians favored the proposition, till a letter arrived from Franklin, urging them to persevere on their original plan.[2] Sears and MacDougall in New-York strenuously resisted concession; but men went from ward to ward to take the opinions of the people; and it was found that eleven hundred and eighty against three hundred were disposed to confine the restriction to tea alone.[3] "If any merchant should presume to break through the non-importation agreement, except in concert

[1] W. S. Johnson to Gov. Trumbull, 6 March, 1770.

[2] Franklin's Works, vii. 468, 469. Compare too, W. S. Johnson to Gov. Trumbull, 21 May, 1770.

[3] C. Colden to Hillsborough, 7 July, 1770. J. Duane to W. S. Johnson, 15 June, 1770.

CHAP. XLIV. 1770. July. with the several Provinces, the goods imported should be burnt as soon as landed, and I am ready to peril my life in the attempt." Such were the words of Isaac Sears at a public meeting of the resolute patriots. The decision was on the balance; an appeal was again taken to the people; and as it appeared that a majority favored resuming importations, the packet of July which had been detained for a few days, sailed before the middle of the month with orders for all kinds of merchandise excepting tea.[1] "Send us your old Liberty Pole, as you can have no further use for it,"[2] said the Philadelphians. The students at Princeton burnt the New-York merchants' letter by the hands of the hangman. Boston tore it into pieces and threw it to the winds.[3] South Carolina, whose patriots had just raised the statue to Chatham, read it with disdainful anger. But there was no help; Lord North had reasoned so far correctly; the non-importation agreement had been sacredly enforced by New-York alone, and now trade between America and England was open in every thing but TEA.

[1] Colden to Hillsborough, 10 July, 1770; A. Colden to A. Todd, 11 July, 1770; James Duane to W. S. Johnson, 9 Dec. 1770.

[2] A Card from the Inhabitants of Philadelphia, &c. July, 1770.

[3] Votes at a full Meeting of the Trade at Faneuil Hall, 24 July, 1770.

CHAPTER XLV.

MARTIAL LAW INTRODUCED INTO MASSACHUSETTS.—HILLSBOROUGH'S ADMINISTRATION OF THE COLONIES CONTINUED.

July—October, 1770.

CHAP XLV. 1770. July.

Greater joy was never shown than prevailed in London at the news that America was resuming commercial intercourse. The occasion invited corresponding concessions, which Lord North would have willingly made; but the majority of his colleagues had been led to consider "the state of the Colony of Massachusetts Bay more desperate than ever;"[1] and on the sixth of July the King in Council gave an order, making a beginning of Martial Law within that Province, and preparing the way for closing the Port of Boston.

Hutchinson paid court by acting in the same spirit; and in July once more summoned the Legislature to Cambridge. For this repeated wrong to the public service of the Colony, he continued to offer no other excuse than the King's will. The highest advocate for the divine right of regal power

[1] State of the Disorders Confusion and Misgovernment, &c. &c.

CHAP. XLV. 1770. July. had never gone so far as to claim, that it might be used at caprice, to inflict wanton injury. There was no precedent for the measure but during the worst of times in England, or in France, where a Parliament had sometimes been worried into a submission by exile.

The Assembly expressed in the strongest terms the superiority of the Legislative body to royal instructions; and in answer to the old question of what is to be done upon the abusive exercise of the prerogative, they went back to the principles of the Revolution, and adopted the words of Locke: "In this as in all other cases, where they have no judge on earth, the people have no remedy but to appeal to Heaven." They drew a distinction between the King and his servants; and attributed to "wicked Ministers" the daring encroachments on their liberty, as well as "the impudent mandate" to one House, "to rescind an excellent resolution of a former one."

Aug Hutchinson made haste to expose his Sovereign personally to contempt. On the third day of August he communicated to the House, that the instruction to rescind, which they had called an impudent mandate, was an order from the King himself, whose "immediate attention," he assured them, they would not be able "to escape." In this manner the royal dignity and character were placed on trial before a colonial Assembly, and Monarchy itself was losing all its halo.

Sept. The session had passed without the transaction of any business, when, near the evening of Saturday, the eighth day of September, Hutchinson received the order which had been adopted in July by the King in Council, and which marks the beginning of a system

CHAP XLV. 1770. Sept.

of measures having for their object the prevention of American Independence. The harbor of Boston was made "the rendezvous of all ships, stationed in North America," and the fortress which commanded it was to be delivered up to such officer as Gage should appoint,[1] to be garrisoned by regular troops, and put into a respectable state of defence.[2] At the same time Hutchinson received from Gage the direction to surrender up Castle William to Dalrymple. But the Charter of Massachusetts purposely and emphatically reserved to its Governor the command of the militia of the Colony and of its forts; the Castle had been built and repaired and garrisoned by the Colony itself at its own expense; to take the command from the Civil Governor and bestow it on the Commander-in-chief, was a plain violation of the Charter, as well as of immemorial usage. For a day Hutchinson hesitated;[3] but what was a scruple about the Charter rights of Massachusetts, compared with the favor of Hillsborough and the King? On second thoughts he resolved to obey the order at once. Early on Monday, Dalrymple hastened to the Castle, provided with a power to substitute regular troops for the provincial sentries. Hutchinson then repaired to the Council Chamber, and enjoining secrecy on the members upon their oaths divulged to them his instructions. The Council was struck with amazement, for the town was very quiet, and the measure seemed a wanton provocation. "Does not the Charter," they

[1] Hillsborough to Hutchinson, July, 1770.

[2] Report of the Committee of the Privy Council, to whom the State of the American Colonies was referred, and which was adopted, 6 July, 1770.

[3] Hutchinson to General Gage, 9 September, 1770.

CHAP. XLV. 1770. Sept. demanded of him, "place the command of the Castle in the Governor?" After a secret discussion which lasted for two hours, till Dalrymple had had time to take possession, he entered his carriage which was waiting at the door, hurried to the Neck, stole into a barge, and was rowed to the Castle. The officers and garrison were discharged without a moment's warning; Hutchinson delivered up the keys to Dalrymple, and in the twilight retired to his country house at Milton.[1] But he was so haunted by fear as to dread being waylaid; and the next day, as he and Bernard had done five years before, he fled for safety to the Castle, where he remained every night for the rest of the week. His fears were groundless. The people of Boston, especially Samuel Adams, were indignant at the breach of their Charter; the act was a commencement of civil war. Yet the last appeal was not to be made without some prospect of success, and the Castle remained in the possession of England for five and a half years.

A fleet in the harbor of Boston, a fort garrisoned and commanded by the regular troops and threatening it at any moment with a total loss of its commerce, were the invention of the Ministry to coerce the town into unresisting obedience. Distrust, injury, and menace were the chosen medicines against rebellion. "As a citizen of the world," cried Turgot, "I see with joy the approach of an event which more than all the books of the philosophers, will dissipate the puerile and sanguinary phantom of a pretended exclusive commerce. I speak of the separation of the British Colonies from their metropolis,

[1] Hutchinson to Sir Francis Bernard, 15 Sept. 1770.

CHAP. XLV. 1770. Sept.

which will soon be followed by that of all America from Europe. Then, and not till then, will the discovery of that part of the world become for us truly useful. Then it will multiply our enjoyments far more abundantly, than when we bought them by torrents of blood."[1]

Oct.

Hillsborough, too, was possessed with the fear, that the idea of independence would indeed be realized, unless he could persuade all but the abettors of "a few desperate men,[2] to see the necessity of restoring the authority of the Supreme Legislature by a reform of the Constitution of the Massachusetts Bay." "No more time," said he, "should be lost in deliberation," and he exerted all his power to establish the binding obligation of the decisions of the Privy Council and the decrees of Parliament.

The very day, on which Hillsborough commenced his fixed purpose of subverting the Constitution of Massachusetts, its two Houses, which had been called for the third time to Cambridge, having summoned all absent members,[3] were keeping a day of fasting, solemn prayer and humiliation. "We have," said Hutchinson, "many people who are enthusiasts, and believe they are contending for the cause of God."[4] Some days after their solemn communing with Heaven, the House, which heretofore had refused to proceed to business away from Boston, expressed alarm at the new, additional and insupportable grievances under which the Colony labored, and after a

[1] Turgot to Tucker. Oeuvres de Turgot, ii. 802.

[2] Hillsborough to Hutchinson, No. 42, 3 October, 1770.

[3] Hutchinson to J. Pownall, Boston, 30 Sept. 1770.

[4] Hutchinson to Whately, 3 Oct. 1770.

CHAP. XLV. 1770. Oct. protest, entered on an inquiry into the state of the Province with a view to a radical redress of its grievances."[1] At the same time Hutchinson, with whom Hillsborough was interchanging private letters, sent word, that "no measure could have been pitched upon more proper than the possession of the harbor of Boston by the King's troops and ships," as a mark of royal resentment, and a preparation for further measures.[2] Conspiring[3] with fiercer zeal than ever against the liberties of his native country, he advised not a mere change of the mode of electing the Council, but "a bill for the vacating or disannulling the Charter in all its parts, and leaving it to the King to settle the Government by a royal Commission." Yet as Hillsborough and the King seemed content with obtaining the appointment of the Council, Hutchinson suppressed his misgivings, considered how the change could be carried into effect, and forwarded lists from which the royal councillors were to be named. "If the kingdom," said he, "is united and resolved, I have but very little doubt, we shall be as tame as lambs." He presented distinctly the option, either to lay aside taxation as inexpedient, and to wait till the Colonies should submit from weariness;—a policy against which all his letters protested;—or to deal with the

[1] Bradford's State Papers, 257, 258. Hutchinson to Hillsborough, 9 October, 1770.

[2] Hutchinson to Lord Hillsborough, Private, Boston, 26 October, 1770. Hillsborough's private letters are missing.

[3] The authorities are, Hillsborough to Hutchinson, 3 October, 1770; Hutchinson to Hillsborough, 8 October, 1770; Same to Same later in October, in Hutchinson's MSS. iii. 22, 23, and printed in the Remembrancer for 1776, i. 158; Hutchinson to Sir Francis Bernard, 20 October, 1770; Hutchinson's private letter to Hillsborough, 26 October, 1770, ii. 181; Hutchinson to an official person not named, I suppose Secretary Pownall, 22 Oct. 1770, and other letters.

CHAP. XLV. 1770. Oct.

inhabitants as being "in a state of revolt."[1] After that should be decided, he proposed to starve the Colony into obedience by narrowing its commerce and excluding it from the fisheries. If this should fail, the military might be employed to act by their own authority, free from the restraints of civil Government.[2] Boston, he thought, should be insulated from the rest of the Colony, and specially dealt with; and he recommended the example of Rome, which, on one occasion, seized the leading men in rebellious Colonies, and detained them in the metropolis as hostages. An Act of Parliament, curtailing Massachusetts of all the land east of the Penobscot, was a supplementary proposition.[3]

Less occasion never existed for martial rule than at Boston. At the ensuing trial of Preston, every indulgence was shown him by the citizens. Auchmuty, his Counsel, had the disinterested assistance of John Adams and Quincy. The prosecution was conducted with languor and inefficiency; the defence with consummate ability; the judges were the partisans of the prisoner; and selected talesmen were put upon the jury. As the slaughter of the citizens took place at night, it was not difficult to raise a plausible doubt, whether it was Preston, or some other person, who had actually cried out to the soldiers to fire; and on that ground a verdict of acquittal was obtained. The public acquiesced; but was offended at the manifest want of uprightness in the Court. Quincy, who

[1] Hutchinson to Sir Francis Bernard, 20 Oct. 1770; in Hutchinson's MS. iii. 26, 27, 28. Compare with it Hutchinson to Sir Francis Bernard, of 4 August, 1770.

[2] Compare Hutchinson to Bernard, 20 Oct. 1770, and Hutchinson's History, iii. 324.

[3] In Letters to Hillsborough, and more distinctly to John Pownall.

CHAP. XLV. 1770. Oct. had taken part in the defence, afterwards denied the propriety of the verdict. "The firmness of the judges" in delivering opinions on "principles of Government," was vaunted to obtain for them all much larger salaries, to be paid directly by the Crown. The Chief Justice, who was a manufacturer, wanted, moreover, money in the shape of pay for some refuse cannon balls which the Province had refused to buy.[1]

The trial of the soldiers, which followed a few weeks after, resulted in a verdict of manslaughter against each one of them who could be proved to have fired.[2]

The self-possession which had marked the conduct of the Town in regard to the trial of Preston, appeared in the measures of the Assembly for the redress of their grievances. In selecting an agent to bring them before the King, Samuel Adams and about one third of the House,[3] following the advice of Joseph Reed of Philadelphia, gave their suffrages for Arthur Lee; but by the better influence of Bowdoin and of the Minister Cooper,[4] Benjamin Franklin, was elected with Arthur Lee as his substitute. Franklin held under the Crown the office of Depu-

[1] Hutchinson to General Gage, Boston, 31 March, 1771.

[2] Hutchinson to Sir Francis Bernard, 6 Dec. 1770, and more fully, 10 Dec. 1770. "If there had been evidence of all having fired, they would have convicted all of manslaughter; but it was agreed on all hands, that no more than seven guns were fired, consequently one was innocent. Two, as several witnesses swore, fired and killed three men. Of the other six, there was no certainty which fired. If they had all been convicted, the jury would certainly have found one guilty who was innocent, and they chose five guilty should escape rather than one innocent be convicted. These are pretty good distinctions for an American jury.

[3] Samuel Adams to S. Sayre, 16 November, 1770. Hutchinson to Gov. Pownall, 11 Nov. 1770.

[4] Samuel Cooper to B. Franklin, 6 November, 1770; in Franklin, vii. 489. Hutchinson to Gov. Pownall, 11 Nov. 1770.

CHAP. XLV. 1770. Oct.

ty Postmaster General for America, and his son was a royal Governor; but his mind had reasoned on politics with the same freedom from prejudice which marked his investigations into the laws of nature; and from questioning the right of Parliament to tax the Colonies externally, he had been led to the conviction, that the Colonies originally were constituted distinct States; that the legislative authority of Parliament over them was a usurpation; that Parliament was not supreme, nor the American Assemblies subordinate; that the American Assemblies with the King, had a true legislative authority, which ought not to be limited by his Parliament in Great Britain; and that the keeping up a standing army in America, without the consent of the colonial Assemblies, had no sanction in the Constitution.[1] From the knowledge that these were his principles, and from confidence in his integrity and ability, the House readily confided the redress of their grievances to his care.[2]

At the time when Franklin was thus called by the people of Massachusetts to be their mediator with the mother country, he was sixty-four years of age. His large experience had ripened his judgment, without impairing the vigor of his mind; and he still retained the kindly benignity of manner, genial humor, and comprehensiveness of observation, which made him every where welcome. The difficult service demanded of him by the Colony of his nativity,

[1] Benjamin Franklin to Samuel Cooper, London, 8 June, 1770; in Franklin's Writings, vii. 475. Compare also Franklin, iv. 408, vii. 392, and vii. 487; and Cooper to Franklin, 15 November, 1770, in Franklin, vii. 490.

[2] See the letter of instructions to B. Franklin, 6 Nov. 1770, written by Samuel Adams.

CHAP. XLV. 1770. Oct.

was rendered with exemplary fidelity and disinterestedness, amidst embarrassment of all kinds. Hutchinson took care to negative all appropriations for his salary;[1] and to remind Hillsborough not to recognise him as an Agent.

[1] Compare Hutchinson to ——, 17 Nov. 1770, and to ——, 26 Nov. 1770.

CHAPTER XLVI.

THE ORIGIN OF TENNESSEE.—HILLSBOROUGH'S ADMINISTRATION OF THE COLONIES CONTINUED.

October, 1770—June, 1771.

CHAP. XLVI. 1770. Oct.

The Colonization of the West was one of the great objects ever promoted by Franklin. No one had more vividly discerned the capacity of the Mississippi valley not only to sustain Commonwealths, but to connect them with the world by commerce; and when the Ministers would have rejected the Fort Stanwix Treaty,[1] which conveyed from the Six Nations an inchoate title to the immense territory southwest of the Ohio, his influence secured its ratification, by organizing a powerful company to plant a Province in that part of the country which lay back of Virginia, between the Alleghanies and a line drawn from the Cumberland Gap to the mouth of the Scioto.[2]

[1] W. S. Johnson to Joseph Chew, 13 Feb. 1770.

[2] See the elaborate Petition of Benjamin Franklin to Congress, Passy, 20 Feb. 1780; not in his Works.

CHAP. XLVI. 1770. Oct. Virginia resisted the proposed limitation of her jurisdiction, as fatal to her interests;[1] earnestly entreating an extension of her borders westward to the Tennessee River. It would be tedious to rehearse the earnest pleas of the Colony; the hesitations of Hillsborough, who wished to pacify her people, and yet to confine her settlements; the entreaties of Botetourt; the adverse Representations of the Board of Trade; the meetings of Agents with the Beloved Men of the Cherokees. On the seventeenth of October, two days after the death of Botetourt, a treaty conforming to the decision of the British cabinet, was made at the Congress of Lochaber,[2] confining the Ancient Dominion on the Northwest to the mouth of the Kenawha, while on the South it extended only to within six miles of the Holston River.[3] The Cherokees would willingly have ceded more land; and when in the following year the line was run by Donelson for Virginia, their Chief consented that it should cross from the Holston to the Louisa,[4] or Kentucky River, and follow it to the Ohio. But the change was disapproved in England, so that the great body of the West, unencumbered by valid titles, was happily reserved for the self-directed emigrant.

The people of Virginia and others were exploring and marking all the richest lands, not only on the Redstone and other waters of the Monongahela, but along the Ohio, as low as the little Kenawha;[5] and

[1] Washington to Botetourt, 15 April, 1770; Writings, ii. 357.

[2] Treaty of Lochaber in Mr. President Nelson's No. 8, of Dec. 1770.

[3] Superintendent Stuart to Lord Botetourt, Lochaber, 25 Oct. 1770.

[4] Lord Dunmore to Hillsborough, March, 1770.

[5] Washington's Diary, in Writings, ii. 531. Washington, ii. 531.

CHAP. XLVI. 1770. Oct.

with each year were getting further and further down the river. When Washington in 1770, having established for the soldiers and officers who had served with him in the French war, their right to two hundred thousand acres in the western valley, went to select suitable tracts, he was obliged to descend to the Great Kenawha. As he floated in a canoe down the Ohio, whose banks he found enlivened by innumerable turkeys and other wild fowl, with many deer browsing on the shore or stepping down to the water's edge to drink, no good land escaped his eye. Where the soil and growth of timber were most inviting, he would walk through the woods, and set his mark on a maple, or elm, a hoop-wood, or ash, as the corner of a soldier's survey;[1] for he watched over the interests of his old associates in arms as sacredly as if he had been their trustee, and never ceased his care for them, till by his exertions, and "by these alone,"[2] he had secured to each one of them, or if they were dead, to their heirs, the full proportion of the bounty that had been promised. His journey to the wilderness was not without its pleasures; he amused himself with the sports of the forest, or observing new kinds of water-fowl, or taking the girth of the largest trees, one of which at a yard from the ground measured within two inches of five and forty feet. His fame had gone before him; the Red Men received him in Council with public honors. Nor did he turn homewards without inquiring of Nicholson, an Indian interpreter, and of Conolly, an intelligent forester, the character of the country further

[1] Washington's Diary, Writings, ii. 528.

[2] Life of Washington by Jared Sparks, i. 119, 120.

CHAP. XLVI. 1770. Nov. west. From these eye-witnesses he received glowing accounts of the climate, soil, good streams and plentiful game that distinguished the valley of the Cumberland. There he was persuaded a new and most desirable Government might be established.[1]

At that time Daniel Boon was still exploring the land of promise.[2] Of forty adventurers who from the Clinch River plunged into the West under the lead of James Knox, and became renowned as "the Long Hunters,"[3] some found their way down the Cumberland to the limestone Bluff, where Nashville stands, and where the luxuriant, gently undulating fields, covered with groves of beech and walnut, were in the undisputed possession of countless buffaloes, whose bellowings resounded from hill and forest.[4]

Sometimes trappers and restless emigrants, boldest of their class, took the risk of crossing the country from Carolina to the Mississippi; but of those who perished by the way, no tradition preserves the names. Others, following the natural highways of the West, descended from Pittsburg, and from Red Stone Creek to Fort Natchez. The pilot, who conducted the party of which Samuel Wells and John MacIntire were the Chiefs, was so attracted by the lands round the Fort, that he promised to remove there in the spring with his wife and family, and believed a hundred families from North Carolina[5] would follow.

The zeal of hunters and emigrants outran the concessions extorted from the Board of Trade. This

[1] Dr. Conolly in Washington, ii. 533.

[2] Boon's Autobiography.

[3] Monette's Valley, i. 355; Butler's Kentucky, 18, 19.

[4] Ramsey's Annals of Tennessee, 105. Haywood's Civil and Political History of Tennessee, 77.

[5] Letter dated Fort Natchez, 19 July, 1770. Compare Hillsborough to Chester, 3 Oct. 1770; Gage to Hillsborough, 24 April, 1770.

CHAP. XLVI. 1770. Nov.

year James Robertson, from the home of the Regulators in North Carolina, a poor and unlettered forester, of humble birth, but of inborn nobleness of soul, cultivated maize on the Watauga. The frame of the heroic planter was robust; his constitution hardy; he trod the soil as if he were its rightful lord. Intrepid, loving virtue for its own sake, and emulous of honorable fame, he had self-possession, quickness of discernment, and a sound judgment. Wherever he was thrown, on whatever he was engaged, he knew how to use all the means within his reach, whether small or great, to their proper end; seeing at a glance their latent capacities, and devising the simplest and surest way to bring them forth; and so he became the greatest benefactor of the early settlers of Tennessee, confirming to them peace, securing their independence, and leaving a name blessed by the esteem and love and praise of a commonwealth.[1]

He was followed to the West, by men from the same Province with himself, where the people had no respite from the insolence of mercenary attorneys and officers, and were subjected to every sort of rapine and extortion.[2] There the Courts of law offered no redress.[3] At the inferior Courts the Justices who themselves were implicated in the pilfering of public money, named the juries. The Sheriff and receivers of taxes were in arrears for near seventy thousand pounds, which they had extorted from the people, and

[1] John Hayward's Civil and Political History of the State of Tennessee, 39, 40.

[2] Governor Martin to the Secretary of State, Hillsborough, 30 August, 1772.

[3] Petition of Orange County to Chief Justice Howard, and to the Associate justices Moore and Henderson, without date; presented perhaps to Henderson, 29 Sept. 1770. See Henderson to Tryon, 29 Sept. 1770, and inclosed in Tryon to Hillsborough, 20 Oct. 1770.

CHAP. XLVI. 1770. Nov. of which more than two thirds[1] had been irretrievably embezzled. In the northern part of the Colony, where the ownership of the soil had been reserved to one of the old proprietaries, there was no land-office;[2] so that the people who were attracted by the surpassing excellence[3] of the land could not obtain freeholds. Every art was employed to increase the expenses of suits at law; and as some of the people in their wretchedness wreaked their vengeance in acts of folly and madness, they were artfully misrepresented as enemies to the Constitution; and the oppressor treacherously acquired the protection which was due to the oppressed. In March, 1770, one of the associate justices reported that they could not enforce the payment of taxes. At the Court in September the Regulators appeared in numbers. "We are come down," they said, "with the design to have justice done;" they would have business proceed, but with no attorney except the King's; and finding that it had been resolved not to try their causes,[4] some of them pursued Fanning and another lawyer, beat them with cowskin whips, and laid waste Fanning's house.[5]

The Assembly which convened in December, at Dec. Newbern, was chosen under a state of alarm and vague apprehension. Tryon had secured Fanning a seat, by chartering the town of Hillsborough as a borough, but the county of Orange, selected Herman Husbands as its Representative, with great unanimity. The

[1] Postscript to Martin to Hillsborough, 30 Jan. 1772.

[2] Tryon to Hillsborough, 12 April, 1770.

[3] Martin to Hillsborough, 10 Nov. 1770, "The super-excellence of the soil."

[4] Judge Henderson to Tryon, 29 Sept. 1770.

[5] Deposition of Ralph McNair, of 9th October, 1770.

CHAP XLVI. 1770. Dec.

rustic patriot possessed a good reputation and a considerable estate, and was charged with no illegal act whatever; yet he was voted a disturber of the public peace; on the twentieth of December was expelled the House;[1] and against the opinion of the Council, and notwithstanding the want of evidence,[2] that he had been even an accessory to the riots at Hillsborough, Tryon seized him under a warrant concerted with the Chief Justice,[3] and kept him in prison without bail.[4]

The Presbyterian party was the strongest in the House;[5] to conciliate its power, a law was passed for endowing Queen's College in the town of Charlotte, Mecklenburg County;[6] a deceitful act of tolerance, which was sure to be annulled by the King in Council. But the great object of Tryon was the riot Act, by which it was declared a felony for more than ten men to remain assembled after being required to disperse. For a riot committed before or after the publication of the Act, persons might be tried in any Superior Court, no matter how distant from their homes, and if within sixty days they did not make their appearance, whether with or without notice, they were to be proclaimed outlaws, and to forfeit their lives with all their property.[7] Such was the san-

[1] Gov. Tryon to Sec. Hillsborough, 31 Jan. 1771.

[2] "No testimony being present to prove him an accessory to the riots at Hillsborough." Tryon to the Sec. 31 Jan. 1771.

[3] Tryon to Hillsborough, 31 Jan. 1771. Letter from Newbern, N. C. 5 Oct. 1770. Letter from a Gentleman in N. C. to his friend in New Jersey respecting the Regulators in North Carolina; in Pennsylvania Journal of 3 Oct. 1771, and in Boston Gazette, of 21 Oct. 1771.

[4] Judge Martin, ii. 269. "Husbands remained several days in jail before he could procure bail." Worse than that; several weeks, and was not bailed at all.

[5] Tryon to Hillsborough, with the laws of the session.

[6] See Acts of the Session. Caruther's Life of Caldwell, 77.

[7] Martin's History of North Carolina, ii. 269, 270.

CHAP. XLVI. 1770. Dec. guinary method by which the wrath of Fanning was to be appeased. In the wish to establish order, full license was given to the ruthlessness of revenge. The Governor also sent letters into the neighboring counties, to ascertain how many would volunteer to serve in a military expedition against "the rebels;" but the Assembly, by withholding grants of money, set itself against civil war.

Tryon's smooth exterior and determined purpose had won for him at the Colonial office the reputation of being the ablest Governor in the thirteen Colonies; the death of Botetourt opened the way for his promotion to the chief magistracy of New-York. The Earl of Dunmore, a needy Scottish peer of the House of Murray, passionate, narrow, and unscrupulous in his rapacity, had hardly taken possession of that Government, when he was transferred to what was esteemed the more desirable one of Virginia. But before he made the exchange, his avarice had involved him in a singular strife. Fees for grants of land had swollen the emoluments of office during the short administration of Colden; Dunmore demanded half of them as his perquisite; and to make sure of four or five thousand pounds, prepared as Chancellor to make, in the King's name, a peremptory award in his own favor. He came over to amass a fortune, and in his passion for sudden gain, cared as little for the policy of the Ministers or his instructions from the Crown, as for the rights of property, the respective limits of jurisdiction of the Colonies, or their civil and political privileges. To get money was the rule of conduct, which included his whole administrative policy.

Dunmore did not remain in New-York long

enough to weary the legislature into a spirited resistance. Its members remained steadfast in their purpose to connect loyalty with their regard for American liberty. On a charge of contempt of their authority, they kept MacDougall[1] in prison during their session; at the same time, adopting the nomination made by Schuyler a year before,[2] they unanimously elected Edmund Burke, for whom his own country had no employment, their Agent in England, allowing "for his services at the rate of five hundred pounds per annum."[3]

This moderation might have persuaded the Ministry to conciliatory measures; it only raised a hope of producing divisions in America, by setting one Province against another. "I can find bones to throw among them, to continue contention and prevent a renewal of their union,"[4] promised Hutchinson, now happy in the assurance of receiving from the tax on tea a salary of fifteen hundred pounds for himself as Governor, while three hundred more were granted to the Lieutenant Governor Oliver, who had long been repining at the neglect of his sufferings in behalf of the Stamp Act. Yet Samuel Adams did not despair. "In every struggle," said he, "this country will approve herself glorious in maintaining and defending her freedom;"[5] and he was sure that the unreasonableness of Great Britain would precipitate the epoch of American Independence. South Carolina received

[1] MacDougall's Account, New Gaol, Dec. 22, 2770, in New-York Gazette of 24 Dec. 1770, and in Boston Gazette, No. 822.

[2] Journals of N. Y. Assembly for 10 Geo. iii. pp. 44, 51, and 59.

[3] Journals 11 Geo. iii. p. 18.

[4] Hutchinson to Mauduit, Boston, Dec. 1770; H. C. iii. 68, 69, 70.

[5] Samuel Adams to John Wilkes, Boston, 27 Dec. 1770.

CHAP. XLVI. 1770. Dec. his letters, still urging union, directing attention to the necessity of finding some more efficacious method of redress than a bare resolution to suspend commerce, and encouraging in the "young men" the ambition "of making themselves masters of the art military."[1]

Zeal for the cause was not wanting in the South. The people had their "tribunes" and most determined leaders in Thomas Lynch, praised by royalists as "a man of sense," and inflexible firmness, Christopher Gadsden, the "enthusiast in the cause," ever suspicious "of British moderation," and John Mackenzie, whose English education at Cambridge furnished him with arguments for the Colonies.[2]

On the thirteenth of December they met the planters, merchants and mechanics of Charleston. Lynch, who had come fifty miles on purpose, exerted all his eloquence; and even shed tears for the expiring liberty of his country. He was seconded by Gadsden and Mackenzie; but South Carolina could neither continue non-importation alone; nor by itself devise a new system. Its association was dissolved, like the rest; the goods of importers which had been stored by the General Committee were delivered up, and in Charleston, the fourth largest city in the Colonies, then having five thousand and thirty white inhabitants, with five thousand eight hundred and thirty-three blacks,[3] commerce resumed its wonted activity in every thing but tea.[4]

For a moment rumors of war between Great

[1] Samuel Adams to Peter Timothy of Charleston, South Carolina, Boston, 21 Nov. 1770.

[2] Lieut. Gov. Wm. Bull, private letter to Hillsborough, 5 Dec. 1770.

[3] State of South Carolina, by Lieut. Gov. Bull, 30 Nov. 1770.

[4] Lieut. Gov. Bull to the Secretary of State, 13 Dec. 1770.

Britain and the united Kings of France and Spain, gave hope of "happy effects."[1] But this also failed. England, following the impulse given by Lord Egmont during the administration of Grenville, had taken possession of the Falkland Islands, as forming the key to the Pacific. Spain, claiming all that part of the world as her own, sent a fleet of five frigates which drove the English from their wooden block-house, and after detaining them twenty days, left them to return to England. The English Ministry, willing to abandon Port Egmont, demanded of the Spanish Government a disavowal of the seizure and its temporary restoration. Spanish pride would have rejected the terms with disdain. "They are the only propositions, which the British Ministry could make;" said Choiseul, scoffing at the Spanish rodomontade. "For heaven's sake," he wrote to the French Minister at London, "do the impossible; and persuade Prince Masserano to follow my instructions rather than those of his own court, which have not common sense." Determined to preserve peace, Choiseul, who would not have feared war for a great cause like the emancipation of the colonial world, checked the rashness of Spain and assumed the direction of its diplomacy.[2] But Weymouth was haughty and unreasonable. "War is inevitable," said Harcourt to Choiseul. "If the English are bent on war," wrote Choiseul to Francès, "all that I can say is unavailing. But you will be witness, that I did not

[1] Compare A. Eliot to T. Hollis, 26 Jan. 1771.

[2] Grimaldi to Masserano, in French Archives; Choiseul to Francès, 6 October, 1770; Choiseul to Francès, 7 October, 1770. Francès to Choiseul, 4 Nov. 1770; Choiseul to Francès, 4 Nov. 1770; Choiseul to Francès, 3 Dec. 1770.

CHAP. XLVI. 1770. Dec.

wish it."[1] Lord North gained honor by allowing Weymouth to retire, and standing firmly for peace; but it was Choiseul's moderation which prevented a rupture. On the twenty-fourth of December the ablest French Minister of the century was dismissed from office and exiled to Chanteloupe, not because he was impassioned for war, as his enemies pretended, but because he was the friend of philosophy, freedom of industry, and colonial independence. Thoroughly a Frenchman, as Chatham was thoroughly an Englishman, he longed to renovate France that she might revenge the wounds inflicted on her glory. For this end he had sought to improve her finances, restore her marine, reform her army, and surround her by allies. Marie Antoinette, the wife of the Dauphin, was a pledge for the friendship of Austria; Prussia was conciliated; while the Family Compact insured at Naples and in the Spanish peninsula the predominance of France, which had nothing but friends from the Bosphorus to Cadiz.

It marks the sway of philosophy that crowds paid their homage to the retiring Statesman; he was dear to the Parliaments he had defended, to men of letters he had encouraged, and to Frenchmen whose hearts beat for the honor of their land in its rivalry with England. His policy was so identified with the passions, the sympathies, and the culture of his country; was so thoroughly national, and so lib-

[1] Choiseul to Francès, 5 December, 1770. Si les Anglais la veulent, [la guerre] tout ce que je mande est inutile; mais vous serez témoin que je ne la voulois pas, comme on le suppose. Compare also the dispatches of the British Ambassador to Lord Weymouth, 14 and 16 December, 1770, which confirm exactly the desire of peace expressed by Choiseul.

eral, that it was sure to return in spite of the royalist party and the Court, and even though he himself was never again to be intrusted with the conduct of affairs. The cause of royalty was, for the time, triumphant in the cabinets; and had America then risen, she would have found no friends to cheer her on.

At the same time the British Ministry attracted to itself that part of the Opposition which was composed of Grenville's friends. Now that he was no more, Suffolk became Secretary of State, instead of Weymouth; and Thurlow being promoted, Wedderburn, whose "credit for veracity" Lord North so lately impeached, and who in his turn had denied to that Minister "honor and respectability,"—refused to go upon a forlorn hope; and with unblushing effrontery, leased his powers of eloquence to the Government in return for the office of Solicitor General.[1] By these arrangements Lord North obtained twelve new votes.[2]

But the moral power of the Ministry gained still more from the vehement clamor with which its opponents condemned the wise settlement of the question respecting the Falkland Islands. Sir Robert Walpole had yielded to a similar clamor, and had yet lost his place; Lord North won the praise of good men by resisting it, and securing peace without a compromise of the public dignity. When the Administration needed for its defence no more than the exposition of the madness of modern wars

[1] King to Lord North, 19 Dec. 1770.

[2] Francès to the Duke de Lavrillière, interim Minister for Foreign Affairs, 12 January, 1771.

CHAP. XLVI. 1771. Jan. in the brilliant and forcible language of the moralist Johnson,[1] the applause of Adam Smith[2] was in accordance with the sentiment of the country.

This was the happiest period in the career of Lord North. His system acquired stability in the confidence of the country; and was sure of majorities in Parliament. No danger hung over him but from his own love of ease. "He was seated on the Treasury bench, between his Attorney and Solicitor General," his equals in ability, but most unlike him in character;[3] and it was his fatal error that he indulged in slumber when America required all his vigilance.

Feb. The Regulators of North Carolina gathered together in the woods on hearing that their Representative had been expelled and arbitrarily imprisoned, and they themselves menaced with exile or death as outlaws. They had labored honestly for their own support; not living on the spoils of other men's labors, nor snatching the bread out of other men's hands. They accepted the maxim, that laws, statutes and customs which are against God's law or nature, are all null; and that the practices of civil officers, who contrary to law as well to reason, justice and equity, exacted illegal taxes and fees from the poor industrious farmers, were guilty of a worse crime than open robbery. They asked no more than that extortioners might be brought to fair trials, and "the collectors of the public money called to proper settlements

[1] Johnson's Thoughts on the Late Transactions respecting Falkland Islands. 1771.

[2] Masere's Occasional Essays and Tracts, 178.

[3] Gibbon's Memoirs of Himself.

of their accounts."[1] Honor and good faith now prompted them to join for the rescue of Husbands. CHAP. XLVI. 1771. Feb.

Tryon was intimidated. Newbern might be attacked and his newly finished palace, source of so much gratification to his vanity, of grievous taxation to the people, might be burned to the ground. Without some manifest sanction of law he dared no longer detain in custody the sturdy Highlander, who had come down under the safeguard of his unquestioned election to the Legislature. Eager to take advantage of the Riot Act, he had by special commission called the Judges to meet at Newbern on the sixth of February. No sooner were they assembled, than he conspired with the Chief Justice to get Husbands indicted for a pretended libel. But the Grand Jury refused to do the work assigned them; and the prisoner was set free.[2]

Angry with the indocile jury, the Governor by a new Commission, called another court for the eleventh of March; against which day he took care, by giving the strictest orders to the Sheriffs, many of whom were defaulters, and by the indefatigable exertions of his own private Secretary, to obtain jurors and witnesses, suited to his purpose.[3] March

The liberation of Husbands having stopped the march of the Regulators, it occurred to some of them on their return to visit Salisbury Superior Court.[4] On the sixth of March, about four or five hundred of them encamped in the woods near the Ferry, on the

[1] Petition signed by one hundred and seventy-four, addressed to Chief Justice Martin, &c. &c.

[2] Tryon to Hillsborough, 12 April, 1771.

[3] Tryon to Hillsborough.

[4] Colonels Frohock and Martin to Gov. Tryon, Salisbury, 18 March, 1771.

CHAP. XLVI. 1771. March

western side of the Yadkin River. "The lawyers are every thing" they complained. "There should be none in the Province." "We shall be forced to kill them all." "There never was such an Act as the Riot Act in the laws of England."[1] This was true; the Counsel to the Board of Trade, making his official report upon that law, declared its clause of outlawry "altogether unfit for any part of the British empire."[2] "We come," said the Chiefs in the Regulators' camp to an officer from Salisbury, "with no intention to obstruct the Court, or to injure the person or property of any one; but only to petition for a redress of grievances against officers taking exorbitant fees." "Why then," it was asked, "are some of you armed?" "Our arms," said they, "are only to defend ourselves." They were told, that no Court would be held on account of the disturbances; but the very persons of whom they complained, finding them "peaceably disposed beyond expectation,"[3] agreed with them, that all differences with the officers of the county of Rowan should be settled by arbitration on the third Tuesday in May. The umpires being named, the Regulators marched through Salisbury, gave three cheers, and quietly returned[4] to their farms, which were the best lands in the whole Province.[5]

Sept.

[1] Deposition of Waightstill Avery. This deposition of one of Tryon's witnesses, taken alone, gives a very wrong view of the case. The letter of Frohock and Martin must be compared. They are adverse witnesses, but far more candid than Avery.

[2] Report of Richard Jackson to the Board of Trade, on the Acts of the North Carolina Session, which began Dec. 5, 1771; 14 February, 1772.

[3] From the letter of Frohock and Martin.

[4] Letters of Tryon and of Martin; Caruthers in Life of Caldwell.

[5] This account, given by the

CHAP. XLVI. 1771. March

But Tryon and Fanning were bent on revenge. On the eleventh of March the Court opened at Newbern; with willing witnesses and a unanimous Grand Jury, sixty-one[1] indictments were readily found for felonies or riots, against the leading Regulators in Orange County, who lived two hundred miles off, and many of whom had been at home during the riots of which they were accused. By law, criminal jurisdiction belonged in the first instance to the district within which offences were charged to have been committed; every one of the indictments was illegal;[2] and yet those charged with felony must appear within sixty days, or a vain and merciless Governor will declare them outlaws.

Armed with this authority to proscribe the principal men among the Regulators, Tryon next received the Grand Jury at the Palace, and volunteered to them to lead troops into the western counties.[3] The obsequious body, passing beyond their proper functions, applauded his purpose; and the Council acquiesced. To obtain the necessary funds, which the Legislature had refused to provide, Tryon created a paper currency by drafts on the Treasury.

April

The Northern Treasurer declined to sanction the illegal drafts; and in consequence, the Eastern counties took no part in the scenes that followed; but the Southern Treasurer complied. From Wilmington a body of militia under the command of Waddel, was

very officers of whom complaint was made, was the statement on the Government side, not of the Regulators. See Frohock and Martin to Tryon, 18 March, 1771.

[1] Tryon to Hillsborough, 12 April, 1771.

[2] Opinion of Maurice Moore, one of the Associate Judges. Jones's Defence, 60.

[3] Tryon to Hillsborough, 1771.

CHAP. XLVI. 1771. May. sent to Salisbury, while Tryon himself, having written a harsh rebuke of the agreement in Rowan County for arbitration, marched into Orange County. His progress was marked by the destruction of wheat fields and orchards, the burning of every house which was found empty; the seizure of cattle, poultry and all the produce of the plantations. The terrified people ran together like sheep chased by a wolf; while Tryon crossed the Eno, and the Haw; and the men who had been indicted at Newbern for felonies, were already advertised as outlaws, when on the evening of the fourteenth, he reached the Great Alamance.

The little army under his command was composed of one thousand and eighteen foot soldiers, and thirty light horse, besides the officers.[1] The Regulators, who had been drawn together not as insurgents but from alarm,—many, perhaps most of them without guns,—may have numbered rather more, and were encamped about five miles to the west of the stream. They gathered round James Hunter as their "general;" and his superior capacity, and dauntless courage, won from the unorganized host implicit obedience and enthusiastic reverence.[2] They were almost in despair, lest the Governor "would not lend a kind ear to the just complaints of the people." Still on the evening of the fifteenth they entreated, that harmony might yet be restored, that "the presaged tragedy of warlike marching to meet each

[1] The number of the army of Tryon is given exactly according to his own statement in a letter from New-York, 1 August, 1771. As the Regulators were not counted, their number is a matter of mere conjecture. Tryon puts it at two thousand. One newspaper account at the time says but three hundred took part in the battle. Compare the judicious Caruthers, Life of Caldwell, 147.

[2] Gov. Martin to Hillsborough, 8 March, 1772.

other might be prevented;" that the Governor would give them leave to present "their Petition," and to treat for peace. CHAP. XLVI. 1771. May.

The next day Tryon crossed Alamance River, and marched out to meet the Regulators. As he approached, James Hunter and Benjamin Merrill,[1] a captain of militia, "a man in general esteem for his honesty, integrity, piety and moral good life," received from him this answer: "I require you to lay down your arms, surrender up the outlawed ringleaders, submit yourselves to the laws, and rest on the lenity of the Government. By accepting these terms in one hour, you will prevent an effusion of blood, as you are at this time in a state of war and rebellion."[2]

The demands were utterly unjustifiable. No one of the Regulators had been legally outlawed; or even legally indicted. The Governor acted against law as against right; and by every rule deserved to be resisted. Yet the Regulators reluctantly accepted the appeal to arms; for they had nothing to hope from victory itself. Their courage was the courage of martyrs.

The action began before noon, by firing a field-piece into the midst of the people. Many of the Regulators, perhaps the larger number, retired; but those who remained, disputed the field for two hours, fighting first in the open ground and then from behind trees, till at last having nearly expended their ammunition,[3] Hunter and his men were compelled to

[1] Letter from North Carolina, 24 July, 1771.

[2] Tryon to the people now assembled in arms, who style themselves Regulators.

[3] Tryon to Hillsborough, "They left behind them little ammunition." Compare Caruthers.

CHAP. XLVI. 1771. May. retreat.[1] Nine of the King's troops were killed, and sixty-one wounded.[2] Of the Regulators, above twenty fell in battle, besides the wounded.[3] Some prisoners were taken in the pursuit. Before sunset, Tryon had returned in triumph to his camp.

The next day James Few, one of the prisoners, was by the Governor's order, hanged on a tree as an outlaw; and his parents ruined by the destruction of their estate. Then followed one proclamation after another,[4] excepting from mercy outlaws and prisoners, and promising it to none others but those who should take an oath of allegiance, pay taxes, submit to the laws, and deliver up their arms.

June. After this Tryon proceeded to the Yadkin to join Waddel, who had incurred some danger of being cut off. Waddel then moved through the South-western counties, unmolested, except that in Mecklenburgh his ammunition was blown up,[5] while Tryon turned back, living at free quarters on the Regulators,[6] forcing them to contribute all kinds of provisions, and burning the houses and laying waste and destroying the plantations of every outlaw.[7]

On the ninth of June he arrived at Hillsborough, where the Court awaited him. His first work was a proclamation inviting "every person" to shoot Herman Husbands, or James Hunter, or Redknap

[1] Letter from North Carolina, 24 July, 1771.

[2] Official return of the killed and wounded.

[3] Martin's Hist. of North Carolina, ii. 282.

[4] Proclamation of Tryon, 17 May, and others.

[5] Tryon's Proclamation of 11 June, excepting from the amnesty, "all concerned in blowing up General Waddel's ammunition in Mecklenburgh.

[6] Tryon to Hillsborough, 1 August, 1771. "The commissary had not occasion to purchase any provision for the troops, from the 16th of May, till they quitted their settlements the 20th of June."

[7] Postscript to the same letter.

Howell, or William Butler; and offering a hundred pounds and a thousand acres of land, as a reward for the delivery of either of them alive or dead. Then twelve men, taken in battle, were tried and brought in guilty of Treason; and on the nineteenth of June, six of them were hanged under the eye of the Governor, who himself marked the place for the gallows, gave directions for clearing the field, and sketched in general orders the line of march of the army to the place of execution, with the station of each company round the gallows. The victims died bravely. It is yet kept in memory, how Benjamin Merrill met his fate in the most heroic manner, sustained by the pious affection of his children, and declaring that he died at peace with his Maker, in the cause of his country.[1]

CHAP. XLVI. 1771. June.

The next day Tryon, having gratified himself with the spectacle, and taking care to make the most of the confiscated lands, which were among the best on the continent, left Hillsborough, and on the thirtieth sailed to take possession of the Government[2] of New-York, leaving the burden of an illegally contracted debt of more than forty thousand pounds. So general was the disgust, that his successor dared not trust the people with the immediate election of a new Assembly,[3] though terror and despair had brought six thousand of the Regulators to submission.[4]

The Governors of South Carolina and of Virginia,

[1] For this there are contemporary statements in letters from North Carolina, of 22 July, and 12 August, 1771; in Boston Gazette, 849, 3, 1; and 853, 2, 3.

[2] Hillsborough to Tryon, 11 Feb. 1771.

[3] Martin to Hillsborough, 1771.

[4] President Hazel of North Carolina Council to Hillsborough, 4 July, 1771.

CHAP. XLVI. 1771. June. were requested not to harbor the fugitives. But the far wilderness offered shelter beyond the mountains, and the savages seemed comparatively mild protectors. Without concert, instinctively impelled by discontent and the wearisomeness of life exposed to bondage, men crossed the Alleghanies and descending into the basin of the Tennessee, made their homes in the valley of the Watauga. There no lawyer followed them; there no King's Governor came to be their Lord; there the flag of England never waved. They rapidly extended their settlements; by degrees they took possession of the more romantic banks of the broader Nollichucky, whose sparkling waters spring out of the tallest mountains in the range. The climate was invigorating; the health-giving westerly wind blew at all seasons; in spring the wild crab apple filled the air with the sweetest of perfumes. A fertile soil gave to industry good crops of maize; the clear streams flowed pleasantly without tearing floods; where the closest thickets of spruce and rhododendron flung the cooling shade furthest over the river, trout abounded. The elk and the red deer were not wanting in the natural parks of oak and hickory, of maple, elm, black ash, and buckeye. Of quails and turkeys and pigeons there was no end. The golden eagle built its nest on the topmost ledge of the mountain, and might be seen wheeling in wide circles high above the pines, or dropping like a meteor upon its prey. The black bear, whose flesh was held to be the most delicate of meats, grew so fat upon the abundant acorns and chestnuts, that he could be run down in a race of three hundred yards; and sometimes the hunters gave chase to the coward panther, strong enough to beat off twenty dogs, yet flying from

CHAP. XLVI.

one. Political wisdom is not sealed up in rolls and parchments. It welled up in the forest, like the waters from the hill side. To acquire a peaceful title to their lands, the settlers despatched James Robertson[1] as their envoy to the Council of the Cherokees, from whom he obtained sincere promises of confidence and friendship, and a lease of the territory of the infant Colony. For government, its members came together as brothers in convention, and already in 1772, they founded a republic by a written association,[2] appointed their own magistrates, James Robertson among the first; framed laws for their present occasions; and "set to the people of America the dangerous example of erecting themselves into a separate State, distinct from and independent of the authority" of the British King.[3]

Fanning who followed Tryon to the North, extolled his patron as the ablest supporter of Government.[4] "I shall leave to your Lordship's reflections the tendency this expedition has had on the frontiers of every Colony in British America," was the self-laudatory remark of Tryon to Hillsborough.[5] The insolent extortioners and officers whom the Regulators had vainly sued for redress, taunted them with their ill fortune, saying, "Alamance is your court of record."[6] Yet the record was not closed. In the old counties of Orange and Mecklenburg, the "over-

[1] Haywood's Hist. of Tennessee, 42.

[2] Haywood's Hist. of Tennessee, 41; J. G. M. Ramsey's Annals of Tennessee, 107.

[3] The nearest contemporary authority is Dunmore to Dartmouth, 16 May, 1774.

[4] New-York Gazette of 9 Sept. 1771.

[5] Tryon to Hillsborough, New-York, 1 August, 1771.

[6] Boston Gazette, 22 July, 1771; 849, 2, 3.

CHAP. XLVI. hill" glades of Carolina, and the little band of mountaineers who planted the commonwealth of Tennessee, a bloodthirsty Governor, in his vengeful zeal for the Crown, had treasured up wrath for the day of wrath.

NOTE.

The successor of Tryon reached Carolina in August, 1771, and drank in all the accounts of the "glorious spirit," which had defeated the Regulators near the Alamance. The next year he made a tour into Orange County. The result of his observations is best given in his own words.

EXTRACT OF A LETTER from JOSIAH MARTIN [the brother of Samuel Martin, who wounded Wilkes in a duel in 1763,] Governor of North Carolina, to the EARL OF HILLSBOROUGH, Secretary of State for the Colonies.

NORTH CAROLINA, HILLSBOROUGH,
August 30, 1772.

* * * * My progress through this country, my Lord, hath opened my eyes exceedingly, with respect to the commotions and discontents that have lately prevailed in it. I now see most clearly, that they have been provoked by insolence, and cruel advantages taken of the people's ignorance by mercenary tricking attorneys, clerks, and other little officers, who have practised upon them every sort of rapine and extortion; by which having brought upon themselves their just resentment, they engaged Government in their defence by artful misrepresentations, that the vengeance the wretched people in folly and madness aimed at their heads, was directed against the constitution; and by this stratagem they threw an odium upon the injured people, that by degrees begot a prejudice, which precluded a full discovery of their grievances. Thus, my Lord, as far as I have been able to discover, the resentment of Government was craftily worked up against the oppressed, and the protection which the oppressors treacherously acquired, where the injured and ignorant people expected to find it, drove them to acts of desperation and confederated them in violence, which as your Lordship knows, induced bloodshed; and I verily believe necessarily. Inquiries of this sort, my Lord, I am sensible are invidious; nor would any thing but a sense of duty have drawn from me these opinions of the principles of the past troubles of this country. * * * *

Diligent inquiry has not as yet brought to light a copy of the written Constitution adopted by the Settlers of Eastern Tennessee. Its existence was ascertained by Haywood, the careful historian of that com monwealth. Ramsey has adopted all that was preserved by Haywood, and has added the results of his own persevering researches. To these authorities I am able to subjoin the evidence of a contemporary witness. In a letter from the Governor of Virginia to the British Secretary of State, pleading warmly in favor of the propriety of making grants of land at the West, in Illinois, he derives his strongest argument from the establishment of this very Republic of Watauga. CHAP. XLVI.

Extract of a letter from the EARL OF DUNMORE, Governor of Virginia, to the EARL OF DARTMOUTH, Secretary of State.

WILLIAMSBURG, 16 May, 1774.

* * * Whatever may be the law with respect to the title, there are, I think, divers reasons which should induce his majesty to comply with the petition, so far at least, as to admit the petitioners and their acquisitions, if not into this government, into some other. For if the title should be thought defective, it would still, at such a distance from the seat of any authority, be utterly impracticable to void it, or prevent the occupying of the lands, which being known to be of an extraordinary degree of fertility, experience shows nothing (so fond as the Americans are of migration,) can stop the concourse of people that actually begin to draw toward them; and should the petition be rejected, your lordship may assure yourself, it is no chimerical conjecture, that, so far from interrupting the progress of their settlement, it would have a direct contrary tendency, by forcing the people to adopt a form of government of their own, which it would be easy to frame in such a manner as to prove an additional encouragement to all the dissatisfied of every other government, to flock to that. In effect, we have an example of the very case, there being actually a set of people in the back part of this colony, bordering on the Cherokee country, who finding they could not obtain titles to the land they fancied, under any of the neighboring governments, have settled upon it without, and contented themselves with becoming in a manner tributary to the Indians, and have appointed magistrates, and framed laws for their present occasions, and to all intents and purposes, erected themselves into, though an inconsiderable, yet a separate State; the consequence of which may prove hereafter letrimental to the peace and security of the other colonies; it at least ets a dangerous example to the people of America, of forming governnents distinct from and independent of his majesty's authority. * * *

CHAPTER XLVII.

GREAT BRITAIN CENTRES IN ITSELF POWER OVER ITS COLONIES. —HILLSBOROUGH'S ADMINISTRATION OF THE COLONIES CONCLUDED.

JUNE, 1771—AUGUST, 1772.

CHAP. XLVII. 1771. June.

THE King steadily pursued the system of concentrating all power over the Colonies; but so gradually that a sudden, complete collision with ancient usage was avoided. If the Charter of the Province had been taken away,[1] even the moderate would have held themselves absolved from their allegiance.[2] But the appointment of a native Bostonian as Governor, seemed to many a pledge of relenting; and his plausible professions hushed the people into silence. "The glorious spirit of liberty is vanquished and left without hope but in a miracle," said desponding patriots. "I confess," said Samuel Adams; "we have, as Wolfe expressed it, a choice of difficulties. Too many flatter themselves that their pusillanimity is true prudence; but in perilous times like these, I cannot con-

[1] Compare Massachusetts Gazette, 21 Jan. 1771.

[2] Compare Brutus in Boston Gazette of 11 Feb. 1771; 827, 1, 1, and of Monday, 4 March, 830, 1, 2; and letters of Eliot and Cooper.

CHAP. XLVII. 1771. June.

ceive of prudence without fortitude."[1] He persevered; but John Adams retired from "the service of the people," and devoting himself to his profession,[2] for a time ceased even to employ his pen in their defence.[3] Otis who had returned to the Legislature, disordered in mind, and jealous of his declining influence, did but impede the public cause. In Hancock, also, vanity so mingled with patriotism, that the Government hoped to separate him from its uncompromising opponents.[4]

The Assembly which for the third year was convened at Cambridge, overruled the advice of Samuel Adams, and was proceeding with business. Yet it adopted the Protest in which he drew the distinction between the existence of a prerogative and its abuse; and significantly inquired, what would follow in England, if a British King should call a Parliament in Cornwall and keep it there seven years. Nor did he omit to expose the rapid consolidation of power in the hands of the executive by the double process of making all civil officers dependent for support solely on the King, and giving to arbitrary instructions an authority paramount to the Charter and the laws.

July.

The Protest had hardly been adopted, when the application of its doctrines became necessary. The Commissioners of the Customs had through Hutchinson[5] applied for an exemption of their salaries from

[1] Compare Samuel Adams to James Warren of Plymouth, 25 March, 1771.

[2] John Adams: Works, ii. 260, 301, 302.

[3] John Adams: Diary, June 22, 1771.

[4] Hutchinson to, ———, 5 June, 1771.

[5] Hutchinson to Hillsborough, 20 Dec. 1769. Opinions of DeGray and Dunning, 13 Feb. 1770.

CHAP. XLVII. 1771. July.

the colonial income tax; and Hillsborough, disregarding a usage of more than fifty years, commanded the compliance of the legislature. The engrossed tax-bill for the year was of the same tenor with the annual Acts from time immemorial. The assessors had moreover rated the Commissioners with extreme moderation. Persons who had less income, were taxed as much as they, so that it did not even appear that any regard was had to their salaries.[1] Paxton's provincial tax for all his personal estate and all his income, was for the last year less than three pounds sterling; and what he paid to the town and county not much more.[2] And to defeat this little tax, in itself so reasonable, so consonant to usage, and in its apportionment so forbearing, Hutchinson, on the fourth of July, greatly against his own judgment, negatived the Bill, and declared his obligation under his instructions to negative any other, drawn in the same usual terms.

The stopping supplies by a veto of the Crown was unknown in England; an order from the King to exempt special individuals from their share of taxation was unconstitutional; the exemption, if submitted to by the Assembly, would have been an acquiescence in an unwarrantable instruction; and a formal recognition of the system of parliamentary taxation. Samuel Adams perceived all the danger, and on the next day, the House replied in his words: "We know of no Commissioners of his Majesty's Customs, nor of any revenue his Majesty has a right to establish in North America; we know and feel a tribute levied

[1] Hutchinson to ——, Boston, 17 July, 1771.

[2] Hutchinson to ——, 19 July, 1771.

CHAP. XLVII. 1771. July.

and extorted from those, who, if they have property, have a right to the absolute disposal of it. To withhold your assent to this bill, merely by force of instruction, is effectually vacating the Charter and giving instructions the force of laws, within this Province. If such a doctrine shall be established, the representatives of a free people would be reduced to this fatal alternative,—either to have no taxes levied and raised at all, or to have them raised and levied in such a way and manner, and upon those only whom his Majesty pleases."[1] At the first meeting of the Assembly, loyalty had visibly prevailed, and the decided patriots were in a minority; necessity had extorted the most explicit assertion of colonial rights, and an unanswerable exposition of the limit of the prerogative. In closing the session Hutchinson put at issue the respect for monarchy itself. "I know," said he, "that your messages and resolves of the last year were very displeasing to the King;[2] I shall transmit my messages, and this your extraordinary answer to be laid before him." Thus the Province was led to speculate on the personal opinions of their Sovereign, and to inquire into the use of regal power itself; while the King regarded the contest with Massachusetts as involving not only the power of Great Britain and the rights of the Crown, but his personal honor.

Wise men saw the event that was approaching, but not that it was so near. "Out of the eater cometh forth meat," said Cooper the clergyman;[3] and Frank-

[1] Message from the House to the Governor, 5 July, 1771.

[2] Bradford's State Papers, 311.

[3] Samuel Cooper to B. Franklin, 10 July, 1771.

CHAP. XLVII. 1771. July. lin foretold a bloody struggle, in which "America's growing strength and magnitude,"[1] would give her the victory. The progress of opinion was marked by the instructions of the House to its Agent, which unreservedly embodied the principle that colonial legislation was free of Parliament and of royal instructions. They were drawn by Samuel Adams, who had long before said in Town Meeting; "Independent we are, and independent we will be." "I doubt," said Hutchinson, "whether there is a greater incendiary than he in the King's Aug. dominions."[2] At least his intrepidity could not be questioned. His language became more explicit as danger drew nearer. In August, Boston saw in its harbor twelve vessels of war, carrying more than two hundred and sixty guns, commanded by Montagu, the brother of Sandwich.[3]

Yet there was no one salient wrong, to attract the sudden and universal attention of the people. The Southern Governors felt no alarm. Eden from Maryland congratulated Hillsborough, on the return of confidence and harmony.[4] "The people," thus Johnson, the Agent of Connecticut wrote after his return home, "appear to be weary of their altercations with the Mother Country; a little discreet conduct on both sides, would perfectly re-establish that warm affection and respect towards

[1] B. Franklin to Committee of Correspondence in Massachusetts, 15 May, 1771.

[2] Hutchinson's letter without date, in Hutchinson's MS. Collections, i. 437. Written between July 29 and August 5, 1771; probably written early in August, 1771.

[3] Boston Gazette, 19 Aug. 1771.

[4] Robert Eden to Hillsborough, 4 August, 1771.

CHAP. XLVII. 1771. Sept.

Great Britain, for which this country was once so remarkable."[1]

Hutchinson, too, reported "a disposition in all the Colonies to let the controversy with the kingdom subside."[2] The King sent word to tempt Hancock by marks of favor. "Hancock and most of the party," said the Governor, "are quiet; and all of them, except Adams, abate of their virulence. Adams would push the Continent into a rebellion to-morrow, if it was in his power."[3] While America generally was so tranquil, Samuel Adams continued musing till the fire within him burned; and the thought of correspondence and union among the friends of liberty flashed upon his mind. "It would be an arduous task," he said, meditating a project which required a year's reflection for its maturity, "to awaken a sufficient number in the colonies to so grand an undertaking. Nothing, however, should be despaired of. We have nothing," he continued, "to rely upon but the interposition of our friends in Britain, of which I have no expectation, or the LAST APPEAL.[4] The tragedy of American freedom is nearly completed. A tyranny seems to be at the very door. They who lie under oppression deserve what they suffer; let them perish with their oppressors. Could millions be enslaved if all possessed the independent spirit of Brutus, who to his immortal Oct.

[1] W. S. Johnson to Alexander Wedderburn, 25 Oct. 1771.

[2] Hutchinson to Gov Pownall, 14 October, 1771.

[3] Hutchinson to John Pownall, Secretary to the Board of Trade, 17 October, 1771.

[4] Ultima ratio. Samuel Adams' Papers. Letter to Arthur Lee, 27 Sept. 1777, from the draft. Compare in Hutchinson's Papers, iii. 236, letter of 30 Sept, 1771. Hutchinson's Papers, iii. 242, 243 and 233, letters of 9 Oct. 1771.

CHAP. XLVII. 1771. Oct. honor, expelled the tyrant of Rome, and his royal and rebellious race? The liberties of our country are worth defending at all hazards. If we should suffer them to be wrested from us, millions yet unborn may be the miserable sharers in the event.[1] Every step has been taken but one; and the last appeal would require prudence, unanimity, and fortitude. America must herself, under God, finally work out her own salvation."[2]

Nov. While these opinions were boldly uttered, Hutchinson, in the annual Proclamation which appointed the Festival of Thanksgiving and which used to be read from every pulpit, sought to ensnare the clergy by enumerating as a cause for gratitude, "that civil and religious liberties were continued," and "trade enlarged." He was caught in his own toils. All the Boston ministers except one refused to read the paper; when Pemberton, of whose church the Governor was a member, began confusedly to do so, the patriots of his congregation, turning their backs on him, walked out of meeting in great indignation; and nearly all the Ministers agreed on the Thanksgiving Day "to implore of Almighty God the restoration of lost liberties."[3]

Dec. Nowise disheartened, Hutchinson waited eagerly and confidently "to hear how the extravagance of the Assembly in their last session would be resented by the King;" now striving to set Hancock more and

[1] Samuel Adams in the Boston Gazette, of 14 Oct. 1771.

[2] Samuel Adams to Arthur Lee, Boston, 31 Oct. 1771. Life of Arthur Lee, ii. 186; Compare Hutchinson to R. Jackson, October, 1771.

[3] Cooper to Gov. Pownall, 14, S. Adams's Papers, ii. 338; also ii. 297. Life of Arthur Lee, ii. 186. S. Adams to Henry Marchant, 7 January, 1772.

more against Adams; now seeking to lull the people into security; now boasting of his band of writers on the side of Government, Church, a professed patriot, being of the number; now triumphing at the spectacle of Otis, who was carried into the country, bound hand and foot as a maniac; now speculating on the sale of cheap teas at high prices; now urging the Government in England to remodel all the New England Provinces, even while he pretended that they were quiet and submissive. His only fears were lest the advice he had sent to the Ministry should become known in America, and lest Temple, who had gone to England and bore him contemptuous hatred, should estrange from him the confidence of Whately.

Confirmed by the seeming tranquillity in America, and by the almost unprecedented strength of the Ministry in Parliament, Hillsborough gave free scope to the conceit, wrongheadedness, obstinacy and passion, which marked his character, and perplexed and embarrassed affairs by the perverse and senseless[1] exercise of authority. To show his firmness, he still required the Legislature of Massachusetts to exempt the Commissioners from taxation, or the tax bill should be negatived; while Gage was enjoined to attend to the security of the fortress in Boston harbor.

In Georgia, Noble Wimberly Jones, a man of exemplary life and character, had been elected Speaker. Wright, who reported him to be "a very strong Liberty Boy," would not consent to the choice; and the House voted the interference a

[1] B. Franklin to S. Cooper, 5 February, 1771.

CHAP. XLVII. 1771. Dec. breach of their privileges.[1] Hillsborough had censured their unwarrantable and inconsistent arrogance.[2] He now directed the Governor "to put his negative upon any person whom they should next elect for Speaker, and to dissolve the Assembly in case they should question the right of such negative." [3]

1772. Jan. The affections of South Carolina were still more thoroughly alienated. Its public men were ruled by their sense of honor, and felt a stain upon it as a wound. A Carolinian in the time of Lyttleton, had been abruptly dismissed from the King's Council; and from that day it became the pride of native Carolinians not to accept a seat in that body.[4] The members of the Assembly "disdained to take any pay for their attendance." [5] Since March 1771, no legislative Act had been perfected,[6] because the Governor refused to pass any appropriations which should cover the grant of the Assembly to the Society for the Bill of Rights; but the patriot planters ever stood ready to lend their private credit and purses to the wants of their own colonial Agents or Committees. To extend the benefit of Courts of Justice into the interior, the Province, at an expense of five thousand pounds,[7] bought out the monopoly of Richard Cumberland as Provost by patent for the whole; and had offered to establish salaries for the Judges, if the Commissions of those Judges were but made permanent as in England. At last, in 1769,

[1] Sir James Wright to Hillsborough, 28 February, 1771.

[2] Hillsborough to Sir James Wright, 4 May, 1771.

[3] Hillsborough to Habersham, 4 Dec. 1771, and 7 August, 1772.

[4] Correspondence of Lieut. Gov. Bull.

[5] State of South Carolina, 1770.

[6] Statutes at large, iv. 331.

[7] Ramsey's History of South Carolina, ii. 126.

CHAP. XLVII. 1772. Jan.

trusting to the honor of the Crown, they voted perpetual grants of salaries. When this was done, Rawlins Lowndes and others, their own judges, taken from among themselves, were dismissed; and an Irishman, a Scotchman, and a Welshman were sent over by Hillsborough to take their places.[1] "We, none of us," said the planters, "can expect the honors of the State; they are all given away to worthless, poor sycophants."[2] The Governor, Lord Charles Greville Montagu, had no Palace at Charleston; he uttered a threat to convene the South Carolina Assembly at Port Royal, unless they would vote him a house to his mind.[3] This is the culminating point of administrative insolence.

March. The system of concentrating all colonial power in England was resisted also at the West.[4] In Illinois the corruption and favoritism of the military commander compelled the people to a remonstrance. The removal of them all to places within the limits of some established Colony, was the mode of pacification which Hillsborough deliberately approved. The Spanish jurisdiction across the river offered so near a sanctuary, that such a policy was impracticable. An establishment by the Crown upon the lowest plan of expense, and without any intermixture of popular power, was thought of. "A regular constitutional Government for them," said Gage, "cannot be sug-

[1] Compare List of Judges in South Carolina Statutes at large, i. 439; Ramsey, i. 214, ii. 126.

[2] Compare Quincy's Quincy, 106, 07, 116.

[3] Montagu to Hillsborough, 26 September, 1771; Hillsborough to Montagu, 4 December, 1771. Same to Same, 11 January, 1772; Montagu to Hillsborough, 27 July, 1772.

[4] Gage to Hillsborough, 4 March, 1772. Compare Gage to Hillsborough, 6 August, 1771; Hillsborough to Gage, 4 Dec. 1771, and 18 April, 1772.

CHAP. XLVII. 1772. March

gested. They don't deserve so much attention." "I agree with you," rejoined Hillsborough; "a regular Government for that District would be highly improper." The people of Illinois, weary of the shameless despotism which aimed only at forestalling tracts of land, the monopoly of the Indian trade, or the ruin of the French villages, took their cause into their own hands; they demanded institutions like those of Connecticut, and set themselves inflexibly against any proposal for a Government, which should be irresponsible to themselves. In 1771, they had assembled in a General Meeting, and had fixed upon their scheme; they never departed from it; "expecting to appoint their own Governor and all civil Magistrates."[1] The rights of freemen were demanded as boldly on the Prairies of Illinois as in Carolina or New England. Towards the people at Vincennes, Hillsborough was less relenting; for there was no Spanish shore to which they could fly. They were, by formal proclamation, peremptorily commanded to retire within the jurisdiction of some one of the Colonies.[2] But the men[3] of Indiana were as unwilling to abandon their homes in a settlement already seventy years old,[4] as those of Illinois to give up the hope of freedom. The spirit of discontent pervaded every village in the wilderness; and what allegiance would men of French origin bear to a British King who proposed to take away their estates and to deny them liberty? The log cabins having been planted,

[1] Hamilton to Gage, 8 Aug. 1772.

[2] Proclamation of 8 April, 1772. Compare Gage to Hillsborough, 4 March, 1772.

[3] Compare Inhabitants of Vincennes to Gage, 18 Sept. 1772, and Memorial of the same date.

[4] "Notre établissement est de soixante et dix années," Memorial, 18 Sept. 1772.

CHAP. XLVII. 1772. April.

and hopes of self-government called into existence, it was beyond the power of the British King to remove the one or the other.

The inhabitants of Virginia were controlled by the central authority on a subject of still more vital importance to them and their posterity. Their halls of legislation had resounded with eloquence directed against the terrible plague of negro slavery. Again and again they had passed laws, restraining the importations of negroes from Africa; but their laws were disallowed. How to prevent them from protecting themselves against the increase of the overwhelming evil was debated by the King in Council, and on the tenth day of December, 1770, he issued an instruction, under his own hand, commanding the Governor, "upon pain of the highest displeasure, to assent to no law, by which the importation of slaves should be in any respect prohibited or obstructed."[1] In April 1772, this rigorous order was solemnly debated in the Assembly of Virginia. "They were very anxious for an Act to restrain the introduction of people, the number of whom already in the Colony, gave them just cause to apprehend the most dangerous consequences, and therefore made it necessary that they should fall upon means not only of preventing their increase, but also of lessening their number. The interest of the country," it was said, "manifestly requires the total expulsion of them."[1]

Jefferson, like Richard Henry Lee, had begun his

[1] Order in Council of 9 December, 1770. George R. Additional instructions to our Lieutenant and Governor General, of our Colony and Dominion of Virginia in America, 10 December, 1770.

[2] Dunmore to Hillsborough, 1 May, 1772. Anthony Benezet to Granville Sharp, 14 May, 1772.

CHAP. XLVII. 1772. April. legislative career by efforts for emancipation. To the mind of Patrick Henry, the thought of slavery darkened the picture of the future, even while he cherished faith in the ultimate abolition of an evil, which, though the law sanctioned, religion opposed.[1] To have approached Parliament with a Petition against the Slave-Trade might have seemed a recognition of its supreme legislative power; Virginia, therefore, resolved to address the King himself, who in Council had cruelly compelled the toleration of the nefarious traffic. They pleaded with him for leave to protect themselves against the crimes of commercial avarice, and these were their words:

"The importation of slaves into the Colonies from the Coast of Africa, hath long been considered as a trade of great inhumanity; and, under its present encouragement, we have too much reason to fear, will endanger the very existence of your Majesty's American dominions. We are sensible that some of your Majesty's subjects in Great Britain may reap emoluments from this sort of traffic; but when we consider, that it greatly retards the settlement of the Colonies with more useful inhabitants, and may in time have the most destructive influence, we presume to hope that the interest of a few will be disregarded, when placed in competition with the security and happiness of such numbers of your Majesty's dutiful and loyal subjects.

"Deeply impressed with these sentiments, we most humbly beseech your Majesty to remove all those restraints on your Majesty's Governors of this Colony

[1] Compare Patrick Henry to Anthony Benezet, 18 Jan. 1773; in Robert Vaux's Life of Benezet.

which inhibit their assenting to such laws, as might check so very pernicious a commerce." CHAP. XLVII. 1772. May.

In this manner Virginia led the host, who alike condemned slavery and opposed the Slave-Trade. Thousands in Maryland and in New Jersey, were ready to adopt a similar Petition; so were the Legislatures of North Carolina, of Pennsylvania, of New-York. Massachusetts, in its towns and in its Legislature, unceasingly combated the condition as well as the sale of slaves. There was no jealousy among one another in the strife against the crying evil; Virginia harmonized all opinions, and represented the moral sentiment and policy of them all. When her Prayer reached England, Franklin through the Press called to it the sympathy of the people; again and again it was pressed upon the attention of the Ministers. But the Government of that day was less liberal than the tribunals; and while a question respecting a negro from Virginia led the courts of law to an axiom, that, as soon as any slave set his foot on English ground, he becomes free, the King of England stood in the path of humanity, and made himself the pillar of the colonial Slave-Trade. Wherever in the Colonies a disposition was shown for its restraint, his servants were peremptorily ordered to maintain it without abatement. But he blushed to reject the solemn appeal of Virginia personally to himself, and evaded a reply.[4]

For the last five years there had been no contested election in Boston. Deceived by the apparent tranquillity, the friends of Government attempted to

[1] Hillsborough to Dunmore, 1 July, 1772.

CHAP. XLVII. 1772. May. defeat the choice of Samuel Adams as Representative. The effort failed; he had more than twice and a half as many votes as his opponent,[1] and the malice of his enemies rendered him still dearer to the people.

June. The Legislature was for the fourth year, convened at Cambridge; but the Governor had grown weary of his pretensions, and with a very ill grace, against his declared purpose, adjourned the session to the accustomed House in Boston. The long altercation on that subject subsided; but the system of British supremacy was sure to produce new collisions.

Inhabitants of Providence, in Rhode Island, had in the last March, complained to the Deputy Governor of the conduct of Lieutenant Dudingston, Commander of the Gaspee, who obstructed their vessels and boats, without showing any evidence of his authority. Hopkins, the Chief Justice, on being consulted, gave the opinion, "that any person who should come into the Colony and exercise any authority by force of arms, without showing his commission to the Governor, and if a Custom House officer, without being sworn into his office, was guilty of a trespass, if not piracy." The Governor, therefore, sent a sheriff on board the Gaspee, to ascertain by what orders the Lieutenant acted; and Dudingston referred the subject to the Admiral.

The Admiral answered from Boston: "The Lieutenant, Sir, has done his duty. I shall give the King's officers directions, that they send every man taken in molesting them to me. As sure as the people of Newport attempt to rescue any vessel, and any of them

[1] Boston Gazette, 11 May, 1772; 892, 3, 2.

[2] Compare W. S. Johnson to R. Jackson, 30 May, 1772.

CHAP XLVII. 1772. June.

are taken, I will hang them as pirates."[1] Dudingston seconded the insolence of his superior officer, insulted the inhabitants, plundered the islands of sheep and hogs, cut down trees, fired at market boats, detained vessels without a colorable pretext, and made illegal seizures of goods of which the recovery cost more than they were worth.[2]

On the ninth of June, the Providence Packet was returning to Providence, and proud of its speed, went gayly on, heedless of the Gaspee. Dudingston gave chase. The tide being at flood, the Packet ventured near shore; the Gaspee confidently followed; and drawing more water ran aground on Nauquit, a little below Pantuxet. The following night a party of men in six or seven boats, led by John Brown and Joseph Brown of Providence, and Simeon Potter of Bristol, boarded the stranded schooner, after a scuffle in which Dudingston was wounded, took and landed its crew, and then set it on fire.[3] The whole was conducted on a sudden impulse;[4] yet Sandwich who was spoken of for the place of Colonial Secretary of State, resolved never to leave pursuing the Colony of Rhode Island, until its Charter should be taken away.[5] "A few punished at Execution Dock, would

[1] Montagu to J. Wanton, Esq., Boston, 8 April, 1772. J. Wanton to Rear Admiral Montagu, 8 May, 1772.

[2] Gov. Wanton to Sec. of State, 16 June, 1772. Statements of Darius Sessions and Chief Justice Hopkins to Chief Justice Horsmanden in January, 1773.

[3] Lieutenant Dudingston to Admiral Montagu, 12 June, 7772; William Checkley to Commissioner of Customs, 12 June, 1772; Governor Wanton to Hillsborough, 16 June, 1772; Admiral Montagu to Hillsborough, 12 June and 11 July, 1772; Deposition of Aaron, a negro, 11 July, 1772; Letter of Charles Dudley, 23 July, 1772.

[4] Representation to the King of the Commissioners of Inquiry, 22 June, 1773.

[5] Hutchinson to Samuel Hood, 2 Sept. 1772. Remembrancer for 1776, ii. 60.

CHAP. XLVII. 1772. June. be the only effectual preventive of any further attempt," wrote Hutchinson, who wished to see a beginning of taking men prisoners, and carrying them directly to England.[1] There now existed a statute authorizing such a procedure. Two months before, the King had assented to an Act for the better securing Dock-yards, ships and stores, which extended to the Colonies, made death the penalty for destroying even the oar of a cutter's boat, or the head of an empty cask belonging to the fleet, and subjected the accused to a trial in any county in Great Britain.

July. Of this statute, which violated every safeguard of justice and might be still more mischievous as a precedent, the Assembly of Massachusetts at that time took no notice, confining its attention to the gradual change in the Constitution of the Colony, effected by the payment of the King's civil officers through warrants under his sign manual, drawn on a perennial fund raised by an Act of Parliament. They regarded the Charter as "a most solemn compact," which bound them to Great Britain. By that Charter they held, they were to have a Governor and Judges, over whom the power of the King was protected by the right of nomination, the power of the Colony by the exclusive right of providing support. These views were embodied[2] by Hawley in a Report to the Assembly,[3] and on the tenth of July, adopted by a vote of eighty-five to nineteen. It followed, and was so

[1] T. Hutchinson to Capt. Gambier, Boston, 30 June, 1772; in Hutchinson's Papers, iii. 354, 355; and Remembrancer for 1776, ii. 56.

[2] Hutchinson's History, iii. 358.

[3] Report and Resolutions of 10 July, 1772; in Bradford, 325

CHAP. XLVII. 1772. July.

resolved, that a Governor who like Hutchinson was not dependent on the people for support, was not such a Governor as the people had consented to, at the granting of the Charter; the House most solemnly protested "that the innovation was an important change of the Constitution, and exposed the Province to a despotic administration of Government." The inference was unavoidable. If the principle contained in the Preamble to Townshend's Revenue Act should be carried out, obedience would no longer be due to the Governor, and the rightful dependence on England would be at an end.

Deceived by the want of organized union among the Colonies, Hutchinson sent word to Hillsborough, that "if the nation would arouse and unite in measures to retain the Colonies in subordination, all this new doctrine of independence would be disavowed, and its first inventors be sacrificed to the rage of the people whom they had deluded."[1] The Secretary, on his part, was proceeding with eager haste to carry Townshend's system into effect; and on the seventh of August, he announced, that the King, with the "entire concurrence of Lord North,[2] had made provision for the support of his law servants in the Province of Massachusetts Bay."[3] It was almost a special provision for Hutchinson's family. It marks the character of the people, that this act, constituting judges, who held their offices at the King's pleasure,

Aug.

Hutchinson to Secretary John Pownall, 21 July, 1772; in Remembrancer, 1776, ii. 57.

[2] Compare Hillsborough to Hutchinson, 6 June, 1772.

[3] Hillsborough to Lords of Trade, 27 July, 1772, and to Hutchinson, 7 August, 1772.

CHAP. XLVII. stipendiaries of the Crown, was selected as the crisis of revolution.

1772. Aug. Meantime Hillsborough was left with few supporters except the herd of flatterers who had soothed his vanity, and by their misrepresentations made him subservient to their selfishness. The King, having become convinced that he had weakened the respect of the Colonies for a royal Government, was weary of him; his colleagues disliked him, and conspired to drive him into retirement.[1] The occasion was at hand. Franklin had negotiated with the Treasury for a grant to a Company of about twenty-three millions of acres of land, south of the Ohio and west of the Alleghanies; Hillsborough, from the fear that men in the backwoods would be too independent, opposed the project.[2] Franklin persuaded Hertford, a friend of the King's, Gower the President of the Council, Camden, the Secretaries of the Treasury,[3] and others to become shareholders in his scheme; by their influence, the Lords of Council disregarded the adverse report of the Board of Trade, and decided in favor of planting the new Province.[4] Hillsborough was too proud to brook this public insult; and the King, soothing his fall by a patent for a British Earldom, accepted his resignation. But his system remained behind him. When he was gone, Thurlow [5] took care that the grant for the Western Province

[1] Franklin to his Son, 17 August, 1772.

[2] De Guines, French Ambassador, to Aiguillon, 11 August, 1772.

[3] W. Duer to Robert R. Livingston Jr., London, 3 August, 1772.

[4] Order in Council, 14 Aug. 1772. Compare Propositions for the Settlement of Pittsylvania, and the Memorial of Franklin and Wharton to the American Congress.

[5] Knox: Extra Official State Papers, ii. 45.

should never be sealed; and the amiable Dartmouth, who became Secretary for the Colonies, had been taught to believe,[6] like Lord North and the King, that it was necessary to carry out the policy of consolidation, as set forth in Townshend's Preamble. CHAP. XLVII. 1772. Aug.

[1] Compare Dartmouth to Hutchinson, 2 September, 1772. "I have been always taught to believe," &c. &c.

CHAPTER XLVIII.

THE TOWNS OF MASSACHUSETTS HOLD CORRESPONDENCE.

AUGUST, 1772—JANUARY, 1773.

CHAP. XLVIII. 1772. Aug.

"WE must get the Colonies into order, before we engage with our neighbors,"[1] were the words of the King to Lord North in August; and though nothing could be more unlike than the manners of George the Third and Louis the Fifteenth, a cordial understanding sprung up between them, and even gave birth to a project for a treaty of defensive alliance, in order that monarchy might triumph in France over philosophy, in America over the people.

In other affairs Louis the Fifteenth was weak of purpose, on the subject of royal authority he never wavered; he was impatient to be obeyed in all things and by all, and prepared to destroy whatever checked his absolute power. To him Protestants were republicans; and he not only refused to restore for them the edict of Nantz, but would not even legalize their marriages. Bold in doing ill, he violated the Constitu-

[1] The King to Lord North, 1 August, 1772.

tions of Languedoc and Brittany without scruple, employing military force against their States. The Parliament of Paris, even more than the other companies of Judges, tended to become an aristocratic senate, not only distributing justice, but exercising some check on legislative power. Louis the Fifteenth obstinately demanded their unqualified compliance with his will. "Sire," remonstrated the upright magistrate Malesherbes in 1771, "to mark your dissatisfaction with the Parliament of Paris, the most essential rights of a free people are taken from the nation. The greatest happiness of the people is always the object and end of legitimate power. God places the Crown on the head of Kings to preserve to their subjects the enjoyment of life, liberty, and property. This truth flows from the law of God, and from the law of nature; and is peculiar to no Constitution. In France, as in all monarchies, there exist inviolable rights, which belong to the nation. Interrogate, Sire, the nation itself; the incorruptible testimony of its Representatives will at least let you know if the cause which we defend to-day, is that of all this people, by whom you reign, and for whom you reign." "I will never change," replied Louis. Exiling Malesherbes, he overturned all the Parliaments, and reconstructed the Courts. "The Crown is rescued from the dust of the rolls;" cried his flatterers. "It is the tower of Babel," said others; "or chaos come again; or the end of the world." But against the Monarch were his own vices which threw infamy on himself and degraded his power. Libertinage must be observed in an old man, to learn all its baseness. It takes the experience and daring hardihood of sensual age to be thoroughly depraved. In youth

CHAP. XLVIII. 1772. Aug. passion palliates indulgence, which does not seem so irrevocably to imbue and to poison the soul; in the old voluptuary sensuality springs from infidelity in the moral existence, and shows itself in a greedy eagerness to catch at every physical indulgence that can be crowded into declining years. The absolute King of France, now that he was growing old, abandoned himself to unbounded dissoluteness, and while he trembled before the unknown future, and dared not hear death named, he filled his remaining days with lewd pleasure, in which Richelieu, a profligate of seventy-two, was his counsellor. The Puritans of England, when they used the stone altar as a threshold for every foot to trample on, never so insulted an emblem of the Catholic faith, as did "the most Christian King" of France, when he caused an attractive woman to be taken from public licentiousness, consecrated by the sacrament of marriage as the wife of a French nobleman, and then installed in his own palace as his mistress. In return she adored royalty and sided against the philosophers. The power which had been taken from those who by the Constitution should have shared it, was bestowed on her; and in the country of Bossuet and Fenelon, of Montesquieu and Turgot, an abandoned female who pleased the corrupt fancies of an old man, became the symbol and the support of absolute power.

Sept. The King of England likewise had no higher object than to confirm his authority. The ministers of Prussia, Austria and Russia, were signing at St. Petersburg the treaty for the first partition of Poland; he neither questioned its justice nor inquired into its motives. Towards European affairs the British policy was that of inertness and peace. The sovereigns of France and England abandoned their influence in Europe; Poland might perish and one Province after another be wrested from the Porte, that Louis the Fifteenth might not be startled in his voluptuous indulgence, and George the Third obtain undisturbed leisure to reduce America.

There in New England the most austere morality prevailed; the marriage vow was sacred; no corrupt Court tainted innocence; no licentious aristocracy disputed for superiority in excesses. There industry created wealth and divided it between all the children. There every man was or expected to become a freeholder; the owner of the land held the plough; he who held the plough, held the sword also; and the liberty which was the fruit of the sacrifices and sufferings of a revered ancestry, was guarded, under the blessing of God, as a sacred trust for posterity. There, among the hills of Berkshire, Hopkins, discoursing from the pulpit to the tillers of the soil, founded morals on the doctrine of disinterested love; which established it as the duty of every one to be willing to sacrifice himself for the glory of God, the freedom of his country, the well-being of his race.

"It is a people," said Samuel Adams of his countrymen, "who of all the people on the earth, deserve most to be free;"[1] and for a full year he had been maturing a plan by which he might elicit from the inquisitive character and the institutions of New England the means of restoring American liberty. Yet when he first proposed his great invention[2] for organ-

[1] Samuel Adams to Arthur Lee, 3 Nov. 1773.

[2] "This meeting was brought on with an intention to raise a general flame." Hutchinson to Dartmouth, 3 Nov. 1772.

CHAP. XLVIII. 1772. Sept. izing the revolution through Committees of Correspondence to be appointed by the Meetings of the Towns, every one of his colleagues in the delegation from Boston opposed him.[1] Especially Cushing, the Speaker, dissuaded from the movement, and had no confidence in its success.[2] Hancock, also, who disapproved of what seemed to him rash measures, joined with three or four others of the Selectmen of Boston; and they rejected the prayer of the first Petition[3] for a Boston Town-meeting.

Oct. Despondency was a state of mind unknown to Samuel Adams. His stern will seemed guided by light from an eternal and unfailing source, and never faltered. "America may assert her rights by Resolves," said Cushing; "but before enforcing them, she must wait to grow more powerful." "We are at a crisis," it was answered; "this is the moment to decide whether our posterity shall inherit liberty or slavery."

A new Petition, signed by one hundred and six inhabitants,[4]—explaining how the Judges would be corrupted into political partisans by their complete dependence—prevailed with the Selectmen, and a meeting of Boston was summoned for the twenty-eighth of October.

The day came. "We must now strike a home blow," said the boldest, "or sit down under the yoke of tyranny. The people in every town must instruct their Representatives, to send a remonstrance to the

[1] Samuel Cooper to B. Franklin, 15 March, 1773. Boston Gazette, 9 Nov. 1772.

[2] Cushing's Statement to Hutchinson, in Hutchinson to John Pownall, 19 April, 1773.

[3] Hutchinson's History, iii. 361.

[4] Boston Gazette, 26 October, 1772; 916, 2, 3.

King of Great Britain, and assure him (unless their Liberties are immediately restored whole and entire), they will form an independent Commonwealth, after the example of the Dutch Provinces; and offer a free trade to all nations. Should any one Province begin the example, the other Provinces will follow; and Great Britain must comply with our demands, or sink under the united force of the French and Spaniards. This is the plan that wisdom and Providence point out to preserve our rights, and this alone."[1]

CHAP. XLVIII. 1772. Oct.

Towards executing that design Adams moved with calm and undivided purpose; conducting public measures with a caution that left no step to be retraced. The attendance at Faneuil Hall was not great;[2] the town only raised a Committee to inquire of the Governor, if the Judges of the Province had become the stipendiaries of the Crown; after which it adjourned for two days. "This country," said Samuel Adams, in the interval, "must shake off its intolerable burdens at all events; every day strengthens our oppressors, and weakens us; if each town would declare its sense, our enemies could not divide us;"[3] and he urged on Elbridge Gerry of Marblehead, to convoke the citizens of that port.

As the Governor refused to answer the inquiry of the town, they next asked that he would allow the General Assembly to meet on the day to which it had been prorogued.

Nov.

A determined spirit began to show itself in the

[1] Oct. 28, 1772. An American in Boston Gazette, 2 Nov. 1772; 917, 2, 2.

[2] S. Adams to A. Lee, 3 November, 1772.

[3] Samuel Adams to Elbridge Gerry, 29 October, 1772.

CHAP. XLVIII 1772. Nov.

country;[1] yet when on the second of November Boston reassembled, no more persons attended than on ordinary occasions. "If in compliance with your Petition," such was Hutchinson's message to them, "I should alter my determination, and meet the Assembly at such time as you judge necessary, I should, in effect, yield to you the exercise of that part of the prerogative. There would," moreover, "be danger of encouraging the inhabitants of the other towns in the Province to assemble from time to time, in order to consider of the necessity or expediency of a session of the General Assembly, or to debate and transact other matters, which the law, that authorizes towns to assemble, does not make the business of a Town meeting."

By denying the right of the towns to discuss public questions of general interest, the Governor placed himself at variance with the institution of Town Governments, the oldest and dearest and most essentially characteristic of the established rights of New England. The Meeting read over the reply several times, and voted unanimously, "that its inhabitants have, ever had, and ought to have, a right to petition the King or his Representative for the redress or the preventing of grievances; and to communicate their sentiments to other towns."

Samuel Adams[3] then arose, and made that mo-

[1] E. Gerry to S. Adams, Marblehead, 2 Nov. 1772.

[2] Samuel Adams to Elbridge Gerry, 5 Nov. 1772.

[3] Journal of the Boston Committee of Correspondence, Book i. page i. In my account of the proceedings of this Committee, I am guided by its own secret journals which have never seen the light, but are in my possession, together with a very large number of their original papers and drafts. The Journal is in perfect order; the papers in a good state of preservation. Gordon, whose history of the Revolution is of great value, and in some parts of careful accuracy, was ac-

CHAP. XLVIII. 1772. Nov.

tion, which included the whole revolution, "that a Committee of Correspondence be appointed, to consist of twenty-one persons, to state the Rights of the Colonists and of this Province in particular, as men, as Christians, and as subjects, to communicate and publish the same to the several towns in this Province and to the world, as the sense of this town, with the infringements and violations thereof, that have been or from time to time may be made; also requesting of each town a free communication of their sentiments on this subject." The end in view was a general Confederacy against the authority of Parliament; the towns of the Province were to begin; the Assembly to confirm their doings and invite the other Colonies to join.[1]

The motion was readily adopted; but it was difficult to raise the Committee. Cushing, Hancock, and Phillips, three of the four Representatives of

customed before his return to England, to seek and to minute down oral communications, and not sifting them severely, his volumes are not free from gossip. His account of the Committee of Correspondence is imperfect and erroneous. He never had the entire confidence of Samuel Adams and his friends, and was never intrusted with a knowledge of their movements; so that he had to rely on what he could learn of those who were as little in the secret as himself. The statement, i. 312, 313, that the idea of the Committee of Correspondence came from James Warren of Plymouth, is wholly incorrect. The tradition comes to me directly from Samuel Adams through his daughter and the late Samuel Adams Welles, that it was not so; and this may offset any opposite tradition. John Adams says the system of Committees of Correspondence was the invention of Samuel Adams: so Hutchinson wrote. There was no doubt about it. Samuel Adams had for a year been brooding over the scheme. When he had matured it for execution, he communicated it by letters to several, among others to James Warren; and the answers of the latter, which are preserved, show him to have been a willing fellow-laborer in carrying out the measure, which he was so far from having advised, that he at first doubted its efficacy.

[1] Hutchinson to a Friend in England, I suppose Sir Francis Bernard, 14 June, 1773. "I had the fullest evidence," &c. &c.

CHAP. XLVIII. 1772. Nov.

Boston,[1] pleaded private business and refused to serve; so did Scollay and Austin, two of the Selectmen. The name of James Otis who was now but a wreck of himself, appears first on the list; as a tribute to former services. The two most important members were Samuel Adams and Joseph Warren, the first, now recognised as a "masterly Statesman,"[2] and the ablest political writer in New England; the second, a rare combination of gentleness with daring courage; of respect for law with the all-controlling love of liberty. The two men never failed each other; the one growing old, the other in youthful manhood; thinking one set of thoughts; having one heart for their country; joining in one career of public policy and action; differing only in this, that while Warren still clung to the hope of conciliation, Adams ardently desired, as well as clearly foresaw, the conflict for Independence.

On the third of November, the Boston Committee of Correspondence met at the Representatives' chamber, and organized itself by electing the true-hearted William Cooper its clerk. From that moment it constituted a body, called into being by the people, possessing their confidence, and exercising, as occasion demanded, the powers of a legislative and of an executive Council. They next, by a unanimous vote, gave each to the others the pledge of "honor, not to divulge any part of the conversation at their meetings to any person whatsoever, excepting what the Committee itself should make known."

[1] S. Cooper to B. Franklin, 15 March, 1773; Franklin, viii. 37; Hutchinson to John Pownall, 19 April, 1773; Boston Gazette, 918, 2, 2, and other letters.

[2] John Adams: Works, iv. 34.

CHAP. XLVIII. 1772. Nov.

Samuel Adams was then appointed to prepare the statement of the rights of the colonists; and Joseph Warren of the several grievous violations of those rights; while Church, who between such men could not go astray, was directed to draft a letter to the other towns.[1] Meantime Adams roused his friends throughout the Province. No more "complaining," thus he wrote to James Warren of Plymouth; "it is more than time to be rid of both tyrants and tyranny;" and explaining "the leading steps," which Boston had taken, he entreated the co-operation of the old Colony.

The flame caught.[2] Plymouth, Marblehead,[3] Roxbury,[4] Cambridge, prepared to second Boston. "God grant," cried Samuel Adams, "that the love of liberty, and a zeal to support it, may enkindle in every town." "Their scheme of keeping up a correspondence through the Province," wrote Hutchinson in a letter which was laid before the King,[5] "is such a foolish one, that it must necessarily make them ridiculous."[6]

After the report of the Boston Committee was prepared, Otis was appointed to present it to the town.[7] As they chose on this last great occasion of his public appearance to name him with the honors of precedence, history may express satisfaction, that he whose eloquence first awakened the thought of resist-

[1] Journals of the Committee of Correspondence, 3 November, 1772.

[2] James Warren of Plymouth, to S Adams, 8 Nov. 1772.

[3] Elbridge Gerry to S. Adams, 10 Nov. 1772, and 17 Nov. 1772.

[4] S. Adams to Elbridge Gerry, 14 Nov. 1772.

[5] Dartmouth to Hutchinson, 6 January, 1773.

[6] Hutchinson to the Secretary of the Board of Trade, 13 Nov. 1772.

[7] "Samuel Adams had prepared a long report, but he let Otis appear in it." Hutchinson to Gage, 7 March, 1773.

CHAP. XLVIII. 1772. Nov. ance, should have been able to lend his presence and his name to the final movement for union. He was a man of many sorrows; familiar with grief, as one who had known nothing else. Of all who have played a great part in American affairs, his existence was the least enlivened by joy. The burden of his infirmities was greater than he could bear, so that he sank under their weight; his fine intellect became a ruin which reason wandered over but did not occupy, and by its waning light showed less the original beauty of the structure than the completeness of its overthrow. The remainder of his life was passed in seclusion; years afterwards, when his country's independence had been declared, but not for him, he stood one summer's day in the porch of the farm-house which was his retreat, watching a sudden shower. One flash and only one was seen in the sky; one bolt fell, and, harming nothing else, struck James Otis, so that all that was mortal of him perished.—This is he who claimed the ocean as man's free highway; and persuaded to an American union.

On Friday, the twentieth of November, Boston, in a legal Town meeting in Faneuil Hall, received the Report of their Committee. Among the natural rights of the colonists, they claimed a right to life, to liberty, to property; a right to support and defend these; in case of intolerable oppression to change allegiance for their sake; to resume them, if they had ever been renounced; to rescue and preserve them sword in hand.

The grievances of which they complained were the assumption by the British Parliament of absolute power in all cases whatsoever; the exertion of that power to raise a revenue in the Colonies without their consent; the appointment of officers unknown to the Charter to collect the revenue; the investing these officers with unconstitutional authority; the supporting them by fleets and armies in time of peace; the establishment of a civil list out of the unconstitutional revenue even for the Judges whose commissions were held only during pleasure, and whose decisions affected property, liberty and life; the oppressive use of royal instructions; the enormous extension of the power of the Vice Admiralty Courts; the infringement of the right derived from God and nature to make use of their skill and industry, by prohibiting or restraining the manufacture of iron, of hats, of wool; the violence of authorizing persons in the Colonies to be taken up under pretence of certain offences and carried to Great Britain for trial; the claim of a right to establish a Bishop and Episcopal Courts without the consent of the Colony; the frequent alteration of the bounds of Colonies, followed by a necessity for the owners of the land to purchase fresh grants of their property from rapacious governors. "This enumeration," they said, "of some of the most open infringements of their rights, will not fail to excite the attention of all who consider themselves interested in the happiness and freedom of mankind, and will by every candid person be judged sufficient to justify whatever measures have been or may be taken to obtain redress."

Having thus joined issue with the King and Parliament, the inhabitants of the town of Boston voted, by means of Committees of Correspondence, to make an Appeal to all the towns in the Colony, "that the

CHAP. XLVIII. 1772. Nov. collected wisdom and fortitude of the whole people might dictate measures for the rescue of their happy and glorious Constitution." "These worthy New Englanders," cried Chatham, as he read the Report, "ever feel as old Englanders ought to do."[1]

It may reasonably be asked what England was gaining by the controversy with America. The Commissioners of the Stamp Office were just then settling their accounts for their expenses in America; which were found to have exceeded twelve thousand pounds, while they had received for revenue, almost entirely from Canada and the West India Islands, only about fifteen hundred.[2] The result of the tax on tea had been more disastrous. Even in Boston, under the very eyes of the Commissioners of the Customs, seven eighths of the teas[3] consumed were Dutch teas, and in the Southern Governments, the proportion was much greater; so that the whole remittance of the last year for duties on tea and wines and other articles taxed indirectly, amounted to no more than eighty-five[4] or eighty[5] pounds; while ships and soldiers for the support of the collecting officers had cost some hundred thousands, and the East India Company had lost the sale of goods to the amount of two and a half millions of dollars annually.

Dec. England was growing weary of the fruitless strife. Lord North wished it at an end; and Dartmouth, instead of thinking to appeal to Parliament for strin-

[1] Chatham to T. Hollis, Burton Pynsent, 3 Feb. 1773.

[2] B. Franklin to J. Galloway, viii. 24.

[3] Hutchinson to Dartmouth, No. 2, 27 October, 1772.

[4] Franklin's Preface of the British Editor to the Votes and Proceedings of the Town of Boston.

[5] Franklin to Galloway, 2 Dec. 1772.

gent measures, desired the King to "reign in the affections of his people," and would have regarded conciliation as "the happiest event of his life."[1] A Member of Parliament,[2] having discovered through John Temple,[3] that every perverse "measure, and every grievance complained of took their rise not from the British Government, but were projected, proposed to Administration, solicited and obtained by some of the most respectable among the Americans themselves, as necessary for the welfare of that country," endeavored to convince Franklin of the well ascertained fact. Franklin remaining skeptical, he returned in a few days with letters from Hutchinson, Oliver, and Paxton, written to produce coercion. These had been addressed to Whately, who had communicated them to Grenville, his patron, and through him to Lord Temple.[4] They had been handed about, that they might more certainly contribute to effect the end which their writers had in view; and at Whately's death, remained in the possession of others.

[1] Dartmouth to Hutchinson, 9 Dec. 1772.

[2] That it was understood to be a Member of Parliament, appears from John Adams, who cites Franklin as his authority. Such certainly was the opinion of Hutchinson. "A Member of Parliament, by whom they had been communicated to Dr. Franklin." Hutchinson, iii. 418.

[3] That Temple was privy to the plan of getting the letters, we know from Hutchinson and under his own hand. That he kept aloof, and at this time concealed his agency in the matter, appears from his own statement and from that of Franklin. Franklin gave his word not to name his informer. English writers have not noticed, that the English Ministry and Hutchinson seem to have had the means of discovering the secret, that the Ministry discouraged inquiry, and that Temple was subsequently forgiven, and appointed to a good place.

[4] Almon's Biog. Anecdotes, ii. 105; confirmed by the recently printed Grenville Papers, which show that Whately was accustomed to communicate to Grenville what he received from Hutchinson. "Another correspondent, [*i. e.* Hutchinson,] the same gentleman, one of whose letters I lately sent you," &c. &c. Grenville Papers, iv. 480.

CHAP. XLVIII. 1772. Nov. These, which were but very moderate specimens of a most persevering and most extensive Correspondence of a like nature, Franklin was authorized to send, to his constituents not for publication, but to be retained for some months, and perused by the Corresponding Committee of the Legislature, by members of the Council, and by some few others to whom the Chairman of that Committee might think proper to show them.

Dec. Had the conspiracy which was thus laid bare, aimed at the life of a Minister or the King, any honest man must have immediately communicated the discovery to the Secretary of State; to conspire to introduce into America a military Government, and abridge American liberty, was a more heinous crime, of which irrefragable evidence had now come to light. Franklin, as Agent of Massachusetts, made himself the public accuser of those whose guilt was now exposed; and in an official letter sent the proofs of their designs to the Speaker of the Massachusetts House of Representatives, with no concealment or reservation but such as his informer had required. "All good men," wrote Franklin as he forwarded the letters, "wish harmony to subsist between the Colonies and the Mother Country. My resentment against this country for its arbitrary measures in governing us, has been exceedingly abated, since my conviction by these papers that those measures were projected, advised, and called for by men of character among ourselves. I think they must have the same effect with you. As to the writers, when I find them bartering away the liberties of their native country for posts, negotiating for salaries and pensions extorted from the people, and, conscious of the odium these might be attended with, calling for troops to protect and secure the enjoyment of them; when I see them exciting jealousies in the Crown, and provoking it to wrath against so great a part of its most faithful subjects; creating enmities between the different countries of which the empire consists; occasioning a great expense to the old country, for suppressing or preventing imaginary rebellions in the new, and to the new country for the payment of needless gratifications to useless officers and enemies; I cannot but doubt their sincerity even in the political principles they profess, and deem them mere time-servers, seeking their own private emoluments, through any quantity of public mischief; betrayers of the interest not of their native country only, but of the Government they pretend to serve, and of the whole English empire."[1]

CHAP. XLVIII. 1772. Dec.

While the letters were on their way, the towns in the Province were just coming together under the impulse from Boston. The people of Marblehead, whose fishermen were all returned from their annual summer's excursion to the Grand Banks, at a full meeting, with but one dissentient, expressed "their unavoidable disesteem and reluctant irreverence for the British Parliament;" their sense of the "great and uncommon kind of grievance," of being compelled "to carry the produce of Spain and Portugal, received for their fish, to Great Britain, and there paying duties;" how "justly they were incensed at the unconstitutional, unrighteous proceedings" of Ministers, how they "de-

[1] B. Franklin to T. Cushing, 2 Dec. 1772.

CHAP. XLVIII. 1772. Nov. tested the name of a Hillsborough;" how ready they were to "unite for the recovery of their violated rights;" and like Roxbury[1] and Plymouth,[2] they appointed their Committee.[3] Warren of Plymouth exerted himself diligently, but despondingly. "The towns," said he, "are dead; and cannot be raised without a miracle."[4] "I am very sorry to find in you the least approach towards despair," answered Adams. "Nil desperandum is a motto for you and me. All are not dead; and where there is a spark of patriotic fire we will rekindle it." The patriot's noble confidence was justified.[5] In Plymouth itself, "there were ninety to one to fight Great Britain."[6]

Dec. The people of Cambridge, in a full meeting, were "much concerned to maintain and secure their own invaluable rights which were not the gift of Kings, but purchased with the precious blood and treasure of their ancestors;" and they "discovered a glorious spirit like men determined to be free." Roxbury, which had moved with deliberation, found "the rights of the colonists fully supported and warranted by the laws of God and Nature, the New Testament and the Charter of the Province." "Our pious Forefathers," said they, "died with the pleasing hope, that we their children should live free; let none, as they will answer it another day, disturb the ashes of those heroes by selling their birthright."

[1] S. Adams to James Warren, 27 Nov. 1772, and Journals.

[2] Journals of C. C. i. 7.

[3] Journals of C. C. i. 9–14.

[4] James Warren of Plymouth to Samuel Adams, 8 Dec. 1772.

[5] Samuel Adams to James Warren, 9 Dec. 1772.

[6] Judge Oliver of Middleborough to Hutchinson, 16 Dec. 1772.

CHAP. XLVIII. 1772. Dec.

On Monday, the twenty-eighth of December, towns were in session from the Banks of the Kennebec[1] to Buzzard's Bay.[2] The people of Charlestown beheld their own welfare "and the fate of unborn millions in suspense." "It will not be long," said Rochester, "before our assembling for the cause of liberty will be determined to be riotous, and every attempt to prevent the flood of despotism from overflowing our land will be deemed open rebellion." Woolwich, "an infant people in an infant country," did not "think their answer perfect in spelling or the words placed," yet hearty good feeling got the better of their false shame.[3] Does any one ask who had precedence in proposing a Union of the Colonies, and a war for Independence? The thoughts were the offspring of the time; and were in every patriot's breast. It were as well to ask which tree in the forest is the earliest to feel the genial influence of the reviving year. The first official utterance of revolution did not spring from a Congress of the Colonies, or the future chiefs of the Republic; from the rich who falter, or the learned who weigh and debate. The people of the little interior town of Pembroke in Plymouth county, unpretending husbandmen, full of the glory of their descent from the Pilgrims, concluded a clear statement of their grievances with the prediction, that "if the measures so justly complained of were persisted in and enforced by fleets and armies, they must, they will, in a little time issue in the total disso-

[1] Proceedings of the Town of Woolwich, in Journals of the Committee of Correspondence, 240.

[2] Proceedings of the Town of Rochester, Original papers, 772. Journal C. C., 108.

[3] Original Papers, 1003. Journal of C. C., iii. 242.

CHAP. XLVIII. 1772. Dec.

lution of the union between the mother country and the Colonies."[1] And in a louder tone the freemen of Gloucester, accustomed to thoughts as free as the ocean which dashes on their bold shore, and brave as became men who from childhood had in their small fishing boats rode the breakers without fear, declared their readiness to stand for their rights and liberties, which were dearer to them than their lives, and to join with all others in an appeal to the Great Lawgiver, not doubting of success according to the justice of their cause.[2]

Salisbury, a small town on the Merrimack, counselled an American Union.[3] Ipswich, in point of numbers[4] the second town in the Province, advised "that the Colonies in general and the inhabitants of their Province in particular, should stand firm as one man, to support and maintain all their just rights and privileges."[5] In the course of December, the Earl of Chatham was reading several New England writings "with admiration and love;" among others an Election Sermon by Tucker, in which he found "the divine Sydney rendered practical, and the philosophical Locke more demonstrative;"[6] and on the very same day, the people of the little town of Chatham, at the extremity of Cape Cod, were declaring their "civil and religious principles to be the sweetest

[1] Votes and Resolves of Pembroke, 28 December, 1772, in Journals of C. C. i. 44. Compare Wedderburn on Pembroke, in his speech against Franklin.

[2] Journals of the Committee, i. 67. Original Papers, 361.

[3] Original papers, 815.

[4] Committee of Boston to Committee of Ipswich, 8 Jan. 1773; Original Papers, 445; Journal of C. C., v. 364.

[5] Votes and Proceedings of the Town of Ipswich, 28 Dec. 1772; in Journal C. C., 50; Original papers, 441.

[6] Chatham to T. Hollis, 29 Dec. 1772.

and essential part of their lives, without which the remainder was scarcely worth preserving."[1]

"They succeed," wrote Hutchinson plaintively;[2] and he called for aid from Parliament. But the excitement increased still more, when it became known, that Thurlow and Wedderburn had reported the burning of the Gaspee to be a crime of a much deeper dye than piracy,[3] and that the King, by the advice of his Privy Council, had ordered its authors and abettors to be delivered to Rear Admiral Montagu, and, with the witnesses, brought for "condign punishment" to England. To send an American across the Atlantic for trial for his life, was an intolerable violation of justice; Hutchinson urged what was worse, to abrogate the Rhode Island Charter. In this hour of greatest peril, the men of Rhode Island, by the hands of Darius Sessions, their Deputy Governor, and Stephen Hopkins, their Chief Justice, appealed to Samuel Adams for advice. And he answered immediately that the occasion "should awaken the American Colonies, and again unite them in one band; that an attack upon the liberties of one Colony was an attack upon the liberties of all, and that therefore in this instance all should be ready to yield assistance."[4]

Employing this event also to contribute to the great purpose of a general union, the Boston Com-

[1] Proceedings of Chatham, Original Papers, 269; Journal of C. C., ii. 118.

[2] Hutchinson to R. Jackson, 8 Dec. 1772, and to John Pownall, Remembrancer, 1776, ii. 60.

[3] Dartmouth to Hutchinson, 4 Sept. 1772. Same to Wanton, Governor of Rhode Island, 4 September, 1772.

[4] Darius Sessions, Stephen Hopkins, John Cole, and Moses Brown to Samuel Adams, Providence, 25 Dec. 1772. Adams's Reply, 28 Dec.

CHAP. XLVIII. 1772. Dec. mittee as the year went out, were "encouraged by the people's thorough understanding of their civil and religious rights and liberties, to trust in God, that a day was hastening when the efforts of the Colonists would be crowned with success, and the present generation furnish an example of public virtue, worthy the imitation of all posterity."

1773. Jan. In a like spirit, the new and eventful year of 1773 was rung in by the men of Marlborough. "Death," said they unanimously on the first of January, "is more eligible than slavery. A freeborn people are not required by the religion of Jesus Christ to submit to tyranny, but may make use of such power as God has given them to recover and support their laws and liberties." And advising all the Colonies to prepare for war, they "implored the Ruler above the skies, that he would make bare his arm in defence of his church and people, and let Israel go."

"As we are in a remote wilderness corner of the earth, we know but little," said the farmers of Lenox; but they were certain that neither nature nor the God of nature required them to crouch "Issachar-like, between the two burdens" of poverty and slavery. "We prize our liberties so highly," thus the men of Leicester with the districts of Spencer and Paxton spoke modestly and sincerely, "that we think it our duty to risk our lives and fortunes in defence thereof." "For that spirit of virtue which induced your town, at so critical a day to take the lead in so good a cause," wrote the Town of Petersham, "our admiration is heightened, when we consider your being exposed to the first efforts of power. The time may come, when you may be driven from your goodly heritage; if that should be the case, we invite you to

CHAP. XLVIII. 1773. Jan.

share with us in our small supplies of the necessaries of life; and should we still not be able to withstand, we are determined to retire, and seek repose amongst the inland aboriginal natives, with whom we doubt not but to find more humanity and brotherly love, than we have lately received from our Mother Country." "We join with the town of Petersham," was the reply of Boston, "in preferring a life among the savages to the most splendid condition of slavery; but Heaven will bless the united efforts of a brave people."

"It is only some people in the Massachusetts Bay making a great clamor, in order to keep their party alive," wrote time-servers to Dartmouth,[1] begging for further grants of salaries, and blind to the awakening of a nation. Samuel Adams, who thoroughly understood the people of New England, predicted "a most violent political earthquake through the whole British empire."[2] "This unhappy contest between Britain and America," he continued, "will end in rivers of blood; but America may wash her hands in innocence." And informing Rhode Island of the design of "Administration to get their Charter vacated," he advised them to make delay, without conceding any of their rights; and to address the Assemblies of all the other Colonies for support.[3]

[1] W. Franklin to Dartmouth, No. 4, 5 Jan., 1773. Cortland Skinner's Petition for a salary from the Crown.

[2] Samuel Adams to Darius Sessions, 2 Jan. 1773.

[3] Compare Joseph Ward to Ezra Stiles, Boston, 2 Jan. 1773.

CHAPTER XLIX.

VIRGINIA CONSOLIDATES UNION.

JANUARY—JULY, 1773.

CHAP. XLIX. 1773. Jan.

ON the sixth of January, the day on which the Legislature of Massachusetts assembled at Boston, the affairs of America were under consideration in England. The King, who read even the semi-official letters in which Hutchinson described the Boston Committee of Correspondence as in part composed of "deacons" and "atheists," and "blackhearted fellows whom one would not choose to meet in the dark,"[1] "very much approved the temper and firmness" of his Governor, and was concerned lest "the inhabitants of Boston should be deluded into acts of disobedience, and the most atrocious criminality towards individuals;" he found "consolation" in the assurance, that "the influence of the malignant spirits was daily decreasing," and "that their mischievous

[1] Hutchinson to Secretary Pownall, 13 Nov. 1772. That this letter was read by the King, appears from Dartmouth to Hutchinson, 6 Jan. 1773

CHAP. XLIX. 1773. Jan.

tenets were held in abhorrence by the generality of the people."[1] But already eighty towns or more,[2] including almost every one of the larger towns, had chosen their Committees; and Samuel Adams was planning how to effect a union of all the Colonies in Congress.[3] When the Assembly met,[4] the Speaker transmitted the proceedings of the Town of Boston for organizing the provincial Committees of Correspondence to Richard Henry Lee of Virginia.[5]

The Governor, in his Speech to the two Houses, with calculating malice summoned them to admit or disprove the supremacy of Parliament. The disorder in the Government he attributed to the denial of that supremacy, which he undertook to establish by arguments derived from the history of the Colony, its Charter, and English law. "I know of no line," he said, "that can be drawn between the supreme authority of Parliament and the total Independence of the Colonies. It is impossible there should be two independent Legislatures in one and the same State." And "is there," he asked, "any thing which we have more reason to dread than Independence?" He therefore invited the Legislature to adhere to his principles or convince him of his error. Elated with vanity,

[1] Dartmouth to Hutchinson, 6 January, 1773.

[2] Hutchinson to a person unnamed, probably R. Jackson, 19 Feb. 1773. Same to I. Mauduit, 21 Feb. 1773; Same to Dartmouth, 22 Feb. 1773; Same to Gen'l. Mackay, 23 Feb. 1773; Same to Sir Francis Bernard, 23 Feb. 1773.

[3] Hutchinson to Dartmouth, 16 Sept. 1773; "The hint of a Congress is nothing new; it is what they have been aiming at the two last sessions." Same to Same, 7 Jan. 1773; Hutchinson to a person not named, 19 Feb. 1773; Same to I. Mauduit, 21 Feb. 1773; Same to General Mackay, 23 Feb. 1773.

[4] Hutchinson to John Pownall, 24 Feb. 1773.

[5] The letter of Cushing seems to be lost; its purport appears from the unpublished answer of R. H. Lee to T. Cushing, Lee Hall, Potomack Virginia, 13 Feb. 1773.

CHAP. XLIX. 1773. Jan. he was sure in any event of a victory; for if they should disown the opinions of the several towns, he would gain glory in England; if they should avow them, then, said he in a letter which was to go straight to the King, "I shall be enabled to make apparent the reasonableness and necessity of coercion, and justify it to all the world."[1]

The speech was printed and industriously circulated in England; and for a short time made an impression on the minds of many not well acquainted with the dispute. His hearers in Boston saw his indiscretion, and Samuel Adams prepared to "take the fowler in his own snare." No man in the Province had reflected so much as he on the question of the legislative power of Parliament; no man had so early arrived at the total denial of that power. For nine years he had been seeking an opportunity of promulgating that denial as the opinion of the Assembly; and caution had always stood in his way. At last the opportunity had come, and the Assembly with one consent, placed the pen in his hand.

Meantime, the towns of Massachusetts were still vibrating from the impulse given by Boston. "The swords which we whet and brightened for our enemies are not yet grown rusty," wrote the town of Gorham.[3] "We offer our lives as a sacrifice in the glorious cause of Liberty;" was the response of Kittery. "We will not sit down easy," voted Shirley, "until

[1] Hutchinson to John Pownall, Jan 1773, in his Letter Book; and compare Hutchinson to John Pownall, Jan. 1773. In Remembrancer for 1776, ii. 60.

[2] Franklin to T. Cushing, 9 March, 1773; — viii. 35.

[3] Original Papers, 377, 7 Jan. 1773. Original Papers, 455.

our rights and liberties are restored."[1] The people of Medfield would also "have a final period put to that most cruel, inhuman and unchristian practice, the Slave-trade."[2] Acton spoke out concisely and firmly. "Prohibiting slitting-mills," said South Hadley, "is similar to the Philistines prohibiting smiths in Israel, and shews we are esteemed by our brethren as vassals." "We think ourselves obliged to emerge from our former obscurity, and speak our minds with freedom," declared Lunenburg, "or our posterity may otherwise rise up and curse us." "We of this place are unanimous," was the message from Pepperell; "our resentment riseth against those who dare invade our natural and constitutional rights." With one voice they named Captain William Prescott, to be the chief of their Committee of Correspondence; and no braver heart beat in Middlesex than his. Lynn called for a Provincial Convention; Stoneham invited the sister Colonies to harmony; Danvers would have "strict union of all the Provinces on the Continent." "Digressions from compacts," said the men of Princetown, "lessen the connection between the Mother Country and the Colonies."

CHAP. XLIX. 1773. Jan.

South Carolina, too remote for immediate concert, was engaged in the same cause. They marked their affection for Rawlins Lowndes, one of their discarded Judges, and "in great esteem throughout the Province," by electing him the Speaker of their Assembly. The Governor "directed the Assembly to return to their House and choose another;" but they

[1] Shirley to Boston Com. 11 Jan. 1773.

[2] Proceedings of the town of Newfield, 28 Dec. 1772, and 11 January, 1773; Original Papers, 602.

CHAP. XLIX. 1773. Jan.

persisted in their first choice. In consequence Montagu prorogued them, and did it in so illegal a manner, that as a remedy, he dissolved them by a proclamation, and immediately issued writs for choosing a new House;[1] thus carrying the subject home to the thoughts of every voter in the Province.

This controversy was local; the answers of the Legislature of Massachusetts to its Governor's challenge would be of general importance. That of the Council, drafted by Bowdoin, clearly traced the existing discontents to the Acts of Parliament, subjecting the Colonies to taxes without their consent. The removal of this original cause, would remove its effects. Supreme or unlimited authority can with fitness belong only to the Sovereign of the universe; from the nature and end of government, the supreme authority of every government is limited; and from the laws of England, its Constitution and the Provincial Charter, it was shown that the limits of that authority did not include the levying of taxes within the Province. Thus the Council conceded nothing, and at the same time avoided a conflict with the opinions of Chatham, Camden and Shelburne.

The House, in their reply, which Samuel Adams, familiar with the opinions of lawyers, and specially aided by the sound legal knowledge of Hawley, had constructed with his utmost skill at sarcasm, and which, after two days' debate,[2] was unanimously adopted and carried up by its author, chose a differ-

[1] Lord Charles Montagu to the Secretary of State, 21 January, 1773; Charles Garth to Committee of South Carolina, 25 Feb. 1773.

[2] From an original MS. rough record of the doings of the House, in my possession.

CHAP. XLIX. 1773. Jan.

ent mode of dealing with the Governor's positions.[1] Like the Council, they traced the disturbed state of Government to taxation of the colonists by Parliament; but as to the supremacy of that body, they took the Governor at his word. "It is difficult, perhaps impossible," they agreed, "to draw a line of distinction between the universal authority of Parliament over the Colonies, and no authority at all;" and laying out all their strength to prove the only point that Hutchinson's statement required to be proved, that that authority was not universal, they opened the door to his own inference. "If there be no such line," said they, "between the supreme authority of Parliament and the total independence of the Colonies, then, either the Colonies are vassals of the Parliament, or they are totally independent. As it cannot be supposed to have been the intention of the parties in the compact, that one of them should be reduced to a state of vassalage, the conclusion is, that it was their sense, that we were thus independent." "But it is impossible," the Governor had insisted, "that there should be two independent Legislatures in one and the same State." "Then," replied the House, "the Colonies were by their Charters, made distinct States from the Mother Country." "Although there may be but one head, the King," Hutchinson had said, "yet the two legislative bodies will make two governments as distinct as the kingdoms of England and Scotland before the union." "Very true, may it please your Excellency," replied the House; "and if they interfere not with each

[1] For the authorship of the paper see the contemporary letter of Hutchinson to Sir Francis Bernard, 23 February, 1773.

CHAP. XLIX. 1773. Jan. other, what hinders but that, being united in one head and Sovereign, they may live happily in that connection, and mutually support and protect each other?"

"But is there any thing," the Governor had asked, "which we have more reason to dread than Independence?" And the House answered, "There is more reason to dread the consequences of absolute uncontrolled power, whether of a nation or of a Monarch." "To draw the line of distinction," they continue, "between the supreme authority of Parliament, and the total independence of the Colonies would be an arduous undertaking, and of very great importance to all the other Colonies; and, therefore, could we conceive of such a line, we should be unwilling to propose it, without their consent in Congress."

Having thus won an unsparing victory over the logic of Hutchinson by accepting all his premises and fitting to them other and apter conclusions, they rebuked the Governor for having reduced them to the alternative, either of appearing by silence to acquiesce in his sentiments, or of freely discussing the supreme authority of Parliament.

The Governor was overwhelmed with confusion. He had intended to drive them into a conflict with Parliament; and they had denied its supremacy by implication from his own premises, in a manner that could bring censure on no one but himself.

During this controversy a Commission composed of Admiral Montagu, the Vice-Admiralty Judge at Boston, the Chief Justices of Massachusetts, New-York and New Jersey, and the Governor of Rhode Island, met at Newport to inquire into the affair of the Gaspee. Deputy Governor Sessions and Stephen

Hopkins, formerly Governor, now Chief Justice, were the two pillars on which Rhode Island Liberty depended. They notified the Commissioners that there had been no neglect of duty or connivance on the part of the Provincial Government; from which it followed that the presence of the special Court was as unnecessary as it was alarming.

CHAP. XLIX. 1773. Jan.

The Assembly having met at East Greenwich to watch the Commissioners, the Governor laid before it his instructions to arrest offenders and send them for trial to England. The order excited general horror and indignation. The Chief Justice asked directions how he should act. The Assembly referred him to his discretion. "Then," said Hopkins in the presence of both Houses, "for the purpose of transportation for trial, I will neither apprehend any person by my own order, nor suffer any executive officers in the Colony to do it."[1]—"The people would not have borne an actual seizure of persons;" which "nothing but an armed force could have effected." The attempt would have produced a crisis.[2]

The Commissioners elicited nothing and adjourned with bitterness in their hearts. Smyth, the Chief Justice of New Jersey, who had just been put on the civil list, threw all blame on the popular Government of Rhode Island.[3] Horsmanden advised to take away the Charter of that Province, and of Connecticut also; and consolidate the "twins

Feb.

[1] Ezra Stiles to Rev Wm. Spencer, Newport, 16 Feb. 1773. A very long and carefully prepared letter.

[2] Sessions, Hopkins, Cole and Brown, to S. Adams, Providence, 15 Feb. 1773.

[3] Smyth to Dartmouth, 8 Feb. 1773.

CHAP. XLIX. 1773. Feb.

in one royal Government."[1] Yet Connecticut, the land of steady habits, was, at that day, the most orderly and quietly governed people in the world; and the Charter of Rhode Island, in spite of all its enemies, had vitality enough to outlast the unreformed House of Commons.

The bold doctrines of Massachusetts, gained ground, and extended to other Colonies.[2] Hutchinson was embarrassed by the controversy, which he had provoked, and would now willingly have ended. Meantime the House made the usual grants to the Justices of the Superior Court; but[3] the Governor refused his assent because he expected warrants for their salaries from the King.[4] The House replied:[5] "No Judge who has a due regard to justice, or even to his own character, would choose to be placed under such an undue bias, as they must be under by accepting their salaries of the Crown. We are more and more convinced, that it has been the design of Administration, totally to subvert the Constitution, and introduce an arbitrary Government into this Province; and we cannot wonder that the apprehensions of this people are thoroughly awakened." The towns of Massachusetts were all the while continuing their meetings. "The Judges," said the men of Eastham,[6] "must reject the detestable plan with abhorrence, if they would have their memories blessed." "We deny the Parliamentary power of taxing us, being without the realm of England and not

[1] Chief Justice Horsmanden of New-York, to Lord Dartmouth, 20 February, 1773.

[2] W. S. Johnson to John Pownall, 27 Feb. 1773. W. S. Johnson to R. Jackson, 26 Feb. 1773.

[3] Message from the House, 3 Feb. 1773; Bradford, 365.

[4] Message to the House, 4 Feb.

[5] Message from the House, 13 Feb.

[6] Original Papers, 322; 24 Feb. 1773.

represented there;" declared Stoughtenham.[1] "Let the Colonies stand firm as one man," voted Winchendon.[2] "Divine Providence and the necessity of things may call upon us and all the Colonies to make our last Appeal;"[3] wrote the farmers who dwelt on the bleak hills of New Salem.

CHAP. XLIX. 1773. Feb.

Yet Hutchinson seemed compelled to renew his discussion with the Legislature, and in a long argument, which contained little that was new, endeavored to prove that the Colony of Massachusetts was holden as feudatory of the imperial Crown of England, and was therefore under the Government of the King's Laws and the King's Court. Again Bowdoin for the Council, with still greater clearness, affirms that Parliamentary taxation is unconstitutional, because imposed without consent; again Samuel Adams for the House, aided briefly, in Hawley's temporary absence, by the strong natural powers and good knowledge of the laws of John Adams, proves from the Governor's own premises, that Parliament has no supremacy over the Colony, because the feudal system admits no idea of the authority of Parliament.

At the same time both parties looked beyond the Province for aid. Hutchinson sought to intimidate his antagonists, by telling them "that the English Nation would be roused, and could not be withstood," that "Parliament would, by some means or other, maintain its supremacy."[4] To his correspondents in England he sent word what measures should be chosen; advising a change in the political organization of towns;[5] a prohibition of the commerce of Bos-

[1] Journals of C. C. 427.
[2] Journals of C. C. 575.
[3] Original papers, 673.
[4] Hutchinson to J. Pownall, 24 Feb. to Gov. Pownall, 23 Feb. 1773.
[5] Hutchinson to Israel Mauduit, Feb. 1773, and to Bernard, March, 1773.

CHAP. XLIX. 1773. Feb. ton,[1] and the option to the Province between submission and the forfeiture of their rights.[2] "I wish," said he, "Government may be convinced that something is necessary to be done." "We want a full persuasion that Parliament will maintain its Supremacy at all events." "Without it, the opposition here will triumph more than ever."

March The people on their part drew from their institution of Committees of Correspondence throughout the Province, the hope of a union of all the Colonies. "Some future Congress," said they, "will be the glorious source of the salvation of America; the Amphictyons of Greece, who formed the Diet or great Council of the States, exhibit an excellent model for the rising Americans." [3]

Whether that great idea should become a reality depended on Virginia. Its Legislature came together on the fourth of March, full of the love of country. Its Members had authentic information of the proceedings of the town of Boston; and public rumors had reached them of the Commission for inquiry into the affairs of Rhode Island. They had read and approved of the answers which the Council and the House of Massachusetts had made in January to the speech of Hutchinson. They formed themselves, therefore, into a Committee of the whole House on the state of the Colony; and in that Committee Dabney Carr, of Charlotte, a young statesman of brilliant genius as well as of fervid patriotism, moved a series of resolutions for a system of intercolonial

[1] Hutchinson to Bernard, March, 1773.

[2] Hutchinson to Dartmouth, 20 March, 1773.

[3] Oration delivered at Boston, March 5, 1773, by Dr. Benjamin Church.

CHAP. XLIX. 1773. March

Committees of Correspondence. His plan included a thorough union of Councils throughout the Continent. If it should succeed and be adopted by the other Colonies, America would stand before the world as a Confederacy. The measure was supported by Richard Henry Lee, with an eloquence which never passed away from the memory of his hearers; by Patrick Henry with a still more commanding majesty.[1] The Assembly was of one mind; and no person appropriated to himself praise beyond the rest. They did what greatness of mind counselled; and they did it quietly, as if it were but natural to them to act with magnanimity. On Friday the twelfth of March, the Resolutions were reported to the House, and unanimously adopted. They appointed their Committee on which appear the names of Bland and Lee, of Henry, and Carr, and Jefferson. Their Resolves were sent to every Colony, with a request that each would appoint its Committee to communicate from time to time with that of Virginia.[2] In this manner, Virginia laid the foundation of our union.[3] Massachusetts organized a Province; Virginia promoted a confederacy. Were the several Committees but to come together, the world would see an American Congress.

The associates of Dabney Carr were spared for still further service to humanity. He himself was cut down in his prime; and passed away like a shadow; but the name of him, who at this moment of crisis, beckoned the Colonies onward to union, must not perish from the memory of his countrymen.

[1] Letter in Wirt's Life of Henry, 104.

[2] Peyton Randolph, Circular 19 March, 1773.

[3] Hutchinson's Hist. iii. 393.

CHAP. XLIX. 1773. April.

The effect of these Resolutions of the Old Dominion was decisive.[1] In Massachusetts they gladdened every heart. "Virginia and South Carolina by their steady perseverance," inspired the hope, that the fire of Liberty would spread through the Continent.[2] "A Congress and then an Assembly of States," reasoned Samuel Adams, is no longer "a mere fiction in the mind of a political enthusiast." What though "the British nation carry their liberties to market, and sell them to the highest bidder?" "America," said he, repeating the words of Arthur Lee, "America shall rise full plumed and glorious from the mother's ashes."[3]

A copy of the proceedings of Virginia was sent to every town and district in Massachusetts, that "all the friends of American Independence and freedom,"[4] might welcome the intelligence; and as one Meeting after another echoed back the advice for a Congress, they could hardly find words to express how their gloom had given way to light, and how "their hearts even leapt for joy." "We trust the day is not far distant," said Cambridge by the hand of Thomas Gardner, "when our rights and liberties shall be restored unto us, or the Colonies, united as one man, will make their most solemn appeal to Heaven, and drive tyranny from these northern climes."[5]

[1] "Most of the Colonies, if not all, will come into the like resolutions, and if the colonies are not soon relieved, some imagine a Congress will grow out of this measure." T. Cushing to A. Lee, 22 April, 1773.

[2] Samuel Adams to Richard Henry Lee, 9 April, 1773.

[3] Samuel Adams to A. Lee, 9 April, 1773.

[4] Original Papers, 351.

[5] Committee of Correspondence of Cambridge, to Committee of Boston; in the handwriting of Thos. Gardner. Original Papers in my possession.

"The Colonies must assert their liberties whenever the opportunity offers;" wrote Dickinson from Pennsylvania.[1] The opportunity was nearer than he thought; in England Chatham saw plainly, that "things were hastening to a crisis at Boston, and looked forward to the issue with very painful anxiety."[2] It was the King who precipitated the conflict. He had no dread of the interposition of France, for that power, under the Ministry of the day, feared lest the enfranchisement of the Anglo-American Colonies should create a dangerous rival power to itself,[3] and was eager to fortify the good understanding with England by a defensive treaty, or at least by a treaty of commerce.[4] Louis the Fifteenth was resolved at all events to avoid war.[5]

CHAP. XLIX. 1773. April.

From the time therefore that the Representatives of Massachusetts avowed their legislative Independence, the King dismissed the thought of obtaining obedience "by argument and persuasion."[6] The most thorough search was made into every Colonial law that checked or even seemed to check the Slave-trade; and an Act of Virginia, which put no more obstructions upon it, than had existed for a generation, was negatived.[7] Parliamentary taxation was also to be enforced.

The continued refusal of North America to receive tea from England, had brought distress upon the

[1] John Dickinson to Samuel Adams, Fairhill, 10 April, 1773.

[2] Chatham to T. Hollis, 18 April, 1773.

[3] Mémoire sur L'Angleterre, in Angleterre, Tome 502.

[4] Dispatches of Aiguillon to de Guines in March and April 1773.

[5] King to Lord North, 20 April, 1773; and King to Lord North, 25 April, 1773.

[6] Dartmouth to Hutchinson, 10 April, 1773.

[7] Dartmouth to Dunmore, No. 2, 10 April, 1773; Dunmore to Dartmouth, 9 July, 1773.

CHAP. XLIX. 1773. April. East India Company, which had on hand wanting a market great quantities imported in the faith that that agreement could not hold. They were able to pay neither their dividends, nor their debts; their stock depreciated nearly one half; and the Government must lose their annual payment of four hundred thousand pounds. The bankruptcies, brought on partly by this means, gave such a shock to credit, as had not been experienced since the South Sea year; and the great manufacturers were sufferers.[1] The directors came to Parliament with an ample confession of their humbled state, together with entreaties for assistance and relief; and particularly praying that leave might be given to export teas free of all duties to America and to foreign ports. Had such leave been granted in respect of America, it would have been an excellent commercial regulation, as well as have restored a good understanding to every part of the empire.[2]

Instead of this, Lord North proposed to give to the Company itself the right of exporting its teas. The existing law granted on their exportation to America a drawback of three fifths only of the duties paid on importation. Lord North now offered a drawback of the whole. Trecothick in the Committee also advised to take off the import duty in America of three pence the pound, as it produced no income to the revenue; but the Ministry would not listen to the thought of relieving America from taxation. "Then," added Trecothick in behalf of the East India Company,

[1] Compare Franklin to Cushing, to W. Franklin, and to Cooper.

[2] Duke of Grafton's Autobiography, iii. 108. The Duke was then Lord Privy Seal, but not of the Cabinet.

CHAP. XLIX. 1773. April.

"as much or more may be brought into the revenue by not allowing a full exemption from the duties paid here." But Lord North refused to discuss the right of Parliament to tax America; insisting that no difficulty could arise, that under the new regulation America would be able to buy tea from the Company at a lower price than from any other European Nation, and that men will always go to the cheapest market.[1]

May.

The Ministry was still in its halcyon days; no opposition was made even by the Whigs; and the measure which was the King's own,[2] and was designed to put America to the test, took effect as a law from the tenth day of May.[3] It was immediately followed by a most carefully prepared answer from the King to Petitions from Massachusetts, announcing that he "considered his authority to make laws in Parliament of sufficient force and validity to bind his subjects in America in all cases whatsoever, as essential to the dignity of the Crown, and a right appertaining to the State, which it was his duty to preserve entire and inviolate;" that he, therefore, "could not but be greatly displeased with the Petitions and Remonstrance in which that right was drawn into question;" but that he "imputed the unwarrantable doctrines held forth in the said Petitions and Remonstrance, to the artifices of a few."[4] All this while, Lord Dartmouth "had a true desire to see lenient measures adopted towards the Colonies,"[5] not being in

[1] Charles Garth to the Committee of Correspondence of South Carolina, London, 4 May, 1773.

[2] B. Franklin to William Franklin, 14 July, 1773; Compare Anecdotes of Chatham, ii. 240, 241, 242.

[3] 13 Geo. III. Chap. xliv.

[4] Dartmouth to Dr. Franklin, Agent for the late Representatives of the Province of Massachusetts Bay; Whitehall, 2 June, 1773. Dartmouth to Hutchinson, same date.

[5] Grafton's Autobiography.

CHAP. XLIX. 1773. May. the least aware, that he was drifting with the Cabinet towards the very system of coercion against which he gave the most public and the most explicit pledges.

In America men began to prepare for extreme measures. Charles Lee, a British Officer on half-pay, resolved to devote himself "to the cause of mankind and of liberty now attacked in their last and only asylum."[1] "Glorious Virginia," cried the Legislature of Rhode Island, glowing with admiration for "its patriotic and illustrious House of Burgesses;" and this New England Province was the first to follow the example of the Old Dominion, by electing its Committees and sending its Circular through the land.[2]

In Massachusetts, so soon as the Government for the year was organized, the House on the motion of Samuel Adams, and by a vote of one hundred and nine to four, expressed its gratitude to the Burgesses of Virginia for their uniform vigilance, firmness and wisdom, and its hearty concurrence in their judicious and spirited Resolves. And then it elected its Committee of Correspondence, fifteen in number. New Hampshire and Connecticut did the same, so that all New England and Virginia were now one political body, with an organization inchoate, yet so perfect, that, on the first emergency, they could convene a Congress. Every other Colony on the Continent was sure to follow their example.[3]

June. While the patriot party was cheered by the hope of union, the letters of Hutchinson and Oliver which Franklin had sent over to the Speaker of the Massa-

[1] Lee to H. Gates, 6 May, 1773.

[2] Metcalf Bowler to Speaker of the House of N. H. 15 May, 1773.

[3] Letter of Massachusetts to the other Colonies, 3 June, 1773: Bradford, 401.

chusetts Assembly, destroyed their moral power by exposing their duplicity. "Cool, thinking, deliberate villains; malicious and vindictive, as well as ambitious and avaricious," said John Adams, who this year was chosen into the Council but negatived by the governor. "Bone of our bone; flesh of our flesh; born and educated among us," cried others. Hancock, who was angry at being named in the correspondence, determined to lay bare their hypocrisy; and Cooper from the pulpit preached of "the old Serpent, which deceiveth the whole world; but was cast out into the earth and his angels with him."

CHAP. XLIX. 1773. June.

The letters had circulated privately in the Province for more than two months, when on Wednesday the second of June, Samuel Adams read them to the House in secret session. They were by no means among the worst which their authors had written, but they showed a thorough complicity with Bernard and the Commissioners of the Customs, to bring military sway into the Province, and to abridge Colonial liberties by the interposition of Parliament. The House, after a debate, voted by one hundred and one against five, "that the tendency and design of the letters was to subvert the Constitution of the Government, and to introduce arbitrary power into the Province." "I have never wrote any public or private letter that tends to subvert the Constitution," was Hutchinson's message the next day.

The House, on the fourth, sent him a transcript of their proceedings, with the date of his letters that were before them; and asked for copies of these and such others, as he should think proper to communicate. "If you desire copies with a view to make them public," answered Hutchinson after five days'

CHAP. XLIX. 1773. June. reflection, "the originals are more proper for that purpose, than the copies;" and he refused to communicate other letters, declaring that it had not been the design of them "to subvert the constitution of the Government, but, rather to preserve it entire."[1] Then conscious of guilt, he by the very next packet sent word to his confidential friend in London, to burn such of his letters as might raise a clamor, for, said he, "I have wrote what ought not to be made public.[2]

He had written against every part of the Constitution, the elective character of the Council, the annual choice of the Assembly, the New England organization of the towns; had advised and solicited the total dependence of the judiciary on the Crown, had hinted at making the experiment of declaring Martial Law, and of abrogating English liberty; had advised to the restraint of the commerce of Boston and the exclusion of the Province from the fisheries; had urged the immediate suppression of the Charter of Rhode Island; had for years "been begging for measures to maintain the supremacy of Parliament," by making the denial of that supremacy a capital felony; and all for the sake of places for his family and a salary and a pension for himself. To corrupt pure and good and free political institutions of a happy country, and infuse into its veins the slow poison of tyranny, is the highest crime against humanity. And how terribly was he punished! For

[1] Message of the Governor to the House of Representatives, 9 June, 1773; in the Representations, &c. 61.

[2] Hutchinson to Sir Francis Bernard, probably, 14 June, 1773.

CHAP. XLIX. 1773. June.

what is life without the esteem of one's fellow-men! Had he been but honest, how New England would have cherished his memory! Now his gray hairs, which should ever be kept purer than the ermine, were covered with shame; his ambition was defeated, and he suffered all the tortures of avarice trembling for the loss of place. It was Hancock,[1] who, taking advantage of the implied permission of Hutchinson, produced to the House copies of the letters, which were then published and scattered throughout New England and the Continent. A series of Resolves was adopted, expressing their true intent, and was followed by a Petition to the King, that he would remove Hutchinson and Oliver for ever from the Government. The Council in like manner, after a thorough analysis of the real intent of the correspondence, joined in the same prayer. So great unanimity had never been known.

Timid from nature, from age, and from an accusing conscience, Hutchinson bowed to the storm; and expressed his desire to resign. "I hope," he said, "I shall not be left destitute, to be insulted and triumphed over. I fall in the cause of Government; and whenever it shall be thought proper to supersede me, I hope for some appointment;"[2] and calumniating Franklin as one who wished to supplant him in the Government of Massachusetts, he himself made interest for Franklin's desirable office of Deputy Postmaster General.[3]

All the summer long the insidious letters, that

[1] Hutchinson to ——, 6 July, 7773.

[2] Hutchinson to —— [R. Jackson, probably,] 3 July, 1773.

[3] Hutchinson to Sir Francis Bernard, 29 June, 1773.

CHAP. XLIX. 1773. July.

had come to light, circulated through the Province, and were discussed by the single-minded country people during the week, as they made hay or gathered in the early harvest; on Sundays, the ministers discoursed on them, and poured out their hearts in prayers for the preservation of their precious inheritance of liberty. "We devote not only what little we have in the world," said the people of Pearsontown, "but even our lives to vindicate rights so dearly purchased by our ancestors."[1] The town of Abington became convinced that the boasted connection with Great Britain was "not worth a rush."[2] The natural right of mankind to improve the form of Government under which they live,[3] was inculcated even from the pulpit; and at the time when the Pope was abolishing the order of the Jesuits, some of the clergy of Boston predicted that "in fifteen years,"[4] the people of America would mould for themselves a new Constitution.

[1] Original Papers, 705.

[2] Abington to Boston, 29 July, 1773.

[3] Hutchinson to R. Jackson, 12 August, 1773.

[4] Hutchinson to Israel Mauduit, 23 August, 1773.

CHAPTER L.

THE BOSTON TEA PARTY.

AUGUST—DECEMBER, 1773.

CHAP. L. 1773. Aug.

THE East India Company, who were now by Act of Parliament authorized to export tea to America entirely duty free in England, applied to the Treasury in August for the necessary license. They were warned by Americans, that their adventure[1] would end in loss, and some difficulties occurred in details; but the scruples of the Company were overruled by Lord North, who answered peremptorily, "It is to no purpose making objections, for the King will have it so. The King means to try the question with America."[2]

Sept.

The time was short; the danger to Boston imminent; resistance at all hazards was the purpose of its Committee of Correspondence; violent resistance might become necessary; and to undertake it without a certainty of union would only bring ruin on the town and on the cause.

[1] Lee to S. Adams, 22 Dec. 1773.

[2] Almon's Anecdotes and Speeches of the Earl of Chatham, ch. xli. Compare also B. Franklin to his Son William Franklin, 14 July, 1773; Franklin's Writings, viii. 75.

CHAP. L. 1773. Sept.

A Congress, therefore, on "the plan of union proposed by Virginia," was the fixed purpose of Samuel Adams. He would have no delay; no waiting for increased strength; for, said he, "when our liberty is gone, history and experience will teach us, that an increase of inhabitants will be but an increase of slaves." Through the press he appealed to the Continent for a Congress in order to insist effectually upon such terms as would not admit of any other authority within the Colonies than that of their respective Legislatures.[1] It was not possible to join issue with the King more precisely.

The first difficulty to be overcome existed in Boston itself. Cushing, the Speaker, who had received a private letter from Dartmouth, and was lulled into confiding in "the noble and generous sentiments" of that Minister, advised that for the time the people should bear their grievances. "Our natural increase in wealth and population," said he, "will in a course of years settle this dispute in our favor; whereas, if we persist in denying the right of Parliament to legislate for us, they may think us extravagant in our demands, and there will be great danger of bringing on a rupture fatal to both countries." He thought the redress of grievances would more surely come "if these high points about the supreme authority of Parliament were to fall asleep."[2] Against this feeble advice, the Boston Committee of Correspondence aimed at the union of the Province, and "the Confederacy of the whole Continent of America." They

[1] In the Boston Gazette of Monday, 13 Sept. 1773; on second page, 1st and 2d column, 962, 2, 1, and 2. Hutchinson to Dartmouth, 23 Sept., 1773.

[2] T. Cushing to Arthur Lee, 20 Sept. 1773.

refused to waive the claim of right, which could only divide the Americans in sentiment and confuse their counsels. "What oppressions," they asked in their circular to all the other towns, "may we not expect in another seven years, if through a weak credulity, while the most arbitrary measures are still persisted n, we should be prevailed upon to submit our rights, as the patriotic Farmer expresses it, to the tender mercies of the Ministry? Watchfulness, unity and harmony are necessary to the salvation of ourselves and posterity from bondage. We have an animating confidence in the Supreme Disposer of events, that He will never suffer a sensible, brave, and virtuous People to be enslaved."[1] 1773. Sept.

Sure of Boston and its Committee, Samuel Adams next conciliated the favoring judgment of the patriot Hawley, whose influence in the Province was deservedly great, and who had shared with him the responsibility of the measures of the Assembly. "I submit to you my ideas at this time, because matters seem to me to be drawing to a crisis." Such were his words on the fourth, and the thirteenth of October. "The present Administration, even though the very good Lord Dartmouth is one of them, are as fixed as any of their predecessors in their resolution to carry their favorite point, an acknowledgment of the right of Parliament to make laws, binding us in all cases whatever. Some of our politicians would have the people believe, that Administration are disposed, or determined to have all the grievances which we complain of, redressed, if we will only be quiet; Oct.

[1] Committee of Correspondence for the Town of Boston, Circular Letter, 21 September, 1773. Journals of Committee, 234, 235.

CHAP. L. 1773. Oct.

but this would be a fatal delusion. If the King himself should make any concessions, or take any steps, contrary to the right of Parliament to tax us, he would be in danger of embroiling himself with the Ministry. Under the present prejudices, even the recalling an instruction to the Governor is not likely to be advised. The subject matter of our complaint is, not that a burden greater than our proportion was laid upon us by Parliament; such a complaint we might have made without questioning the authority of Parliament; but that the Parliament has assumed and exercised the power of taxing us. His Majesty, in his answer to our late Petitions, implies, that the Parliament is the Supreme Legislature; and that its authority over the Colonies is the Constitution.[1] All allow the Minister in the American Department to be a good man. The Great men in England have an opinion of us, as being a mightily religious people; and suppose that we shall place an entire confidence in a Minister of the same character. In fact, how many were filled with the most sanguine expectations, when they heard, that the good Lord Dartmouth was intrusted with a share in Administration. Yet without a greatness of mind, equal, perhaps superior to his goodness, it will be impossible for him singly to stem the torrent of corruption. This requires much more fortitude, than I yet believe he is possessed of. The safety of the Americans depends upon their pursuing their wise plan of union in principle and conduct."[2]

[1] Samuel Adams to Joseph Hawley, 4 October, 1773; in S. A. Welles, i. 437, 438.

[2] Samuel Adams to Joseph Hawley, 13 October, 1773; S. A. Welles, i. 439, 440.

Such were the thoughts which Samuel Adams unbosomed to his faithful fellow-laborer. The Press[1] which he directed, continued to demand an annual "Congress of American States to frame a Bill of Rights," or to "form an Indpendent State, an American Commonwealth." Union, then, Union, was the first, the last, the only hope for America. Massachusetts, where the overruling will of Samuel Adams swayed the feebler politicians, was thoroughly united. But that was not enough; "we must have a Convention of all the Colonies," he would say to his friends; and the measure was recognised by the royalists as "of all others the most likely to kindle a general flame."[2] His advice was confirmed by the concurrent opinion of Franklin,[3] to whose "greatness"[4] he had publicly paid a tribute. His influence[5] brought even Cushing to act as one of a select Committee with himself and Heath of Roxbury; and they sent forth a secret Circular, summoning all the Colonies to be prepared to assert their rights, when time and circumstances should give to their claim the

[1] Boston Gazette, 964, 2, 2; and 966, 1, 1

[2] Hutchinson to J. Pownall, 18 Oct. 1773.

[3] Franklin to T. Cushing, 7 July, 1773; Hutchinson to Dartmouth, 19 October, 1773.

[4] Samuel Adams in Boston Gazette, 963, 3, 1, 2. See Wedderburne's Speech, 111.

[5] "Others declare they will be altogether independent. Those of the latter opinion have for their head one of the members of Boston [Samuel Adams], who was the first person that openly and in any public assembly declared for a total independence, and who from a natural obstinacy of temper, and from many years' practice in politics, is probably as well qualified to excite the people to any extravagance in theory or practice as any man in America. * * * * Within these seven years his influence has been gradually increasing, until he has obtained such an ascendency as to direct the town of Boston and the House of Representatives, and consequently the Council, just as he pleases." Private Letter of Hutchinson to Lord Dartmouth, 9 Oct. 1773.

CHAP. L. 1773. Oct. surest prospect of success. "And when we consider," they said, "how one great event has hurried on after another, such a time may come and such circumstances take place, sooner than we are now aware of." They advised to contentment with no temporary relief. They explained that the King would certainly maintain the power of Parliament, to extort and to appropriate a tribute from the Colonies; that the connection between Great Britain and America should be broken, unless it could be perpetuated on the terms of equal liberty; that the necessary contest must be entered upon, while "the ideas of liberty" were strong in men's minds; and they closed with desiring each Colony to resist the designs of the English Ministry in allowing the East India Company to ship its teas to America.

That Company was already despatching its consignments simultaneously to Charleston, to Philadelphia, to New-York, and to Boston. The system gave universal offence, not only as an enforcement of the tax on tea, but also as an odious monopoly of trade.[1] Philadelphia, the largest town in the Colonies, began the work of prevention. Its inhabitants met on the eighteenth of October in great numbers at the State House, and in eight resolutions, denied the claim of Parliament to tax America; specially condemned the duty on tea; declared every one who should directly or indirectly countenance the attempt, an enemy to his country; and requested the agents of the East India Company to resign. The movement was so general and so com-

[1] Gen. Haldimand to Dartmouth, 28 Dec. 1773.

manding, that the agents, some cheerfully, others reluctantly, gave up their appointment.[1] Within a few days not one remained. CHAP. L. 1773. Oct.

South Carolina, by her spirit and perseverance, gave now, as she had ever done, evidence that her patriotism would be the support of Union. The Province was at that time in a state of just excitement at the arbitrary act of its Council in imprisoning Thomas Powell, the Publisher of the South Carolina Gazette, for an alleged contempt. The Council was a body in which the distinguished men of that Province scorned to accept a seat; its members were chiefly the Crown officers; and they held their places at the King's pleasure. Their power to imprison on their mere warrant was denied; the prisoner was taken before Rawlins Lowndes and another magistrate on a writ of habeas corpus, and was released.[2] The questions involved in the case were discussed with heat; but they did not divert attention from watching the expected tea ships.

Nov. The "ideas of Liberty" on which resistance was to be founded, had taken deep root in a soil which the Circular of Massachusetts did not reach. At this moment the people of Illinois were most opportunely sending their last message respecting their choice of a Government directly to Dartmouth himself. We have seen how vainly they had reasoned with Gage and Hillsborough for some of the privileges of self-direction. Here, as on other occasions,

[1] French Archives, Angleterre, 503. Garnier to D'Aiguillon, 17 December, 1773, incloses the documents. Gordon's Hist. of Pennsylvania, 481, 482. Hazard's Register of Pennsylvania, ii. 368.

[2] Bull to Dartmouth, 18 Sept. 1773. Drayton's Memoirs, i. 118.

CHAP. L. 1773. Nov.

Dartmouth, with the purest intentions, adopted the policy of his predecessor. He censured "the ideas of the inhabitants of the Illinois District with regard to a civil Constitution as very extravagant;" and rejected their proposition to take some part in the election of their rulers,[1] as "absurd and inadmissible." A plan of Government[2] was therefore prepared of great simplicity, leaving all power with the executive officers of the Crown, and Gage had been summoned to England to give advice on the administration of the Colonies, and especially on the mode of governing the West. It was on the fourth of November, that the fathers of the Commonwealth of Illinois, through their Agent Daniel Blouin, forwarded their indignant protest against the proposed form, which they rejected as "oppressive and absurd," "much worse than that of any of the French or even the Spanish Colonies." "Should a Government so evidently tyrannical be established," such was their language to the British Minister, "it could be of no long duration;"[3] there would exist "the necessity of its being abolished." The words were nobly uttered and were seasonable. The chord of liberty vibrated on the Illinois, and the sympathy of the western villages with freedom was an assurance that they too would join the great American family of Republics.

The issue was to be tried at Boston; its tea-ships were on the water; the Governor himself under the name of his sons was selected as one of the con-

[1] Dartmouth to Gage, 4 Nov. 1772; Gage to Dartmouth, 6 Jan. 1773; Dartmouth to Gage, 3 March, 1773.

[2] Sketch of Government, &c. &c. for Illinois.

[3] Daniel Blouin to Lord Dartmouth, 4 Nov. 1773.

signees; the moment for the decision was hastening on. In the night between the first and second of November, a knock was heard at the door of each one of the persons commissioned by the East India Company, and a summons left for them to appear without fail at Liberty Tree on the following Wednesday, at noon, to resign their commission;[1] printed notices were also posted up, desiring the freemen of Boston and the neighboring towns to meet at the same time and place as witnesses.[2]

On the appointed day, a large flag was hung out on the pole at Liberty Tree; the bells in the Meeting-houses were rung from eleven till noon. Adams, Hancock and Phillips, three of the four Representatives of the town of Boston, the Selectmen, and William Cooper the Town Clerk,[3] with about five hundred more, gathered round the spot. As the consignees did not make their appearance, the Assembly, appointing Molineux, Warren and others a Committee, marched into State Street to the warehouse of Richard Clarke, where all the consignees were assembled. Molineux presented himself for a parley.

"From whom are you a Committee?" asked Clarke. "From the whole people." "Who are the Committee?" "Nothing is now to be kept secret," replied Molineux; "I am one," and he named all the rest. "And what is your request?" Molineux read a paper, requiring the consignee to promise not to sell the teas, but to return them to London in the

[1] Order on Thomas and Elisha Hutchinson, 2 Nov. 1773.

[2] Handbills posted up the 2d and 3d of November, 1773.

[3] Abstract of the Correspondence from America, made by Thurlow and Wedderburn.

CHAP. L. 1773. Nov.

same bottoms in which they were shipped. "Will you comply?" "I shall have nothing to do with you," answered Clarke, roughly and peremptorily.[1] The same question was put to the other consignees, one by one; who each and all answered, "I cannot comply with your demand." Molineux then read another paper, containing a Resolve passed at Liberty Tree, that the consignees who should refuse to comply with the request of the people, were enemies to their country. Descending into the street, he made his report to the people. "Out with them, out with them," was the cry; but he dissuaded from violence.

On the fifth, Boston in a legal Town Meeting, with Hancock for Moderator, adopted the Philadelphia Resolves, and then sent to invite Thomas and Elisha Hutchinson to resign their appointment; but they and all the other consignees, declined to do so, in letters addressed to Hancock, the Moderator. At this, some spoke of "taking up arms," and the words were received with clapping of hands;[3] but the Meeting only voted the answers "daringly affrontive," and then dissolved itself.[4] On the same day the people of New-York assembled at the call of their Committee of Vigilance. Let the tea come free or not free of duty, they were absolutely resolved it should not be

[1] S. Cooper to B. Franklin, 17 Dec. 1773.

[2] Narrative prepared for Gov. Hutchinson by Mr. Benjamin Davis, merchant in Boston, 3 Nov. 1773. Narrative prepared for Gov. Hutchinson, by Joseph Green, Esq.

[3] Hutchinson to Dartmouth, 4 November, 1773.

[4] Hutchinson to ——, 24 Nov. 1773.

[5] Hutchinson to Dartmouth, 6 Nov. 1773; H. 150. Clarke, Faneuil, and Winslow to John Hancock, Moderator, &c., 5 Nov. 1773. Thos. Hutchinson Jr. to John Hancock, &c. &c., 5 Nov. 1773.

landed.[1] After a few days' reflection, the commissioners for that city, finding the discontent universal, threw up their places; yet the Sons of Liberty continued their watchfulness; a paper signed Legion, ordered the pilots not to bring tea-ships above the Hook; and "the Mohawks" were notified to be in readiness, in case of their arrival.[2]

This example renewed the hope, that a similar expedient might succeed in Boston. Members of the Council, of greatest influence, intimated that the best thing that could be done to quiet the people would be the refusal of the consignees to execute the trust; and the merchants, though they declared against mobs and violence, yet as generally wished that the teas might not be landed.[3]

On Wednesday the seventeenth, a ship which had made a short passage from London, brought an authentic account that the Boston tea-ships had sailed; the next day, there was once more a legal Town Meeting to entreat the consignees to resign. Upon their repeated refusal, the town passed no vote and uttered no opinion, but immediately broke up. The silence of the dissolution struck more terror than former menaces. The consignees saw that the legal Town Meeting had finished its work, and that henceforward they were in the hands of the Committee of Correspondence. On Monday the twenty-second, the Committees of Dorchester, Roxbury, Brookline, and Cambridge, met the Boston Committee by invitation

[1] Tryon to Dartmouth, 3 Nov. 1773; Hutchinson to Dartmouth, 4 Nov. 1773. Resolves of the Sons of Liberty of New-York, 29 Nov. 1773.

[2] Leake's Life of Lamb, 76, 77.

[3] Hutchinson to Dartmouth, 15 Nov. 1773.

[4] Hutchinson to Tryon, 21 Nov. 1773.

[5] Consignees' Petition to the Council, 18 Nov. 1773.

CHAP. L. 1773. Nov.

at the Selectmen's Chamber in Faneuil Hall. Their first question was: "Whether it be the mind of this Committee to use their joint influence to prevent the landing and sale of the teas exported from the East India Company?" And it passed in the affirmative unanimously.

A motion next prevailed unanimously for a letter to be sent by a joint Committee of the five towns to all the other towns in the Province. "Brethren," they wrote, "we are reduced to this dilemma, either to sit down quiet under this and every other burden, that our enemies shall see fit to lay upon us, or to rise up and resist this and every plan laid for our destruction as becomes wise freemen. In this extremity we earnestly request your advice."

The Governor in his alarm proposed to flee to "the Castle, where he might with safety to his person more freely give his sense of the criminality of the proceedings."[1] Dissuaded from so abject a display of pusillanimity, he yet never escaped the helpless irresolution of fear. "Nothing will satisfy the people, but reshipping the tea to London," said the Boston Selectmen to the consignees. "It is impracticable," they answered. "Nothing short of it," said the Selectmen, "will be satisfactory. Think, too, of the dreadful consequences that must in all probability ensue on its not being done." After much discussing they "absolutely promised that when the tea arrived, they would immediately hand in proposals to be laid before the town;"[2] negotiating with dishonesty of purpose, only to gain time.

[1] Hutchinson to a friend in Boston, 24 Nov. 1773.

[2] Attested Copy from the Selectmen's Minute book, of their conversation with some of the consignees.

But the true-hearted people were as vigilant as they were determined. The men of Cambridge assembled on the twenty-sixth, and after adopting the Philadelphia Resolves, "very unanimously" voted, "that as Boston was struggling for the liberties of their country, they could no longer stand idle spectators, but were ready on the shortest notice to join with it and other towns in any measure that might be thought proper, to deliver themselves and posterity from slavery."[1] The next day, the town of Charlestown assembled and showed such a spirit, that ever after its Committee was added to those who assumed the executive direction.

The combination was hardly finished, when on Sunday, the twenty-eighth of November, the ship Dartmouth appeared in Boston Harbor with one hundred and fourteen chests of the East India Company's tea. To keep the Sabbath strictly was the New England usage. But hours were precious; let the tea be entered, and it would be beyond the power of the consignee to send it back. The Selectmen held one meeting by day, and another in the evening, but they sought in vain for the consignees, who had taken sanctuary in the Castle.[2]

The Committee of Correspondence was more efficient. They met also on Sunday; and obtained from the Quaker Rotch, who owned the Dartmouth, a promise not to enter his ship till Tuesday;[3] and authorized Samuel Adams to invite the Committees of the five surrounding towns, Dorchester, Roxbury,

[1] Votes of the Town of Cambridge, Original Papers, 231. Journal of Committee of Correspondence, vi. 480.

[2] Attested Copy from the Minute Book of the Selectmen.

[3] Journals of the Committee, vi. 458; Information of Francis Rotch.

CHAP. L. 1773. Nov. Brookline, Cambridge, and Charlestown, with their own townsmen and those of Boston to hold a Mass Meeting the next morning. Faneuil Hall could not contain the people, that poured in on Monday. The concourse was the largest ever known. Adjourning to "the Old South" Meeting-house, Jonathan Williams did not fear to act as Moderator, nor Samuel Adams, Hancock, Young, Molineux, and Warren[1] to conduct the business of the meeting. On the motion of Samuel Adams, who entered fully into the question, the Assembly, composed of upwards of five thousand persons, resolved unanimously, that "the tea should be sent back to the place from whence it came at all events, and that no duty should be paid on it." "The only way to get rid of it" said Young, "is to throw it overboard."[2] The consignees asked for time to prepare their answer; and "out of great tenderness" the body postponed receiving it to the next morning. Meantime the owner and master of the ship were convented and forced to promise not to land the tea. A watch was also proposed. "I," said Hancock, "will be one of it, rather than that there should be none,"[3] and a party of twenty-five persons under the orders of Edward Proctor as its Captain, was appointed to guard the tea-ship during the night.

On the same day, the Council who had been solicited by the Governor and the consignees to assume the guardianship of the tea, coupled their refusal with a reference to the declared opinion of both branches of the General Court, that the tax upon it

[1] Francis Rotch's Information. Andrew Mackenzie's Information.
[2] Captain Hall's Information; [3] Frazier's Deposition.

by Parliament was unconstitutional.[1] The next morning the consignees jointly gave as their answer: "It is utterly out of our power to send back the teas; but we now declare to you our readiness to store them until we shall receive further directions from our constituents;"[2] that is, until they could notify the British Government. The wrath of the Meeting was kindling, when the Sheriff of Suffolk entered with a Proclamation from the Governor, "warning, exhorting and requiring them, and each of them there unlawfully assembled, forthwith to disperse, and to surcease all further unlawful proceedings at their utmost peril." The words were received with hisses, derision, and a unanimous vote not to disperse. "Will it be safe for the consignees to appear in the Meeting?" asked Copley; and all with one voice responded, that they might safely come and return; but they refused to appear. In the afternoon Rotch the owner, and Hall the master of the Dartmouth, yielding to an irresistible impulse, engaged that the tea should return as it came, without touching land or paying a duty. A similar promise was exacted of the owners of the other tea-ships whose arrival was daily expected. In this way "it was thought the matter would have ended."[3] "I should be willing to spend my fortune and life itself in so good a cause,"[4] said Hancock, and this sentiment was general; they all voted "to carry their Resolutions into effect at the risk of their lives and property."

[1] Hutchinson to Tryon, 1 Dec. 1773.

[2] Thomas and Elisha Hutchinson &c. to John Scollay, 29 Nov. 1773.

[3] S. Cooper to B. Franklin, 17 Dec. 1773.

[4] Hutchinson to ——, 3 Dec. 1773.

CHAP. L. 1773. Nov. Every ship owner was forbidden on pain of being deemed an enemy to the country to import or bring as freight any tea from Great Britain, till the unrighteous Act taxing it should be repealed, and this vote was printed and sent to every sea-port in the Province, and to England.

Six persons were chosen as post-riders, to give due notice to the country towns of any attempt to land the tea by force, and the Committee of Correspondence, as the executive organ of the Meeting, took care that a military watch was regularly kept up by volunteers armed with muskets and bayonets, who at every half hour in the night regularly passed the word "all is well," like sentinels in a garrison. Had they been molested by night, the tolling of the bells would have been the signal for a general uprising. An account of all that had been done, was sent into every town in the Province.

Dec. The ships after landing the rest of their cargo, could neither be cleared in Boston with the tea on board, nor be entered in England, and on the twentieth day from their arrival would be liable to seizure. "They find themselves," said Hutchinson, "involved in invincible difficulties." Meantime in private letters he advised to separate Boston from the rest of the Province; and to commence criminal prosecutions against its patriot sons.[1]

The spirit of the people rose with the emergency. Two more tea-ships which arrived were directed to anchor by the side of the Dartmouth at Griffin's wharf, that one guard might serve for all. The peo-

[1] Hutchinson to Sir Francis Bernard, 3 Dec. 1773; Compare too Hutchinson to Mauduit, 7 Dec. 1773.

ple of Roxbury on the third of December, voted that they were bound by duty to themselves and posterity to join with Boston and other sister towns, to preserve inviolate the liberties handed down by their ancestors. The next day the men of Charlestown, as if foreseeing that their town was destined to be a holocaust, declared themselves ready to risk their lives and fortunes. On Sunday, the fifth, the Committee of Correspondence wrote to Portsmouth in New Hampshire, to Providence, Bristol, and Newport in Rhode Island, for advice and co-operation. On the sixth, they entreat New-York, through MacDougall and Sears, Philadelphia, through Mifflin and Clymer, to insure success by "a harmony of sentiment and concurrence in action."[1] As for Boston itself, the twenty days are fast running out; the consignees conspire with the Revenue officers to throw on the owner and master of the Dartmouth the whole burden of landing the tea, and will neither agree to receive it, nor give up their bill of lading, nor pay the freight.[2] Every movement was duly reported,[3] and "the town became as furious as in the time of the Stamp Act."[4]

CHAP. L. 1773. Dec.

On the ninth, there was a vast gathering at Newburyport, of the inhabitants of that and the neighboring towns, and none dissenting, they agreed to assist Boston, even at the hazard of their lives. "This is not a piece of parade;" they say, "but if an occasion should offer, a goodly number from among us will hasten to join you."[5]

[1] Letter to MacDougall and Sears, 6 Dec. 1773.

[2] Questions proposed by Captain Hall and his owner, and Answers given by the tea consignees.

[3] Journal of the Com. of Corr. for 7 Dec. vi. 461.

[4] Hutchinson to Mauduit, 7 Dec. 1773.

[5] Original Papers, 670.

CHAP. L. 1773. Dec.

On Saturday the eleventh, Rotch, the owner of the Dartmouth, is summoned before the Boston Committee with Samuel Adams in the Chair; and asked why he has not kept his engagement, to take his vessel and the tea back to London, within twenty days of its arrival. He pleaded that it was out of his power. "The ship must go," was the answer; "the people of Boston and the neighboring towns, absolutely require and expect it;" and they bade him ask for a clearance and pass, with proper witnesses of his demand. "Were it mine," said a leading merchant, "I would certainly send it back."[1] Hutchinson acquainted Admiral Montagu with what was passing; on which the Active and the Kingfisher, though they had been laid up for the winter, were sent to guard the passages out of the harbor. At the same time orders were given by the Governor to load guns at the Castle, so that no vessel, except coasters, might go to sea without a permit. He had no thought of what was to happen; the wealth of Hancock, Phillips, Rowe, Dennie, and so many other men of property, seemed to him a security against violence;[2] and he flattered himself,[3] that he had increased the perplexities of the Committee."

The decisive day draws nearer and nearer; on the morning of Monday, the thirteenth, the Committees of the five towns are at Faneuil Hall, with that of Boston. Now that danger was really at hand, the men of the little town of Malden offered their

[1] Journal of the Committee of Correspondence, vi. 463. Rotch's Information before the Privy Council.

[2] Hutchinson to Mauduit, Dec. 1773; to ———, 30 Dec. 1773; to Sir F. Bernard, 1 Jan. 1774.

[3] Hutchinson to Lord Dartmouth, 14 Dec. 1773; Boston Gazette, 13 Dec. 1773.

CHAP. L. 1773. Dec.

blood and their treasure; for that which they once esteemed the Mother Country, had lost the tenderness of a parent, and become their great oppressor.[1] —"We trust in God," wrote the men of Lexington, "that should the state of our affairs require it, we shall be ready to sacrifice our estates and every thing dear in life, yea, and life itself, in support of the common cause."[2]—Whole towns in Worcester County were on tiptoe to come down.[3] "Go on, as you have begun," wrote the Committee of Leicester on the fourteenth; "and do not suffer any of the teas already come or coming to be landed, or pay one farthing of duty. You may depend on our aid and assistance when needed."[4]

The line of policy adopted was, if possible, to get the tea carried back to London uninjured in the vessel in which it came. A Meeting of the people on Tuesday afternoon directed and as it were "compelled" Rotch, the owner of the Dartmouth, to apply for a clearance. He did so, accompanied by Kent, Samuel Adams, and eight others as witnesses. The Collector was at his lodgings, and refused to answer till the next morning; the Assemblage, on their part, adjourned to Thursday the sixteenth, the last of the twenty days, before it would become legal for the Revenue officers to take possession of the ship, and so land the teas at the Castle. In the evening, the Boston Committee finished their preparatory Meetings. After their consultation on Monday with the Committee of the five towns, they had been together that day and the next, both morning

[1] Journal of C. C. 501.
[2] Original Papers, 495.
[3] J. Adams: Works, ix. 335.
[4] Journal of C. C. vii. 603.

CHAP. L. 1773. Dec. and evening; but during the long and anxious period, their Journal has only this entry: "No business transacted, matter of record."[1]

At ten o'clock on the fifteenth, Rotch was escorted by his witnesses to the Custom-house, where the Collector and Comptroller unequivocally and finally refused to grant his ship a clearance, till it should be discharged of the teas.

Hutchinson began to clutch at victory; for, said he, it is notorious the ship cannot pass the Castle without a permit from me, and that I shall refuse. On that day, the people of Fitchburg pledged their word "never to be wanting according to their small ability;" for "they had indeed an ambition to be known to the world and to posterity as friends to liberty." The men of Gloucester also expressed their joy at Boston's glorious opposition, cried with one voice that "no tea subject to a duty should be landed in their town," and held themselves ready for the last appeal.

The morning of Thursday the sixteenth of December, 1773, dawned upon Boston, a day by far the most momentous in its annals. Beware, little town; count the cost, and know well, if you dare defy the wrath of Great Britain, and if you love exile and poverty and death rather than submission. The town of Portsmouth held its Meeting on that morning, and, with six only protesting, its people adopted the principles of Philadelphia, appointed their Committee of Correspondence, and resolved to make common cause with the Colonies. At ten

[1] Journal of Committee of Correspondence, vi. 463, 464.

o'clock the people of Boston with at least two thousand men from the country, assembled in the Old South. A report was made that Rotch had been refused a clearance from the Collector. "Then," said they to him, "protest immediately against the Custom-house, and apply to the Governor for his pass, so that your vessel may this very day proceed on her voyage for London."

The Governor had stolen away to his country house at Milton. Bidding Rotch make all haste, the Meeting adjourned to three in the afternoon. At that hour Rotch had not returned. It was incidentally voted, as other towns had already done, to abstain totally from the use of tea; and every town was advised to appoint its Committee of inspection, to prevent the detested tea from coming within any of them. Then, since the Governor might refuse his pass, the momentous question recurred, "Whether it be the sense and determination of this body to abide by their former Resolutions with respect to the not suffering the tea to be landed." On this question Samuel Adams and Young[1] addressed the Meeting, which was become far the most numerous ever held in Boston, embracing seven thousand men.[2] There was among them a patriot of fervid feeling; passionately devoted to the liberty of his country; still young; his eye bright, his cheek glowing with hectic fever. He knew that his strength was ebbing. The work of vindicating American freedom must be done soon, or he will be no party to the great achievement. He rises, but it is to restrain, and

[1] Dr. Wm. Tyler's Deposition.

[2] S. Adams to A. Lee, 21 Dec. 1773.

CHAP. L. 1773. Dec.

being truly brave and truly resolved, he speaks the language of moderation: "Shouts and hosannas will not terminate the trials of this day, nor popular resolves, harangues, and acclamations vanquish our foes. We must be grossly ignorant of the value of the prize for which we contend, of the power combined against us, of the inveterate malice and insatiable revenge which actuate our enemies, public and private, abroad and in our bosom, if we hope that we shall end this controversy without the sharpest conflicts. Let us consider the issue, before we advance to those measures, which must bring on the most trying and terrible struggle this country ever saw." Thus spoke the younger Quincy. "Now that the hand is to the plough," said others, "there must be no looking back,"[1] and the whole Assembly of seven thousand voted unanimously that the tea should not be landed.

It had been dark for more than an hour. The Church in which they met was dimly lighted; when at a quarter before six Rotch appeared, and satisfied the people by relating that the Governor had refused him a pass, because his ship was not properly cleared. As soon as he had finished his report, Samuel Adams rose and gave the word: "This Meeting can do nothing more to save the country."[2] On the instant a shout was heard at the porch; the war-whoop resounded; a body of men, forty or fifty[3] in number, disguised as Indians, passed by the door; and encouraged by Samuel Adams, Hancock and others, repaired to Griffin's wharf, posted guards to

[1] William Turner's Deposition.
[2] Francis Rotch's Information before the Privy Council.
[3] J. D. Whitworth's Deposition.

1773. Dec.

prevent the intrusion of spies, took possession of the three tea-ships, and in about three hours, three hundred and forty chests of tea, being the whole quantity that had been imported, were emptied into the bay without the least injury to other property. "All things were conducted with great order, decency, and perfect submission to government."[1] The people around, as they looked on, were so still, that the noise of breaking open the tea-chests[2] was plainly heard. A delay of a few hours would have placed the tea under the protection of the Admiral at the Castle. After the work was done, the town became as still and calm, as if it had been holy time. The men from the country that very night carried back the great news to their villages.

The next morning the Committee of Correspondence appointed Samuel Adams and four others, to draw up a declaration of what had been done. They sent Paul Revere as express with the information to New-York and Philadelphia.

The height of joy that sparkled in the eyes and animated the countenances and the hearts of the patriots as they met one another, is unimaginable.[3] The Governor, meantime, was consulting his books and his lawyers to make out, that the Resolves of the meeting were treasonable. Threats were muttered of arrests; of executions; of transportation of the accused to England; while the Committee of Correspondence pledged themselves to support and vindicate each other and all persons who had shared in their effort. The country was united with the town,

[1] John Adams to James Warren, 17 Dec. 1773.

[2] Hugh Williamson's Deposition.

[3] S. Adams to A. Lee, 21 Dec.

CHAP. L. 1773. Dec.

and the Colonies with one another more firmly than ever.[1] The Philadelphians unanimously approved what Boston had done.[2] New-York,[3] all impatient at the winds which had driven its tea-ship off the coast, was resolved on following the example.

In South Carolina the ship with two hundred and fifty-seven chests of tea, arrived on the second of December; the spirit of opposition ran very high; but the consignees were persuaded to resign, so that though the Collector after the twentieth day seized the dutiable article, there was no one to vend it or to pay the duty, and it perished in the cellars where it was stored.

Late on Saturday, the twenty-fifth, news reached Philadelphia, that its tea-ship was at Chester. It was met four miles below the town, where it came to anchor. On Monday, at an hour's notice, five thousand men collected in a Town Meeting; at their instance, the consignee who came as passenger resigned; and the Captain agreed to take his ship and cargo directly back to London; and to sail the very next day.[4] "The Ministry had chosen the most effectual measures to unite the Colonies. The Boston Committee were already in close correspondence with the other New England Colonies, with New-York and Pennsylvania. Old jealousies were removed and perfect harmony subsisted between all."[5] "The heart of the King was hardened against them like that of Pha-

[1] Cooper to Franklin, 17 Dec. 1773; S. Adams to James Warren, 28 Dec. 1773.

[2] Clymer and Mifflin to S. Adams.

[3] Haldimand to Dartmouth, 28 Dec. 1773.

[4] Geo. Clymer and Thomas Mifflin to Samuel Adams, 27 Dec. 1773.

[5] S. Adams to James Warren, 28 Dec. 1773.

raoh;"[1] and none believed he would relent. Union, therefore, was the cry; a union which should reach "from Florida to the icy plains" of Canada. "No time is to be lost," said the Boston Press; "a Congress or a Meeting of the American States is indispensable; and what the people wills, shall be effected."[2] Samuel Adams was in his glory.[3] He had led Boston to be foremost in duty, and cheerfully offer itself as a sacrifice for the liberties of mankind. CHAP. L. 1773. Dec.

[1] Compare A. Lee to S. Adams, Dec. 1773.

[2] Boston Gazette, 27 Dec. 1773; 977, 1, 2 and 3.

[3] Hutchinson to ——, 30 Dec. 1773.

CHAPTER LI.

THE KING IN COUNCIL INSULTS THE GREAT AMERICAN PLEBEIAN.

DECEMBER, 1773—FEBRUARY, 1774.

CHAP. LI. 1773. Dec.

THE just man covered with the opprobrium of crime and meriting all the honors of virtue, is the sublimest spectacle that can appear on earth. Against Franklin were arrayed the Court, the Ministry, the Parliament, and an all-pervading social influence; but he only assumed a firmer demeanor and a loftier tone. On delivering to Lord Dartmouth the Address to the King for the removal of Hutchinson and Oliver, he gave assurances, that the people of Massachusetts aimed at no novelties; that "having lately discovered the authors of their grievances to be some of their own people, their resentment against Britain was thence much abated." The Secretary promised at once to lay the Petition before the King, and expressed his "pleasure" at the communication as well as his "earnest hope" for the restoration "of the most perfect tranquillity and happiness." It had been the unquestionable duty of the Agent of the Province to communi-

CHAP. LI. 1773. Dec.

cate proof that Hutchinson and Oliver were conspiring against its Constitution; to bring censure on the act, it was necessary to raise a belief that the evidence had been surreptitiously obtained. To that end Hutchinson was unwearied in his entreaties; but William Whately the Banker, who was his brother's xecutor, was persuaded that the letters in question had never been in his hands, and refused to cast imputations on any one.

The newspaper Press was therefore employed to spread a rumor that they had been dishonestly obtained through John Temple. The anonymous calumny which was attributed to Bernard, Knox, and Mauduit, was denied by one calling himself "a Member of Parliament," who also truly affirmed, that the letters which were sent to Boston, had never been in the executor's hands. Again the Press declared, what was also true, that Whately, the executor, had submitted files of his brother's letters to Temple's examination, who, it was insinuated, had seized the opportunity to purloin them. Temple repelled the charge instantly and successfully.[1] Whately, the executor, never made a suggestion that the letters had been taken away by Temple, and always believed the contrary;[2] but swayed not so much by the solicitations of Hutchinson and Mauduit, as by his sudden appointment as a banker to the Treasury, he published an evasive card, in which he did not relieve Temple from the implication.

[1] J. Temple to the Public Advertiser, 8 Dec. 1773; and for further reiterated denials, see Almon's Biog. Anec. 238, 243, 245, 246, 249, 250, 251. 252. If he had gone for letters to perfect files, he might have found very much better ones for his purpose.

[2] Hutchinson's History, iii. 416, and 418.

CHAP. LI. 1773. Dec. A duel followed between Temple and Whately, without witnesses; then newspaper altercations on the incidents of the meeting; till another duel seemed likely to ensue. Cushing, the timid Speaker of the Massachusetts Assembly, to whom the letters had been officially transmitted, begged that he might not be known as having received them, lest it should be "a damage" to him; the Member of Parliament, who had had them in his possession, never permitted himself to be named; Temple, who risked offices producing a thousand pounds a year, publicly denied "any concern in procuring or transmitting them." To prevent bloodshed, Franklin assumed the undivided responsibility, from which every one else was disposed to shrink. "I," said he, "I alone am the person who obtained and transmitted to Boston the letters in question."[1] His ingenuousness exposed him to "unmerited abuse" in every company and in every newspaper, and gave his enemies an opening to reject publicly the Petition; which otherwise would have been dismissed without parade.[2]

1774. Jan. On Tuesday the eleventh of January, Franklin for Massachusetts, and Mauduit, with Wedderburn, for Hutchinson and Oliver, appeared before the Privy Council. "I thought," said Franklin, "that this had been a matter of politics, and not of law, and have not brought any counsel." The hearing was, therefore, adjourned to Saturday the twenty-ninth. Meantime the Ministry and the courtiers expressed their

[1] B. Franklin, Agent for the House of Representation of the Massachusetts Bay, to the Printers of the Public Advertiser. The faultless poet of Rome would have approved this act of Franklin. "Me, me, adsum qui feci, in me convertite ferrum."

[2] Annual Register for 1774, page 86; "unmerited abuse."

rage against him; and talked of his dismissal from office, of his arrest,[1] and imprisonment at Newgate; of a search among his papers for proofs of Treason; while Wedderburn openly professed the intention to inveigh personally against him. He was also harassed with a subpœna from the Chancellor, to attend his Court at the suit of William Whately, respecting the letters.

The public sentiment was, moreover, embittered by accounts that the Americans would not suffer the landing of the tea. The zeal of the Colonists was unabated. On New-Year's eve, a half chest of tea, picked up in Roxbury, was burned on Boston Common; on the twentieth, three barrels of Bohea tea were burned in State Street. On the twenty-fifth John Malcolm, a North Briton, who had been aid to Governor Tryon in his war against the Regulators, and was now a preventive officer in the Customs, having indiscreetly provoked the populace, was seized, tarred and feathered, and paraded under the gallows.

The General Court also assembled, full of a determination to compel the Judges to refuse the salaries proffered by the King. Enough of the prevalence of this spirit was known in England, to raise a greater clamor against the Americans, than had ever before existed. Hypocrites, traitors, rebels and villains were the softest epithets applied to them;[2] and some menaced war, and would have given full scope to sanguinary rancor. On the twenty-seventh, the

[1] Franklin to Cushing, 15 Feb. 1774; in Works iv. 108, confirmed by the letter of Dartmouth to Gen. Gage, of 3 June, 1774.

[2] Nicholas Ray to W. S. Johnson, London, 4 April, 1774.

CHAP. LI. 1774. Jan. Government received official information,[1] that the people of Boston had thrown the tea overboard, and this event swelled the anger against the Americans.

In this state of public feeling, Franklin on the twenty-ninth, assisted by Dunning and John Lee, came before the Privy Council, to advocate the removal of Hutchinson and Oliver, in whose behalf appeared Israel Mauduit, the old adviser of the Stamp Tax; and Wedderburn the Solicitor General. It was a day of great expectation. Thirty-five Lords of the Council were present; a larger number than had ever attended a hearing; and the room was filled with a crowded audience, among whom were Priestley, Jeremy Bentham and Edmund Burke.

The Petition and accompanying papers having been read, Dunning asked on the part of his clients the reason of his being ordered to attend.[2] "No cause," said he, "is instituted; nor do we think advocates necessary; nor are they demanded on the part of the Colony. The Petition is not in the nature of accusation, but of advice and request. It is an Address to the King's wisdom, not an application for criminal justice; when referred to the Council, it is a matter for political prudence, not for judicial determination. The matter, therefore, rests wholly in your Lordships' opinion of the propriety or impropriety of continuing persons in authority, who are represented by legal bodies, competent to such representation, as having (whether on sufficient or insufficient grounds) entirely forfeited the confidence of the Assemblies

[1] Hutchinson to Dartmouth, 17 Dec. 1773, received 27 January, 1774.

[2] Shelburne to Chatham, 3 Feb. 1774.

whom they were to act with, and of the people whom they were to govern. The resolutions on which that representation is founded, lie before your Lordships, together with the letters from which they arose.

"If your Lordships should think that these actions which appear to the Colony Representative to be faulty, ought in other places to appear meritorious, the Petition has not desired that the parties should be punished as criminals for these actions of supposed merit; nor even that they may not be rewarded. It only requests that these gentlemen may be removed to places where such merits are better understood, and such rewards may be more approved."[1] He spoke well, and was seconded by Lee.[2]

The question as presented by Dunning, was already decided in favor of the Petitioners; it was the universal opinion that Hutchinson ought to be superseded. Wedderburn changed the issue, as if Franklin were on trial; and in a speech which was a continued tissue of falsehood and ribaldry, turned his invective against the Petitioners and their Messenger. Of all men, Franklin was the most important in any attempt at conciliation. He was the Agent of the two great Colonies of Massachusetts and Pennsylvania, and also of New Jersey and Georgia; was the friend of Edmund Burke, who was Agent for New-York. All the troubles in British colonial policy had grown out of the neglect of his advice, and there was no one who could have medi-

[1] Report of the speech of the Counsel of the Province, in a letter from Edmund Burke, the Agent of the Colony of New-York to the Committee of Correspondence of the New-York Assembly.

[2] Burke to Rockingham, 1 or 2 of Feb. 1774; in Corr. i. 453.

CHAP. LI. 1774. Jan.

ated like him between the Metropolis and the Americans. He was now thrice venerable, from genius, fame in the world of science, and age, being already nearly threescore years and ten. This man Wedderburn, turning from the real question, employed all the cunning powers of distortion and misrepresentation to abuse. With an absurdity of application which the Lords of the Privy Council were too much prejudiced to observe, he drew a parallel between Boston and Capri, Hutchinson and Sejanus, the humble Petition of the Massachusetts Assembly, and a verbose and grand epistle of the Emperor Tiberius. Franklin, whose character was most benign, and who from obvious motives of mercy had assumed the sole responsibility of obtaining the letters, he described as a person of the most deliberate malevolence, realizing in life what poetic fiction only had penned for the breast of a bloody African. The speech of Hutchinson, challenging a discussion of the Supremacy of Parliament, had been not only condemned by public opinion in England, but disapproved by the Secretary of State; Wedderburn pronounced it "a masterly one," which had "stunned the faction." Franklin, for twenty years had exerted his wonderful powers as the great conciliator, had never once employed the American press to alarm the American people, but had sought to prevent the Parliamentary taxation of America, by private and successful remonstrance during the time of the Pelhams; by seasonable remonstrance with Grenville against the Stamp Act; by honest and true answers to the inquiries of the House of Commons; by the best of advice to Shelburne. When sycophants sought by flattery to mislead the Minister for America, he had given correct information and safe counsel to the Ministry of Grafton, and repeated it emphatically, and in writing to the Ministry of North; but Wedderburn stigmatized this wise and hearty lover of both countries as "a true incendiary." The letters which had been written by public men in public offices on public affairs, to one who formed an integral part of the body that had been declared to possess absolute power over America, and which had been written for the purpose of producing a tyrannical exercise of that absolute power, he called private. Hutchinson had solicited the place held by Franklin, from which Franklin was to be dismissed; this fact was suppressed, and the wanton falsehood substituted, that Franklin had desired the Governor's office, and had basely planned "his rival's overthrow." Franklin had inclosed the letters officially to the Speaker of the Massachusetts Assembly, without a single injunction of secrecy with regard to the sender; Wedderburn maintained that they were sent anonymously and secretly; and by an argument founded on a misstatement, but which he put forward as irrefragable, he pretended to convict Franklin of having obtained the letters by fraudulent and corrupt means, or of having stolen them from the person who stole them.[1]

CHAP. LI. 1774. Jan.

The Lords of Council as he spoke, cheered him on by their laughter; and the cry of "Hear him, Hear him," burst repeatedly from a body, which professed to be sitting in judgment as the highest Court of Appeal for the Colonies, and yet encouraged the advocate of one of the parties to insult a public envoy,

[1] Wm. Temple's, Franklin, ii. 401.

CHAP. LI. 1774. Jan. present only as the person delivering the Petition of a great and loyal Colony. Meantime the gray-haired Franklin, whom Kant, the noblest philosopher of that age, had called the modern Prometheus, stood conspicuously erect, confronting his vilifier and the Privy Council, compelled to listen while calumny, in the service of lawless force, aimed a death-blow at his honor, and his virtues called on God and man to see how unjustly he suffered.

The reply of Dunning, who was very ill and was fatigued by standing so long,[1] could scarcely be heard; and that of Lee produced no impression. There was but one place in England where fit reparation could be made; and there was but one man who had the eloquence and the courage and the weight of character to effect the atonement. For the present, Franklin must rely on the approval of the monitor within his own breast. "I have never been so sensible of the power of a good conscience," said he to Priestly; "for if I had not considered the thing for which I have been so much insulted, as one of the best actions of my life, and what I should certainly do again in the same circumstances, I could not have supported it." But it was not to him, it was to the people of Massachusetts, and to New England, and to all America, that the insult was offered through their Agent.

Franklin and Wedderburn parted; the one to spread the celestial fire of freedom among men; to

[1] On this hearing, besides the newspaper reports of the day, the accounts by witnesses are: The pamphlet of Mauduit and Wedderburn; Franklin's Report as Agent to his Constituents; Account left by Franklin; Edmund Burke as Agent of New-York to his Constituents, Feb. 1774; Same to Rockingham; Same to Charles Lee; Dartmouth to Hutchinson; Arthur Lee to Samuel Adams, 31 January, 1774; Letter of Priestly, 10 Nov. 1802; Observations of Edward Bancroft.

make his name a cherished household word in every nation of Europe; and in the beautiful language of Washington, "to be venerated for benevolence, to be admired for talents, to be esteemed for patriotism, to be beloved for philanthropy;" the other childless, though twice wedded, unbeloved, wrangling with the patron who had impeached his veracity, busy only in "getting every thing he could"[1] in the way of titles and riches, as the wages of corruption Franklin when he died, had nations for his mourners, and the great and the good throughout the world as his eulogists; when Wedderburn died, there was no man to mourn; no senate spoke his praise; no poet embalmed his memory; and his King, hearing that he was certainly dead, said only, "He has not left a greater knave behind him in my dominions."[2] The report of the Lords which had been prepared beforehand, was immediately signed; and "they went away, almost ready to throw up their hats for joy, as if by the vehement Philippic against the hoary-headed Franklin, they had obtained a triumph."[3]

And who were the Lords of the Council, that thus thought to mark and brand the noblest representative of free labor who for many a year had earned his daily bread as apprentice, journeyman, or mechanic, and "knew the heart of the working man,"[4] and felt for the people of whom he remained one? If they who upon that occasion pretended to sit in judgment had never come into being, whom among them all would humanity have missed? But how would it have suffered if Franklin had not lived!

[1] Geo. III. in Campbell.
[2] Brougham on Loughborough.
[3] C. J. Fox's Speeches, vi. 527.
[4] Kingsley's Alton Locke.

CHAP. LI. 1774. Jan. The men in power who on that day sought to rob Franklin, of his good name, wounded him on the next in his fortunes,[1] by turning him out of his place in the British American Post Office. That institution had yielded no revenue till he organized it, and yielded none after his dismissal.

Feb. On Tuesday the first of February, the Earl of Buckinghamshire, who had attended the Privy Council, went to the House of Lords, "to put the Ministry in mind that he was to be bought by private contract."[2] Moving for the Boston Correspondence, he said, "The question is no longer about the liberty of North America, but whether we are to be free or slaves to our Colonies. Franklin is here, not as the Agent of a Province, but as an Ambassador from the States of America. His embassy to us is like nothing but that sent by Louis XIV. to the Republic of Genoa, commanding the doge to come and appease the Grand Monarch, by prostrating himself at Versailles."—"Such language is wild," replied the Earl of Stair. "Humanity, commercial policy, and the public necessities dictate a very contrary one."—"I would not throw cold water on the noble Lord's zeal," said the good Lord Dartmouth; as he made the request that further despatches might be waited for.

Superior to injury, Franklin, or as Rockingham called him, the "magnanimous" "old man,"[3] still sought for conciliation, and seizing the moment when he was sure of all sympathies, he wrote to his constituents to begin the work, by making compensation to

[1] Mignet's Life of Franklin.

[2] The phrase is Edmund Burke's, Burke to Rockingham, Tuesday night, February 2, 1774; Burke's Corr. i. 452. [Tuesday was Feb. 1.]

[3] Albemarle, ii. 302.

CHAP. LI. 1774. Feb.

the East India Company before any compulsive measures were thought of.[1] But events were to proceed as they had been ordered. Various measures were talked of for altering the Constitution of the Government in Massachusetts, and for prosecuting individuals. The opinion in town was very general, that America would submit; that Government was taken by surprise when they repealed the Stamp Act, and that all might be recovered.[2]

The King was obstinate, had no one near him to explain the true state of things in America, and admitted no misgivings except for not having sooner enforced the claims of authority. On the fourth day of February, he consulted the American Commander-in-Chief who had recently returned from New-York. "I am willing to go back at a day's notice," said Gage, "if coercive measures are adopted. They will be lions, while we are lambs; but if we take the resolute part, they will undoubtedly prove very meek. Four regiments sent to Boston will be sufficient to prevent any disturbance." The King received these opinions as certainly true; and wished their adoption. He would enforce the claim of authority at all hazards.[3] "All men," said he, "now feel, that the fatal compliance in 1766 has increased the pretensions of the Americans to absolute independence."[4] In the letters of Hutchinson, he saw nothing to which the least exception could be taken;[5] and condemned the Address of Massachusetts, of

[1] Franklin to Thomas Cushing, Samuel Adams, John Hancock, William Phillips. MS. letter in my possession.

[2] Shelburne to Chatham, Chat. Corr. iv. 324.

[3] Dartmouth to Haldimand, 5 Feb. 1774.

[4] From letters communicated to me by Lady Charlotte Lindsay.

[5] Hutchinson's Diary.

CHAP. LI. which every word was true, as the production of "falsehood and malevolence."

1774. Feb. Accordingly on the seventh day of February, in the Court at St. James's, the report of the Privy Council was read, embodying the vile insinuations of Wedderburn; and the Petition which Franklin had presented, and which expressed the exact truth, was described as formed on false allegations, and was dismissed by the King as "groundless, vexatious and scandalous."

CHAPTER LII.

THE CRISIS.

FEBRUARY—MAY, 1774.

CHAP. LII. 1774. Feb.

THE passions of the British Ministry were encouraged by the British people, who resented the denial of its supremacy and made the cause of Parliament its own.[1] The current ran against the Americans; and the Ministry, overruling the lingering scruples of Dartmouth and Lord North, decided that there existed a rebellion which required not conciliation but coercion. Inquiries were made with the object of enabling the King to proceed in "England against the ringleaders," and inflict on them immediate and exemplary punishment. But after laborious examinations before the Privy Council, and the close attention of Thurlow and Wedderburn, it appeared that British law and the British Constitution set bounds to the anger of the Government, which gave the first evidence of its weakness by acknowledging a want of power to wreak its will.

During the delay attending an appeal to Parlia-

[1] Edmund Burke in VanSchaack's VanSchaack, 19, and Vardell, 26.

CHAP. LII. 1774. Feb.

ment, pains were taken to quiet the Bourbon powers. The Secretary of State would speak with the French Minister of nothing but harmony. "Never," said he in like manner to Pignatelli,[1] the Representative of Spain, "never was the union between Versailles, Madrid and London, so solid; I see nothing that can shake it." Yet the old distrust lurked under the pretended confidence.[2]

The Government at the time encountered no formidable opposition. One day in February, Charles James Fox, who was of the Treasury Board, severely censured Lord North for want of decision and courage. The King was "greatly incensed at his presumption." "That young man," said the King, "has so thoroughly cast off every principle of common honor and honesty, that he must become as contemptible as he is odious." He was therefore dismissed from office at this critical moment in American affairs; and being unconnected, he was left free to follow his own bold and generous impulses. He was soon "to discover powers for regular debate, which neither his friends hoped nor his enemies dreaded." He could not only take the vast compass of a great question, but with singular and unfailing sagacity, could detect the decisive point on which it turned. In his habits, he delighted in excess; he squandered recklessly at the gaming table, what his father had taken anxious years to hoard; but with all his vices and extravagance, "perhaps no human being was ever more perfectly exempt from the taint of malevolence, vanity, or falsehood." Disinterested

[1] Garnier to the Duke D'Aiguillon, 4 Feb. 1774.

[2] Rochfort to Stormont, 18 March, 1774.

observers already predicted, that he would one day be classed among the greatest statesmen of his country.[1]

The cause of liberty obtained in him a friend who was independent of party allegiance and traditions, just at the time when the passion for ruling America by the central authority was producing anarchy in the Colonies. In South Carolina, whose sons esteemed themselves disfranchised on their own soil by the appointment of strangers to every office, the Governor had for four years negatived every tax-bill in the hope of controlling the appropriations. In North Carolina, the law establishing courts of justice had expired; in the conflict of claims of power between the Governor and the Legislature, every new law on the subject was negatived, and there were no courts of any kind in the Province.[2] The most orderly and best governed part of Carolina was the self-organized Republic of Watauga, beyond the mountains, where the settlements were extending along the Holston, as well as south of the Nollichucky.

Every where an intrepid, hardy and industrious population, heedless of proclamations, was moving westward through all the gates of the Alleghanies;

[1] Parmi ceux qui annoncent des talens, M. Charles Fox est le seul qui en montre de distingués. Il a beaucoup d'esprit, de force d'eloquence, et malgré le dérangement, sans exemple de sa conduite et de ses affaires, la nation est naturellement disposée à la confiance sur tout ce qu'il veut lui persuader. Si ses premiers pas dans les affaires sont marqués par les succès, il pourra produire un jour dans son pays des effets pareils à ceux qui y ont a jamais illustré la carrière politique de Milord Chatham." Written in 1773 by the French Ambassador De Guines. Mémoire sur l'Angleterre; In the French Archives, Angleterre, Tom. 502.

[2] Martin to Dartmouth, 25 Dec. 1773. Quincy's Quincy, 121, 123.

CHAP. LII. 1774. Feb. seating themselves on the New River and the Green Briar, on the branches of the Monongahela, or even making their way to the Mississippi; accepting from nature their title-deeds to the unoccupied wilderness. Connecticut kept in mind, that its Charter bounded its territory by the Pacific. Its daring sons held possession of the Wyoming Valley; and learned already to claim lands westward to the Mississippi, "seven or eight hundred miles in extent of the finest country and happiest climate on the Globe. In fifty years," said they, "our people will be more than half over this tract, extensive as it is; in less than one century, the whole may become even well cultivated. If the coming period bears due proportion to that from the first landing of poor distressed fugitives at Plymouth, nothing that we can in the utmost stretch of imagination fancy of the state of this country at an equally future period, can exceed what it will then be. A commerce will and must arise, independent of every thing external, and superior to any thing ever known in Europe, or of which a European can have an adequate idea." Thus the statesmen of Connecticut pleased themselves with pictures of the happiness of their posterity; and themselves enjoyed a vivid vision of "the glory of this New World."[1] Already the commerce of Philadelphia and New-York had outgrown the laws of trade; and the Revenue officers in those places, weary of attempts to enforce them, received what duties were paid almost as a favor.

Nor was the spirit of independence confined to the western woodsmen; the New England people

[1] From letters written in February, 1774.

who dwelt on each side of the Green Mountains, resisted the jurisdiction which the Royal Government of New-York would have enforced even at the risk of bloodshed; and administered their own affairs by means of permanent Committees.

CHAP. LII. 1774. Feb.

The people of Massachusetts knew that "they had passed the river and cut away the bridge."[1] Voting the Judges of the Superior Court ample salaries from the colonial treasury, they called upon them to refuse the corrupting donative from the Crown. Four of them yielded; Oliver the Chief Justice alone refused; the House, therefore, impeached him before the Council, and declared him suspended till the issue of the impeachment. They began also to familiarize the public mind to the thought of armed resistance, by ordering some small purchases of powder on account of the Colony, to be stored in a building of its own; and by directing the purchase of twelve pieces of cannon. "Don't put off the boat till you know where you will land," advised the timid. "We must put off the boat," cried Boston patriots, "even though we do not know where we shall land."[2] "God will bring us into a safe harbor," said Hawley.[3] "Anarchy itself," repeated one to another, "is better than tyranny."[4]

March

The proposal for a General Congress was deferred to the next June; but the Committees of Correspondence were to prepare the way for it.[5] A circular let-

[1] J. Adams, ix. 333.

[2] Thos. Hutchinson to Col. Williams, Boston, 23 Feb. 1774.

[3] Communicated to me by the late Jonathan Dwight, Senior, of Springfield, a contemporary of Hawley.

[4] Hutchinson to Col. Williams.

[5] Hutchinson to Dartmouth, 28 March.

CHAP. LII. 1774. March

ter explained why Massachusetts had been under the necessity of proceeding so far of itself, and entreated for its future guidance the benefit of the councils of the whole country. The firmness was contagious. Hancock, on the fifth of March, spoke to a crowded audience in Boston: "Permit me to suggest a general Congress of deputies from the several Houses of Assembly on the Continent, as the most effectual method of establishing a union for the security of our rights and liberties." "Remember," he continued, "from whom you sprang. Not only pray, but act; if necessary, fight and even die for the prosperity of our Jerusalem;" and as he pointed out Samuel Adams, the vast multitude seemed to promise that in all succeeding times the great patriot's name, and "the roll of fellow-patriots, should grace the annals of history." Nor did a doubt exist that "the present noble struggle would terminate gloriously for America."

"We must not boast, as he who putteth off the harness," said Samuel Adams. "It is our duty at all hazards to preserve the public liberty;" and in the name of Massachusetts, he prepared her last instructions to Franklin.[1] "It will be in vain," such were his solemn words officially pronounced, "for any to expect that the people of this country will now be contented with a partial and temporary relief; or that they will be amused by Court promises, while they see not the least relaxation of grievances. By means of a brisk correspondence among the several towns in this Province, they have wonderfully animated and

[1] S. Adams: Draft of letter to Franklin, 28 March.

enlightened each other. They are united in sentiments, and their opposition to unconstitutional measures of Government is become systematical. Colony begins to communicate freely with Colony. There is a common affection among them; and shortly the whole Continent will be as united in sentiment and in their measures of opposition to tyranny, as the inhabitants of this Province. Their old good will and affection for the parent country are not totally lost; if she returns to her former moderation and good humor, their affection will revive. They wish for nothing more than a permanent union with her upon the condition of equal liberty. This is all they have been contending for; and nothing short of this will or ought to satisfy them."

Such was the ultimatum of America, sent by one illustrious son of Boston for the guidance of another. But the Ministry would not be warned. The sense of the English people was manifestly with them;[1] they were persuaded that there was no middle way, that procrastination and irresolution had produced numberless evils, but never yet cured one;[2] that the American Continent would not interpose to shield Boston from the necessity of submission.[3]

On the seventh of March Dartmouth and North presented to the two Houses a message from the King. "Nothing," said Lord North, "can be done to re-establish peace without additional powers from Parliament."—"The question now brought to issue,"

[1] Compare Rochford to Stormont, 20 May, 1774; Burke to New-York, 6 April.

[2] Compare Stormont to Rochford, 23 March, 1774.

[3] Arthur Lee to S. Adams, 18 March, 1774; Franklin to Cushing, 2 April, 1774; and Shelburne to Chatham, 3 Feb. 1774.

CHAP. LII. 1774. March said Rice, on moving the Address, which was to pledge Parliament to the exertion of every means in its power, "is, whether the Colonies are or are not the Colonies of Great Britain." Nugent, now Lord Clare, entreated that there might be no divided counsels. "On the repeal of the Stamp Act," said Dowdeswell, "all America was quiet; but in the following year you would go in pursuit of a pepper-corn, —you would collect from pepper-corn to pepper-corn, —you would establish taxes as tests of obedience. Unravel the whole conduct of America; you will find out the fault is at home." "The dependence of the Colonies is a part of the Constitution," said Pownall, the former Governor of Massachusetts. "I hope, for the sake of this country, for the sake of America, for the sake of general liberty, that this Address will go with a unanimous vote."

As nothing was proposed but to carry out the Declaratory Act, no man in England could so little find fault with the principle of the proposed measures, as Edmund Burke; he only taunted the Ministry with their wavering policy. Lord George Germaine derived all the American disturbance from the repeal of the Stamp tax. Conway pleaded for unanimity. "I speak," said William Burke, "as an Englishman; we applaud ourselves for the struggle we have had for our Constitution; the Colonists are our fellow-subjects; they will not lose theirs without a struggle." Barré applauded the good temper with which the subject had been discussed, and refused to make any opposition. "The leading question," said Wedderburn, who bore the principal part in the debate, "is the dependence or independence of America." The Address was adopted without a division.

CHAP. LII. 1774. March

The next day letters arrived from America, manifesting no change in the conduct of the Colonies. Calumny, with its hundred tongues, exaggerated the turbulence of the people, and invented wild tales of violence. The jests of the Crown officers among one another were repeated as solemn truths. It was said at the palace, and the King believed, that there was in Boston a regular Committee for tarring and feathering; and that they were next, to use the King's expression, "to pitch and feather" Hutchinson himself.[1] The press was also employed to rouse the national pride, till the zeal of the English people for maintaining English supremacy became equal to the passions of the Ministry. Even the merchants and manufacturers were made to believe that their command of the American market depended on the enforcement of the British claim of authority.

It was, therefore, to a Parliament and people as unanimous as when in Grenville's day they sanctioned the Stamp Act, that Lord North, on the fourteenth of March, reserving the measures of a more permanent character, opened the first branch of his American plan, for the instant punishment of Boston. The privilege of its harbor was to be discontinued; and the port closed against all commerce, not merely till it should have indemnified the East India Company, but until the King should be satisfied that for the future it would obey the laws. He invited all branches of the Government, all political parties, alike those who denied and those who asserted the right to tax,—Members of Parliament, Peers, Merchants, all

[1] Minutes of a conversation of the King with Hutchinson, just after Hutchinson's arrival from America.

CHAP. LII. 1774. March

ranks and degrees of people,—to proceed steadily and universally in the one course of maintaining the authority of Great Britain. Yet it was noticed, that he spoke of the indispensable necessity of vigorous measures with an unusual air of languor and moderation.[1]

This appeal was successful. Of the few who belonged to the Rockingham party, Cavendish approved the measure, which was but a corollary from their own Declaratory Act. "After having weighed the noble Lord's proposition well," said even Barré, "I cannot help giving it my hearty and determinate affirmative. I like it, adopt and embrace it for its moderation." "There is no good plan," urged Fox, "except the repeal of the taxes forms a part of it." "The proposition does not fully answer my expectations," said John Calvert; "seize the opportunity, and take away their Charter."

On the eighteenth Lord North by unanimous consent presented to the House the Boston Port Bill. To its second reading, George Bynge was the only one who cried no. "This Bill," said Rose Fuller, in the debate on the twenty-third, "shuts up one of the ports of the greatest commerce and consequence in the English Dominions in America. The North Americans will look upon it as a foolish act of oppression. You cannot carry this Bill into execution but by a military force." "If a military force is necessary," replied Lord North, "I shall not hesitate a moment to enforce a due obedience to the laws of this country." Fox, seizing the very point of

[1] Edmund Burke to the Committee of New-York, 6 April, 1774.

the question, would have softened the Bill by opening the port on the payment of indemnity to the East India Company; and he took care that his motion should appear on the journal. "Obedience," replied Lord North, "obedience, not indemnification, will be the test of the Bostonians." "The offence of the Americans is flagitious," said Van. "The town of Boston ought to be knocked about their ears and destroyed. Delenda est Carthago. You will never meet with proper obedience to the laws of this country, until you have destroyed that nest of locusts." The clause to which Fox had objected, was adopted without any division, and with but one or two negatives.

The popular current, both within doors and without, set strongly against America. It was only for the acquittal of their own honor and the discharge of their own consciences,[1] that two days later, on the third reading, Dowdeswell and Edmund Burke, unsupported by their former friends, spoke very strongly against a Bill, which punished the innocent with the guilty, condemned without an opportunity of defence, deprived the laborer and the sailor of bread, injured English creditors by destroying the trade out of which the debts due them were to be discharged, and ultimately oppressed the English manufacturer. "You will draw a foreign force upon you," said Burke; "I will not say where that will end, but think, I conjure you, of the consequences." "The Resolves at Boston," said Gray Cooper, "are a direct issue against the Declaratory Act;" and half the Rockingham party went with him. Rose Fuller

[1] Edmund Burke to his New-York Constituents.

CHAP. LII. 1774. March opposed the Bill, unless the tax on tea were also repealed. Pownall was convinced that the time was not proper for a repeal of the duty on tea. "This is the crisis," said Lord North, who had by degrees assumed a style of authority and decision. "The contest ought to be determined. To repeal the tea duty or any measure would stamp us with timidity." "The present Bill," said Johnstone, late Governor of West Florida, "must produce a Confederacy and will end in a general revolt." But it passed without a division, and very unfairly went to the Lords as the unanimous voice of the Commons. The King cheered his Minister on by sneers at "the feebleness and futility of the Opposition." [1]

In the midst of the general anger, a book was circulating in England, on the interest of Great Britain in regard to the Colonies, and the only means of living in peace and harmony with them, which judged the past and estimated the future with contemplative calmness and unerring sagacity. Its author Josiah Tucker, Dean of Gloucester, a most loyal churchman, though an apostle of Free Trade, saw clearly, that the reduction of Canada had put an end to the sovereignty of the Mother Country; that it is in the very nature of all Colonies, and of the Americans more than others, to aspire after independence. He would not suffer things to go on as they had lately done, for that would only make the Colonies more headstrong; nor attempt to persuade them to send over a certain number of deputies or representatives to sit in Parliament, for the prosecution of that scheme

[1] King to Lord North, 23 March, 1774.

could only end in furnishing a justification to the Mother Country for making war against them; nor have recourse to arms, for the event was uncertain, and England if successful, could still never treat America as an enslaved people, or govern them against their own inclinations. There remained but one wise olution; and it was to declare the North American Colonies, to be a free and independent people. CHAP. LII. 1774. March

"If we separate from the Colonies," it was objected, "we shall lose their trade." "Why so?" answered Tucker. "The Colonies will trade even with their bitterest enemies in the hottest of a war, provided they shall find it their interest so to do. The question before us will turn on this single point: Can the Colonists, in a general way, trade with any other European State to greater advantage than they can with Great Britain? If they cannot, we shall retain their custom;" and he demonstrated that England was for America, the best market and the best storehouse; that the prodigious increase of British trade was due not to prohibition, but to the suppression of various monopolies, and exclusive companies for foreign trade; to the repeal of taxes on raw materials; to the improvements, inventions and discoveries for the abridgment of labor; to roads, canals, and better postal arrangements. The measure would not decrease shipping and navigation, or diminish the breed of sailors.

But "if we give up the Colonies," it was pretended, "the French will take immediate possession of them." "The Americans," resumed Tucker, "cannot brook our Government; will they glory in being numbered among the slaves of the grand Monarch?" "Will you leave the Church of England in America to suffer per-

CHAP. LII. 1774. March secution?" asked the Churchmen. "Declare North America independent," replied Tucker, "and all their fears of ecclesiastical authority will vanish away; a Bishop will be no longer looked upon as a monster but as a man; and an Episcopate may then take place." No Minister, he confessed, would dare, as things were then circumstanced, to do so much good to his country; neither would their opponents wish to see it done; and "yet," he added, "measures evidently right will prevail at last."

An honest love of liberty revealed the same truth to John Cartwright. The young enthusiast was firmly persuaded that the species, as well as individuals of mankind, obtains knowledge, wisdom, and virtue progressively, so that its latter days will be more wise, peaceable, and pious, than the earlier periods of its existence. He was destined to pass his life in efforts to purify the British Constitution, which, as he believed, had within itself the seeds of immortality. With the fervid language of sincerity he now advocated the freedom of his American kindred; and proclaimed American independence to be England's interest and glory.[1]

Thus spoke the forerunners of free trade and reform. But the infatuated people turned from them to indulge unsparingly in ridicule and illiberal jests on the Bostonians, whom the iron hand of power was extended to chastise and subdue. At the meeting of the Commons, on the twenty-eighth, Lord North asked leave to bring in a Bill for regulating the government of the Province of Massachusetts Bay.

[1] Cartwright's American Independence, &c. Letter vi. March 27, 1774.

On this occasion, Lord George Germaine showed himself anxious to take a lead. "I wish," said he, "to see the Council of that country on the same footing as that of other Colonies. Put an end to their Town Meetings. I would not have men of a mercantile cast every day collecting themselves together and debating about political matters. I would have them follow their occupations as merchants, and not consider themselves as Ministers of that country. I would wish that all corporate powers might be given to certain people in every town, in the same manner that corporations are formed here. Their grand juries, their petty juries, require great regulation. I would wish to bring the Constitution of America, as similar to our own as possible; to see the Council of that country similar to a House of Lords in this; to see Chancery suits determined by a Court of Chancery. At present their Assembly is a downright clog; their Council thwart and oppose the security and welfare of that Government. You have, sir, no Government, no Governor; the whole are the proceedings of a tumultuous and riotous rabble, who ought, if they had the least prudence, to follow their mercantile employment, and not trouble themselves with politics and government, which they do not understand. Some gentlemen say, 'Oh, don't break their charter; don't take away rights granted them by the predecessors of the Crown.' Whoever wishes to preserve such Charters, I wish him no worse than to govern such subjects. By a manly perseverance, things may be restored from anarchy and confusion to peace, quietude, and obedience."

"I thank the noble Lord," said Lord North, "for every one of the propositions he has held out; they

CHAP. LII. 1774. March

are worthy of a great mind; I see their propriety, and wish to adopt them;" and the House directed North, Thurlow, and Wedderburn to prepare and bring in a bill accordingly.

On the twenty-ninth of March, the Boston Port Bill underwent in the House of Lords a fuller and fairer discussion. The rightness of mind of Rockingham impelled him to resist it with firmness, and the Duke of Richmond ardently supported him. "Nothing can justify the Ministers hereafter," said Temple, "except the town of Boston proving in an actual state of rebellion." The good Lord Dartmouth, who sincerely desired to see lenient measures adopted, showed his disposition by calling what passed in Boston commotion, not open rebellion. Lord Mansfield, a man "in the cool decline of life," acquainted only with the occupations of peace, a civil magistrate, covered with judicial purple and ermine that should have no stain of blood, with eyes broad open to the consequences, rose to take the guidance of the House out of the hands of the faltering Minister. "What passed in Boston," said he, "is the last overt act of High Treason, proceeding from our over lenity and want of foresight. It is, however, the luckiest event that could befall this country, for all may now be recovered. Compensation to the East India Company I regard as no object of the Bill.[1] The sword is drawn,[2] and you must throw away the scabbard.[3] Pass this Act, and you will be passed the Rubicon.[4] The Americans will then know that we shall tempo-

[1] Shelburne to Chatham, 4 April, 1774; in Chatham's Corr. iv. 339.

[2] Life of Lord Mansfield in Almon's Biographical Anecdotes, i. 35.

[3] Speech of Barré, 2 May, 1774.

[4] Garnier to D'Aiguillon, 8 April.

rize no longer; if it passes with tolerable unanimity, Boston will submit, and all will end in a victory without carnage."[1] In vain did Camden meet the question fully, and return very nearly to his former principles; in vain did Shelburne prove the tranquil and loyal condition in which he had left the Colonies on giving up their administration. There was no division in the House of Lords, and its Journal, like that of the Commons, declares that the Boston Port Bill passed unanimously. The King in person made haste to give it his approval. Boston has now no option but to claim entire independence, or to approach the throne as a penitent, and promise for the future passive "obedience" to British "laws" in all cases whatsoever. 1774. March

The immediate repeal of the tax on tea and its Preamble remained the only possible avenue to conciliation. It was moved by Rose Fuller on the nineteenth of April, and gave rise to a long and animated debate. The subject in its connections was the gravest that could engage attention, involving the prosperity of England, the tranquillity of the British empire, the principles of colonization, and the liberties of mankind. But Cornwall, speaking for the ministers, stated the question to be simply, "whether the whole of British authority over America should be taken away." On this occasion, Edmund Burke, indignant at the tyranny that was menaced, pronounced an oration such as had never been heard in the British Parliament. His boundless stores of knowledge came obedient at his command; and his April.

[1] Shelburne to Chatham.

CHAP. LII. 1774. April. thoughts and arguments, the facts which he cited, and his glowing appeals, fell naturally into their places; so that his long and elaborate speech seemed to burst from his mind as one harmonious and unbroken emanation. He first demonstrated that the repeal of the tax would be productive of unmixed good; he then surveyed comprehensively the whole series of the Parliamentary proceedings with regard to America, in their causes and their consequences. After exhausting the subject, he entreated Parliament to "reason not at all," but to "oppose the ancient policy and practice of the empire, as a rampart against the speculations of innovators on both sides of the question."

"Again and again," such was his entreaty, "revert to your old principles—seek peace and ensue it—leave America, if she has taxable matter, to tax herself. Be content to bind America by laws of trade; you have always done it. Let this be your reason for binding their trade. Do not burden them by taxes; you were not used to do so from the beginning. Let this be your reason for not taxing. These are the arguments of states and kingdoms. Leave the rest to the schools. The several provincial Legislatures ought all to be subordinate to the Parliament of Great Britain. She, as from the throne of Heaven, superintends and guides and controls them all. To coerce, to restrain and to aid, her powers must be boundless."

Such was the adjustment which was advocated by Burke. He left questions of right to the schools, and proposed to conform Colonial Government to the facts of the past. It was all that America had been for ten years soliciting; it was advice to which des-

CHAP. LII. 1774. April.

potism itself might have listened, for it contained a sanction of all established power. It might at once have been received by the New Tory party, the conservative party of England. They must soon make it their own, and one day must accept its author as their champion against revolution and reform. But at the moment his heart gained a partial victory over his theories.

During the long debate the young and fiery Lord Carmarthen had repeated what so many had said before him. "The Americans are our children, and how can they revolt against their parent? If they are not free in their present state, England is not free; because Manchester, and other considerable places, are not represented."—"So then," retorted Burke, "because some towns in England are not represented, America is to have no Representative at all. They are 'our children;' but when children ask bread, we are not to give a stone. Is it because the natural resistance of things and the various mutations of time hinders our Government, or any scheme of Government, from being any more than a sort of approximation to the right, is it therefore that the Colonies are to recede from it infinitely? When this child of ours wishes to assimilate to its parent, are we to give them our weakness for their strength? our opprobrium for their glory? and the slough of slavery which we are not able to work off, to serve them for their freedom?" The words fell from him as burning oracles. It appeared as if he was lifted upward to gaze into futurity, and while he spoke for the rights of America, he seemed to prepare the way for renovating the Constitution of England. Yet it was not so. Though more than half a century had

CHAP. LII. 1774. April. intervened, Burke would not be wiser than the whigs of the days of King William. It was enough for him if the Aristocracy applauded. He did not believe in the dawn of a new light, in the coming on of a new order, though a new order of things was at the door, and a new light had broken. He would not turn to see, nor bend to learn, if the political system of Somers, and Walpole, and the Pelhams, and their adherents was to pass away; if it were so, he himself was determined not to know it, but "rather to be the last of that race of men." As Dante is the poet who sums up the civilization of his times, so that the departed spirit of the Middle Age seems still to live in his immortal verse, so Burke portrays in his pages all the lineaments of that Old Whig Aristocracy which in its day had achieved mighty things for liberty and for England. He that will study under its best aspect the enlightened character of England in the first half of the eighteenth century, the wonderful intermixture of privilege and prerogative, of aristocratic power and popular liberty, of a free Press and a secret House of Commons, of an established church and a toleration of all Protestant sects, of a fixed adherence to prescription and liberal tendencies in administration, must give his days and nights to the writings of Edmund Burke. But time never keeps company with the mourners; it flies from the memories of the expiring past, though they may be clad in the brightest colors of imagination; it leaves those who stand still to their despair; and itself hurries on to fresh fields of action and scenes for ever new.

Resuming the debate, Fox said earnestly, "If you

persist in your right to tax the Americans, you will force them into open rebellion." On the other hand, Lord North asked that his measures might be sustained with firmness and resolution; and then, said he, "there is no doubt but peace and quietude will soon be restored." "We are now in great difficulties," said Dowdeswell, speaking for all who adhered to Lord Rockingham; "let us do justice before it is too late." But it was too late. Even Burke's object had been only "to refute the charges against that party with which he had all along acted." After his splendid eloquence no more divided with him than forty-nine, just the number that had divided against the Stamp Act, while on the other side stood nearly four times as many. "The repeal of the tea tax was never to be obtained, so long as the authority of Parliament was publicly rejected or opposed."

With ten thousand regulars," said the creatures of the Ministry, "we can march through the Continent." To bring Boston on its knees and terrify the rest of America by the example, Gage, the military Commander-in-Chief for all North America, was commissioned as the civil Governor of Massachusetts also, and was sent over with four regiments to enforce submission. He was directed to shut the port of Boston, and having as a part of his instructions the opinion of Thurlow and Wedderburn that acts of High Treason had been committed there, he was directed to take measures for bringing the ringleaders to condign punishment. Foremost among these, Samuel Adams was marked out for sacrifice as the chief of the revolution. "He is the most elegant writer, the most sagacious politician, and celebrated patriot, per-

CHAP. LII. 1774. April. haps of any who have figured in the last ten years,"[1] is the contemporary record of John Adams. "I cannot sufficiently respect his integrity and abilities," said Clymer of Pennsylvania; "all good Americans should erect a statue to him in their hearts."[2] Time proved that he had been right, even where his conduct had been questioned; and many in England "esteemed him the first politician in the world."[3] He saw clearly that "the rigorous measures of the British administration would the sooner bring to pass" the first wish of his heart, "the entire separation and independence of the Colonies, which Providence would erect into a mighty empire."[4] Indefatigable in seeking for Massachusetts the countenance of her sister Colonies,[5] he had no anxiety for himself; no doubt of the ultimate triumph of freedom; but as he thought of the calamities that hung over Boston, he raised the prayer, "that God would prepare that people for the event, by inspiring them with wisdom and fortitude."

The members of the Committee knew how momentous was the revolution which they were accomplishing. "We have enlisted," they said, "in the cause of our country, and are resolved at all adventures to promote its welfare; should we succeed, our names will be held up by future generations with that unfeigned plaudit, with which we now recount the great deeds of our worthy ancestors."[1]

[1] From the minute in the handwriting of John Adams, dated 29 April, 1774.

[2] Clymer to Quincy, 1774.

[3] Quincy's Quincy, 258.

[4] S. Adams to A. Lee, April.

[5] S. Adams to John Dickinson, 21 April, 1774.

[1] The Committee of Boston, to the Gentlemen Committee of Correspondence for the Town of Winchendon, 5 April, 1774.

Meantime, New-York gave proof that the union was perfect; on the nineteenth, while the House of Commons was voting not to repeal the duty on tea, its people sent back the tea-ship which had arrived but the day before; and eighteen chests of tea, found on board of another vessel, were hoisted on deck and emptied into "the slip."

America had chosen her part, so too had the British Ministry. The second penal Bill for the Government of Massachusetts Bay, which was introduced into Parliament on the twenty-eighth, without any hearing or any notice to the Province, abrogated so much of its Charter as gave to its Legislature the election of the Council; abolished Town Meetings except for the choice of town officers, or on the special permission of the Governor; conferred on the executive the power of appointing and removing the Sheriffs at pleasure; and transforming the trial by jury into a snare for the people, it intrusted the returning of juries to the dependent Sheriff. This Bill, too, notwithstanding the earnest resistance of Dunning, passed the Commons by a vote of more than three to one.

A third penal measure, which had been questioned by Dartmouth, and recommended by the King, transferred the place of trial of any magistrates, Revenue officers, or soldiers, indicted for murder or other capital offence in Massachusetts Bay, to Nova Scotia[1] or Great Britain. As Lord North brought forward this wholesale Bill of indemnity to the Governor and soldiers, if they should trample upon the people of Boston and be charged

[1] King to Lord North, on Dartmouth's Scruples.

CHAP. LII. 1774. April. with murder, it was noticed that he trembled and faltered at every word; showing that he was the vassal of a stronger will than his own, and vainly struggled to wrestle down the feelings which his nature refused to disavow. "If the people of America," said Van, "oppose the measures of Government that are now sent, I would do, as was done of old, in the time of the ancient Britons; I would burn and set fire to all their woods, and leave their country open. If we are likely to lose it, I think it better lost by our own soldiers, than wrested from us by our rebellious children." "The Bill is meant to enslave America," said Sawbridge with only forty to listen to him. "I execrate the present measure," cried Barré; "you have had one meeting of the Colonies in Congress; you may soon have another. The Americans will not abandon their principles; for if they submit they are slaves."

Yet the Bill passed the Commons by a vote of more than four to one. But evil when it comes, is intermixed with good; the ill is evanescent, the good endures. The British Government inflamed the passions of the English people against America, and courted their sympathy; as a consequence, the secrecy of the debates in Parliament came to an end; and this great change in the political relation of the Legislature to public opinion, was conceded by a Tory Government, seeking strength from popular excitement. The concession was irrevocable.

A fourth measure legalized the quartering of troops within the town of Boston. The fifth statute professed to regulate the Government of the Province of Quebec. The nation which would not so much as legally recognise the existence of a Catholic in Ireland, from political considerations sanctioned on the Saint Lawrence "the free exercise of the religion of the Church of Rome, and confirmed to the clergy of that Church their accustomed dues and rights." So far the act was merciful; but it extended the boundaries of the Government to the Ohio and the Mississippi, and over the vast region, which included, besides Canada, the area of the present States of Ohio, Michigan, Indiana, Illinois, and Wisconsin, it decreed an arbitrary rule. The establishment of Colonies on principles of liberty is "the peculiar and appropriated glory of England,"[1] rendering her venerable throughout all time in the history of the world. The office of peopling a Continent with free and happy commonwealths was renounced. The Quebec Bill which quickly passed the House of Lords, and was borne through the Commons by the zeal of the Ministry and the influence of the King, left the people who were to colonize the most fertile territory in the world without the writ of Habeas Corpus to protect the rights of persons, and without a share of power in any one branch of the Government.

In this manner Great Britain, allured by a phantom of absolute authority, made war on human freedom. The liberties of Poland had been sequestered, and its territory began to be parcelled out among the usurpers. The aristocratic privileges of Sweden had been swept away by treachery and usurpation. The Free Towns of Germany, which had preserved in that empire the example of Republics, were, "like so many dying sparks that go out one after another."

[1] Edmund Burke.

CHAP. LII. 1774. April. Venice and Genoa had stifled the spirit of independence in their prodigal luxury. Holland was ruinously divided against itself. In Great Britain the House of Commons had become so venal, that it might be asked, whether a body so chosen and so influenced was fit to exercise legislative power even within the realm. If it shall succeed in establishing by force of arms its "boundless" authority over America, where shall humanity find an asylum? But this decay of the old forms of liberty was the symptom and the forerunner of a new creation. The knell of the ages of servitude and inequality was rung; those of equality and brotherhood were to dawn.

As the fleets and armies of England went forth to consolidate arbitrary power, the sound of war every where else on the earth died away. Kings sat still in awe, and nations turned to watch the issue.